Starting and Managing a Nonprofit Organization

A Legal Guide

Fifth Edition

Bruce R. Hopkins

WILEY

John Wiley & Sons, Inc.

Library of Congress Cataloging-in-Publication Data:

Hopkins, Bruce R.
    Starting and managing a nonprofit organization: a legal guide / Bruce R. Hopkins.—5th ed.
        p. cm.
    Includes index.
    ISBN 978-0-470-39793-0 (pbk.)
    1. Nonprofit organizations—Law and legislation—United States. 2. Nonprofit organizations—Taxation—Law and legislation—United States. I. Title.
    KF1388.H66 2009
    346.73'064—dc22

                                                                    2008042573

Printed in the United States of America

10 9 8 7 6 5 4 3 2 1

To my parents, Frederick and Jane, who, as teachers, professional and otherwise, encouraged me, in their own way and in ways they may not realize, to write this book, with love.

Contents

CONTENTS

Preface

This book was conceived nearly 20 years ago; the conception remains a vividly memorable experience. Its incubation occurred during a speech before managers of relatively small nonprofit organizations. I had been assigned some esoteric topic on the law of tax-exempt organizations and was about five minutes into my presentation when suddenly—to my chagrin—I realized, from the glazed-over looks, that few people in the audience had even the faintest idea what I was talking about. The remainder of them did not seem to care. Preservation instincts took over. The assignment was hopeless, so I abandoned my intended remarks. (I literally threw my notes on the floor, at least generating—to my relief—a little laughter.) Instead, we talked about what my audience really wanted to hear: some of the basics of the laws affecting nonprofit organizations.

The experience was not a measure of the level of intelligence of that particular audience; rather, it reflects the fact that those who manage nonprofit organizations—particularly the smaller ones—often lack understanding of the basics of the laws that regulate their operations and the legal problems that may be awaiting them in their blissful ignorance. A massive gap exists between the wish lists and the legal expertise of many of those responsible for the fate of nonprofit organizations. The law can either help them achieve their goals or prevent them from succeeding.

I was struck by the thought that there was a need for a basic summary of the laws that affect the operation of nonprofit organizations. The summary I envisioned would have no citations or footnotes—just readable text.

I had no shortage of questions from my practice, speeches over the years, and 21 years of teaching a law school course on tax-exempt organizations. I began recalling and noting these questions and was surprised to realize how the same ones are asked again and again. Even though I have practiced law in excess of 35 years, I still find myself asked many of the same basic questions. This book has been written to provide answers to those questions.

The questions are fundamental and important, but they reveal tremendous confusion. The confusion is understandable: The law in this field is confusing—even overwhelming. The ultimate purposes of this book are to decipher the Internal Revenue Code as it affects nonprofit organizations; to translate the intricacies of the law in these areas and try to make them understandable to nonlawyer managers of "nonprofits"; and otherwise to help to close the gap between goals and knowledge in nonprofit organizations.

The law affecting nonprofit organizations is volatile. Ongoing change in this field of law is a constant, and many regulatory changes lie ahead. I have tried to make the book sufficiently general to withstand most of this change. Yet, once the basics in this field are grasped, some readers may want more detail and more current information. My monthly newsletter, *Bruce R. Hopkins' Nonprofit Counsel* (Wiley), is a useful resource for keeping up with legal developments that affect nonprofit organizations.

For some readers, there may be more in the book than they need at this time, particularly if they are just beginning to establish a nonprofit organization or they are thinking about doing so. Let me offer this perspective for the newcomer to the world, and the law, of nonprofit organizations. There are many types of nonprofit organizations. Nearly always, those who start a nonprofit organization want it to be tax-exempt. At a minimum, they want it to be eligible to receive tax-deductible contributions. They equate *nonprofit* organizations with *tax-exempt* organizations and perhaps with *charitable* organizations.

For those who already know that they want a charitable entity, Chapter 4 can be skimmed as a review. For others, Chapter 4's inventory of the various types of tax-exempt organizations is the place to begin.

A fictional "Campaign to Clean Up America" is used throughout as an illustration of how to organize and qualify a tax-exempt charitable organization. Most individuals, when planning to establish a nonprofit organization, are thinking in terms of a charity, even if that thinking is only subconscious. Rarely have they selected between a *public* versus a *private* charity. Usually, they are thinking about the establishment of a *foundation*.

The first question for an individual interested in establishing a nonprofit organization should be: What is the nonprofit organization going to do? Just like starting a for-profit business, the first step is to determine the organization's functions, then match the category of tax-exempt status (if any) to the organization's purposes and functions. Too often, individuals start with a round-peg nonprofit organization (usually, a charitable one) and try to force it into the square-hole requirements of the law imposed on that type of organization.

A *charity* will not fit the requirements of all. Here are some of the other choices:

- *Advocacy organizations.* These groups attempt to influence the legislative process or the political process, or otherwise champion particular positions. They may call themselves social welfare organizations or political action committees. Not all advocacy is lobbying. and not all political activity is political campaign activity. Some of this program can be accomplished through a charitable organization, but that outcome is rare where advocacy is the organization's primary undertaking. In some instances, two nonprofit organizations are used, to have it both ways—a blend of charitable and advocacy activities.

- *Membership groups.* Some nonprofit organizations—associations, veterans' groups, and fraternal organizations—are structured as membership organizations. This is not to say that a charitable organization may not be structured as a membership entity; it can, but there are other categories of membership groups. Frequently, these are business leagues.

- *Social or recreational organizations.* Nonprofit organizations may be organized as formal social clubs (like country clubs, and tennis and golf clubs), or hobby, garden, or sports tournament organizations. The key factor is their primary purpose; some social activity can be tolerated in charitable groups. There is some overlap with other categories—for example, a social organization can be structured as a membership entity.

- *Satellite organizations.* Some nonprofit organizations are deliberately organized as auxiliaries or subsidiaries of other organizations. Examples of these organizations include title-holding companies, the various types of cooperatives, and retirement and other employee benefit funds. The parent organization may be a for-profit entity, such as a business corporation with a related foundation.

- *Employee benefit funds.* The world of compensation is intricate, regardless of whether the employer is a for-profit or nonprofit organization. Various current and deferred benefits for employees are provided, including retirement and profit-sharing programs. These programs—or "plans"—are often financially supported by benefit funds. When properly organized and operated, these funds are tax-exempt entities.

Once the category of tax-exempt organization has been decided, the reader can turn to Chapter 5, which discusses the concepts of *private inurement* and *private benefit*. Among other things, it offers an explanation of the basic distinctions between non-profit and for-profit organizations. An understanding of these distinctions may well prevent some difficulties later on. An understanding of the private inurement doctrine is necessary because it applies to most tax-exempt organizations. The private benefit doctrine, by contrast, applies only to charitable organizations. Also in this chapter is a summary of the *intermediate sanctions* rules—a significant package of statutory law that affects charitable and social welfare organizations.

If the organization will engage in attempts to influence legislation, a jump ahead, for a reading of Chapter 14, is essential. If the organization is to engage in efforts to intervene or participate in political campaign activities, a perusing of Chapter 15 is necessary.

For charitable organizations, another jump ahead in the book may be in order. Because all charitable organizations are presumed to be *private foundations* and because there is little advantage in being so classified, most charitable entities strive to avoid private foundation status if they can. A review of the basic differences between *public* and *private* charities, included in Chapter 7, is important at the outset.

In addition to being tax-exempt, an organization may have charitable donee status. Not every tax-exempt organization can receive tax-deductible gifts, but many can. Chapter 4 identifies those that are charitable donees; Chapter 11 provides the basic charitable giving rules. An organization's charitable giving program ideally will include at least the rudiments of a planned giving program; this type of giving is described in Chapter 19. If a charitable gift solicitation program is planned, the organization must keep in mind the state and federal laws pertaining to fundraising. These laws are summarized in Chapter 12.

Nearly all charitable organizations must obtain a ruling from the Internal Revenue Service (IRS) that they are tax-exempt and eligible to receive deductible gifts. Most other categories of tax-exempt organizations may wish to obtain IRS rulings but are not required to do so. The process of obtaining such a ruling is the subject of Chapter 6, obviously a necessary chapter for new organizations. Readers will find it helpful to have a copy of IRS Form 1023 at hand when they reach this chapter. (The current form is dated June 2006.)

Another key chapter is Chapter 9, which outlines the various returns and reports that a tax-exempt organization must file, under both federal and state law. The principal form in this regard is Form 990. This return recently was significantly redesigned. Readers should have the most current form at hand when reading this chapter.

These days, the matter of governance is the hottest law issue for nonprofit organizations. Thus, Chapters 8 and 22 are essential reading.

Chapter 25 may be the most riveting chapter for those who are serving (or are thinking of serving) on boards of directors and/or as officers in nonprofit organizations. The chapter deals with personal liability (as does Chapter 8) and how to avoid it.

The balance of the book can be read when the topics are relevant for particular situations. For example, Chapter 11 focuses on the charitable giving rules, Chapter 12 concerns fundraising regulation, Chapter 13 pertains to the unrelated business rules, and Chapter 17 deals with the use of subsidiaries. Chapter 18 details involvements in partnerships.

Other chapters (16, 21, and 23) pertain to somewhat more esoteric topics—principally, donor-advised funds, tax shelters, insurance schemes, commerciality, and competition with for-profit organizations. Chapter 24 addresses a subject nonprofit entities dread the most: an IRS audit.

An inherent dilemma faces those involved with startups of nonprofit organizations: How is an organization to progress if it does not absorb and act on new information? Yet how can it avoid stagnating in frustration and not progressing at all, if it is overwhelmed with unnecessary detail, particularly in the beginning stages?

The trick, of course, is balance, and that balance lies in understanding the basics. As an example, take the topic of Chapter 19, planned giving. Assume that, in the face of all reasonable advice, the management of a charitable organization refuses to entertain even a preliminary thought about launching a planned giving program at this time. It may be hoped, nonetheless, that there is an employee or a trustee who has tried to at least understand what planned giving is and has become aware of the basic terms. Even if the managers of a charitable organization elect to decline a planned giving program for now, at a minimum they will have some idea of what they are turning down.

Those who are tempted to spurn Chapter 19 should spend a few minutes reviewing the topics it covers:

- The basic concept of planned giving
- The likelihood of securing a planned gift immediately
- The reasons for not postponing the advent of a planned giving program
- The charitable remainder trust
- The charitable gift annuity
- The pooled income fund
- The charitable lead trust
- The use of insurance as the basis for a charitable gift
- The integration of estate planning and charitable giving
- The need for an endowment for the organization
- The existing fundraising resources that might more productively be devoted to a planned giving program

Someday, someone may ask a trustee, officer, or employee of a charitable organization: "Do you have a charitable remainder trust program?" It would be nice for the potentially hapless respondent to have some idea of what a charitable remainder trust is.

The same may be said with respect to compensation issues. *Excessive compensation*, discussed in Chapter 5, may seem almost laughable as a problem for those starting a nonprofit organization, particularly a charitable one. But, the years sail by quickly and sudden economic success is not confined to dot.com companies. Thus, the following questions should at least be kept in mind:

- What is the difference between private inurement and private benefit?
- Who are the insiders or disqualified persons with respect to the organization?
- Does the organization have a conflict of interest policy?
- Could a transaction be construed as an excess benefit transaction?
- Does the organization participate in a revenue-sharing transaction?
- Is any effort being made to comply with the rebuttable presumption?
- Has the composition and/or the functioning of the board of directors been evaluated in light of these rules?

Still, the same may be said for the definitions of subsidiaries or partnerships. (See Chapters 17 and 18.) Those starting a nonprofit organization may believe (and rightly so) that the use of a taxable subsidiary or an involvement in a joint venture is the farthest thing from their minds. Still, it would be good to know at least the basics regarding the use of a subsidiary. For example:

- Would the tax-exempt status of the organization be disturbed, enhanced, or preserved if one or more activities were housed in a separate organization?
- Aside from tax considerations, do management or other factors dictate the use of a subsidiary?
- How is the subsidiary to be funded, for initial capitalization and/or ongoing operations?
- How does the parent organization maintain control over the subsidiary?
- What circumstances might cause the activities of the subsidiary to be attributed to the tax-exempt parent?

Regarding partnerships, a wise newcomer will contemplate such fundamentals as

- The purpose of using a partnership (frequently simply a financing device)
- The difference between a general partnership and a limited partnership
- When property is best acquired by a partnership rather than by a participating nonprofit organization
- When to use (and when not to use) a for-profit partner

- How and why it may be beneficial for a nonprofit organization to lease property from a partnership in which it is a partner
- When to become involved in a joint venture—and when not to
- The circumstances where involvement by the exempt organization in a partnership might cause the organization to endanger or forfeit its tax-exempt status

Thus, each chapter is designed to have some practical import, and, for newcomers, some chapters are of greater necessity than others. This Preface serves as a guide to the must-read chapters and pleads with readers not to abandon the rest. When in doubt on the meaning of a word or phrase, the glossary is available.

No book is a substitute for good legal or other professional advice. Some managers of nonprofit organizations are afraid to seek advice—out of embarrassment for asking "dumb questions" or fear of the costs involved. An operator of a nonprofit organization may not even realize the presence of a legal problem. This book is intended to ease those fears and close those gaps.

BRUCE R. HOPKINS
Kansas City, Missouri
December 2008

Acknowledgments

This book is possible because of the contributions of many people: clients, participants at conferences and seminars, students, colleagues, and my wife. As to the latter, Bonnie J. Buchele, Ph.D., has been and is a director and/or officer of several nonprofit organizations; herewith, many questions and much free legal advice.

Many at John Wiley & Sons, Inc., have played significant roles in the development and production of this book. The process started with Jeffrey W. Brown, who offered indescribable assistance with this and other projects over several years. He guided the preparation of the first edition. Then, Marla J. Bobowick stepped in, continuing the Wiley tradition of encouragement and support. It was during her years of service that Wiley undertook publication of my newsletter, *Bruce R. Hopkins' Nonprofit Counsel*. She guided preparation of the second edition. Thereafter, the task of guiding me through the third edition fell to Martha Cooley, who did a terrific job (after recovering from the shock of receiving the manuscript unsolicited). Today, the individual who directs the majority of my writing time is Susan McDermott, who also is always there with support and assistance. Susan has overseen the fourth and fifth of these editions. I acknowledge the contributions of all four of these wonderful individuals with thanks.

I further acknowledge a considerable debt to the copyeditor for the first and second editions of this book: Maryan Malone, then of Publications Development Company of Texas. Practicing law and writing legal documents over many years has not aided my book-writing style. To compensate, Maryan worked tirelessly to rid the text of nearly all of its "lawyerese." Thanks again, Maryan; I never envied you your job. I hope the subsequent editions have not undone your work too much.

Still others at Wiley who have contributed considerably to this project are Robin Goldstein (third edition), Louise Jacob (fourth edition), and Natasha A. S. Wolfe (this edition).

B.R.H.

Starting a Nonprofit Organization

CHAPTER ONE

What Is a
Nonprofit Organization?

One of the most striking features of life as we settle into the third millennium is the awesome sweep of reform around the world. Freedom of thought and action is now permitted in societies that previously knew only totalitarianism and suppression. Frequently, a country earns the label *emerging democracy* by introducing startling economic and political changes. Sometimes, this is accomplished by elections; sometimes, a revolution is necessary. The collapse of the former U.S.S.R., along with the struggles toward freedom and economic betterment in the several countries that were once part of it, is a prime example of these reforms.

Countries that are planning transitions to a democratic state are discovering a fact that some Western countries learned a long time ago: To create and maintain economic and political freedom, which is the essence of a true democracy, the power to influence and cause changes cannot be concentrated in one sector of that state or society. There must be a *pluralization of institutions* in society, which is a fancy way of saying that the ability to bring about changes and the accumulation of power cannot belong to just one sector—namely, the government. A society that has achieved this type of pluralization is sometimes known as a *civil society*.

A strong democratic state has three sectors: a government sector, a private business sector, and a nonprofit sector. Each sector must function effectively and must cooperate with the others, to some degree, if the democracy is to persist for the good of the individuals in the society. A democratic society must be able to make and implement policy decisions with the participation of all three sectors. Ideally, a democratic society can solve some of its problems with minimal involvement of government if there is a well-developed and active nonprofit sector—charitable, educational, scientific, and religious organizations; associations and other membership organizations; advocacy groups; and similar private agencies.

Of all countries, the United States has the most highly developed sector of nonprofit organizations. The reach of the U.S. government is often curbed by the activities of nonprofit organizations, but that is a prime mark of a free and otherwise democratic society. The federal, state, and local governments acknowledge this fact (sometimes grudgingly) by exempting most nonprofit organizations from income and other taxes and, in some instances, allowing tax-deductible gifts to them. These tax enhancements are crucial for the survival of many nonprofit organizations.

When an individual in the United States perceives either a personal problem or one involving society, he or she does not always have to turn to a government for the problem's resolution. The individual, acting individually or with a group, can attempt to remedy the problem by turning to a nongovernmental body. There are obvious exceptions to this sweeping statement: Governments provide a wide range of services that individuals cannot, such as national defense and foreign policy implementations. Still, in U.S. culture, more so than in any other, an individual is often likely to use nongovernmental means to remedy, or at least address, personal and social problems.

A BIT OF PHILOSOPHY

For most Americans, this mind-set stems from the very essence of our political history—distrust of government. We really do not like governmental controls; we prefer to act freely, as individuals, to the extent it is realistic and practical to do so. As the perceptive political philosopher Alexis de Tocqueville wrote in 1835, "Americans of all ages, all conditions, and all dispositions constantly form associations" (meaning nonprofit organizations) and "[w]henever at the head of some new undertaking you see the government in France, or a man of rank in England, in the United States you will be sure to find an association." About 150 years later, John W. Gardner, founder of Common Cause, observed: "In the realm of good works this nation boasts a unique blending of private and governmental effort. There is almost no area of educational, scientific, charitable, or religious activity in which we have not built an effective network of private institutions."

This "effective network of private institutions" (the nation's nonprofit organizations) is called the *independent sector*, the *voluntary sector*, or the *third sector* of U.S. society. For-profit organizations are the business sector; the governmental sector is made up of the branches, departments, agencies, and bureaus of the federal, state, and local governments.

Nonprofit organizations, particularly charitable ones, foster pluralization of institutions and encourage voluntarism. Society benefits not only from the application of private wealth to specific public purposes but also from the variety of programs that individual philanthropists, making gifts of all sizes, make available for support. Program choice–making is decentralized, efficient, and more responsive to public needs than the cumbersome and less flexible government allocation process. As John Stuart Mill once observed, "Government operations tend to be everywhere alike. With individuals and voluntary associations, on the contrary, there are varied experiments, and endless diversity of experience."

Contemporary writing is replete with statements of these fundamental principles. Here are some examples:

> . . . the associative impulse is strong in American life; no other civilization can show as many secret fraternal orders, businessmen's "service clubs," trade and occupational associations, social clubs, garden clubs, women's clubs, church clubs, theater groups, political and reform associations, veterans' groups, ethnic societies, and other clusterings of trivial or substantial importance.—*Max Lerner*

> . . . in America, even in modern times, communities existed before governments were here to care for public needs.—*Daniel J. Boorstein*

> . . . voluntary association with others in common causes has been thought to be strikingly characteristic of American life.—*Merle Curti*

We have been unique because another sector, clearly distinct from the other two [business and government], has, in the past, borne a heavy load of public responsibility.—*Richard C. Cornuelle*

The third sector is . . . the seedbed for organized efforts to deal with social problems.—*John D. Rockefeller*

. . . the ultimate contribution of the Third Sector to our national life—namely, what it does to ensure the continuing responsiveness, creativity and self-renewal of our democratic society.—*Waldemar A. Neilsen*

. . . an array of its [the independent sector's] virtues that is by now fairly familiar: its contributions to pluralism and diversity, its tendency to enable individuals to participate in civic life in ways that make sense to them and help to combat that corrosive feeling of powerlessness that is among the dread social diseases of our era, its encouragement of innovation and its capacity to act as a check on the inadequacies of government.—*Richard W. Lyman*

The problems of contemporary society are more complex, the solutions more involved and the satisfactions more obscure, but the basic ingredients are still the caring and the resolve to make things better.—*Brian O'Connell*

NONPROFIT ORGANIZATIONS AND LAW

The English language does not serve us well in this context, in that the term *nonprofit organization* is often misunderstood. This term does not refer to an organization that that is prohibited by law from earning a *profit* (that is, an excess of gross earnings over expenses); *nonprofit* does not mean *no profit*. In fact, it is quite common for nonprofit organizations to generate profits. (Those make the better clients.) Rather, the definition of nonprofit organization essentially relates to requirements as to what must be done with the profit earned or otherwise received. This fundamental element of the law is found in the doctrine of *private inurement* (see Chapter 5).

The word *nonprofit*, by the way, should not be confused with the term *not-for-profit* (although it often is). (For inexplicable reasons, the accounting profession prefers the phrase *not-for-profit*.) The former describes a type of organization; the latter describes a type of activity. For example, in the federal income tax setting, expenses associated with a not-for-profit activity (namely, one conducted without the requisite profit motive, as in the nature of a hobby) are not deductible as business expenses.

The concept in law of a nonprofit organization is best understood through a comparison with the concept of a *for-profit* organization. A fundamental distinction between the two types of entities is that the for-profit organization has *owners* that hold the equity in the enterprise, such as stockholders of a corporation. The for-profit organization is operated for the economic benefit of its owners; the profits of the business undertaking are passed through to them, such as by the payment of dividends on shares of stock. That is what is meant by the term for-profit organization: It is an entity that is designed to generate a profit for its owners. The transfer of the profits from the organization to its owners is pure private inurement—the inurement of net earnings to them in their private (personal) capacity. For-profit organizations are *supposed* to engage in private inurement.

By contrast, a nonprofit organization is not permitted to distribute its profits (net earnings) to those who *control* it, such as directors and officers. Normally, a nonprofit entity does not have *owners*; a few states allow nonprofit corporations to issue non–dividend paying stock. The U.S. Supreme Court has contemplated this point only once, writing that a "nonprofit entity is ordinarily understood to differ from a for-profit corporation principally because it is barred from distributing its net earnings, if any, to individuals who exercise control over it, such as members, officers, directors, or trustees."

Simply stated, a nonprofit organization is an entity that is not permitted to engage in forms of private inurement. This is why the private inurement doctrine is the substantive defining characteristic that distinguishes nonprofit organizations from for-profit organizations for purposes of the law. To reiterate: Both nonprofit and for-profit organizations are legally able to generate a profit. Yet, as the comparison between the two types of organizations indicates, there are two categories of profit: one is at the *entity* level and one is at the *ownership* level. Both categories of entities can yield entity-level profit; the distinction between the two types of entities pivots on the latter category of profit.

Why, then, the confusion as to the meaning in law of the term *nonprofit organization*? The answer: For-profit and nonprofit organizations often *look alike*. (This fact is behind, for example, today's raging debates about the difference between tax-exempt and for-profit hospitals and exempt credit unions and commercial banks.) The characteristics of the two categories of organizations are often identical, in that both mandate a legal form (see discussion following), have directors (or trustees) and officers, have employees (and thus pay compensation and other employee benefits), face essentially the same expenses (such as for occupancy, supplies, travel, and, yes, legal and other professional fees), make investments, enter into contracts, can sue or be sued, produce goods and/or services, and (as noted) generate profits.

LEGAL FORM

What form should a prospective nonprofit organization take? A lawyer may say, "It must be a separate legal entity." What does that mean?

A nonprofit organization generally must be one of three types: a corporation: a trust, or an "other" (usually an unincorporated association). In recent years the *limited liability company* has emerged as a possible form. (Occasionally, a nonprofit organization is created by a legislature.) A common element in each is that there should be a creating document (*articles of organization*) and a document containing operational rules (*bylaws*).

Keep in mind that before an organization can be tax-exempt, it must be a non-profit organization. Nonprofit organizations are basically creatures of state law; tax-exempt organizations are basically subjects of federal tax law. State tax exemption tends to follow the contours of the federal tax law (although the real estate tax exemption rules are likely to be more stringent).

Once the decision has been made to form a nonprofit organization, the legal form of the organization must be considered. This is basically a matter of state law; the laws of the state in which the headquarters is based will govern this decision.

Assuming that the nonprofit organization is expected to qualify as a tax-exempt organization under both federal and state law, it is essential to see whether a particular form of organization is dictated by federal tax law. In most cases, federal law is neutral on the point. In a few instances, however, a specific form of organization is required to qualify as a tax-exempt organization. For example, a federal government instrumentality and a title-holding organization must, under federal tax law, be formed as corporations, while entities such as supplemental unemployment benefit organizations, Black Lung benefit organizations, and multiemployer plan funds must be formed as trusts. A multibeneficiary title-holding organization can be formed as either a corporation or a trust. On occasion, a federal law other than the tax law will have a direct bearing on the campaign regulation laws; corporations cannot make political campaign contributions. A political committee may have to avoid the corporate form.

These are relatively technical types of nonprofit organizations; the vast majority need not be created by a mandated form. Thus, in the absence of a federal (or state) law requiring a particular form for the organization, the choice is made by those who are establishing the entity.

There are several factors to take into account in selecting the form of a nonprofit organization. Given the reality of our litigious society, personal liability looms as a major element in the decision. *Personal liability* means that one or more managers of a nonprofit organization (its trustees, directors, officers, and/or key employees) may be found *personally* liable for something done or not done while acting on behalf of the organization. (See Chapter 25.)

THE FOUR I'S

Some of this exposure to personal liability can be limited by one or all of the following: indemnification, insurance, immunity, and incorporation.

Indemnification occurs (assuming indemnification is legal under applicable state law) when the organization agrees (usually by provision in its bylaws) to pay the judgments and related expenses (including legal fees) incurred by those who are covered by the indemnity, when those expenses are the result of a misdeed (commission or omission) by those persons while acting in the service of the organization. The indemnification cannot extend to criminal acts and may not cover certain willful acts that violate civil law. Because an indemnification involves the resources of the organization, the real value of an indemnification depends on the economic viability of the organization. In times of financial difficulties for a nonprofit organization, an indemnification of its directors and officers can be a classic "hollow promise."

Insurance is similar to indemnification. Instead of shifting the risk of liability from the individuals involved to the nonprofit organization, however, the risk of liability is shifted to an independent third party—an insurance company. Certain risks, such as criminal law liability, cannot be shifted via insurance. The insurance contract will likely exclude from coverage certain forms of civil law liability, such as libel and slander, employment discrimination, and antitrust matters. Even where adequate coverage is available, insurance can be costly; premiums can easily amount to thousands of dollars annually, even with a sizeable deductible.

Immunity is available when state law provides that a class of individuals, under certain circumstances, is not liable for a particular act or set of acts or for failure to undertake a particular act or set of acts. Several states have enacted laws for officers and directors of nonprofit organizations, protecting them in case of asserted civil law violations, particularly where these individuals are functioning as volunteers.

Incorporation is the last of the four I's. This additional form of protection against personal liability is discussed next, as part of the summary of the type of legal entity known as the *corporation*.

THE CORPORATION

A *corporation* is regarded as a separate legal entity. Liability is generally confined to the organization and does not normally extend to those who manage it. For this reason alone, a nonprofit organization should probably be incorporated.

Incorporation has another advantage. The state nonprofit corporation law may provide answers to many of the questions that inevitably arise when forming and operating a nonprofit organization. Here are some examples:

- How many directors must the organization have? What are their voting rights? How is a quorum ascertained? How is notice properly given? What is the length and number of their terms of office?

- What officers must the organization have? What are their duties? What is the length and number of their terms of office? Can more than one office be held by the same individual?

- How frequently must the governing board meet? Must the board members always meet in person, or can the meetings be by telephone conference call or video teleconferencing? Can the board members vote by mail or unanimous consent? Can they use proxies?

- If there are members, what are their rights? When must they meet? What notice of the meetings must be given? How can they vote?

- What issues must be decided by members (if any)? By directors?

- May there be an executive committee of the governing board? If so, what are its duties? What limitations are there on its functions?

- What about other committees, including an advisory committee? Which are standing committees?

- How are the organization's governing instruments amended?

- How must a merger of the organization occur?

- What is the process for dissolving the organization? For distributing its assets and net income on dissolution?

Nearly every state has a nonprofit corporation act. The answers to these and many other questions may be found in that law. If the organization is not a corporation, these and other questions are usually unanswered under state law. The organization must then add to its rules the answers to all the pertinent questions (assuming they can be anticipated) or live with the uncertainties.

There is a third reason for the corporate form: More people will know what the entity is. People are familiar with corporations. The IRS knows corporations. Private foundations understand corporations as potential grantees. In general, the work in which the nonprofit organization will be functioning is compatible with the concept of a corporation.

In contrast to the three advantages of incorporation—limitation against personal liability, availability of information concerning operations, and the comfort factor—what are the disadvantages of incorporation? Generally, the advantages far outweigh the disadvantages. The disadvantages stem from the fact that incorporation entails an affirmative act on the part of the state government: It "charters" the entity. In exchange for the grant of corporate status, the state usually expects certain forms of compliance by the organization, such as adherence to rules of operation, an initial filing fee, annual reports (which are public documents), and annual fees. These costs are frequently nominal, however, and the reporting and disclosure requirements are usually not extensive.

A nonprofit organization that is a corporation is formed by preparing and filing *articles of incorporation*, with its operating rules embodied in *bylaws*. The contents of the articles of incorporation, dictated in part by state law, will usually include

- The name of the organization
- A general statement of its purposes
- The name(s) and address(es) of its initial director(s)
- The name and address of its registered agent
- The name(s) and address(es) of its incorporator(s)
- Language referencing the applicable federal tax law requirements

The bylaws of an incorporated nonprofit organization will usually include provisions with respect to

- Its purposes (it is a good idea to restate them in the bylaws)
- The election and duties of its directors
- The election and duties of its officers
- The role of its members (if any)
- Meetings of members and directors, including dates, notice, quorum, and voting
- The role of excessive and other committees
- The role of its chapters (if any)
- The function of affiliated organizations (if any)
- The organization's fiscal year
- Language referencing the applicable federal tax law requirements (again, a good idea to repeat this in the bylaws)

Some organizations adopt operational rules and policies stated in a document that is neither articles of incorporation nor bylaws. These rules may be more freely amended than articles or bylaws. They should not, however, be inconsistent with the articles or bylaws.

THE TRUST

A nonprofit organization may be formed as a *trust*. This is rarely an appropriate form for a nonprofit organization other than a charitable entity or some of the funds associated with employee plans. Many private foundations, for example, are trusts. Those created by a will are known as testamentary trusts.

Most nonprofit organizations, however, particularly those that will have a membership, are ill-suited to be structured as trusts.

The principal problem with structuring a nonprofit organization as a trust is that most state laws concerning trusts are written for the regulation of charitable trusts. These rules are rarely as flexible as contemporary nonprofit corporation acts, and frequently impose fiduciary standards and practices that are more stringent than those for nonprofit corporations.

A nonprofit organization that is to be a trust is formed by the execution of a *trust agreement* or a *declaration of trust*. Frequently, only one trustee is necessary—another reflection of the usual narrow use of trusts.

The trustees of a trust do not have the protection against personal liability that is afforded by the corporate form.

Although a fee to the state is rarely imposed upon the creation of a trust, most states impose on trusts an annual filing requirement for the trust agreement or declaration of trust.

It is unusual—although certainly permissible—for the trustee(s) of a trust to adopt a set of bylaws.

THE UNINCORPORATED ASSOCIATION

The final type of the usual nonprofit organization is the *unincorporated association*.

To the uninitiated, a nonprofit corporation and a nonprofit unincorporated organization look alike. For example, a membership association has the same characteristics, whether or not it is incorporated. The shield against individual liability provided by the corporate form, however, is unavailable in an unincorporated association.

An unincorporated association is formed by the preparation and adoption of a *constitution*. The contents of a constitution are much the same as the contents of articles of incorporation; the contents of bylaws of an unincorporated association are usually the same as those of a nonprofit corporation.

It is relatively uncommon for an unincorporated association to have to register with and annually report to a state (other than for fundraising regulation purposes; see Chapter 12).

Occasionally, nonprofit organizations will have articles of incorporation, a constitution, and bylaws. This is technically improper. For an incorporated nonprofit organization, the constitution is a redundancy.

Trusts and unincorporated associations are likely to have less contact with the state than nonprofit corporations, but this advantage is usually overshadowed by more substantive disadvantages.

In some states (e.g., California and New York), the nonprofit corporation and trust law is far more refined. Careful examination of these and other relevant laws is essential when an organization is to be formed in, or to operate in, one or more of these states. In addition, some states have far more stringent laws concerning mergers and dissolutions.

In summary, as a general rule a nonprofit organization has clear advantages if it is organized as a corporation. Nonetheless, the facts and circumstances of each situation must be carefully examined to be certain that the most appropriate form is selected.

LOCATION

The starting point for organizing a nonprofit organization is the law of the state. But which state? Although it can operate in more than one jurisdiction, an organization can be created or formed under the law of only one jurisdiction (at a time). In most instances, this means selecting the jurisdiction in which the organization will be headquartered.

Because the process of qualifying an organization to do business in a state is about the same as incorporating it, there usually is no point in forcing the organization to comply with the laws of two states. There are exceptions to this rule: A stock-based nonprofit organization may be appropriate, or perhaps only one director is desired. Another consideration is the degree of regulation imposed by the office of a state's attorney general or comparable agency; this element varies widely from state to state. If an organization is formed in one state but has offices in one or more other states, this duplication of effort is unavoidable.

A caution: If a nonprofit organization is formed in one jurisdiction and the plan is to qualify it in another, be certain that the organization will meet the requirements of the law of the state of qualification. For example, not all states allow a nonprofit organization formed as a corporation with stock to qualify.

Checklist

- ❑ Form of organization:
    - ❑ Corporation
    - ❑ Unincorporated association
    - ❑ Trust
    - ❑ Other
- ❑ Type of articles of organization:
    - ❑ Articles of Incorporation
    - ❑ Constitution
    - ❑ Declaration of trust
    - ❑ Trust agreement
    - ❑ Other
- ❑ Date organization formed _____
- ❑ Place organization formed _____
- ❑ States in which qualified to do business _____
- ❑ Date(s) of amendment of articles _____
- ❑ Date operational rules (e.g., bylaws) adopted _____
- ❑ Date(s) of amendment of rules _____

❏ Membership: Yes _____ No _____

❏ If yes:

Annual meeting date _____

Notice requirement _____

❏ Chapters: Yes _____ No _____

❏ Affiliated organizations _____

❏ Committees: _____

    ❏ Executive

    ❏ Nominating

    ❏ Development (fundraising)

    ❏ Finance and/or Audit

    ❏ Long-Range Planning

    ❏ Other(s)

❏ Fiscal year _____

CHAPTER TWO

Starting a Nonprofit Organization

Being enthusiastic, imaginative, and creative about establishing a nonprofit organization is one thing. Actually forming the entity and making it operational is quite another matter.

For better or worse, the exercise is much like establishing one's own business. It is a big and important undertaking, and it should be done carefully and properly. The label *nonprofit* does not mean "no planning." Forming a nonprofit organization is as serious as starting up a commercial company.

It is important when setting up an organization to remember that in some instances, the same activity or activities may be undertaken in a for-profit or nonprofit organization. Other considerations come into play as well, such as whether the motive for starting the organization is *profit* (so that money can be taken out as dividends or money can be made when the stock is sold). In a rare instance, the choice of entity may be dictated by the realities of initial financing. (In an example of the latter, some individuals in New York City decided to establish a Museum of Sex. The original plan was that the museum would be nonprofit but the initial funding could not be obtained because prospective donors and private foundations were leery of the concept. So, the founders attracted capital and made it a for-profit museum.)

Many nonprofit organizations are started on a shoestring; the individuals involved undertake tasks they would never do if they were starting a commercial enterprise. One of the reasons is a widespread *nonprofit mentality*—a belief that because the undertaking is nonprofit, it need not pay for services rendered. Encumbered with this view, the sponsors of the organization will, in abundant good faith and with the best of intentions seek—or even expect—free assistance. Sometimes, this attitude carries over to the acquisition of equipment and supplies.

In some instances, this nonprofit mentality is wonderful. It enables a skilled manager to parlay a horde of earnest volunteers into a magnificent service-providing organization. Truly skilled managers are rare, however, and anyone considering organizing and operating a nonprofit organization is well advised not to skimp on hiring three consultants: a lawyer, an accountant, and a fundraiser. The professional services of these individuals are crucial. The old adage, "You get what you pay for," is amply applicable here.

AN ILLUSTRATION: A NEW ORGANIZATION

Let's reduce the role of nonprofit organizations to a more practical level. What problems in society trouble you? How would you solve these problems if:

Sufficient money were available to fund the programs you feel are needed?

No governmental agency were to become directly involved?

Suppose you decide that something must be done nationwide about littering. You intensely dislike the cluttering of the environment with an assortment of bottles, cans, and other trash, and you resent those who do the littering. You realize that this is not a problem that you can conquer singlehandedly, and you suspect (correctly) that there is not much money in the coffers of your town, county, state, or federal treasuries to be used for more trash control. Yet you suspect (also correctly) that others in your community and around the nation feel the same about the accumulating litter as you do.

In the best tradition of problem solving in the United States, you decide to form an organization to "do something." In your opinion, the trash problem can be solved in two basic ways: pickup and disposal, and public education. You envision scores of volunteers who will comb the streets, parks, and other areas of their communities, picking up trash and distributing antilitter literature. Your hope is that greater sensitivity to the trash problem will inhibit littering and encourage citizens to be more willing to clean up their communities and keep them clean.

Being not one of the rich and famous, you begin thinking about how you will fund this organization and the specific nature of its programs. As your plans take shape, you mention your ideas to a neighbor, who is a labor-relations lawyer. He has only a vague idea of what to recommend, but he helps you contact one of his law partners who practices in the field of corporate and tax law.

While you are driving to the first appointment, your car radio delivers a fundraising message on behalf of a charitable organization that has a catchy name and some memorable slogans. Suddenly, you realize that your organization-to-be must likewise be a charitable one (to be exempt from taxes and to receive deductible gifts) and that it needs a suitable name. By the time you reach the lawyer's office, you know what the name will be: "Campaign to Clean Up America."

The lawyer is a specialist in the field of nonprofit, tax-exempt organizations. She takes down from her bookshelf a 1977 report by a body known as the Commission on Private Philanthropy and Public Needs, and reads this passage:

> The practice of attending to community needs outside of government has profoundly shaped American society and its institutional framework. . . . This vast and varied array is, and has long been widely recognized as part of the very fabric of American life. It reflects a national belief in the philosophy of pluralism and in the profound importance to society of individual initiative.

Next, she produces a copy of congressional testimony in 1973, when George P. Shultz, then Secretary of the Treasury, said that charitable organizations "are an important influence for diversity and a bulwark against overreliance on big government."

Then, as befits a lawyer, she reaches into the casebooks. A federal court of appeals, in the context of explaining the rationale for tax-exempt status for nonprofit organizations, had this to say:

> [O]ne stated reason for a deduction or exemption of this kind is that the favored entity performs a public service and benefits the public or relieves it of a burden which otherwise belongs to it.

For further backup, the lawyer turns to a U.S. Supreme Court decision:

> The State has an affirmative policy that considers these groups as beneficial and stabilizing influences in community life and finds this classification [tax exemption] useful, desirable, and in the public interest.

She then reads from a federal district court opinion concerning the charitable contribution deduction. The court stated that the reason for the deduction has "historically been that by doing so, the Government relieves itself of the burden of meeting public needs which in the absence of charitable activity would fall on the shoulders of the Government."

By this time, your enthusiasm and vision are nearly boundless. Here you are, thinking and acting in the finest American traditions: approaching and solving a problem, invoking the principles of pluralism and voluntarism, demonstrating your care and "resolve to make things better"—all without government help. You're relieving government of a responsibility that society must assume. You feel that, almost singlehandedly, you are ensuring the "continuing responsiveness, creativity, and self-renewal of our democratic society."

Twenty minutes later, however, your soaring enthusiasm for ridding the United States of its litter has plummeted into deep confusion. What seemed like such a wonderful concept has been quickly and repeatedly punctured with swirls of advice about state corporate law intricacies, warnings of personal liability, gobbledygook about the law of deductible charitable giving, babble about related and unrelated activities, something about state regulation of fundraising, talk of a Form 1023 and Form 990, and—here the lawyer has totally lost you—a discourse on private inurement and private benefit, and something called intermediate sanctions, the distinctions between private foundations and public charities, and rules regarding the disclosure of tax documents.

Discouraged, and rapidly abandoning any more thoughts about saving your country from the onslaught of more rubbish, you dejectedly mumble something about paying a fee for the consultation and prepare to leave. Sensing your dejection and despair, the lawyer assures you that, although the startup may be more complex than you thought, you have a good idea and she can help you (for a reasonable fee) through the maze of laws to your goal. Implicitly trusting her, you agree to proceed. In a few short months, you have a successful, nationwide, multimillion-dollar charitable organization to combat the blight of trash in the American environment. In fact, you have quit your job and are now the full-time, paid president of the Campaign to Clean Up America.

AN INITIAL CHECKLIST

Looking back, you review the questions that you and the lawyer resolved:

- What should be the form of the organization? Why? In what jurisdiction should it be formed?

- Who should be its directors and officers? Why? What about their personal liability? Should there be employees? Consultants? Compensation arrangements?

- What will be the organization's activities? Will some of them be unrelated businesses?

- How will the organization achieve its goals at the community level? Will it have chapters? Members? In either case, what will be the criteria?

- How can the organization be exempt from federal and state taxation?

- How will the organization be funded? By gifts? By grants? By income from the performance of exempt functions? By endowment income? By unrelated income?

- Will the organization be public or private?

- To what extent will gifts to the organization be deductible?

- What reports must be filed with federal and state governmental agencies?

- What are the applicable laws on fundraising requirements?

- Do the doctrines of private inurement or private benefit have any applicability to what the organization will be doing?

- Are there any aspects of the organization's operations that might trigger application of the intermediate sanctions penalties?

- Can or should the organization engage in lobbying or political campaign activities?

- Is there a need for a separate fundraising foundation?

- Should a for-profit subsidiary be established?

- Would it be appropriate for the organization to "partner" with one or more other organizations?

You're aware that there are subsidiary questions within each of these categories. Numerous other questions have come up since you became president. Some are on your desk now, and you surmise (all too correctly) that many others lie ahead.

FOCUS: Campaign to Clean Up America

After consideration of all of the relevant factors, the decision is made (in conformance with the lawyer's advice) to form the Campaign to Clean Up America (CCUA) as a nonprofit corporation. The aspect of limited personal liability is of particular interest, and you can see few disadvantages to incorporation of the entity. (Regarding personal liability, the lawyer advises the use of an indemnification provision and points out that in some instances, under Missouri law, directors and officers of nonprofit organizations are immunized from personal liability.) You instruct the lawyer to prepare the articles of incorporation for the CCUA and to incorporate it in your home state of Missouri.

BOARD OF DIRECTORS

Every nonprofit organization—irrespective of form—must have at least one director (or trustee). Few nonprofit organizations, however, have just one *manager*. (In tax-law language, directors, officers, and key employees are managers.)

The directors are those who set policy for and generally administer the organization (see Chapter 8). The word *generally* is used here because day-to-day management is supposed to be the province of the employees and, sometimes, the officers. The directors are the policymakers of the organization—they develop plans for the organization and oversee its affairs. In reality, it is difficult to set a precise line of demarcation as to where the scope of authority of the board of directors stops and the authority of the officers begins. The authority of directors and officers in relation to the authority of employees is equally hard to separate. All too frequently, authority or "territory" is resolved on an occasion-by-occasion basis—in the political arena, not the legal one—by the sheer force of personalities.

Although many state nonprofit corporation laws require at least three directors, many nonprofit organizations have far larger governing boards. State laws never set a maximum number of nonprofit organization directors. The optimum size of a governing board of a nonprofit organization depends on many factors.

One factor that affects the size of a nonprofit organization's governing board is the manner in which its membership is elected. If there are bona fide members of the nonprofit organization, it is likely that these members will elect some or all of the members of the governing board. This election may be conducted by mail ballot, online, or by voting at an annual meeting. In some instances, the board may include some ex officio positions (such as one or more of the officers, one or more past presidents, or individuals who hold positions in a separate but related organization). It is quite possible, however, for a nonprofit organization with a membership to have a governing board that is not elected by that membership.

In the absence of a membership (or if the membership has no vote on the matter), the governing board of a nonprofit organization may be a *self-perpetuating board*. In this case, the initial board may continue with those whom it elects and with subsequent boards. Again, there may be one or more ex officio positions.

In many nonprofit organizations, the source of the membership of the governing board is preordained. Some examples include the typical membership organization that elects the board (for example, a trade association, a country club, or a veterans' organization); a hospital, college, or museum that has a governing board generally reflective of the community; and a private foundation that has one or more trustees who represent a particular family or a corporation.

Politics is a dominant factor in board elections. Some membership organizations, for example, may appear to have an "open" election system, yet the process is controlled by a small group that functions as the nominating committee. Some advocacy groups may feature a membership that is not a true membership at all and a governing board that is tightly controlled by a small group of insiders.

The combinations of ways to generate members of a governing board are numerous. One fundamental principle to keep in mind is that, except in the rare instance of a stock-based nonprofit corporation, no one owns a nonprofit organization. *Control* of a nonprofit organization, however, is another matter. A membership may control a nonprofit organization without owning it; more frequently, the board of directors controls a nonprofit organization, regardless of the presence of a membership.

The selection of directors and the control of a nonprofit organization are of particular consequence in a single-purpose organization that is started by one individual or a close-knit group. The people who launch a nonprofit organization do not want to put their blood, sweat, tears, and dollars into the organization, only to watch others assume control over it. Yet these founders usually want a "representative" governing board, which, if created, would clearly put them in a minority, without control.

One solution to this problem may be an advisory committee—a group of individuals who do not substitute for the board of directors but provide technical input on the organization's programs. Because the members of an advisory committee lack voting rights, their number is governed only by what is practical. Committee members serve without the threat of personal liability that may accrue to directors and officers and without incurring the larger set of responsibilities held by the directors. By having an advisory committee, an organization can surround itself with prominent names in the field. The roster can lead to some impressive stationery!

The board of directors may decide to have a chair (or chairperson or chairman) of the board. This individual presides over board meetings. The chair position is not usually an officer position (although it can be made one). The position may (but need not) be authorized in the organization's bylaws.

A board of directors (or trustees) of a nonprofit organization usually acts by means of in-person meetings (a quorum must be present). Where state law allows, the members of the board can act at a meeting held via a conference telephone call (where all participants can hear each other) or by unanimous written consent. These alternative procedures must also be authorized in the bylaws. Unless there is a specific authorization in the law, directors of a nonprofit organization may not vote by proxy, mail ballot, e-mail, or telephone calls (other than a conference call). (These limitations do not normally apply to voting by members, which is why some nonprofit organizations have a membership composed solely of the board of directors.)

Checklist

❑ Board of directors (trustees):

Origin _____

Number _____

Quorum _____

Voting power _____

Terms of office _____

Annual meeting date _____

Notice requirement _____

❑ Chair of board: Yes _____ No _____

FOCUS: Campaign to Clean Up America

How should the Campaign to Clean Up America (CCUA) organize its governing board? Assume that you wish to retain control and that the state law under which the CCUA is formed requires at least three directors (recall that the CCUA was formed as a nonprofit corporation). You are one of the three. The other two spots may be filled by your spouse, best friend, lawyer, accountant, or someone else whom you trust. Thus, as a matter of fact (but not necessarily of law), you presumably are in control of the CCUA.

This approach has some deficiencies. Because loyalties can shift, you can never be certain that you are in fact always in control. Your ability to advance the cause may be hindered in the absence of a "public" board. In addition, the Internal Revenue Service (IRS) may allege the presence of private benefit or private inurement if the governing board is too small and incestuous.

Here are some options:

- Form the CCUA in a state that requires only one director, then become qualified to function in the state from which it will operate.

- Form the CCUA In a state that allows nonprofit corporations to issue stock. You become the sole stockholder, the bylaws are written so that the directors of the CCUA are selected by the shareholder, and the CCUA then becomes qualified to function in the state from which it will operate.

- Create an intimate, small (for example, three-person) board, to be accompanied by a separate advisory committee composed of "outsiders"; the advisory committee has no binding vote as to corporate policy.

- Elect the governing board of the CCUA by a membership vote or by some other means that is representative of those interested in the cause, and trust your political skills to enable you to retain operational control.

After due consideration, you doubt your political acumen and you incorporate the CCUA in the state where you live (Missouri). You name as the three initial board members yourself, your spouse, and a close personal friend. (You invited your lawyer to be on the board, but she declined on the grounds of potential personal liability and a conflict of interest.) The bylaws of the CCUA are written to provide for a self-perpetuating board and to create an advisory committee that is generally representative of the antitrash cause. You resolve that you will, someday, make the governing board of the CCUA more representative of its constituency.

In the meantime, you are not Interested in a membership with full voting rights. You begin thinking about how a nonvoting membership would enable you to build a network of individuals who could serve the CCUA as volunteers at the local level. These individuals could become the heart of a very important group: the CCUA's regular donors.

OFFICERS

Nearly every nonprofit organization has *officers*. The classic exception is the trust, which usually has only one or more trustees (and no officers).

As with the board of directors, levels of authority of officers are difficult to articulate. In a nonprofit organization that has members, directors, officers, and employees, setting a clear distinction as to who has the authority to do what is nearly impossible. General principles can be stated, but they usually prove useless in practice. For example, it can be stated that the members set basic policy and the board of directors sets additional policy, but within the policy parameters established by the membership. The officers then implement policy; the employees also implement policy, albeit more on a day-to-day basis. Yet the reality is that, at all four levels, policy is established. Worse, at all four levels, policy is implemented.

In a typical nonprofit organization, for example, who decides which new programs will be undertaken, who is hired and fired as employees, what will be the nature of the retirement plan arrangements, who the lawyers and accountants will be, along with the type of fundraising program, the format of the journal, or the organization's physical location? Depending on the circumstances, the answer may be the members, the board, the chair of the board, the president, the vice-president, the executive director, or any number of others!

For the most part, the answers to these questions relate to politics and personalities. A nonprofit corporation statute may spell out the duties of directors and officers, but these are broad ranges of responsibilities. Who is to stop a board majority that wants a green tint to an organization's newsletter rather than a blue one? Or the board majority that wants the organization to use the services of a particular bank, lawyer, or pension plan administrator? Yet, in many a nonprofit organization, the directors and officers are mere putty in the hands of the executive director or president. By contrast, many nonprofit organizations have volunteer members of the board of directors, each of whom believes it is his or her duty to delve deeply into the day-to-day management of the organization.

One cannot generalize on the origins of officers, except to say that they are usually elected, either by the membership or by the board of directors. Some may be appointed by other officers who are elected.

The common patterns include the following:

- A membership elects the directors and the officers.
- A membership elects the directors and the directors elect the officers.
- A self-perpetuating board elects the officers.
- In any of the foregoing combinations, some of the officers may be appointed.

The governing instruments of the organization (usually the bylaws) should identify the offices of the organization, state the duties and responsibilities of the officers, provide for the manner of their selection, state the terms of the offices, address the matter of reelections to office, and so forth. Some organizations find it useful to stagger the terms of office so that only a portion of the board is up for election at any one time, thereby providing some continuity of service and expertise. A popular model is a nine-member board, each member having a three-year term, with one-third of the board elected or reelected annually. In some states, the nonprofit corporation's law imposes some requirements for officers, terms of office, and the like.

For example, in a typical pattern, a membership elects a board of directors. The directors elect a president, secretary, and treasurer. The president appoints an assistant treasurer, an assistant secretary, and an executive director. A variation is to have the members directly elect the officers. Another common pattern is for an organization to have a self-perpetuating board of directors that elects the officers. For the most part, the law allows a nonprofit organization to use whatever governing structure it wants.

Normally, a chair of the board is not a corporate officer. He or she is selected by the board of directors as its leader. In many nonprofit organizations, the chair of the board and the president are the same individual. In others, the chair of the board assumes the responsibilities normally expected of a president. Sometimes, the person normally termed an executive director is labeled the president. Here, too, the possibilities are numerous. How can the roles of a chair of the board and a president be differentiated? What is the difference between an executive director and an executive vice-president?

Can a strong, aggressive chair dominate the board of directors, the officers, and the staff? Can a strong, aggressive executive director dominate the other staff members, the officers, and the board of directors? The answer to both questions is Yes.

Particularly if the organization is a corporation, state law usually requires at least certain officers. In general, the same individual can hold more than one office—the positions of secretary and treasurer are commonly combined. The president and the secretary, however, should not be the same individual. This duality is prohibited in many states. Frequently, legal documents require these two officers' separate signatures.

Officers are officers of the organization. They are not officers of the board of directors or board of trustees.

Checklist

❏ Officers:

Origin _____

Titles:

    ❏ President

    ❏ Other title for President

    ❏ Vice-President(s)

    ❏ Treasurer

    ❏ Secretary

    ❏ Other(s)

Terms of office _____

FOCUS: Campaign to Clean Up America

The Campaign to Clean Up America decided to have its board of directors elect the officers. The officers must be members of the board. You are elected the president and your spouse is elected the secretary-treasurer. Given the size of the organization at this time, there is no need to have a chair of the board or a vice president.

ORGANIZATIONAL MINUTES

Another document—in addition to the articles of organization and the bylaws—that is important when forming a nonprofit organization is the *organizational minutes*. If there is a membership, there should be organizational minutes of that body. The same is true with respect to the board of directors. If there is no membership, the only organizational document will be that of the board of directors.

In this document (or documents), the following actions, at a minimum, will be reflected: ratification of the adoption of the articles of organization; adoption of the bylaws; election of the officers; passage of the requisite resolution(s) for the establishment of a bank account (or accounts); passage of resolutions selecting legal counsel, an accountant, and perhaps a fundraising consultant; and authorization of reimbursement of expenses incurred in establishing the entity. (The bank that is selected will provide the form of the resolution(s) that it wishes passed.) Organizational minutes may reflect other actions, such as a discussion of program activities, development of the fundraising program, and/or development of various policies (see Chapter 22).

All minutes of meetings concerning a nonprofit organization are important, but the organizational minutes have particular significance. Minutes need not be filed with the IRS when pursuing recognition of tax-exempt status (see Chapter 6) but are important documents in other settings, such as an IRS audit. A current and complete minute book, reflecting explanation of material transactions, can go a long way toward shortening (or even forestalling) an audit. For example, in the intermediate sanctions setting (see Chapter 5), if an IRS agent sees an organization's minutes which fully explain the reasons for a transaction with a disqualified person, coupled with the requisite other documentation, the treasured rebuttable presumption of reasonableness may discourage any further inquiry.

Minutes should be kept in a minute book, along with other important documents (including the articles of organization and bylaws). Minute books can be purchased commercially. A simple ring binder will suffice, but the formality of a true minute book seems to get an organization's recordkeeping off to a good start. To be useful, a minute book needs to be maintained, although there is nothing inherent in a good minute book that will cause an organization's operations to be successful.

IDENTIFICATION NUMBER

Every nonprofit organization must have an *employer identification number* (EIN). This number is assigned by the IRS and is acquired by filing a properly completed Form SS-4. This form may be filed as soon as the entity is formed or with the application for recognition of tax-exempt status. (The bank will want the number as part of the process of opening the organization's account.)

There is much confusion about the employer identification number, also known as the *taxpayer identification number*. Part of the confusion comes from its names. The number is required even though the organization does not have any employees and is not a "taxpayer."

As discussed in Chapter 3, a "tax-exempt number" is a myth. A tax-exempt organization must have an IRS-assigned identification number, but the number has nothing to do with tax-exempt status. An identification number is required of every entity, whether it is a corporation, an unincorporated association, a trust, a partnership, a limited liability company, some other type of venture, or an estate.

LIABILITY REVISITED

A vehicle that is becoming quite popular with tax-exempt organizations is the *single-member limited liability company*. (The *multimember limited liability company* is discussed in Chapter 18.)

For the most part, a limited liability company (LLC) is treated for federal tax purposes like a partnership, which is to say that the entity itself is not taxable. If an LLC has only one member, it is *disregarded* for tax purposes. Yet, it is still an entity for liability law purposes. Tax-exempt organizations can exploit this unique dichotomy to provide additional protection against organizational liability.

Here are six examples of use of this planning technique:

1. A charitable organization may accept a gift of property that carries with it exposure of the charity to legal liability (such as for environmental hazards). Each of the contributed properties can be placed in a single-member LLC, thereby offering protection in relation to each of the other properties and providing the charity with overall liability protection.

2. A charity was working with a city government to transform a decrepit downtown area. It organized a single-member LLC to operate a parking facility. The charity was held by the IRS to be lessening the burdens of the government by providing the parking in this fashion.

3. A tax-exempt museum owned and operated a racetrack and a campground in a single-member LLC. The IRS ruled that these activities were related businesses (see Chapter 12).

4. A charity developed and operated a student housing project for an exempt college in a single-member LLC. In this fashion, it issued bonds and provided temporary construction jobs and permanent employment opportunities in the community.

5. A charitable organization that provided educational opportunities to low-income and other students, including housing, provided facilities for various colleges, with the ownership and operation of each facility being placed in a single-member LLC.

6. A tax-exempt university was having severe financial difficulties with its business school. (Its law school was booming.) The institution sought relief from a private foundation in the form of substantial grants. The foundation, being entrepreneurial in spirit, did not want to just throw money at the school; it thus agreed to help but only if it could also manage the school. Desperate, the university agreed; the foundation created and funded a single-member LLC to administer the business school. (It is not every day that one sees a private foundation managing a program of a public charity; see Chapter 7.)

Even though activities and/or assets are in a single-member LLC, where a tax-exempt organization is the sole member, the activities and assets are reported on the exempt organization's annual information return (see Chapter 9). Again, this unusual treatment is accorded because this type of LLC is a disregarded entity.

CHAPTER THREE

Debunking Some Myths and Misperceptions

Those who manage and consult with nonprofit organizations all too frequently misunderstand the nature of the entities they are working with and the law that applies to them. This chapter is offered with the hope that it will, at least for the readers, put an end to these myths and misunderstandings.

MYTH 1: NONPROFIT AND NOT-FOR-PROFIT ARE THE SAME

Nonprofit is the proper term. Many laws and lawyers (and others) use the term *not-for-profit* when they mean nonprofit. Accountants, for example, tend to prefer the term not-for-profit. This is understandable, because of the confusion surrounding what the term *nonprofit* means (see Myth 2). The term not-for-profit is properly used to refer to an activity that is engaged in without a profit motive (that is, a hobby), where the expenses involved do not qualify for the business expense deduction. This term was not intended (at least not in tax law parlance) to describe a type of organization. (See Chapter 1.)

MYTH 2: NONPROFIT ORGANIZATIONS CANNOT EARN A PROFIT

Nothing could be further from the truth. A nonprofit organization can enjoy a profit (more income than expenses); no organization can operate in the red for very long. The difference between nonprofit and for-profit organizations lies in what should be done with the profit. Nonprofit organizations use profits to advance their programs. For-profit organizations distribute their profits to their owners; in a corporation, dividends are paid to stockholders. This is why the fundamental legal distinction between the two types of entities is the doctrine of private inurement. (See Chapters 1 and 5.)

MYTH 3: AN ORGANIZATION MUST BE INCORPORATED TO BE TAX-EXEMPT

In general, this is not the law. As discussed in Chapter 2, a tax-exempt organization generally may take one of three forms. Incorporation may be (and usually is) desirable, but generally it is not mandatory. The federal tax law, however, occasionally mandates that certain tax-exempt organizations be incorporated, such as instrumentalities of the United States and single-parent title-holding organizations.

MYTH 4: EVERY NONPROFIT ORGANIZATION QUALIFIES AS A TAX-EXEMPT ORGANIZATION

This is not the case. Nearly every tax-exempt organization is a nonprofit organization, but not all nonprofit organizations are eligible to be tax-exempt. The concept of a nonprofit organization is broader than that of a tax-exempt organization. (See Chapter 5.) Some types of nonprofit organizations (such as mutual, self-help entities) do not, as a matter of federal law, qualify for tax-exempt status.

MYTH 5: BEING TAX-EXEMPT MEANS THAT THE ORGANIZATION DOES NOT HAVE TO PAY ANY TAXES

As Chapters 7, and 13 to 16 indicate, this is certainly not the case—and those chapters relate only to federal income and excise taxes. Even with complete exemption from federal taxation, an organization may still have exposure to state or local income, sales, use, or property taxation. Moreover, several civil law penalties (not really taxes, but payments to a government nonetheless) are applicable to nonprofit organizations.

MYTH 6: ALL TAX-EXEMPT ORGANIZATIONS ARE ELIGIBLE TO RECEIVE CONTRIBUTIONS THAT ARE DEDUCTIBLE FOR FEDERAL INCOME TAX PURPOSES

Not true. Just as nonprofit organizations are a larger universe than tax-exempt organizations, tax-exempt organizations are a larger universe than organizations that are eligible to receive deductible contributions. (The types of tax-exempt organizations that may receive contributions that are deductible for federal income tax purposes are referenced in Chapter 11.)

MYTH 7: A TAX-EXEMPT ORGANIZATION MUST HAVE A RULING FROM THE IRS STATING THAT IT IS TAX-EXEMPT

For the most part, this is not the law. First, the IRS does not grant tax-exempt status— Congress does that; the IRS grants *recognition* of tax-exempt status. (See Chapter 6.) Second, this grant of recognition from the IRS is generally made by means of a *determination letter*, which technically is not a ruling. Third, only four types of tax-exempt organizations are required to have a determination letter: charitable organizations, credit counseling organizations, voluntary employees' beneficiary associations, and supplemental unemployment benefit trusts. For other tax-exempt organizations, the pursuit of recognition of tax-exempt status is optional. (Political organizations, however, to be tax-exempt, are required to file a notice, on Form 8871, with the IRS.) This is not to say that a tax-exempt organization should not seek a determination letter if it does not have to (since in many cases that is advisable); the point simply is that, generally, a determination letter is not mandatory.

MYTH 8: THERE IS SOMETHING CALLED A *TAX-EXEMPT NUMBER*

This is not true. As discussed in Chapter 2, every nonprofit organization (tax-exempt or not) must have an IRS-assigned identification number, but that number has nothing to do with tax-exempt status.

MYTH 9: ONLY CHARITABLE ORGANIZATIONS ARE ELIGIBLE TO RECEIVE CONTRIBUTIONS THAT ARE DEDUCTIBLE FOR FEDERAL INCOME TAX PURPOSES

Not true. Congress has provided charitable donee status for organizations in addition to those that are normally regarded as charitable organizations. In addition to organizations that are charitable, educational, religious, scientific, and the like, deductible charitable gifts may be made to governmental bodies, veterans' organizations, fraternal organizations, and cemetery companies. (See Chapter 11.)

MYTH 10: A CHARITABLE ORGANIZATION CANNOT ENGAGE IN LEGISLATIVE ACTIVITIES

False. A charity is permitted to engage in far more lobbying efforts than most people realize. Indeed, under some circumstances, a charitable organization can spend more than one-fifth of its funds for legislative ends. (See Chapter 14.)

MYTH 11: A CHARITABLE ORGANIZATION CANNOT ENGAGE IN POLITICAL ACTIVITIES

Again, not true. A charity cannot engage in political campaign activities without loss of its tax-exempt status (and eligibility to receive deductible contributions), but it can engage in certain types of political activities. This practice may trigger a tax—but not loss of exemption. Also, a charity can use a political action committee to engage in political activities that are not political campaign activities. (See Chapter 15.)

MYTH 12: ONLY THE STATES REGULATE THE PROCESS OF FUNDRAISING BY CHARITABLE ORGANIZATIONS

This is not true. There is no federal charitable solicitations act (at least not yet), but the federal authorities have devised a variety of ways to regulate charitable fundraising (see Chapter 12), primarily through the federal tax system.

MYTH 13: STATE REGULATION OF FUNDRAISING FOR CHARITABLE PURPOSES HAS DECLINED

Wrong. This is a boom area of the law. States that previously lacked fundraising regulation statutes now enact them, and states that have them are finding ways to make them tougher. (See Chapter 12.)

MYTH 14: NONPROFIT ORGANIZATIONS HAVE FEWER REPORTING OBLIGATIONS THAN FOR-PROFIT ORGANIZATIONS

Of all the myths, this one might seem—on its face—to make the most sense. It is, however, certainly wrong. Despite the favors the law frequently bestows on nonprofit organizations, the reporting requirements are not one of them, particularly when the organization is tax-exempt. The annual information return that most tax-exempt organizations have to file with the IRS (see Chapter 9) is far more extensive than the tax returns most commercial businesses must file. In addition, several state annual reports may be required (if the organization is doing business in more than one state) along with the state annual charitable solicitation act reports (perhaps over 40 of them). (See Chapter 12.)

MYTH 15: A NONPROFIT ORGANIZATION MUST BE REPRESENTED BY A PROFESSIONAL (LAWYER OR ACCOUNTANT) TO SECURE RECOGNITION OF TAX-EXEMPT STATUS FROM THE IRS

Although the professionals may wish it otherwise, there is no requirement that a professional be involved in this process. A nonprofit organization may secure recognition of tax-exempt status on its own. In complex circumstances (and circumstances may be more complex than most people may realize), however, a nonprofit organization usually will be far better off using the services of a competent professional who charges a reasonable fee to see that the task is done correctly. (The lawyer or other professional involved should be asked, in advance, for an estimate of total fees and expenses.) If mistakes are made, it is more costly to undo them and otherwise rectify the situation than it is to pay a fair fee to do the tax exemption application properly from the beginning. This reality is even more compelling now that the IRS is more intensely scrutinizing applications for recognition of exemption.

MYTH 16: ALL LAWYERS AND ACCOUNTANTS ARE COMPETENT TO REPRESENT A NONPROFIT ORGANIZATION

As society becomes more complex and as fields of practice become correspondingly more specialized, this statement is becoming more and more a myth. A lawyer, for example, may be an excellent practitioner in the field of labor law, securities law, patent law, admiralty law, or domestic relations law, but that does not mean that he or she is competent to represent a nonprofit organization. Even a corporate or tax lawyer may not have the requisite expertise. Just as you would not go to a brain surgeon for a coronary bypass operation, you should not go to a divorce lawyer when you need help with a nonprofit or tax-exempt organization.

MYTH 17: IT IS EASY TO FIND A LAWYER OR ACCOUNTANT WHO IS COMPETENT TO REPRESENT NONPROFIT, TAX-EXEMPT ORGANIZATIONS

Related to Myth 16, this myth is too frequently untrue. There is no convenient master list of these specialists. Some lawyers and accountants who do not practice in this field are not shy about referring nonprofit organizations to practitioners who specialize in this area of the law. Other professionals, however, are not that self confident: They are unwilling to lose a client or prospective client to someone else, even if it is in the best interest of the organization. To find a lawyer or accountant who serves nonprofit organizations on a regular basis, you should talk to those involved with other nonprofit organizations and learn whom they rely on for legal and accounting services. An alternative is to attend one or more seminars or conferences concerning nonprofit organization matters where lawyers and accountants are presenting; on these occasions, you can see your prospective professional advisors in action. Most lawyers and accountants who are good at what they do will tell you that referrals are their best source of new business.

MYTH 18: ALL FUNDRAISERS ARE EQUAL IN COMPETENCE

This untruth rivals and magnifies Myths 16 and 17. Not only are there good and bad, ethical and unethical fundraisers, there are good ones with important subspecialties. Fundraising consultants can be excellent when it comes to direct mail, special events, capital campaigns, fee-for-service projects, or planned giving, but rarely will one consultant have any true expertise in more than one or two of these areas. Your direct mail consultant probably knows nothing about planned giving. Look for a fundraiser with expertise in working with comparable types of organizations, such as colleges, hospitals, symphony orchestras, or professional societies. A *fundraiser* may in reality be a *solicitor*, and you'll be faced with other problems.

MYTH 19: THE IRS IS ALWAYS RIGHT

Usually, the IRS is right, at least in the tax-exempt organizations context. Once in a while, nonetheless, the IRS will err. As an example, the IRS has been known to take an erroneous position on an issue at the district office level, only to be overruled by its National Office in Washington, D.C. Generally, the quality of IRS personnel is good; it is exceptionally high at the National Office. The point is that, although the IRS is usually correct, an answer received from the IRS in response to a particular inquiry may be less than fully accurate. With few exceptions, IRS personnel do not provide tax planning services.

MYTH 20: THERE IS NO HUMOR IN THE FEDERAL TAX LAW BEARING ON TAX-EXEMPT ORGANIZATIONS

Actually, this myth comes closer to the truth than any of the others. There are, however, a few exceptions.

The federal tax law definition of the term *agricultural* includes the art or science of "harvesting . . . aquatic resources." The comparable definition under the postal laws includes the art or science of "harvesting . . . marine resources." It is not clear why this distinction is made, but, because the word *aquatic* means "pertaining to water" and the word *marine* means "pertaining to the sea," an organization engaged in or associated with the harvesting of fresh waters can acquire classification as an agricultural organization for federal tax purposes but will fail to do so under the postal law, which emphasizes salt waters.

Maybe this one will spark more mirth. A variety of types of organizations are exempt from the unrelated income rules. One of them is a category of radio station operated by a nonprofit organization that satisfies certain criteria. The three basic tests that must be met under these rules are worded so that only one radio station qualifies. The criteria are phrased in such a way that the first letter of each of the three tests identifies a call letter of the beneficiary radio station (WWL, operated by Loyola University in New Orleans, Louisiana).

Try this one. The IRS is unhappy when organizations, claiming to be tax-exempt but lacking a determination letter (see Myth 7), file an annual information return (see Chapter 9); the agency seems to have trouble correlating these returns with its other records (if any) as to these filers. The IRS decided the solution to this problem was to reject the returns (even though the organizations were legally required to file them). So, the IRS would simply mail them back! The position of the IRS was, yes, the law mandates the filing of these returns but nothing in the statute requires the IRS to *accept* them! (To its credit, the agency has quietly abandoned this policy.)

Humor can creep in when the IRS is naming its annual information returns and tax returns. Political organizations—run for the benefit of or in opposition to *pols*—are required to file an annual return named, appropriately enough, Form 1120-POL. The return filed by small organizations, which is only two pages so as to make it *easy* for them, is named Form 990-EZ.

MYTH 21: TO BE CHARITABLE, AN ORGANIZATION CANNOT CHARGE FEES

This has never been the law, but you wouldn't know that, given today's discourse. Many nonprofit organizations charge fees for services rendered or products sold. Tax-exempt schools, colleges, universities, hospitals, theaters, museums, symphony orchestras and other orchestras, and myriad other public charities do it. Yet, in the minds of some, this is evidence of commercial activity and undue competition with for-profit organizations. Some profess to be confused, unable to differentiate between for-profit businesses and nonprofit groups that "look like" for-profits. Charitable status is predicated on what is done with the money, not where it comes from. Fee-for-service charities are expressly provided for in the federal tax law (see Chapter 7).

MYTH 22: TO BE CHARITABLE, AN ORGANIZATION MUST GIVE SOMETHING AWAY

This notion (the flip side of Myth 21) does not reflect the law either, although many policymakers believe that it does. Some charities operate on a no-charge or low-charge basis, but that is not the sole way to be charitable. (It can be tough to make ends meet if no funds are coming in.) The Supreme Court of Minnesota classically demonstrated this confusion as to what the law is in a well-publicized decision rendered in December 2007. That court held that a nonprofit day care agency was not exempt from property taxes because—gasp—it is operated on a fee basis. The court wrote: "The extent to which the recipients of the charity are required to pay for the assistance received tests for a value that is fundamental to the concept of charity— that is, whether the organization gives away anything." Should this suddenly become the law, the ranks of the tax-exempt charitable sector would be massively decimated.

MYTH 23: EVERYONE LOVES NONPROFIT ORGANIZATIONS

This should be true. What's not to like? How can anyone dislike an organization that is operating on a nonprofit basis, engaging in programs that are beneficial to the public? Unfortunately, the statement is not true. Indeed, the nonprofit community, particularly the charitable sector, is under attack today at unprecedentedly high levels and for innumerable reasons.

Some of this enmity is coming from the staff of the Senate Finance Committee, which is examining many organizations and issues. As to the former, the Committee has investigated the American National Red Cross, Nature Conservancy, the Smithsonian Institution, and the Statue of Liberty Foundation. It is currently looking into the operations and finances of six evangelical ministries (churches). As to the latter, the Committee is focusing on governance of nonprofit organizations, tax exemption criteria for hospitals, and use of college and university endowments. The Committee was the proponent of massive legislation enacted in 2006, some of it quite harmful to the charitable community (see, e.g., Chapter 7).

The IRS, stepping up its audit activities (see Chapter 24), is also studying the matter of the tax-exempt status of hospitals and of higher education institutions' use of endowment funds. In addition, the agency is examining community foundations, executive compensation, governance issues, supporting organizations, tax-exempt bond financing recordkeeping, and nonprofit organizations' involvement in tax shelters. The IRS's massive redesign of the general annual information return (see Chapter 9) will be causing considerable angst for tax-exempt organizations for years to come.

The courts, as well, are not feeling too charitable these days, particularly in cases involving property tax exemptions for tax-exempt organizations. This is most obvious in the health care context, where the courts are having trouble understanding why fee-based hospitals, clinics, and the like should be exempt. In one case, a court, in approving revocation of a property tax exemption for a hospital, wrote: "The term charitable has become magical gibberish to sanctify any socially beneficial use of property that a court deems worthy of subsidy."

Other components of Congress, state attorneys general, tax assessors, and the media are scrutinizing charitable and other nonprofit organizations. (The main headline of the *New York Times* on Memorial Day 2008 was "Tax Exemptions of Charities Face New Challenges," with the sub-headline: "Worry for Nonprofits.") An argument can be made that much of this reflects overkill and loss of perspective. Nonetheless, these days there is far from universal love for nonprofit organizations.

MYTH 24: THE IRS IS THE ONLY PART OF THE FEDERAL GOVERNMENT INVOLVED IN THE REGULATION OF NONPROFIT ORGANIZATIONS

That is not the case. Other federal departments, agencies, and regulatory commissions with something to say about the operations of nonprofit organizations include the Department of Justice, the Department of Housing and Urban Development, the Department of the Treasury, the Federal Communications Commission, the Federal Election Commission, the Federal Trade Commission, the U.S. Postal Service, and the Securities and Exchange Commission.

MYTH 25: ONLY TECHNICAL PERSONNEL (SUCH AS LAWYERS AND ACCOUNTANTS) NEED TO KNOW THE INFORMATION IN THIS BOOK

This may be the greatest misperception of all. Too many professionals serving nonprofit organizations are functioning without this necessary information. This book is designed to provide the basics of the law of the various subjects covered, in the belief that *everyone* seriously serving one or more nonprofit organizations—particularly directors and officers, but also fundraisers, managers, employees, and consultants—should understand the points of law surveyed.

Indeed, if a lawyer or accountant is using this book to gain information, the nonprofit organization–client could be on the brink of serious trouble. The technical person hired by the nonprofit organization should be researching and studying some of this author's other books. (The list of publications on law topics, including several titles that have annual updates, is referenced at www.wiley.com.) This book surveys the basics of nonprofit law for everyone else.

PART TWO

Being Nonprofit, Legally

CHAPTER FOUR

Nonprofit Organizations: Much More than Charity

True or false?

- The concepts of the nonprofit organization and the tax-exempt organization are the same.
- Nonprofit/tax-exempt organizations mean charitable organizations.

Neither statement is true. As explained previously (see Chapter 1), the idea of a nonprofit organization is broader than that of a tax-exempt organization. This chapter summarizes the different types of tax-exempt organizations. The charitable entity is the best known type of exempt organization, but there are many other types.

The type of a tax-exempt organization is determined largely by the nature of its purposes. Thus, to qualify as an exempt entity, the organization must satisfy the appropriate *primary purpose test*. Indeed, the primary purpose test may determine whether a nonprofit organization can qualify as any type of exempt organization.

Because they are so popular, charitable organizations will be discussed first. The federal tax law uses the term *charitable* in two ways. The broader definition encompasses all organizations that are eligible to receive deductible contributions. Used this way, charitable includes entities that are religious, educational, scientific, and the like, as well as certain fraternal, cemetery, and veterans' organizations. To get technical for a moment, most of these organizations (not the fraternal, cemetery, and veterans' groups) are *501(c)(3) organizations*—they are governed by Section 501(c)(3), one of the most widely recognized provisions of the Internal Revenue Code.

In the narrower definition, the term *charitable organization* is restricted to organizations that match the descriptions of that type of entity under the law.

CHARITABLE ORGANIZATIONS

The federal tax law definition of a charitable organization contains at least 15 different ways for a nonprofit entity to be charitable. These characteristics, found in the income tax regulations, IRS rulings, and federal and state court opinions, include relieving the poor or distressed or the underprivileged; advancing religion, education, or science; lessening the burdens of government; beautifying and maintaining a community; preserving natural beauty; promoting health, social welfare, environmental conservancy, arts, or patriotism; caring for orphans or animals; promoting, advancing, and sponsoring amateur sports; and maintaining public confidence in the legal system. Those most widely claimed are discussed in the discussion that follows.

The *relief of poverty* is perhaps the most basic and historically founded form of charitable activity. Originally, it meant largely the distribution of money or goods to the poor. In contemporary times, particularly as government has assumed some of this function, it means more the provision of services. This type of charitable entity might feed the homeless or provide them shelter, operate a counseling center, provide vocational training, supply employment assistance, provide low-income housing, or offer transportation services.

The *relief of the distressed* is a considerably misunderstood way to be charitable. Too many associate *distressed* with *impoverishment*. To be sure, one way to be distressed is to be financially distressed (although one can be only temporarily financially distressed). An individual can, however, be physically or emotionally distressed. The confusion as to the scope of the concept of distressed was, most unfortunately, displayed in the aftermath of the terrorist attacks against the U.S. in 2001, when there was a huge outcry and battle as to who was entitled to relief funds—and pursuant to what criteria. While the law tends to precisely define the term *poor*, the concept of the term *distressed* is largely undefined and expansive.

The *advancement of religion*, as a charitable activity, frequently pertains to collateral activities of churches. For example, charitable organizations of this nature may maintain church buildings, monuments, or cemeteries; distribute religious literature; or supplement salaries. These organizations may conduct programs unique to a particular religion, operate a retreat center, or maintain a religious radio or television station.

The *advancement of education*, as a charitable activity, includes providing student assistance; advancing knowledge through research; or disseminating knowledge by means of publications, seminars, lectures, and the like. This type of charitable function may be a satellite activity of a particular educational institution, such as a university, library, or museum.

The *advancement of science*, as a charitable activity, includes activities devoted to the furtherance or promotion of science and the dissemination of scientific knowledge. Frequently, this type of charitable function involves conducting or disseminating the results of research.

The characteristic of *lessening the burdens of government* includes the erection or maintenance of public buildings, monuments, or works. This type of organization's activities must parallel those that a governmental unit considers to be its burden and must actually diminish that burden. Charitable organizations of this type, for example, help finance assistance to police and firefighters, public transportation, recreational centers, and internship programs. They may provide public parks, preserve a lake, or beautify a city.

The charitable activity of *community beautification and maintenance*, and the preservation of natural beauty, somewhat overlaps the concept of lessening the burdens of government. An organization that is charitable under this definition is one that may maintain community recreational facilities, assist in community beautification activities, or work to preserve and improve public parks.

The *promotion of health* is a separately recognized charitable purpose; in this context, public and mental health are included. This function includes the establishment and maintenance of institutions and organizations such as hospitals, clinics, homes for the aged, and similar treatment or residential centers. Other illustrations of health-providing (or health-promoting) organizations are health maintenance organizations, drug abuse treatment centers, blood banks, hospices, and home health agencies. The advancement of medical and similar knowledge through research, and, generally, the maintenance of conditions conducive to health are included. Classification of an organization as a tax-exempt hospital or a medical research organization is an automatic pathway to avoidance of private foundation status. (See Chapter 7.)

The *promotion of social welfare* is one of the most indefinite categories of charitable endeavors. In the law of trusts, the concept of promotion of social welfare can include such purposes as the promotion of temperance or national security or the erection or maintenance of tombs and monuments. In the federal tax law context, the term embraces activities designed to accomplish charitable purposes, lessen neighborhood tensions, eliminate prejudice and discrimination, defend human and civil rights secured by law, and combat community deterioration and juvenile delinquency.

An organization that endeavors to *promote environmental conservation* might engage in a range of activities to preserve and protect the natural environment for the benefit of the public. The IRS has recognized an express national policy of conserving the nation's unique natural resources; this type of organization serves to implement that policy.

The *promotion of patriotism* is a charitable objective; organizations that, in the words of one IRS ruling, "inculcate patriotic emotions" are charitable. This type of organization may assist in the celebration of a patriotic holiday, provide a color guard, or underwrite flag-raising ceremonies.

The *promotion of the arts* includes activities such as operating a theater (for plays, musicals, concerts, and the like), working to encourage the talent and ability of young artists, promoting filmmaking, sponsoring festivals or exhibits, or otherwise promoting public appreciation of one of the arts.

The purposes and activities of a nonprofit organization may involve more than one of these various ways to be charitable. For example, the hypothetical Campaign to Clean Up America (CCUA) has been formed to beautify communities, preserve natural beauty, lessen the burdens of government, and advance education. In addition, it promotes social welfare, protects the natural environment, and, in some instances, promotes health. (See Chapter 6 for the CCUA's programs.)

When the IRS classifies an organization as a tax-exempt entity because it is charitable (using that term in its broader sense), it does not specifically determine the type(s) of charity it may be. The categories just discussed, however, enable an organization to describe its charitable activities to the IRS (and others) in terms that conform to the federal tax law requirements.

EDUCATIONAL ORGANIZATIONS

Educational organizations include schools, colleges, universities, libraries, museums, and similar institutions. To be a "formal" educational institution, an organization must have a regularly scheduled curriculum, a regular faculty, and a regularly enrolled body of students in attendance at the place where the educational activities are carried on.

Formal educational entities are, by reason of their functions, exempted from classification as private foundations. (See Chapter 7.) Beyond these formal educational institutions, however, are a wide variety of organizations that are educational in nature.

One way to be educational, for federal tax law purposes, is to instruct or train individuals for the purpose of improving their capabilities. Within this category are organizations that provide instruction or training on a particular subject (although they may not have a regular curriculum, faculty, or student body). For example, organizations that operate apprentice training programs; correctional or rehabilitation centers; internship programs; or seminars, conferences, and lectures are educational. In addition, educational entities can include those that engage in study and research.

Another way to be educational is to instruct the public on subjects that are useful to the individual and beneficial to the community. Within this classification are organizations that provide counseling services, offer instruction on various subjects, endeavor to instruct the public in the field of civic betterment, publish materials for distribution, or engage in study and research. For publishing activities to be considered educational functions, the content of the publications must follow methods generally accepted as educational in character, the distribution of the material must be necessary or valuable in achieving the organization's tax-exempt purposes, and the manner in which the distribution is accomplished must be distinguishable from ordinary commercial practices.

There can be a fine line of distinction between an educational activity and a taxable business. (See Chapter 13.) Sometimes it is difficult to distinguish between an educational undertaking and one that amounts to propagandizing—the zealous endorsement of a particular idea or doctrine in a manner that is not reasonably objective or balanced. (See Chapter 14.) It is often impossible (and unnecessary) to differentiate between organizations that are charitable because they advance education and those that are educational. The CCUA would be both charitable (it advances education) and educational (it instructs the public on subjects that are beneficial to the community).

In addition, tax-exempt organizations are not supposed to engage in activities that are contrary to public policy. Thus, exemption does not extend to groups that promote violence, illegal discrimination, and other law-breaking activities. Occasionally, civil law (and sometimes even criminal law) violations occur, perhaps in the form of civil disobedience, where the organizations involved believe (or at least assert) that what they are doing is educational. Tax exemption is not a shelter for property-damaging activities, assault, kidnapping, fraud, and the like.

RELIGIOUS ORGANIZATIONS

Religious organizations are the oldest form of tax-exempt organization. Unlike other areas of the law of tax-exempt organizations, religious organizations defy definition. This is due in large part to the First Amendment to the U.S. Constitution, which bars Congress from making any law that would establish religious organizations or prohibit the free exercise of religion.

The U.S. Congress, the Department of the Treasury, and the IRS have all backed away from attempting to define the word *religion* (or *religious*). The courts are supposed to steer clear of definitions of the term as well. The U.S. Supreme Court has written that freedom of thought and religious belief "embraces the right to maintain theories of life and of death and of the hereafter which are rank heresy to followers of the orthodox faiths," and that if judges undertake to examine the truth or falsity of religious beliefs, "they enter a forbidden domain."

With this in mind, one federal district court said that it will not consider the "merits or fallacies of a religion," nor will it "praise or condemn a religion, however excellent or fanatical or preposterous it may seem." The U.S. Tax Court observed that it is "loath to evaluate and judge ecclesiastical authority and duties in the various religious disciplines." One aspect of the matter is clear: for tax and other law purposes, religious belief is not confined to "theistic" belief. Another district court noted that "an activity may be religious even though it is neither part of nor derives from a societally recognized religious sect."

Some courts, however, have ventured into the "forbidden domain." One wrote that religious belief is "a belief finding expression in a conscience which categorically requires the believer to disregard elementary self-interest and to accept martyrdom in preference to transgressing its tenets." Another court found an activity to be religious because it was centered around belief in a higher being "which in its various forms is given the name 'god' in common usage." Even the U.S. Supreme Court has placed emphasis on belief in a "supreme being" and has looked to see whether "a given belief that is sincere and meaningful occupies a place in the life of its possessor parallel to that filled by the orthodox belief in God" and whether the belief occupies in the life of the individual involved "'a place parallel to that filled by . . . God' in traditional religious persons."

There are many kinds of religious organizations; the most common form is referred to as a church (including synagogues and mosques). But, here again, the federal tax law lacks a crisp definition of the word *church*. The IRS has informally defined a church as an organization that satisfies at least some of the following criteria: a distinct legal existence, a recognized creed and form of worship, a definite and distinct ecclesiastical government, a formal code of doctrine and discipline, a distinct religious history, a membership not associated with any other church or denomination, a complete organization of ordained ministers ministering to their congregations and selected after completing prescribed courses of study, a literature of its own, established places of worship, regular congregations, regular religious services, Sunday schools for the religious instruction of the young, and schools for the preparation of its ministers.

Some courts are building on these informal criteria. For example, the U.S. Tax Court has concluded that, to be a church, an organization must have, at a minimum, the "existence of an established congregation served by an organized ministry, the provision of regular religious services and religious education for the young, and the dissemination of a doctrinal code." On another occasion, the Tax Court concluded that a "church is a coherent group of individuals and families that join together to accomplish the religious purposes of mutually held beliefs" and that a "church's principal means of accomplishing its religious purposes must be to assemble regularly a group of individuals related by common worship and faith."

Over the ensuing years, however, the IRS has added criteria and become more rigid (and inconsistent) in its interpretation of the term *church*. It is currently the position of this agency that, to be a church, an organization must—in addition to being *religious*—have a defined congregation of worshippers, an established place of worship, and regular religious services. Some of the criteria in the original 14-element list have been downgraded in importance, as being common to tax-exempt organizations in general.

Other types of religious organizations, for tax purposes, include conventions of churches, associations of churches, integrated auxiliaries of churches, religious orders, apostolic groups, missionary organizations, bible and tract societies, and church-run organizations, such as schools, hospitals, orphanages, nursing homes, publishing entities, broadcasting entities, and cemeteries.

The law has become clouded in this area, because of the tax abuses involved in the establishment of certain alleged "churches." Many entities have been declared to be nonexempt on the finding that they are "personal churches."

In recent years, the IRS has had difficulty administering the law in this area because a substantial amount of fraud and other abuse in the nonprofit world is done in the name of religion. Charlatans pose as clergy, and phony churches are being peddled as tax shelters. (One alleged religious organization held "worship services" on a boat in the middle of a beautiful bay; the worshippers spent much time in the water. The organization's name formed the acronym SCUBA.) New religions (some genuine), mail-order ministries, and televangelism are making IRS agents' lives difficult.

SCIENTIFIC ORGANIZATIONS

A scientific organization engages in scientific research or is otherwise operated for the dissemination of scientific knowledge. A tax-exempt scientific organization must be organized and operated to serve the public interest.

No definition of the term *scientific* in the tax-exempt organizations context has come from Congress, the Department of the Treasury, or the IRS. One dictionary states that *science* is a "branch of study in which facts are observed, classified, and, usually, quantitative laws are formulated and verified; [or which] involves the application of mathematical reasoning and data analysis to natural phenomena." One federal court has stated that the term *science* means the "process by which knowledge is systematized or classified through the use of observation, experimentation, or reasoning."

In this area, the focus is largely on the concept of *research*. This term lacks precise definition in this setting as well. Generally, the concept differentiates between *fundamental* and *basic* research, as opposed to *applied* or *practical* research. While all research may be scientific for purposes of the law of tax-exempt organizations, applied or practical research is suspect. Thus, scientific research does not include activities ordinarily carried on in connection with commercial operations—for example, the testing or inspection of materials or products, or the designing or construction of equipment or buildings.

Certain nonprofit organizations—principally universities and independent research institutions—are today engaging in research activities that have significant commercial applications. The law is having difficulty distinguishing between activities that are truly "research" and those that are more in the nature of testing products for marketing. As businesses, nonprofit organizations, and governments team up to make and commercially market discoveries (known as *technology transfer*), the law will have to sort out tax-exempt from taxable activities.

OTHER CHARITABLE ORGANIZATIONS

A nonprofit organization may be charitable for federal tax purposes because it is a literary organization. Or, it may be charitable by reason of the fact that it operates to prevent cruelty to children or animals, or because it qualifies as an amateur sports organization.

Some organizations operated as cooperatives can qualify as charitable entities—for example, cooperative hospital service organizations and cooperative educational service organizations. These organizations are subject to strict rules, to maintain their eligibility for tax-exempt status.

Organizations that test for public safety are eligible for tax-exempt status as charitable organizations. This type of charitable organization, however, is ineligible to receive contributions that are deductible as charitable gifts.

ONGOING CONTROVERSIES

It would be highly misleading to suggest that these categories of tax-exempt charitable entities are nicely discrete and definable. That is certainly not the case; like much of the law in general, matters in these contexts are in constant flux, even turmoil. Not only are new applications of these principles of law evolving, the IRS sometimes takes it on itself to change its policy as to when (or if) a type of entity can qualify as a charitable one.

As an illustration, consider the credit counseling organization. Long regarded as tax-exempt charitable organizations by the courts and (reluctantly) the IRS, in recent years the IRS decided that too many of these entities had gone commercial, gotten too deep into credit repair, with insufficient attention to consumer counseling and education. (The worst, according to the IRS, are those who peddle so-called *debt management plans*.) The IRS launched one of its most massive examination programs, roaming the nation and revoking or denying the exempt status of nearly every credit counseling group. This carnage abated only after Congress stepped in and legislated criteria for exempt consumer credit counseling organizations.

Another example is the down-payment assistance organization. This type of entity, which the IRS has regarded as tax-exempt and charitable for many years, provides grants to mostly low-income individuals and families to enable them to make a down payment when purchasing their (usually first) homes. In some instances (and there are various versions of this approach), the funding of these grants is derived from the home sellers. The IRS, abruptly reversing course, decided that this funding mechanism provides unwarranted private benefit (see Chapter 5) to the sellers, and is busy revoking and denying exempt status in this setting as well. (Efforts to explain to the IRS that, to have home buyers (a public policy the federal government has fostered for decades) there must be home sellers have been unavailing.)

SOCIAL WELFARE ORGANIZATIONS

Traditionally, a social welfare organization is one that, in the language of the tax regulations, functions to advance the "common good and general welfare," and seeks "civic betterments and social improvements." This type of organization is expected to engage in activities that benefit the community in its entirety, rather than merely its own membership or other select groups of individuals or organizations.

A contemporary use of the social welfare organization is as an advocacy entity. The term *social welfare* can be broader than the term *charitable* (even though, as discussed previously, the concept of *charitable* includes the promotion of social welfare). Social welfare organizations can engage in an unlimited amount of legislative activity without endangering their tax-exempt status, and they can permissibly engage in some political campaign activity. Consequently, some charitable organizations link up with related social welfare organizations as a means of engaging in more lobbying activities than the charitable organizations are allowed to undertake directly.

Like many other tax-exempt organizations, social welfare entities may not engage in transactions that constitute private inurement (see Chapter 5) and may not operate unrelated businesses as a primary activity. The only type of social welfare organization to which contributions are deductible is a veterans' organization (see the section on that topic further on in this chapter).

BUSINESS LEAGUES

The federal tax law uses the anachronistic term *business leagues* to describe what are known today as trade, business, and professional associations. The private inurement doctrine applies to them.

A business league is a group of persons (an *association*) who have some common business interest; the purpose of the league is to promote that common interest. Its activities (if it is to be tax-exempt) are directed to the improvement of business conditions of one or more lines of business, as distinguished from the performance of particular services for individual persons.

These organizations are membership service entities. They are usually dues-based; in exchange for their dues, members receive a package of services. These can include one or more publications, an annual meeting, seminars and workshops, lobbying, trade shows, and research. A caution: If members are required to pay additional fees for discrete services (such as advertising or various types of consultancies), the IRS may take the position that the rendering of those "extra" services amounts to one or more unrelated businesses (see Chapter 13).

A unique category of association is accorded specific mention as a tax-exempt entity in the Internal Revenue Code: professional football leagues.

CHAMBERS OF COMMERCE

A tax-exempt chamber of commerce is an organization that has a common business interest—the general economic welfare of a community. The organization's efforts are directed at promotion of the common economic interests of all of the commercial enterprises in a given trade community. Similar to the exempt chamber of commerce is a board of trade or a real estate board.

SOCIAL CLUBS

Social clubs are basically tax-exempt, although, unlike most forms of exempt organizations, their investment income is taxable. A social club is a nonprofit organization, operated for pleasure, recreation, and social purposes, that is usually principally supported by membership dues, fees, and assessments. The exempt club must have an established membership, personal contacts, and fellowship.

The private inurement doctrine is applicable to tax-exempt social clubs. Also, the law limits the extent to which an exempt social club can make its facilities available to the general public.

Tax-exempt social clubs include country clubs, golf and tennis clubs, college and university fraternities and sororities, clubs promoting an interest in specific sports, garden clubs, and hobby clubs.

LABOR ORGANIZATIONS

Federal tax law provides tax-exempt status for labor organizations. The purposes of these organizations are (1) to better the conditions of workers, (2) to improve the grade of their products, and (3) to develop a higher degree of efficiency in particular occupations. The most common example of this type of organization is a labor union, which bargains collectively with employers to secure better working conditions, wages, and similar benefits.

The private inurement doctrine is applicable to labor organizations.

AGRICULTURAL ORGANIZATIONS

Like labor organizations, tax-exempt agricultural organizations must have as their purposes the betterment of the conditions of those engaged in the exempt pursuit, the improvement of the grade of their products, and the development of a higher degree of efficiency in the particular occupation.

For this purpose, the term *agricultural* includes (but is not limited to) the art or science of cultivating land, harvesting crops or aquatic resources, or raising livestock. The IRS, however, will not grant agricultural status to an organization whose principal purpose is to provide a direct business service for its members' economic benefit. The private inurement doctrine is applicable in this context.

HORTICULTURAL ORGANIZATIONS

The definition of a horticultural organization is much like that of the labor and agricultural organizations. For tax purposes, the term *horticultural* means the art or science of cultivating fruits, flowers, and vegetables. The private inurement doctrine is applicable.

U.S. INSTRUMENTALITIES

A corporation that is organized pursuant to an act of Congress, is an "instrumentality" of the United States, and is specifically classified as an instrumentality under federal tax law, is an exempt organization. Certain federal credit unions are exempt under this rule.

SINGLE-PARENT TITLE-HOLDING CORPORATIONS

A corporation that is organized for the exclusive purposes of holding title to property, collecting income from the property, and turning the net income over to a tax-exempt organization is itself tax-exempt. An organization is ineligible for tax exemption under this rule if it has two or more unrelated parents.

Title-holding corporations generally may not engage in any business other than that of holding title to property. These organizations can be particularly useful in holding title to property that may attract liability, such as swimming pools and parks.

MULTIPARENT TITLE-HOLDING ORGANIZATIONS

Tax exemption is available for a multiparent title-holding organization. This is an entity organized and operated for the exclusive purposes of acquiring and holding title to real property, collecting income from the property, and remitting the entire amount of income from the property (less expenses) to one or more qualified tax-exempt organizations that are shareholders of the title-holding corporation or beneficiaries of the title-holding trust. This category of tax-exempt organization was created in response to an IRS position. The IRS held that a title-holding company that was otherwise eligible for tax exemption under preexisting law (see previous discussion) could not be exempt if two or more of its parent organizations were unrelated.

LOCAL EMPLOYEES' ASSOCIATIONS

A local association of employees, with membership limited to the employees of a designated employer or employers in a particular municipality, is a form of tax-exempt organization. The private inurement doctrine is applicable.

FRATERNAL BENEFICIARY SOCIETIES

Federal tax law provides tax-exempt status for fraternal beneficiary societies, orders, or associations operating under the lodge system or for the exclusive benefit of the members of a fraternal organization that operates under the lodge system. The purpose of such groups is to provide for the payment of life, sick, accident, or other benefits to the members of the society, order, or association, or their dependents.

Contributions to a fraternal beneficiary society are deductible where the gift is to be used exclusively for charitable purposes.

DOMESTIC FRATERNAL SOCIETIES

Tax exemption is available for domestic fraternal societies, orders, or associations operating under the lodge system, if their net earnings are devoted exclusively to charitable purposes and if they do not provide for the payment of life, sick, accident, or other benefits to members. An organization not providing these benefits but otherwise qualifying as a fraternal beneficiary society qualifies as a domestic fraternal society.

VOLUNTARY EMPLOYEES' BENEFICIARY ASSOCIATIONS

The law of tax-exempt organizations and the law of employee benefits are intertwined in many ways. Thus, pension funds and other funds that are part of an employee benefit program are forms of tax-exempt organizations. There are several of these exempt entities, including the following six types of tax-exempt organizations.

Federal tax exemption is available for voluntary employees' beneficiary associations (VEBAs) that provide for the payment of life, sickness, accident, or other benefits to members or their dependents or designated beneficiaries. The private inurement doctrine is applicable to VEBAs.

A VEBA is an increasingly popular vehicle for the provision of benefits to employees (usually of a common employer). Eligibility for membership may be restricted by geographic proximity or by objective conditions or limitations reasonably related to employment. Eligibility for benefits may be restricted by objective conditions relating to the type or amount of benefits offered.

Most VEBAs are subject to certain nondiscrimination requirements.

SUPPLEMENTAL UNEMPLOYMENT BENEFIT TRUSTS

Tax exemption is available for certain trusts forming part of a plan providing for the payment of supplemental unemployment compensation benefits (SUB). Among other requirements, a SUB must be part of a plan that does not discriminate in favor of supervisory or highly compensated employees and that requires determination of benefits according to objective standards. SUBs are intended to provide benefits to laid-off (and perhaps ill) employees, frequently in conjunction with other payments such as state unemployment benefits.

BLACK LUNG BENEFITS TRUSTS

Income tax exemption is available for a qualifying trust used by a coal mine operator to self-insure for liabilities under federal and state Black Lung benefits laws. A coal mine operator may be located in a state deemed not to provide adequate workers' compensation coverage for pneumoconiosis. Under federal law, the operator must secure, via commercial insurance or self-insuring, the payment of benefits for which the operator may be found liable under the Black Lung statute.

MULTIEMPLOYER PENSION PLAN TRUSTS

Also tax-exempt under federal law is a trust established by the sponsors of a multiemployer pension plan as a vehicle to accumulate funds in order to provide withdrawal liability payments to the plan.

TEACHERS' RETIREMENT FUND ASSOCIATIONS

Federal tax law allows tax-exempt status to teachers' retirement fund associations of a purely local character, if there is no private inurement (other than through the payment of retirement benefits) and the income consists wholly of amounts received from public taxation, amounts received from assessments on the teaching salaries of members, and income from investments.

BENEVOLENT OR MUTUAL ORGANIZATIONS

Exemption is available for benevolent life insurance associations of a purely local character, mutual ditch or irrigation companies, mutual or cooperative telephone companies, or similar organizations, if 85 percent or more of the income is collected from members for the sole purpose of meeting losses and expenses.

CEMETERY COMPANIES

A cemetery company is exempt from federal income taxation if it is owned and operated exclusively for the benefit of its members and if it is not operated for profit. The private inurement doctrine is expressly applicable. A tax-exempt cemetery generally is an entity that owns a cemetery, sells lots in it for burial purposes, and maintains these and the unsold lots in a state of repair and upkeep appropriate to, in the words of the IRS, a "final resting place."

Contributions to tax-exempt cemetery companies are deductible for federal income tax purposes.

CREDIT UNIONS

Credit unions that do not issue capital stock and that are organized and operated for the mutual benefit of their members and not for purposes of profit are tax-exempt under federal law. Usually these organizations are chartered under state law. As noted previously, those formed under federal law are likely to be tax-exempt as "instrumentalities" of the United States.

In recent years, tax-exempt credit unions allegedly have strained the bounds of their mutuality or, in the view of critics, have pushed beyond these bounds. They are providing financial, insurance, and other services that may be more for the benefit of the public than merely the credit union membership. The IRS has weighed into this controversy, concluding that many of these new services are forms of unrelated business (see Chapter 13). All of this has triggered a major controversy, with commercial banks asserting that these credit unions are no longer eligible for exempt status.

MUTUAL INSURANCE COMPANIES

Tax exemption is available for an insurance company or association (other than a life insurance company or association) if the gross receipts of the company for the tax year involved do not exceed $600,000 and more than 50 percent of the receipts consists of premiums. For a mutual insurance company to be exempt, however, its gross receipts for the tax year cannot exceed $150,000, and more than 35 percent of the receipts must consist of premiums. This category of tax-exempt organization is available not only to qualified mutual property and casualty organizations but also to qualified stock property and casualty organizations.

CROP OPERATIONS FINANCE CORPORATIONS

Federal tax law provides exemption for corporations that are organized by a tax-exempt farmers' cooperative, or its members, for the purpose of financing the ordinary crop operations of the members or other producers, and that are operated in conjunction with this type of a cooperative. Under certain circumstances, this entity may issue capital stock.

VETERANS' ORGANIZATIONS

Federal tax law provides exemption for a post or organization of veterans, or an auxiliary unit or society, or a trust or foundation formed for the entity, as long as it is organized in the United States or any of its possessions. At least 75 percent of its members must be past or present members of the armed forces of the United States, and substantially all of the other members must be individuals who are either cadets or spouses, widows, or widowers of such past or present members or of cadets. The private inurement doctrine is applicable.

A special provision in the unrelated income tax rules exempts from taxation income that is derived from members of these organizations and is attributable to payments for life, accident, or health insurance coverage for members or their dependents, where the profits are set aside for charitable purposes. (See Chapter 13.)

Contributions to veterans' organizations are generally deductible. Some veterans' groups are tax-exempt as social welfare or charitable entities.

FARMERS' COOPERATIVES

Farmers' cooperatives are exempt from federal income tax. These cooperatives are farmers', fruit growers', or similar associations organized and operated on a cooperative basis for (1) marketing the products of members or other producers and returning to them the proceeds of sales, less the necessary marketing expenses, on the basis of either the quantity or the value of the products furnished by them; or (2) purchasing supplies and equipment for the use of members or other persons and turning over the supplies and equipment to them at actual cost plus necessary expenses.

One of the many other requirements if a farmers' cooperative seeks tax-exempt status, is that any excess of gross receipts over expenses and payments to patrons must be returned to the patrons in proportion to the amount of business done for them. If a farmers' cooperative issues stock and wishes to remain tax-exempt, substantially all of the capital stock must be owned by producers who market their products or purchase their supplies and equipment through the cooperative.

SHIPOWNERS' PROTECTION AND INDEMNITY ASSOCIATIONS

Federal tax law provides that gross income does not include the gross receipts of nonprofit shipowners' mutual protection and indemnity associations. The private inurement doctrine is applicable. These organizations are, however, taxable on income from interest, dividends, and rents.

POLITICAL ORGANIZATIONS

Tax exemption is basically available for a political organization. This entity is a political party, committee, association, fund, or other organization formed and operated primarily for the purpose of directly or indirectly accepting contributions and/or making expenditures for an *exempt function*. An exempt function includes influencing or attempting to influence the selection, nomination, election, or appointment of any individual to any federal, state, or local public office in a political organization, or the election of presidential or vice-presidential electors. The political organization thus includes political action committees (PACs) or, more technically, separate segregated funds.

Income of a political organization, other than income from an exempt function, is taxable. This type of taxable revenue includes investment income.

HOMEOWNERS' ASSOCIATIONS

A homeowners' association is tax-exempt if it satisfies the following basic requirements:

- It must be organized and operated to provide for the acquisition, construction, management, maintenance, and care of association property.
- At least 60 percent of the association's gross income for the year must consist of exempt function income.
- At least 90 percent of the annual expenditures of the association must be used to acquire, construct, manage, maintain, and care for or improve its property.
- Substantially all of the dwelling units in a condominium project or the lots and buildings in a subdivision, development, or similar area, must be used by individuals for residences.
- The private inurement doctrine is expressly applicable.

Only the exempt function income of a homeowners' association escapes taxation; the remainder (including investment income) is fully taxed. This exemption must be elected.

PREPAID TUITION PROGRAMS

Qualified tuition programs are tax-exempt. These programs are established and maintained by a state agency or colleges and universities, under which individuals may (1) purchase tuition credits or certificates on behalf of a designated beneficiary that entitle the beneficiary to the waiver or payment of certain higher education expenses of the beneficiary, or (2) make contributions to an account that is established for the sole purpose of meeting these higher education expenses. Expenses that are eligible for this type of program are tuition, fees, books, and equipment required for the enrollment or attendance at a college, university, or certain vocational schools.

These purchases and contributions may be made only in money. A specified individual, generally, must be designated as the beneficiary at the commencement of participation in the program. A distribution is includable in the gross income of the distributee in the manner prescribed under the annuity taxation rules, unless the income is excluded by law from taxation (such as a scholarship).

OTHER TAX-EXEMPT ORGANIZATIONS

This chapter has taken a fast sweep through the various types of organizations that are conventionally described as tax-exempt. Many other entities, under federal law, are also exempt from taxes.

Governmental entities, such as states, political subdivisions of states, and other governmental bodies, whether termed *agencies, bodies*, or *instrumentalities*, have tax-exempt status because of the doctrine of intergovernmental immunity.

Tax-exempt status is accorded the funds underlying employee benefit plans, such as retirement and profit-sharing plans.

Other organizations that, in effect, are tax-exempt are partnerships (see Chapter 18), certain small business corporations, limited liability companies, some cooperatives (other than those discussed previously), and planned giving vehicles (see Chapter 19) such as charitable remainder trusts and pooled income funds.

This brief survey of tax-exempt organizations illustrates the vast array of non-profit entities that Congress has decided merit tax-exempt status. These organizations range far beyond the charitable entities and similar groups that are commonly thought of as nonprofit organizations.

FOCUS: Campaign to Clean Up America

The facts surrounding the Campaign to Clean Up America (CCUA) illustrate the application and interrelationship of at least some of these rules. The CCUA is a charitable organization, in the broader sense of that term; it is actually both a charitable and an educational entity.

Suppose you were to decide that the CCUA should engage in a greater degree of legislative activities than is allowed to charitable organizations. You could establish a related social welfare organization to conduct those activities. The social welfare organization might then establish a political action committee (PAC). Alternatively, the CCUA could establish a PAC to engage in political activities other than political campaign activities.

Still other tax-exempt organizations may be involved. In launching its planned giving program, the CCUA may establish a pooled income fund and (ideally) spawn many charitable remainder trusts. (See Chapter 17.) As it grows, it will have retirement and other benefit programs for its employees; the underlying funds of those programs will be tax-exempt. The time may come when a title-holding organization is appropriate.

As discussed throughout the chapter, today's tax-exempt organization is often part of a group of related organizations, some nonprofit (and tax-exempt) and some for-profit.

CHAPTER FIVE

Nonprofits and Private Benefit

One of the fundamental requirements for qualification as a nonprofit organization is also one of the most misunderstood. There is enormous misperception of the term *nonprofit*. An entity must be nonprofit before it can be tax-exempt, so it is important to understand what the ramifications of *nonprofit* are. The meaning of the term is found in another confusing term: *private inurement*. Most nonprofit organizations are subject to the *private inurement doctrine*, which deals with the unique difference between nonprofit and for-profit organizations (see Chapter 1).

The private inurement doctrine is applicable to nearly all types of tax-exempt organizations. It is most significant, however, for charitable organizations. By contrast, for a few types of nonprofit organizations—for example, employee benefit trusts, social clubs, and cemetery companies—private benefit is the exempt function.

PRIVATE INUREMENT

The federal law of tax exemption for charitable and other exempt organizations requires that each of these entities be organized and operated so that "no part of . . . [its] net earnings . . . inures to the benefit of any private shareholder or individual." Literally, this means that the profits of a charitable organization may not be passed along to individuals in their private capacity, in the way that dividend payments are made to shareholders. In actual fact, the private inurement rule, as expanded and amplified by the IRS and the courts, today means much more.

(a) Charitable Organizations

The contemporary concept of private inurement is broad and wide-ranging. Lawyers for the IRS have advised that inurement is likely to arise where the financial benefit represents a transfer of the organization's financial resources to an individual solely by virtue of the individual's relationship with the organization, and without regard to accomplishing exempt purposes." The IRS's lawyers thereafter more bluntly have stated that the inurement prohibition "serves to prevent anyone in a position to do so from siphoning off any of a charity's income or assets for personal use." These descriptions are correct for today's private inurement doctrine, but it is a substantial embellishment of the original statutory rule.

The contemporary meaning of the thoroughly antiquated statutory private inurement language is scarcely reflected in its literal form and transcends the nearly century-old formulation; what the doctrine means today is that none of the income or assets of a tax-exempt organization subject to the inurement doctrine may be permitted to directly or indirectly unduly benefit an individual or other person who has a close relationship with the organization, when he, she, or it is in a position to exercise a significant degree of control over it.

The essence of the private inurement concept is to ensure that a charitable organization is serving public interests, *not* private interests. To be tax-exempt, an organization must establish that it is not organized and operated for the benefit of private interests—designated individuals, the creator of the entity or his or her family, shareholders of the organization, persons controlled (directly or indirectly) by private interests, or any persons having a personal and private interest in the activities of the organization.

One of the ways the law determines the presence of any proscribed private inurement is to look to the ultimate purpose of an organization. If its basic purpose is to benefit individuals in their private capacity, then it cannot be tax-exempt as a charitable organization (and probably not as any other type of exempt organization), even though it may be performing exempt activities. Conversely, although the IRS officially believes the private inurement proscription is absolute, incidental benefits to private individuals could possibly not defeat tax exemption, as long as the organization otherwise qualifies for exempt status.

Is private inurement the same as commercial activities? Not necessarily. A charitable organization may usually engage in commercial activities in order to achieve a larger exempt purpose. The existence of a single commercial or otherwise nonexempt and substantial *purpose*, however, will destroy or prevent the exemption.

(b) Other Tax-Exempt Organizations

As noted (see Chapter 4), the applicability of the private inurement doctrine is not confined to charitable organizations. Most of the other principal types of exempt organizations are also caught up in this body of law. These include social welfare organizations, labor organizations, business leagues, social clubs, some employee benefit funds, and veterans' organizations.

Almost all of the law concerning private inurement, however, has developed in the context of charitable organizations. Thus, those applying this aspect of the law to other types of exempt organizations must look to developments in the realm of charitable entities.

(c) Insiders

The federal securities laws that govern business corporations target the notion of an *insider*—someone who has a special and close relationship with a corporation, frequently because he or she is a director, officer, and/or significant shareholder. Thus, for example, the securities laws prohibit *insider trading*. The private inurement rules, using the phrase *private shareholder or individual*, mirror the insider concept.

An *insider* for private inurement purposes refers to an organization's directors, trustees, and officers. It also encompasses key employees, particularly where they have duties or responsibilities normally vested in officers. Further, the family members of insiders and entities controlled by insiders (business corporations, partnerships, trusts, and estates, for example) are covered. One of the hot issues of the day is whether, or the extent to which, a vendor of services can be an insider (because of the extent of control over the organization) and the circumstances under which this occurs. Vendors of this type include fundraising and management companies.

The inurement doctrine prohibits a transaction between a tax-exempt organization subject to the rule and a person who is an insider, where the latter is able to cause the organization's net earnings to be turned to private purposes as the result of his or her control or influence. The IRS, in adopting this view, once observed that, as a general rule, "[a]n organization's trustees, officers, members, founders, or contributors may not, by reason of their position, acquire any of its funds." Stating its view another way, the IRS has rather starkly said that "[t]he prohibition of inurement, in its simplest terms, means that [with exceptions] a private shareholder or individual cannot pocket the organization's funds."

Private inurement involves two necessary components. The private person (insider) to whom the benefit inures must have the ability to control or otherwise influence the actions of the charitable organization and must do so to cause the private benefit to come into existence. Second, the benefit must be intentionally conferred by the influenced organization and as opposed to being a permissible form of private benefit or a coincidental result.

The self-dealing rules that are applicable to private foundations represent a formal statement of the private inurement doctrine. (See Chapter 7.) An impermissible transaction must involve, in addition to the charitable entity (the foundation), *disqualified persons* (directors, trustees, officers, key employees, substantial contributors, their family members, and the family members of those whom they control).

(d) Standard of Reasonableness

People can receive private benefits in many ways; private inurement can take many forms. Still, a charitable organization may incur ordinary and necessary operating expenditures without losing its tax-exempt status. It may pay compensation, rent, interest, and maintenance costs without penalty, because these expenses, even if paid to persons in their private capacity, further the organization's exempt purposes. The costs, however, must be justifiable and be for *reasonable* amounts.

The matter of *reasonableness* is one of *fact*, not *law*. The exercise in determining what is reasonable is closely akin to *valuation*. Lawyers are not usually trained or experienced in making these judgments. In complex instances, the services of an independent, competent consultant may be warranted. The law that is developing in the intermediate sanctions setting (see discussion following) is helping to define the parameters of the term *reasonable*.

(e) Compensation

The most common form of private inurement is excessive and unreasonable compensation. When a charitable organization pays an employee a salary, it is paying a portion of its earnings to an individual in his or her private capacity. Payment of reasonable compensation, however, is allowable; it is not private inurement. Compensation becomes private inurement when the payment is excessive and unreasonable—and is made to an insider.

Many court cases involve the payment of high compensation to the founder of an organization or the family members. Whether the compensation paid is reasonable is a question of fact, to be decided in the context of each case. Generally, under the law, allowable compensation is ascertained by comparing the compensation paid to individuals who have similar responsibilities and expertise in the same or comparable communities. Other factors are the need of the organization for a particular individual's services, the amount of time devoted to the job, and whether the compensation was approved by an independent (as opposed to a captive) board.

The comparison is easier said than done; the key is the *reasonableness* of the compensation. As the U.S. Tax Court observed, the law "places no duty on individuals operating charitable organizations to donate their services; they are entitled to reasonable compensation for their services." Likewise, a congressional committee report contained the observation that "an individual need not necessarily accept reduced compensation merely because he or she renders services to a tax-exempt, as opposed to a taxable, organization."

Two aspects of compensation can make it unreasonable and excessive. One is the sheer amount of the compensation, in absolute terms. A federal court, in finding private inurement because of excessive compensation, characterized the salaries as being "substantial" amounts. Other courts tolerate "substantial" amounts of compensation, where the employees' services and skills warrant that level of payment. Some courts evidence a distinct bias when it comes to compensation paid by nonprofit organizations: They believe it should be lower than that paid by for-profit organizations, even though all other material elements of the compensation may be the same.

In many cases, it has been found that an insider was receiving high cash compensation in addition to other financial benefits from a charity (such as fees, commissions, and royalties), and that family members were also participating in the largess. Most of the cases denying tax exemption to religious organizations do so on the ground that the founders are engaging in private inurement transactions, including unwarranted levels of compensation.

The other aspect of compensation that can lead to private inurement is the manner in which the amount is calculated. The courts and the IRS may challenge compensation arrangements that are predicated on a percentage of gross receipts. Case law on this point is inconsistent and unclear, but, under a rule developed by the U.S. Tax Court, private inurement will not be found simply because a commission system is used; the important fact is still the reasonableness of the compensation actually paid. The Tax Court, however, found private inurement in a compensation arrangement based on a percentage of gross receipts, where no upper limit was placed on total compensation. In another instance, a court focused on the reasonableness of the percentage, not the reasonableness of the amount paid.

The special rules applying to self-dealing by private foundations may be used as a guide for determining whether private inurement exists. The rules allow compensation arrangements where the payments are reasonable and not excessive.

As a general proposition, then, a charitable, organization may, without causing undue private inurement, pay reasonable compensation to its employees, suppliers, and consultants—even those who are its insiders. This compensation may be in the form of salaries, wages, or fees. It can also include benefits such as insurance, deferred compensation, or pension and retirement benefits.

(f) Rents and Loans

A charitable organization generally may lease property and pay rent. The private inurement doctrine, however, requires that the rental arrangement be beneficial and suitable to the organization, and that the rental payments be reasonable. (Inflated rental prices may well amount to a private benefit inuring to the lessor.) Loan arrangements between a private foundation and its disqualified persons are generally acts of self-dealing, and the rules that govern potential private inurement in other settings apply here.

Rental arrangements and terms of a loan involving a charitable organization should be financially advantageous to the organization and in line with its exempt purposes. Where the charity is the borrower, the interest charges, amount of security, repayment period, terms of repayment, and other aspects of the loan must be reasonable. The scrutiny will heighten where an insider is borrowing from the charity. If a loan from a charity is not repaid on time, questions of private inurement will likely be raised. A federal court once observed that the "very existence of a private source of loan credit from [a charitable] organization's earnings may itself amount to inurement of benefit." Once again, the self-dealing rules can offer general guidance.

Some charitable organizations are called on to guarantee the debt of another entity, such as a related nonprofit or even a for-profit organization. The terms of such an arrangement must be carefully reviewed. If the loan guarantee does not advance exempt purposes or cannot be characterized as a reasonable investment, private inurement may be occurring.

(g) Services

For charitable organizations, the interaction of the private inurement rules and the provision of services can be quite confusing. Many charitable organizations provide services in the ordinary advancement of their exempt functions. An organization cannot qualify as a charitable entity, however, where its primary purpose is the provision of services to individuals in their private capacity. By contrast, individuals can be benefited by a charity where they constitute members of a charitable class (such as the poor or students), are considered merely instruments or means to a charitable objective, or are receiving private benefit that is merely incidental. (In this situation, where insiders are not involved, there may be *private benefit*, which usually is not as objectionable as *private inurement*. See the following examples.)

Some illustrations have occurred in case law:

- Generally, organizations operated to advance the arts are charitable; however, a cooperative art gallery that exhibits and sells its members' works was held not to be a charitable entity because it was serving the private interests of its members.

- Quite frequently, the rendering of housing assistance for low-income families qualifies as a charitable undertaking; yet an organization that provides such assistance but gives preference for housing to employees of a particular organization was found to be advancing private, not charitable, interests.

- The operation of a private school can be a charitable program; but an organization that provides bus transportation for children attending a private school was held not to be tax-exempt because it was relieving the children's parents of their responsibility to transport their children to school.

- An organization primarily engaged in the testing of drugs for commercial pharmaceutical companies was ruled not to be engaged in scientific research but to be serving the private interests of the manufacturers.

- An association of professional nurses that operates a nurses' registry was ruled to be affording greater employment opportunities for its members and thus to be substantially operated for private ends.

(h) Social Welfare Organizations

Social welfare organizations, like most forms of tax-exempt organizations, cannot be operated primarily for private gain. The private inurement doctrine is applicable to these types of nonprofit entities. For example, homeowners' associations may be exempt as social welfare organizations only if they are engaged in the promotion of the common good and general welfare of a community. If they operate for the benefit of a select group of individuals, they are not exempt.

A social welfare organization can use the criterion that it must not be operated primarily for the economic benefit or convenience of its members. Many cooperative entities fail to be social welfare organizations because, in the words of a federal court, they are operated "primarily to benefit the taxpayer's membership economically." A federal appellate court denied social welfare status to a mutual assistance organization established by a church because its policies and practices benefited a "select few"—its members—rather than a larger public.

As is the case with membership associations in general, the rendering of services to members does not necessarily bring a denial or loss of social welfare status. An organization may be able to qualify as a social welfare organization where its services are equally available to members and nonmembers.

As stated earlier in discussing charitable organizations, the private inurement rules for social welfare organizations are not the same as the restrictions on commercial practices. The federal tax law, however, expressly states that an exempt social welfare organization may not be organized or operated to carry on a business with the general public as though it were a for-profit entity. In addition, a social welfare organization (as well as a charitable organization) will lose or be denied tax-exempt status if a substantial part of its activities consists of the provision of commercial-type insurance.

(i) Trade and Business Associations

The federal tax law governing the activities of tax-exempt trade, business, and professional associations (business leagues) forbids inurement of the net earnings of these organizations to individuals in their private capacities. At first glance, this rule may seem somewhat anomalous, when the purpose of these associations is to promote the common business interests of the membership. Why would anyone join an association of this type if the benefits it can offer its members are off limits?

There is an important distinction between improving business conditions of a line of business (a business league's primary purpose; see Chapter 4) and performing services for members to the point where private inurement results. The federal tax law prohibits such associations from carrying on *business activities for profit*.

One tax rule applicable to business leagues is often misunderstood and ignored: A tax-exempt business league may not perform *particular* services for individual persons. In practice, this prohibition is enforced only where these services are the primary function of an association. It can be difficult, in a specific instance, to distinguish between performing particular services and engaging in activities directed to the improvement of business conditions.

An activity of a business league is exempt where the activity benefits the membership as a group, rather than in individual capacities. The benefit to the group occurs where the business league provides a product or service to its members for a fee, and the benefit is not directly proportional to the fee. One federal court stated, "the activities that serve the interests of individual . . . [members] according to what they pay produce individual benefits insufficient to fulfill the substantial relationship test, since those activities generally do not generate inherent group benefits that inure to the advantage of its members as members."

(j)   Labor and Other Organizations

Labor organizations, which frequently are unions, are much like business leagues: They operate to better the working conditions and economic opportunities of employees. Labor organizations are often membership groups that provide services to their members. The federal tax law forbids the net earnings of a labor organization from inuring to the benefit of persons in their private capacity.

The private inurement constraint also specifically applies to social clubs, agricultural and horticultural organizations, voluntary employees' beneficiary associations, certain teachers' retirement fund associations, veterans' organizations, shipowners' protection and indemnity associations, and homeowners' associations.

The distinctions between public and private benefit are evident in the law pertaining to other types of tax-exempt organizations. The net earnings of local associations of employees must be devoted to charitable purposes. The same "reverse inurement" rule applies to domestic fraternal societies, which are prohibited from paying life, sick, accident, or other benefits to their members.

In another twist on the prohibition of private benefits flowing from tax-exempt organizations, the law mandates that the economic benefits flowing out of employee benefit plans cannot discriminate in favor of highly compensated employees. This is particularly true with respect to voluntary employees' beneficiary associations and supplemental unemployment benefit trusts.

The federal tax law governing other exempt organizations simply states that they may not be operated "for profit." Cemetery companies and certain credit unions are subject to that general prohibition.

(k)   Private Benefit Tax-Exempt Organizations

Several types of tax-exempt organizations have, as their tax-exempt function, the provision of "private" benefits. These organizations serve to advance private ends; they do not transfer funds to individuals in their private capacity.

The most notable "private benefit" tax-exempt organizations provide economic benefits to employees, either during difficult personal times or at retirement. For example, the funds underlying retirement, pension, and profit-sharing plans are those of tax-exempt organizations. Other employee benefit organizations are voluntary employees' beneficiary associations, which provide life, sick, accident, and other benefits to their members and dependents; supplemental unemployment benefit trusts, which provide unemployment compensation benefits to employees; Black Lung benefits trusts, which fund employer liabilities for pneumoconiosis under federal and state Black Lung benefits laws; and multiemployer pension plan trusts, which are designed to improve retirement income security under private multiemployer pension plans.

Other private benefit programs can be undertaken by tax-exempt fraternal and other organizations. For example, fraternal beneficiary societies that operate under the lodge system provide for the payment of life, sickness, accident, and other benefits to their members and dependents, as do some veterans' organizations. Benevolent life insurance associations provide life insurance coverage to their members. Cemetery companies own and operate cemeteries for ultimate use by their members. Exempt credit unions provide financial services to their members, as do crop operations finance corporations. Farmers' cooperatives, shipowners' protection and indemnity associations, and homeowners' associations also function on behalf of their members.

The type of tax-exempt organization where private benefit is most blatant—permissibly—is the social club. The private inurement doctrine expressly applies, but exempt social clubs (country clubs, gourmet clubs, sports clubs, and so on) are organized and operated for the pleasure and recreation of their members. Nonprofit fraternities and sororities are usually classified as social clubs for federal tax purposes. A social club will lose its tax-exempt status if it makes its facilities unduly available to the general public.

The private inurement doctrine has several specific applications to social clubs. One emerges when an exempt club generates too much nonmember income and the membership gains a subsidy in the form of reduced dues and improved facilities. Or, a club with more than one class of member may attempt to have the dues payments of one class operate to subsidize the members of another class. In more conventional terms, private inurement can exist when a social club engages in undue dealings with its members, such as regular sales of liquor for consumption off the club's premises.

(l) Sanction

The sanction for violation of the private inurement doctrine is loss or denial of the organization's tax-exempt status. There is no other penalty; there is no sanction imposed on the insider who received (and presumably retained) the unwarranted benefit.

The private inurement doctrine and the intermediate sanctions rules (see discussion following), however, have much in common. The general expectation is that the IRS will first apply intermediate sanctions, invoking private inurement principles only in egregious cases. Nonetheless, it is certainly possible for the IRS to apply both bodies of law, thus penalizing both the insider or insiders who obtained the excess benefit and the tax-exempt organization that provided it.

PRIVATE BENEFIT

The body of law that concerns *private benefit* is somewhat different from the law encompassed by private inurement.

(a) General Rules

The private benefit doctrine, created largely by the courts, is more sweeping; it covers a wider range of activities. Most significantly, the private benefit rule can operate without the involvement of an insider. As the IRS stated the matter, the private benefit doctrine applies to "all kinds of persons and groups." The doctrine is, however, applicable only to tax-exempt charitable organizations, although the IRS from time to time tries to extend the doctrine to other types of exempt organizations, such as social welfare entities.

The private benefit rule was illustrated by a case involving a nonprofit school. Individuals were trained there to become political campaign consultants, but the graduates of the school nearly always ended up working for candidates of the same political party. The school's instructional activities did not constitute political campaign activity (see Chapter 15), but the judge wanted to deny tax-exempt status. He ruled that the school could not be tax-exempt because it provided private benefits in the form of assistance to the political candidates by the school's alumni. (If this private benefit rule was applied literally, there would not be many tax-exempt schools.)

In recent years, the private benefit doctrine has emerged as a potent force in the law concerning charitable organizations. No longer is the doctrine applied only where individuals are benefited. Private benefit can also occur where the beneficiary is a for-profit corporation, as the joint venture cases (see discussion following) attest. Indeed, the IRS, supported to some degree by a court, has aggressively begun finding impermissible private benefit conferred by charitable entities on other types of tax-exempt organizations (such as social welfare organizations and associations).

Matters have evolved to the point where the IRS is applying the private benefit doctrine to achieve certain ends in the governance setting (see Chapter 8). Although the doctrine is supposed to be applied as a sanction, that is, only when some form of unwarranted benefit actually occurs, today's IRS asserts that the doctrine is applicable where private benefit *might* or *could* occur. Thus, the IRS is issuing private letter rulings holding that the private benefit doctrine applies, to deny tax exemption, when a charitable organization refuses to adopt a conflict-of-interest policy (see Chapter 22) or have an independent board (neither of which is required by law).

The private benefit doctrine presents a proverbial trap for the unwary. The private inurement doctrine may not apply because there is no insider involved. The intermediate sanctions rules or private foundation self-dealing rules may not apply because there is no disqualified person or an exception may be available. Nonetheless, the analysis should not stop—the lawyer or other advisor should press on, to determine whether the private benefit doctrine is applicable.

As is the case with the private inurement doctrine, the sole sanction for violation of the private benefit doctrine is loss or denial of the organization's tax-exempt status.

JOINT VENTURES

Charitable organizations are increasingly involved in partnerships with individuals or in other joint ventures with individuals or for-profit entities. Real estate ventures in which a charitable organization is the general partner in a limited partnership are common. Partnerships and similar vehicles are discussed in Chapter 18; the topic here is the IRS's concern about private benefit in joint ventures.

In a general partnership, all of the partners are subject to liability for the acts committed in the name of the partnership. In a limited partnership, which will have at least one general partner, the limited partners are essentially investors; their liability is confined to the extent of their investment. As investors, the limited partners expect to experience a return on their investment. Meanwhile, the general partner(s) in a limited partnership has the responsibility to operate the partnership in a successful manner—which includes seeing to it that the limited partners achieve an economic return that is worth the commitment of their capital.

In this structure and set of expectations, the IRS sees private benefit lurking. In its worst light, a limited partnership with a charitable organization at the helm can be construed as the running of a business (the partnership) for the benefit of private interests (the limited partners). This is rarely the case in the context of nonprofit organizations. A partnership (general or limited) is basically a financing entity—a means to an end. In this instance, a charitable organization is able to attract the funds of others for a legitimate purpose. Like the borrowing of money from a bank (where the charity pays interest), a charitable organization/general partner must pay the limited partners for its use of their money. But, because in the partnership structure the general partner is functioning in an active (not passive) manner, the IRS finds private benefit when the limited partners are paid but not when the bankers are paid.

When it went to litigation, the IRS lost nearly every case. The position of the IRS has now evolved to this point: A charitable organization will lose its tax-exempt status if it participates as a general partner in a limited partnership, unless the purpose of the partnership is the advancement of charitable purposes. Even a charity that passes that test will forfeit tax exemption if it is not protected against the day-to-day duties of administering the partnership or if the payments to the limited partners are excessive.

Despite its ferocious stance against charitable organizations in partnerships, the IRS has yet (since losing all but one of a string of cases) to deny or revoke exempt status to a charitable organization that has ended up in a limited partnership as general partner. To date, the IRS has always found the partnership to be engaged in charitable purposes. By dramatic contrast, the IRS is having considerable success in situations where a tax-exempt charitable organization is involved in a joint venture (usually where the venture vehicle is a limited liability company) to the extent that the entirety of the entity is in the venture. If the charitable organization loses control of its resources to (or, as one court put it, "cedes its authority" to) one or more for-profit companies, the charity will lose its tax-exempt status.

Thus, charitable organizations should be cautious when entering into any form of joint venture or partnership, in whatever capacity. They should avoid conferring private benefit on persons or otherwise being used to generate unwarranted benefits to persons in their private capacities.

INTERMEDIATE SANCTIONS

One of the most dramatic statutory additions to the federal tax law directly affecting nonprofit organizations was the enactment of the intermediate sanctions rules. This development, in 1996, was historic, bringing into federal tax law one of the most significant bodies of regulation affecting charitable organizations ever enacted. These sanctions are designed to curb abuses in the arena of private inurement using a mechanism other than revocation of the charitable organization's tax exemption. They are applicable with respect to all public charitable organizations and tax-exempt social welfare organizations. These two categories of organizations are termed *applicable tax-exempt organizations*.

In the past, revocation of an offending charitable organization's tax-exempt status did not solve the problem. The person receiving the undue benefit continued to retain it; the beneficiaries of the charitable organization's program were the ones who were hurt in the aftermath of loss of exemption. Intermediate sanctions are *intermediate* in the sense that they will be imposed on directors, officers, key employees, or other types of disqualified persons who engage in inappropriate private transactions (rather than the exempt organization).

The heart of this body of tax law is the *excess benefit transaction*. A transaction is considered an excess benefit transaction if an economic benefit is provided by an applicable tax-exempt organization directly or indirectly to, or for the use of, a disqualified person, if the value of the economic benefit provided exceeds the value of the consideration received by the exempt organization for providing the benefit. The principal focus of intermediate sanctions is on instances of unreasonable compensation—where a person's level of compensation is deemed to be in excess of the value of the economic benefit derived by the organization from the person's services. In that regard, an economic benefit may not be treated as compensation for the performance of services unless the organization clearly indicated its intent to so treat the benefit.

The concept of the excess benefit transaction includes any transaction in which the amount of any economic benefit provided to, or for the use of, a disqualified person is determined in whole or in part by the revenues of one or more activities of the organization, where the transaction is reflected in tax regulations and results in private inurement.

A *disqualified person* generally is any person who was, at any time during the five-year period ending on the date of the transaction, in a position to exercise substantial influence over the affairs of the organization. The term *disqualified person* also includes members of the family of someone who is a disqualified person under the general rule and organizations (corporations, partnerships, trusts) in which these persons own more than 35 percent of the stock or other interest.

A disqualified person who benefited from an excess benefit transaction is subject to an initial tax equal to 25 percent of the amount of the excess benefit. Moreover, this person will be required to return the excess benefit amount to the tax-exempt organization. An *organization manager* (usually a director or officer) who participated in an excess benefit transaction, knowing that it was such a transaction, is subject to an initial tax of 10 percent of the excess benefit. An additional tax may be imposed on a disqualified person where the initial tax was imposed and the appropriate correction of the excess benefit transaction did not occur. In this situation, the disqualified person is subject to a tax equal to 200 percent of the excess benefit involved.

A fascinating (and huge) exception to the intermediate sanctions rules is the *initial contract* exception. These rules do not apply to a fixed payment made by an applicable tax-exempt organization to a disqualified person pursuant to the first contract between the parties. A *fixed payment* is an amount of money or other property specified in the contract involved, or determined by a fixed formula specified in the contract, which is to be paid or transferred in exchange for the provision of specified services or property. An *initial contract* is a binding written contract between an applicable tax-exempt organization and a person who was not a disqualified person immediately prior to entering into the contract. (This exception is informally referred to as the *first bite* exception, the parallel drawn with the law of dogs.)

If a transaction creating a benefit was approved by an independent board, or an independent committee of the board, a presumption arises that the terms of the transaction are reasonable. The burden of proof would then shift to the IRS, which would then have to overcome (rebut) the presumption to prevail. This presumption may cause a restructuring of the boards of directors or trustees of many charitable organizations.

The concept of the excess benefit transaction could apply in the context of payments for fundraising services. One circumstance would be the receipt of funds by an employee of the exempt organization. Another circumstance would be payment to an independent contractor, such as an outside fundraising company. The sanctions apply to disqualified persons, such as an individual who is in a position to exercise substantial influence over the affairs of the organization.

In many respects, the concept of the excess benefit transaction is based on existing law concerning private inurement. The statute, however, expressly states that an excess benefit transaction also includes any transaction in which the amount of any economic benefit provided to a disqualified person is determined, at least in part, by the revenues of the organization. These transactions are referenced in the legislative history of the intermediate sanctions as *revenue-sharing arrangements*.

The IRS and the courts have determined that a variety of revenue-sharing arrangements do not constitute private inurement. This includes arrangements where the compensation of a person is ascertained, in whole or in part, on the basis of the value of contributions generated. The legislative history of the sanctions states that the IRS is not bound by these prior determinations when interpreting and applying intermediate sanctions.

Once the final tax regulations were issued (in early 2002), IRS enforcement of the intermediate sanctions rules began in earnest. Private letter rulings are beginning to appear, as are court cases. This body of law may be expected to be one of the most active of the overall federal law of nonprofit organizations in the coming years.

INUREMENT AND INTERMEDIATE SANCTIONS

Federal tax regulations provide the criteria the IRS uses in deciding whether to revoke exempt status, on the ground of private inurement, where there has been an excess benefit transaction. These regulations provide that, in determining whether to continue to recognize the tax exemption of a charitable entity that engages in an excess benefit transaction and apply only the intermediate sanctions rules, the IRS will consider all relevant facts and circumstances, including

- The size and scope of the organization's regular and ongoing activities that further exempt purposes, before and after one or more excess benefit transactions have occurred

- The size and scope of one or more excess benefit transactions in relation to the size and scope of the organization's regular and ongoing exempt functions

- Whether the organization has been involved in multiple excess benefit transactions

- Whether the organization has implemented safeguards that that are reasonably calculated to prevent excess benefit transactions

- Whether the excess benefit transaction has been corrected or the organization has made good-faith efforts to seek correction from the disqualified person or persons who benefited from the excess benefit transaction. (See Chapters 20 and 21.)

With this development (in 2008), it is now official: There is such a thing as incidental private inurement (in the sense of inurement that can occur without leading to revocation or denial of tax exemption—at least in the charitable context).

APPEARANCES

Occasionally, a nonprofit organization engages in activities that, to some, are *wrong* or *unethical*. This description does not necessarily mean that the activities are illegal or contrary to tax-exempt status.

Consider, for example, a charge of *conflict of interest*. This accusation is leveled at a person who is on both sides of a transaction—for example, a member of the board of directors of a nonprofit organization who provides consulting services to the organization for a fee. The term conflict of interest connotes wrongful activity; it is a derogatory phrase. It is, however, often *not* a violation of law; rather, it is a state of affairs that looks suspicious and thus raises questions of "appearances." Some nonprofit organizations have conflict-of-interest policies that are designed to prevent even an appearance of wrongdoing. Conflicts of interest can be indications of private inurement or private benefit.

Other circumstances that may cause questions as to "appearances" are having two or more members of the same family on the board or on the payroll of a nonprofit organization; luxurious travel and accommodations arranged for board members or staff; club memberships and other such perquisites for the officers of a nonprofit organization; and an array of taxable subsidiaries and joint ventures. A nonprofit organization can suffer at the hands of the media and in many other ways, if appearances suggest wrongdoing. This fact is being exacerbated as the IRS and others push charitable organizations into following *best practices*, which may preclude engaging in certain activities, even if they are legal. Organizations are finding that a defense based on the niceties of legal distinctions only invites further chiding.

As the federal law of tax-exempt organizations evolves, the private inurement/private benefit constraint is becoming more stringent. Entire classes of organizations have lost their tax exemption as the result of this evolutionary process. Homeowners' associations ceased being exempt social welfare organizations (although Congress stepped in and gave them their own exemption category). Veterans' organizations that provide benefits to their members and dependents were likewise extricated from the social welfare exemption (although, again, Congress intervened). So-called "self-interest" organizations, which provide sickness and death benefits to members (such as individuals within a particular ethnic group) and their beneficiaries, are no longer exempt as social welfare organizations. (In this instance, Congress has let the IRS's policy decision stand.)

FOCUS: Campaign to Clean Up America

The Campaign to Clean Up America (CCUA), as a charitable organization, is subject to the rule that its net earnings may not inure to the benefit of individuals in their private capacities. Because the CCUA is a public charity, the intermediate sanctions rules, rather than the self-dealing rules, apply.

Application of the private inurement doctrine to the CCUA first requires an assessment of who its insiders are. The most likely insiders are founders, directors, and officers, and at the CCUA, the same individual may be serving in two or all three capacities. You, as the founder of the CCUA, and as a director and an officer (president) are obviously an insider. (In the parlance of the intermediate sanctions rules, you are a disqualified person.) So, too, is your spouse, who is a director and officer (and may be a cofounder as well). Other directors and officers are insiders, and key employees and substantial contributors are potential insiders.

The other principal aspect of private inurement lies in the transactions, if any, between the CCUA and Its insiders. You and the other directors and/or officers may function as employees and may be receiving a salary. To avoid the intermediate sanctions penalties and/or private inurement, the compensation must be reasonable and not excessive. Because of the self-dealing taint of this type of compensatory arrangement, the IRS will likely give it more than passing scrutiny, so you and the other insiders would be wise to develop a substantive rationale for the salary amounts.

You happen to lease space to use as an office for your business. You decide to sublease space to the CCUA for Its offices, at least until the organization has the wherewithal to locate in independent quarters. The CCUA can pay you rent without endangering its tax exemption, as long as the rental rate is reasonable. Again, the arrangement may well be subject to strict scrutiny, so you must be prepared to justify the normality of the rental rates.

You are contributing money to the CCUA, as are others, but it needs more funding now. You can lend money to the CCUA, at interest. With the private inurement doctrine and intermediate sanctions in the picture, however, the interest rate must be reasonable, and you must be able to justify the interest rate selected.

The law theoretically tolerates rentals or loans from the CCUA, but these activities are not advisable for you or other insiders. If they are done, the charges must be reasonable. Moreover, the other terms of the arrangement (self-dealing) must be reasonable as well—the rental term and/or the borrowing term, and, in the case of the loan, the repayment terms and the security provided.

For the CCUA (and other public charities), with the current emphasis on scrutiny for instances of private inurement and the potential of applicability of the intermediate sanction penalties, the types and number of its transactions with insiders must be approached guardedly. Moreover, there are limits as a matter of practicality. It is *possible* for the CCUA to lawfully employ every insider and each of his or her family members, but it would be imprudent, and your lawyer advises a minimization of that employment practice. She recites to you and the other directors a litany of court cases where tax exemption was lost or denied because the nonprofit organization involved was a nest of self-dealing and had incestuous employment practices. You decide to avoid that fate.

During the course of its existence, the CCUA will purchase goods and services, equipment, furniture, supplies, and the like. It will likely pay fees to consultants (such as lawyers, accountants, and fundraisers, and, perhaps, investment counselors and management consultants). In these respects, the CCUA is no different than a for-profit organization. The private inurement constraint, however, never goes away. When the consultants or vendors are insiders, the CCUA should always be in a position to justify both the relationship and the amounts paid. The law does not require "competitive bidding" on purchases and fee assignments, but, for nonprofit organizations, a good rule of thumb is to minimize, if not avoid, self-dealing transactions. Even if the transactions are legal, nothing can spoil a good fundraising campaign more than adverse publicity about intrafamily business dealings.

For example, one of the programs of the CCUA is trash collection, using volunteers. To facilitate this program and at the same time to generate publicity about the organization, you decide that the CCUA will purchase plastic trash bags, bearing its name and logo, for distribution and use by the volunteers. Your brother-in-law owns a company that manufactures lawn maintenance supplies, including trash bags; the CCUA purchases the bags from his company. If the company gives the CCUA a discount, such as for purchasing in bulk, the acquisition of the bags from that particular company is not a transgression of the private inurement doctrine. But, if the bags are sold to the CCUA at a mark-up substantially in excess of the retail market price, an excess benefit transaction or private inurement would occur. Even if the purchase of the bags was for a fair price (or at a discount), the launching of the CCUA, its programs, and its fundraising effort could be hindered. Members' or volunteers' gossip might reach an enterprising reporter, and the organization could face an accusation of being manipulated for private gain.

The absence of private gain is what separates the CCUA and other nonprofit organizations from for-profit businesses. Charitable and similar organizations are expected to serve the *public*, not private individuals. If the CCUA wishes to further an activity that would best be housed in a for-profit entity, it should explore the establishment of a for-profit subsidiary. (See Chapter 17.)

CHAPTER SIX

From Nonprofit to Tax-Exempt

Under the federal income tax system, every element of gross income received—whether by a corporate entity or an individual—is subject to taxation, unless an express statutory provision exempts from tax either that form of income or that type of person.

Many types of nonprofit organizations are eligible for exemption from the federal income tax. (See Chapter 4.) The exemption is not automatic, however; exemption is not available merely because an organization has been set up and is not operated as a for-profit organization. Organizations become tax-exempt when they meet the requirements of the particular statutory provision that provides for the exempt status.

RECOGNITION OF TAX-EXEMPT STATUS

Whether a nonprofit organization is entitled to tax exemption, initially or on a continuing basis, is a matter of law. The U.S. Congress defines the categories of organizations that are eligible for tax exemption; it is up to Congress to determine whether an exemption from tax should be continued, in whole or in part, or whether a tax exemption should be created. Except for state and local governments, no entities have a constitutional right to a tax exemption.

The IRS does not *grant* tax-exempt status. (See Myth 7 in Chapter 3.) Congress grants it, under sections of the Internal Revenue Code that it has enacted. The function of the IRS is to *recognize* tax exemption.

When an organization applies to the IRS for a ruling or determination regarding its tax-exempt status, it is requesting the IRS to recognize a tax exemption that already exists (assuming the organization qualifies). It is not asking the IRS to grant tax exemption. Subsequently, the IRS may determine that an organization, which it once recognized as being tax-exempt, is no longer entitled to exempt status and may revoke its prior recognition of exempt status.

Most nonprofit organizations that are eligible for a tax exemption do not need to have their exemption recognized by the IRS. When should a nonprofit organization seek an IRS determination? Management personnel must decide, taking into account their own degree of confidence in the organization's eligibility for the exemption and the costs associated with the application process. Most organizations in this position elect to pursue recognition of tax-exempt status.

Charitable organizations, certain credit counseling entities, and certain employee benefit organizations must file (successfully) with the IRS for recognition of their exemption. Entities such as social welfare organizations, labor organizations, trade and professional associations, social clubs, and veterans' organizations may, but need not, file an application for recognition of tax-exempt status. (Political organizations, however, are required to file a notice (Form 8871) with the IRS to be tax-exempt.)

A request for recognition of tax exemption generally is commenced by filing a form, entitled "Application for Recognition of Exemption." Charitable organizations file Form 1023; most other organizations file Form 1024. (In rare instances, neither form is used; the filing is done by letter.)

The IRS can revoke recognition of exemption for good cause (such as a change in the law), but an organization that has been recognized by the IRS as being tax-exempt can rely on that determination as long as there are no substantial changes in its character, purposes, or methods of operation. If material changes occur, the organization should notify the IRS and may have to undergo a reevaluation of its exempt status.

APPLICATION PROCEDURE

The IRS has developed procedures by which a ruling or determination letter may be issued to an organization that is filing for recognition of its tax-exempt status. The organization must file an application with the IRS at its service center in Cincinnati, Ohio. The determination of exemption will be issued by that office unless the application presents a matter of some controversy or involves an unresolved or novel point of law. In that case, the application will be sent for resolution to the National Office of the IRS in Washington, D.C.

Organizations should allow several months for the processing of an application for recognition of tax exemption. It is the contemporary practice of the IRS to closely examine these applications. Applicants should not be surprised to receive one or more lists (perhaps an extensive one) of questions from the agency, seeking additional information. A procedure for expedited consideration is available in extreme cases, but the IRS is reluctant to consider applications out of the order in which they are received.

A favorable ruling or determination will be issued, as long as the application and supporting documents establish that the organization meets the particular statutory requirements. The application must include a statement describing the organization's purposes, copies of its governing instruments (such as, in the case of a corporation, its articles of incorporation and bylaws), and either a financial statement or a proposed multiyear budget.

The application filed by a charitable organization must also include a summary of the sources of its financial support, its fundraising program, the composition of its governing body (usually a board of directors), its relationship with other organizations (if any), the nature of its services or products, and the basis for any charges for them, and its membership (if any).

The IRS is generally free to seek and obtain other information it deems necessary for a determination or ruling, and it frequently does so. The ability of the IRS to pursue additional information is not unlimited, however, and the courts have held that recognition of exemption must be granted once an organization makes the requisite "threshold showing."

If the application is not complete, the IRS will return the application and all supporting documents to the organization and instruct it to file again, by submitting a complete application.

The proper preparation of an application for recognition of exemption involves far more than merely filling in the blanks of a government form. The process is similar to the preparation of a prospectus in conformance with the federal securities laws requirements, and every statement made in the application should be carefully considered. The prime objective should be to be accurate; all material facts must be fully and fairly disclosed. Determining which facts are material requires careful judgment.

The phrasing of the answers to questions in the application can be extremely significant. The exercise is more one of "art" than "science." Whoever prepares the form should be able to anticipate any concerns the contents of the application may cause, see that the application is prepared properly, and yet minimize, if not completely avoid, conflict with the IRS. Organizations that are entitled to a particular tax exemption have often been denied recognition of tax-exempt status because poor or wrong wording in their application enabled the IRS to build a case against their exemption.

Preparing an application for recognition of exemption is a useful exercise. It forces an organization to think through what it wants to do, how its activities will be financially supported, and other aspects of its organization and operation. Frequently, the language developed in preparing the application can be useful in grant applications and fundraising appeals. Sometimes, preparation of the application causes an organization to focus on significant aspects of its organization and operation that it would otherwise ignore.

Preparation of an application is even more important for charitable organizations. The information filed with the IRS is used to make three sets of determinations: whether the organization will be recognized as tax-exempt, whether it will be eligible to receive deductible charitable contributions (and sometimes to what extent), and whether the organization will be a public charity or a private foundation.

A nonprofit organization does not need to retain the services of a lawyer or other professional for preparation of an application for recognition of exemption (see Myth 15 in Chapter 3). Because of the complexities involved, however, it is a good idea to at least have a professional who understands the process (see Myth 16) review the documents before they are filed. In many instances, a lawyer is involved during the entire process, beginning with preparation of the governing instruments.

An application for recognition of exemption should be regarded as an important legal document and prepared accordingly. Throughout an organization's existence, this document will be subject to review. A nonprofit organization is required to provide a copy of this application, along with supporting documents and related correspondence, to anyone who asks for it (see discussion following).

A nonprofit organization seeking recognition of its tax-exempt status has the burden of proving that it satisfies all of the requirements of the particular exemption provision. If the application process is not initially successful, the organization has certain appeals rights within the IRS. If the organization fails to successfully navigate the administrative process, there are opportunities to pursue the matter in federal court.

APPLICATION FORM

This section provides guidance for preparing an application for recognition of tax exemption. (The following section shows some sample answers, using the facts involving the Campaign to Clean Up America.) Because it is more complex, Form 1023 will be used for analysis rather than Form 1024. (The current Form 1023 is dated June 2006.)

The application will require some attachments. These may be identified and keyed into the form as Exhibit A, Exhibit B, and so on. Some answers will be longer than the space provided on the form. These can also be provided as attachments.

(a) Part I

Part I of the Form 1023 requests basic information about the organization, such as its name and address (including website address). Every nonprofit organization must have an *employer identification number* (even if there are no employees). The number is obtained by filing Form SS-4 (see Chapter 2). Form SS-4 may be filed as soon as the organization is formed and organized. Thus, question 4 should be answered by inserting the number.

The contact person (question 6) may be someone directly involved with the organization, such as an officer or director, or an independent representative of the organization, such as a lawyer or accountant. If such a representative is being used (question 7), he or she must be granted a power of attorney, which is filed on Form 2848 and attached to the application.

The organization must state the month in which its annual accounting period ends (question 5). The determination of a fiscal year should be given some thought; most organizations prefer the calendar year (in which case, the answer is 12). Whatever period is selected, the organization should be certain that the same period is stated on Form SS-4 and used when compiling its multiyear budget (Part III).

The date of formation must be recorded (question 11). If the organization is incorporated, this date will be the date the state agency issued the certificate of incorporation. This date is significant in relation to the 27-month rule (see the discussion following).

(b) Part II

Part II of the Form 1023 requires the organization to report as to its organizational structure (that is, its *type*). To file this application, the organization must be able to report that it is a nonprofit corporation, limited liability company, unincorporated association, or trust. (The application states that an entity cannot file it unless it is one of these four types.)

If the organization is a corporation, it must attach a copy of its articles of incorporation, the certificate of incorporation, and any amendments to the articles. If the entity is a limited liability company, the documents to be attached are copies of the articles of organization, certificate of filing with the state, any operating agreement, and any amendments to the articles. If the organization is an unincorporated association, the application must include copies of the articles of association (which may be labeled a constitution) and any amendments. If the organization is a trust, it must include a copy of the trust agreement and any amendments. A copy of the organization's bylaws, if any, must also be filed with the application.

(c) Part III

Part III focuses on required provisions in the applicant's organizing document. (Indeed, the application is not supposed to be filed unless the applicant can check the boxes in lines 1 and 2a.) One provision that must be cited (line 1) is the statement of exempt purpose. The other provision this part highlights (line 2b) is the reference to the entity's dissolution clause.

(d) Part IV

For many organizations, Part IV of the Form 1023 will be the most important portion of the application. It can also be the most difficult to prepare and the most sensitive, in terms of disclosure to the public and potential trouble with the IRS.

The organization, using an attachment, must provide a narrative description of its past, present, and planned activities. Representative copies of newsletters, brochures, and similar documents may accompany this description, which is expected to be "thorough and accurate." Usually, the description is an essay that summarizes the organization's programs. It should be carefully written. Good practice is to open with a brief description of the organization's purposes and follow with paragraphs summarizing its program activities. This response should be as full as is reasonable.

(e) Part V

Part V is one of the trickiest and most complex portions of the application. This concerns compensation and other financial arrangements with the organization's trustees, directors, officers, employees, and independent contractors.

The organization must list the names, titles, and mailing addresses of its trustees, directors, and officers, and their total annual compensation (line 1a). Also to be listed are the names, titles, and mailing addresses of the organization's five most highly compensated employees (receiving over $50,000 annually) (line 1b), and the names, business names, and mailing addresses of its five most highly compensated independent contractors (receiving over $50,000 annually) (line 1c).

The organization must indicate and discuss whether its trustees, directors, and officers are related through family or business relationships, or are related to any most highly compensated employees or independent contractors. Any business relationship between the organization and its trustees, directors, and officers must be identified. (line 2.) A list must be attached showing the name, qualifications, average hours worked, and duties of these trustees, directors, officers, employees, and independent contractors; in addition, reporting must be made of these persons' receipt of compensation from related organizations (line 3).

In establishing compensation for these five categories of persons, the organization is asked whether it follows a conflict-of-interest policy, engages in advance approval of compensation arrangements, documents compensation arrangements, has written records as to compensation arrangements, and how it sets compensation that is reasonable (line 4). The organization is also asked whether it has adopted a conflict-of-interest policy and, if not, how it determines whether persons who have a conflict of interest will not have influence in setting their compensation and/or with respect to business deals involving the organization (line 5).

The organization is asked about non-fixed compensation arrangements and purchase or sale of goods or services from or to insiders, as well as leases, other contracts, loans, or other agreements with insiders or entities controlled by insiders (lines 6–9).

(f) Part VI

Part VI concerns the provision of benefits by the organization. A question (line 1a) inquires as to program activities that entail the provision of goods, services, or funds to individuals. Another question asks whether the organization's programs limit the provision of goods, services, or funds to a specific individual or group of individuals (line 2). A further question pertains to whether individuals receiving program benefits have a family or business relationship with any of the organization's trustees, directors, officers, highest compensated employees, or highest compensated independent contractors (line 3).

(g) Part VII

Part VII concerns the organization's history; this consists of two parts. The IRS wants to know whether the applicant organization is a *successor organization*—namely, whether it has taken or will take over the activities of another organization, has taken over at least 25 percent of the fair market value of the net assets of another organization, or was established on the conversion of an organization from for-profit to nonprofit status (line 1, Schedule G). The application also inquires as to whether the application is being submitted more than 27 months after the end of the month in which the entity was formed (line 2, Schedule E).

(h) Part VIII

Part VIII of the Form 1023 looks at a variety of *specific activities* the organization may be conducting, such as political campaign activities (see Chapter 15), legislative activities (see Chapter 14), gaming activities (see Chapter 13), fundraising activities (see Chapter 12), economic development, joint ventures (see Chapter 18), ownership or rights in intellectual or other property, international operations, the making of grants and loans, and activities in conjunction with other organizations.

(i) Part IX

Part IX concerns financial data, such as a statement of revenue and expenses (or a proposed budget) or a balance sheet. The organization is asked to explain whether there have been any substantial changes in its assets or liabilities since the end of its filing period.

(j) Part X

Part X concerns the organization's public charity or private foundation status (see Chapter 7). The organization is to indicate whether it is a foundation or public charity and, if the latter, the category of public charity. Additional questions apply to publicly supported charitable organizations.

(k) Schedules

Form 1023 is accompanied by a host of other schedules concerning churches and certain other religious organizations (Schedule A), schools (including colleges and universities) (B), hospitals and medical research organizations (C), supporting organizations (D), organizations that maintain homes for the elderly or provide low-income housing (F), and entities that provide scholarships and fellowships (H).

(l)   Follow-Up Questions

Regarding follow-up questions, the IRS tends to use sets of questions drawn up as forms. Two types of activities, scholarships and research, are detailed here to illustrate the questions and information that will have to be dealt with. If the applicant organization is to have a *scholarship program*, here are the typical questions it will have to answer:

- Describe the class of eligibles, or potential recipients, of the organization's grants.

- Indicate whether there are any restrictions or limitations on who may make application for a scholarship or whom the organization will consider as possible grantees.

- Who makes the selection of eventual recipients from the class of eligibles? If these people are related to the organization, give complete details.

- List and describe all criteria used by the selection committee in selecting recipients from the class of eligibles.

- Will any grants be made to spouses, children, descendants, spouses of children or of descendants, or other persons disqualified in relationship to the organization, its directors, or its officers?

- Describe how the scholarship program is publicized to ensure that all eligible individuals are reasonably likely to be informed of the availability of the scholarship aid.

- Will all grants be limited to students attending qualified educational institutions?

- Will the organization provide aid to students both as grants and as loans?

- If loans are to be made, describe the interest rates (if any) applicable to any loans to be given, how such interest rates are determined, and the terms of repayment of the loans.

- Explain the follow-up procedures in place to ensure that all scholarship funds will be used for the stated purposes.

- Explain the procedures that will be followed if a misuse of funds is discovered.

- Will funds be paid to the individual students, or will they be paid directly to the school the students will be attending?

- When did the organization begin giving scholarship aid?

- How many scholarships have been given?

- Provide a list of all grant recipients together with an indication of how much money was received by each recipient.

If the applicant organization is to have a research program, here are the questions it will likely have to answer:

- Describe the nature of the research engaged in or contemplated.

- Describe research projects completed or presently being engaged in.

- How and by whom are research projects determined and selected?

- Does the organization have, or is it contemplating having, contract or sponsored research? If so, submit the names of past sponsors or grantors, the terms of the contract or grant, and copies of any executed contracts or grants.

- Summarize the disposition made or to be made of the results of the research, including whether preference has been or will be given to any organization or individual, either as to results or timing of the release of results.

- Who will retain ownership or control of any patents, copyrights, processes, or formulas resulting from the research?

- Submit copies of publications or other media showing reports of the research activities.

- If the organization is engaged in medical research, is the research performed in connection with a hospital?

(m) Specific Questions

Part VIII, question 15, can be very important for some organizations. As a general rule, it does not matter whether the charitable organization has a special relationship with, or is controlled by, another organization. For example, some charitable organizations are controlled by other types of tax-exempt organizations, such as social welfare organizations or trade associations (see Chapter 4), or are controlled by for-profit corporations, such as corporation-related foundations. This question usually has no "right" or "wrong" answer. If the organization has an interlocking directorate, it is good practice to refer to the provision in the governing instruments that describes the overlap of directors.

Some caution may be required when responding as to whether the organization is an *outgrowth* of another (Part VII, question 1). A typical problem arises where the applicant organization is a corporation and the other organization is an unincorporated organization and has been operating as a charitable entity, without recognition of tax-exempt status.

Part VII, question 2, can be of no importance or it can be of extreme importance, depending on the circumstances. The basic *27-month rule* is that the recognition of exemption will be retroactive to the date of formation of the organization, if the application is filed with the IRS within 27 months from the end of the month in which the organization was established. (This is why the date inserted in response to question 11 of Part I can be of importance.) For example, if the organization is created on January 15, 2009, and the application for recognition of exemption is filed before April 30, 2010, the recognition of exemption (if granted) will be retroactive to January 15, 2009, regardless of when the determination is made by the IRS. If the application is filed on or after May 1, 2010, the recognition of exemption may be effective only as of the date the application was received by the IRS.

As for tax-exempt status, the 27-month rule may not be of any particular importance because the organization can qualify as a tax-exempt social welfare organization until the date of its classification as a charitable organization. (Remember, social welfare organizations do *not* have to have a ruling recognizing their exempt status.) This alleviation of the tax exemption problem, however, does not help with the organization's posture as a charitable donee (or, if applicable, as a non-private foundation). Donors making gifts during the interim period will, upon audit, find their charitable deductions disallowed. Private foundations making grants during the interim period may be subject to taxation for failure to exercise *expenditure responsibility*. (See Chapter 7.) Thus, an organization desiring to be recognized as a charitable organization from the outset must file a completed application for recognition of tax exemption prior to the expiration of the 27-month period.

If the applicant charitable organization is a private foundation, the answer to Part X, question 1a is "yes." If the organization is seeking classification as a private operating foundation, it should so indicate in response to question 2 and then complete a special schedule.

If the applicant organization believes it can avoid private foundation status, however, it must indicate which of nine public charity classifications it is requesting (question 5). An organization that qualifies as a tax-exempt school, hospital, other institution, or a supporting organization (see Chapter 7) will be recognized by the IRS as a public charity at the time exempt status is recognized. Matters can become more complex for new charitable organizations that are seeking classification as publicly supported organizations because they lack any financial history evidencing public support.

Either type of publicly supported organization (see Chapter 12) must demonstrate its initial qualification for nonprivate foundation status by convincing the IRS that it will receive the requisite extent of public support. This is done by submitting a proposed budget. This budget should summarize contemplated types of revenue (such as gifts, grants, exempt function revenue, and investment income) and types of expenses (such as expenditures for programs, compensation, occupancy, telephones, travel, postage, and fund-raising). The applicant organization should be certain that the fiscal year used to develop the budget is the same period referred to in the response to question 5 of Part I.

Prior to law that took effect in 2008, an organization that wanted to be recognized by the IRS as a publicly supported charity had to go through a two-step process. First, the organization had to declare, as part of the application process, that it expected to be publicly supported on an ongoing basis. Second, following a five-year period, the organization had to make a filing with the IRS demonstrating its compliance with the applicable public support test. The determination letter issued to a successful applicant was, as to public charity status, an *advance ruling*. Another ruling, issued after expiration of the five-year period (the *advance ruling period*), was termed a *definitive ruling*.

Pursuant to this new approach, an organization will be classified as a publicly supported charity if, as part of the process for seeking recognition of tax exemption, it can show that (in addition to qualification for tax exemption) it can reasonably be expected to be publicly supported during its first five years. The organization has public charity status for this five-year period irrespective of the amount of public support it received. This new set of rules eliminated the advance ruling process and the subsequent filing requirement for new organizations seeking tax-exempt charitable status.

Beginning with the organization's sixth year, it must establish (if it can) that it meets the applicable public support test by showing that it is publicly supported; this is evidenced on Form 990, Schedule A (see Chapter 9). The organization will not owe a private foundation investment income tax or private foundation termination tax with respect to its first five years. Beginning with the organization's sixth year, for every year as to which it cannot establish that it is a public charity, it will be classified as a private foundation and thus potentially liable for private foundation taxes (see Chapter 7).

The advance ruling pertains only to the applicant organization's status as a publicly supported entity; it is not an advance ruling on its tax-exempt status or charitable donee status. The advance ruling period is probationary or conditional as to *public charity* status. Once the advance ruling period expires and the organization has in fact received adequate public support during the five-year period, that fact will be reported to the IRS. A definitive ruling that the organization is a publicly supported charity will then be issued by the IRS. The advance ruling is conditional; the definitive ruling is permanent (unless upset by a subsequent loss of qualification or change in the law).

A publicly supported charitable organization must, during and after the expiration of the advance ruling period (on an ongoing basis), continue to show that it qualifies as a publicly supported charity (assuming it wants to retain that status). This is done by reporting the financial support information as part of the annual information return (see Chapter 9).

It does not matter which type of publicly supported organization the charitable entity is at any point in its existence; the principal objective is to qualify, at any one time, under one category or another. Thus, an organization can "drift" from one classification of publicly supported organization to another throughout its duration. A charitable organization can, without harm, select one category of publicly supported organization when it completes Part X and satisfy the requirements of the other category only as of the close of the advance ruling period.

As discussed in Chapter 7, the two basic categories of publicly supported organizations are sometimes referred to as *donative publicly supported charities* and *service provider publicly supported charities*. A charitable organization can, at any time in its existence, qualify as one or both of these types of public charities without concern. It does not matter which category the organization complies with as of the end of any year, nor does it matter which category the organization initially selected (and to which the IRS agreed).

The IRS, private foundations, and major donors do not usually care why the organization is publicly supported—they simply want to have the assurance that it is.

If an organization selects a category of publicly supported charitable organization when it prepares Part X, and then finds that it has not met either set of requirements for publicly supported status at the close of the advance ruling period, it will be categorized as a private foundation, unless it can demonstrate that it is eligible for otherwise avoiding private foundation status. This can be done if the organization qualifies as an entity such as a church, school, hospital, or supporting organization (see discussion following).

An applicant organization that qualifies as a church, school, hospital, supporting organization, or the like, is eligible to receive a definitive ruling at the outset. Its financial support is not the factor used in classifying it as a public entity. Instead, its public status derives from what it does programmatically.

(n) Application as Portrait

This application, if properly completed, amounts to a rather complete portrait of the applicant organization. It is important to devote proper time and thought to the preparation of the form. It is, as noted subsequently, a public document and, during the course of the organization's existence, copies may be requested by prospective donors or grantors or representatives of the media.

A ruling from a governmental agency is only as good as the facts on which it is based. If the material facts of a charitable organization change, the determination letter granting recognition of tax-exempt status may become void. It will then be necessary to contact the IRS and arrange for review, to ensure ongoing tax-exempt status.

(o) Disclosure

The application for recognition of tax exemption is a public document and thus is subject to the same disclosure and document dissemination requirements that apply with respect to annual information returns (see Chapter 9).

FOCUS: Campaign to Clean Up America

The Campaign to Clean Up America (CCUA), desiring to be a charitable and publicly supported organization, must complete and file Form 1023. The following answers to selected questions in Form 1023 Illustrate the form and content of these answers for any applicant organization. Questions that require particularly fact-specific answers have not been included.

Part IV
The CCUA would respond to Part IV as follows:

As the name of the organization indicates, the purpose of the Campaign to Clean Up America is to rid the cities, towns, suburbs, and other areas of the United States of trash, debris, and other litter. It is the vision of those who have formed the organization that the beauty of the urban areas and landscapes of this country should not be tarnished, or hidden, by accumulations of garbage and other trash.

It is the belief of the CCUA that much of the solution to the nation's trash problem lies in Individuals' attitudes and mind-sets. An area that is clean is less likely to be trashed than one that is already littered. A community whose occupants are sensitized to the litter accumulation problem is less likely to be full of trash than the one whose occupants have subconsciously repressed the ugly sights. A community whose members are willing to rid the area of trash, and keep it that way, will be a far more beautiful place to live and work, and be proud of, than one that is constantly strewn with litter.

Therefore, the focus of the CCUA will always be on the prevention of littering and the pick-up of litter where it is found. As to the latter, the CCUA will, on a community-by-community basis, organize teams of volunteers who will pick up trash so as to keep their community clean and scenic. It will supply these teams with the equipment necessary to achieve this end, including rakes, shovels, gloves, trash bags, and safety signs to alert traffic that Clean Up America teams are at work in their community. If funding permits, the CCUA will provide members of these teams with "Clean Up America" tee-shirts, to both stimulate spirit in their volunteer work and advertise the programs of the CCUA.

(Continued)

The CCUA will provide these teams with information as to organizational techniques, safety matters, and ideas for coordinating their efforts with local governmental officials. This latter aspect will be of importance in organizing means of trash disposal. The CCUA will also provide the teams with practical guidelines on matters such as trespassing, personal safety, and similar aspects that involve considerations of law.

The CCUA will endeavor to prevent littering from occurring in the first instance through public education programs. These will consist of the distribution of literature, media advertising, and community meetings. The public education aspect of the CCUA's program will be intertwined with its fundraising program. Essentially, the public education component of the CCUA's efforts will be directed to ways to sensitize individuals to the problem of litter accumulation, in the hope that they will not litter, will be moved to dispose of litter caused by others, and will join a CCUA volunteer team to make and keep their community trash free.

It is the belief of the CCUA that a community that is physically attractive (litter free) is a community that will have other desirable attributes that contribute to a better way of life for its members.

The CCUA will undoubtedly engage in some attempts to influence legislation, mostly at the local level, such as laws to toughen the fines for littering and to force trucks to travel with their loads covered. Any such activities, however, will be insubstantial in relation to total activities.

The CCUA may engage in some activities that may constitute unrelated business. For example, the CCUA may sell trash bags (bearing its name and an antilitter message) to the general public. Again, any unrelated business activities will be insubstantial In relation to total activities.

Part VIII, Question 4a

The CCUA would answer question 4a of Part VIII as follows:

The fundraising program of the Campaign to Clean Up America is in the process of formulation. The CCUA will commence its fundraising program with selective mailings and other attempts to reach the general public (such as brochures, flyers, and newspaper advertisements). The CCUA will endeavor to secure gifts of money and property, including charitable bequests. The CCUA will soon commence a planned giving program and will likely, in the future, begin a capital campaign. The CCUA is in the process of retaining the services of a professional fundraising consultant but an agreement has not been executed as yet. A copy of the first fundraising letter that has been developed is attached as Exhibit X.

Part IX

The CCUA would not file any financial statement in Part IX. Instead, It would provide a three-year budget, showing its financial support and its anticipated expenditures.

Attachments to Form 1023

The attachments to Form 1023 can be as important—if not more important—as the contents of the form itself, particularly the statement of activities (the response to Part IV). A review of the attachments to accompany Form 1023, submitted on behalf of the CCUA, serves as a basic checklist for all of these submissions:

- Form 2848 (power of attorney) (if applicable).
- A check in payment of the user fee (Form 1023, Part XI).
- Conformed copy of organizing document (e.g., articles of incorporation).
- Conformed copy of rules of operation (e.g., bylaws).
- Form 872-C (in duplicate).

- Other attachments, such as copies of solicitations for financial support, list of directors and officers, any management agreement or lease, any schedule of membership fees and dues, and any descriptive literature for prospective members.

- A cover letter to the IRS, stating exactly what is being requested. If expedited consideration of the application is being requested, this is the place to include that statement. It is also good practice to include a request for an administrative hearing in the event the IRS decides to (initially at least) rule adversely with respect to the organization.

BIZARRE IRS POSITIONS

The IRS has some inexperienced and not well-trained tax law specialists reviewing applications for recognition of exemption. On occasion, these reviewers display ignorance of the law or invoke their personal judgment as to what the law should be. Applicant nonprofit organizations need to proceed cautiously when caught up in these circumstances.

Here are some examples of bizarre positions of the IRS:

- An organization was advised that, to obtain recognition of tax exemption, it must expand its board of directors, "so control no longer rests with related individuals." With the exception of supporting organizations (see Chapter 7), there is no such requirement in the federal tax law.

- In a variant of the foregoing, a tax law specialist advised that the organization's board structure "must be changed to allow members of the general public to control the organization." Again, there is no such rule.

- A tax law specialist advised that an exempt organization is forbidden to allow its directors to vote on their compensation. That is not the case.

- A tax law specialist opined that a majority of an organization's board must not be salaried by the organization. There is no such rule.

- A tax law specialist advised that a majority of an organization's board may not be related to salaried personnel or to parties providing services. That is not the law.

- A specialist advised that, to be recognized as exempt, the organization must adopt a conflict-of-interest policy. Outside the health care context, this is not a requirement for tax-exempt status.

- A specialist stated that an exempt organization may not be controlled by a for-profit corporation. This is not true.

- A specialist stated that, as a condition of exemption, the organization must provide a statement from each of its board members that "makes it clear" that they are aware of the intermediate sanctions rules (see Chapter 5). There is no such requirement.

- Some reviewers request copies of the resumes of the organization's directors and officers. One IRS questioner noted that these resumes should "focus on their professional experience and training" in relation to these individuals' "oversight" of the organization. The federal tax law does not require that, as a condition of exemption, an organization's managers have experience and training that comports with the organization's affairs. Ignorance, lack of schooling, apathy, or low IQ are not bars to service.

Judgment is required in differentiating between the demands of IRS tax law specialists that are legitimate and those that are not. In the interest of obtaining a ruling, the organization may decide to capitulate. Otherwise, these mistaken efforts should be resisted. (This is easier to do when a professional advisor is involved.) A technique that can be effective is to advise the specialist that, unless he or she revises the erroneous view, the organization will take the matter to his or her supervisor, or, if necessary, to the IRS in Washington, D.C. That approach frequently motivates the specialist to rethink the initial position.

GROUP EXEMPTION

An underutilized procedure allows a charitable (or other) organization to be tax-exempt without having to file an application for recognition of tax exemption. This procedure is tax exemption on a *group* basis.

For the procedure to be available, there must be a *group*, which must consist of a *central* (or parent) organization and at least one *subordinate* (or affiliated) organization. An affiliated organization is a chapter, local, post, or like entity that is affiliated with and subject to the general supervision or control of a central organization—usually a state, regional, or national organization. (The term *affiliated* is not defined in this context but usually entails a mix of funding and decision making.) In this way, an organization is recognized as exempt by reason of its relationship with the parent organization, in addition to its own qualifying activities.

The group exemption requires the parent organization to evaluate, responsibly and independently, the tax-exempt status of its subordinate organizations, using applicable organizational and operational tests. The parent organization must annually certify to the IRS the specific organizations that are part of the group. Private foundations and foreign organizations may not be included in these groups.

A central organization may be involved in more than one group exemption arrangement; for example, a charitable parent organization may have both charitable and social welfare organization affiliates. Alternatively, a central organization may be subordinate to another central organization or a state organization that has subordinate units may be affiliated with a national organization. All of the subordinate organizations in the group must have the same category of tax-exempt status, but the tax-exempt status of the central organization may be different from that of the subordinates.

EXEMPTIONS FROM FILING

A few categories of organizations are exempted from filing an application for recognition of exemption with the IRS. These entities are considered tax-exempt as charitable organizations, even though they do not file a Form 1023:

- A church, an interchurch organization, a local unit of a church, a convention or association of churches, or an integrated auxiliary of a church

- An organization that is not a private foundation or a supporting organization (see Chapter 7) and normally has gross receipts of not more than $5,000 in each tax year
- An organization that is a subordinate organization covered by a group exemption, but only if the central organization timely submits a return covering the subordinates

CHAPTER SEVEN

Charities: Public or Private?

One of the great myths about tax-exempt organizations is that they are not taxable. (See Chapter 3, Myth 5.) The truth is, they can be taxable. In some situations, they may be subject to heavy taxation. Moreover, the individuals involved—founders, officers, or directors—can also be taxable. Of all types of tax-exempt organizations, the degree of potential taxation is most stringent for private foundations.

WHAT IS A PRIVATE FOUNDATION?

The term *private foundation*, used generically in the nonprofit organization community for decades, was not defined in the Internal Revenue Code until 1969. At that time, Congress was on an antifoundation rampage, legislating against foundations in every way it could think of. Congress wanted to be certain that each charitable organization that was not clearly *public* (as explained subsequently) would be treated as a private foundation; it wanted that term to be as all-encompassing as possible. Indeed, in its search for a way to cast a superwide net, it could not write a definition of the term *private foundation*. Instead, it wrote a definition of what a private foundation is not.

Under the federal tax law, every charitable organization—every church, university, hospital, or local community group—is presumed to be a private foundation. Each charitable organization must either rebut that presumption (and become public) or exist as a private foundation.

Despite the intricacies of the tax law, the concept of a *private foundation* is simple. The typical private foundation has four fundamental characteristics:

1. It is a charitable organization and thus subject to the rules applicable to charities generally.

2. Its financial support came from one source, usually an individual, family, or company.

3. Its annual expenditures are funded out of earnings from investment assets, rather than from an ongoing flow of contributions (in this way, a private foundation is much the same as an endowment fund).

4. It makes grants to other organizations for charitable purposes, rather than operate its own programs.

A hybrid entity called a *private operating foundation* (a blend of a private foundation and a public charity) conducts its own programs but has most of the other features of a private foundation (see discussion following).

There is no legal advantage to private foundation status. These are some of the disadvantages:

- A need to comply with a battery of onerous rules, such as prohibitions on self-dealing, insufficient grants for charitable purposes, excess business holdings, jeopardizing (highly speculative) investments, and certain types of grants
- A tax on net investment income
- Extensive reporting responsibilities
- Narrow limitations on gift deductibility
- The reality that private foundations are highly unlikely to make grants to other private foundations

The word *private*, as used here, means that funding comes from a single source. *Private* has nothing to do with the composition of an organization's board of directors or trustees. There is a fairly widespread belief that an advantage to private foundation status is an ability to function "in private,"—that is, without scrutiny from outsiders. Quite the opposite is often true.

A lawyer or other professional helping a new charitable organization through the tax law maze can provide no greater service than steering the organization away from private foundation status when appropriate.

AVOIDING PRIVATE FOUNDATION STATUS

Three principal types of charitable organizations are not private foundations and thus are *public charities*: the *institutions* of the charitable world, the *publicly supported* charities, and the *supporting organizations*. To avoid being a private charity, an organization must demonstrate public involvement, public financial support, or an operating relationship with a public (or certain other) organization.

(a) Institutions

Federal tax law identifies certain institutions within the philanthropic sector that are exempted from the private foundation rules and taxes:

- Churches, or conventions or associations of churches
- Operating educational institutions, such as universities, colleges, and schools
- Operating health care providers (including hospitals) and certain medical research organizations
- Governmental units, whether federal or state

(b) Publicly Supported Organizations

One of the chief characteristics of a private foundation is that it is or was funded from one source. One way for an organization to be classed as a public charity is to draw its funding from many sources (the public). An organization is not a private foundation if it is publicly supported.

There are two basic types of publicly supported organizations. The law has not assigned either of them a name, so we will call them *donative* charities and *service-provider* charities. These classifications are flawed—most publicly supported charities receive a blend of gifts, grants, and fee-for-service revenue (as well as investment income)—but they serve to identify the two types of charities.

(i) Donative Charities. A donative charity is one that *normally* receives a *substantial part* of its support from one or more governmental units in the form of grants, or from direct or indirect contributions from the *public*.

Most donative organizations must derive at least one-third of their financial support (the *support ratio*) from eligible governmental or public sources. The normal time span for measuring the organization's support is its most recent five (since 2008) fiscal years (the *support computation period*).

Public support comes from individuals, trusts, corporations, or other legal entities. The total amount of contributions from any one donor during the support computation period is not public support to the extent that the amount exceeds 2 percent of the organization's total support received during that period. The 2 percent limitation generally does not apply to support received from other donative organizations or from governmental units. All grant support from these two sources is public support.

Donors who have a defined relationship to one another (such as husband and wife) must share a single 2 percent limitation. Multiple contributions from any one source are aggregated over the support computation period.

When it is identifying income in the computation of its support ratio, an organization cannot include amounts received from the exercise or performance of its tax-exempt functions. An organization will not, however, meet the *support test* if it receives almost all of its support from its related activities and only an insignificant amount from governmental units and/or the general public.

An organization's lawyer or accountant should be consulted on whether the support-ratio test requirements have been met. A formula fraction called a *support fraction* will be applied by the professional, using the organization's specific revenues in each category.

Here is an example illustrating how these rules work. A charitable organization received, during its most recent five years, the total sum in the form of gifts and grants of $400,000. Thus, to qualify as this type of public charity, its public support must be at least $134,000 (one-third of $400,000). To see whether that goal was met, the charity applies the 2 percent rule. Two percent of $400,000 is $8,000. Thus, as a general rule, support from a donor or grantor will be public support to the extent that it is no more than $8,000. A donor who gave $5,000 provided $5,000 in public support; a donor who gave $10,000 provided $8,000 in public support. Funds from other donative charities or government entities (if grants) are not limited by the 2 percent rule. Each donor's gift must be evaluated in this fashion to determine whether the $134,000 minimum goal was reached. One outcome might be 15 donors who gave $8,000 each (a total of $120,000) and a $20,000 government grant, resulting in $140,000 of public support—and satisfaction of the test.

An organization that meets a public support test for its current tax year is treated as a publicly supported entity for that year and the immediately succeeding tax year. For example, a calendar-year organization that meets a public support test for 2011, based on the five-year computation period 2007-2011, is a public charity for 2011 and

2012. If this organization cannot meet a public support test for 2012, based on the computation period consisting of 2008-2012, it nonetheless will be a public charity for 2012 because it met a public support test for 2011, based on the computation period of 2007-2011. If, however, the organization cannot meet a public support test for 2013, based on the 2009-2013 computation period, the organization will become a private foundation as of January 1, 2013. Because an organization that cannot meet a public support test for its current tax year is at risk of classification as a private foundation as of the first day of its subsequent tax year, the IRS has observed that organizations "may wish to carefully monitor their public support calculations."

(ii) Service-Provider Charities. A service-provider charitable organization normally receives more than one-third of its support from gifts and grants, membership fees, and/or gross receipts from the performance of exempt functions. Amounts that are eligible are derived from *permitted sources*: governmental agencies, the three basic types of institutions (churches, educational institutions, and health care/medical research entities), donative charities, and persons who are not *disqualified persons* (description follows).

To qualify as a service-provider charitable organization, no more than one-third of the organization's support can come from investment income.

Both the donative organization rules and the service-provider organization rules measure support over the most recent five (since 2008) years, and both utilize a one-third support fraction.

There are, however, some major differences. Exempt function revenue can count as public support for the service-provider organization, but only to the extent that the revenue from any one source does not exceed the greater of $5,000 or 1 percent of the organization's support for the year involved.

The rules limit gifts and grants to service-provider charitable organizations. Public support cannot come from *disqualified persons*: an organization's directors and officers, members of their families, any controlled person, or a substantial contributor (whether an individual, trust, estate, corporation, or other entity). A *substantial contributor* is a person who contributes or bequeaths an aggregate amount of more than $5,000, where that amount is more than 2 percent of the total contributions in addition to bequests received by the organization.

Here is an example (as similar to the previous one as possible) illustrating how these rules work. A charitable organization received, during its most recent five years, the total sum, in the form of gifts and grants, of $400,000. Thus, to qualify as this type of public charity, its public support must be at least $134,000 (one-third of $400,000). To determine whether that goal was met, the charity subtracts gifts made by disqualified persons from its total gifts. Each donor's gift must be evaluated in this fashion to determine whether the $134,000 minimum goal was reached. One outcome might be 15 donors, none of whom are disqualified persons, who gave $8,000 each (a total of $120,000) and a $20,000 government grant, resulting in $140,000 of public support—and satisfaction of the test. Or, the $20,000 may have been in the form of qualifying exempt function revenue.

(c) Supporting Organizations

The third category of charitable organization that is *not* a private foundation is the *supporting organization*, an entity that is related, structurally or operationally, to one or more institutions, publicly supported organizations, or certain noncharitable organizations (namely, social welfare or labor organizations or business leagues). (For simplicity, these institutions and publicly supported organizations will be referred to collectively as *public charities*.) A supporting organization must be organized, and at all times operated, in an active relationship with one or more qualified supported entities.

The relationship must be one of three types; as outlined in the following table, the interaction is different for each type.

Supporting Organization Relationship	Effect
Operated, supervised, or controlled by one or more supported organizations	Substantial direction of policies, programs, and activities by the supported organization(s); similar to parent–subsidiary corporation relationship (Type I)
Supervised or controlled in connection with one or more supported organizations	Common supervision or control by the persons heading both the supporting organization and the supported organization(s); similar to "brother–sister" relationship (Type II)
Operated in connection with one or more supported organizations	Supporting organization responsive to and functionally integrated with supported organization(s) (Type III)
Operated in connection with one or more supported organization(s)	Nonfunctionally integrated (Type III)

A supporting organization may not be controlled directly or indirectly by one or more disqualified persons.

In 2006, Congress passed new law, much of it rather intricate, in connection with supporting organizations. Some of this law involved application of certain of the private foundation rules to supporting organizations. Other law brought in specific application of the intermediate sanctions rules (see Chapter 5). The most stringent provisions of new law are directed at Type III supporting organizations, particularly those that are not functionally integrated with a supported organization.

A grant-making private foundation (as contrasted with a private operating foundation) may not treat as a qualifying distribution (see discussion following) an amount paid to a Type III supporting organization that is not a functionally integrated Type III supporting organization or to any other type of supporting organization if a disqualified person with respect to the foundation directly or indirectly controls the supporting organization or a supported organization of the supporting organization. An amount that does not count as a qualifying distribution under this rule is regarded as a taxable expenditure (see discussion following).

An organization is not considered to be operated, supervised, or controlled by a qualified supported organization (the general criterion for a Type I organization) or operated in connection with a supported organization (the general criterion for Type IIIs) if the organization accepts a contribution from a person (other than a qualified supported organization) who, directly or indirectly, controls, either alone or with family members and/or certain controlled entities, the governing board of a supported organization. A supporting organization is considered not to be operated in connection with a supported organization unless the supporting organization is operated only in connection with one or more supported organizations that are organized in the United States.

The private foundation excess business holdings rules (see discussion following) are applicable to Type III supporting organizations, other than functionally integrated Type III supporting organizations. Until more specific guidance is issued, a *functionally integrated Type III supporting organization* is a Type III supporting organization that is not required by the tax regulations to make payments to supported organizations. Solely for purposes of certain due diligence requirements (see discussion following), an entity is a functionally integrated Type III supporting organization if it is engaged in activities for or on behalf of a supported organization that are activities to perform the functions of, or to carry out the purposes of, a supported organization and, but for the involvement of the supporting organization, would normally be engaged in by the supported organization (the *but for* test).

These excess business holdings rules also apply to a Type II supporting organization if the organization accepts a contribution from a person (other than a public charity that is not a supporting organization) who controls, either alone or with family members and/or certain controlled entities, the governing body of a supported organization of the supporting organization. Nonetheless, the IRS has the authority not to impose the excess business holdings rules on a supporting organization if the organization establishes that the holdings are consistent with the organization's tax-exempt status.

A Type III supporting organization must apprise each organization that it supports of information regarding the supporting organization in order to help ensure the responsiveness by the supporting organization to the needs or demands of the supported organization(s). A Type III supporting organization that is organized as a trust must establish to the satisfaction of the IRS that it has a sufficiently close and continuous relationship with the supported organization so that the trust is responsive to the needs or demands of the supported organization.

An excise tax is imposed on disqualified persons if they engage in one or more excess benefit transactions with public charities and/or social welfare organizations. (This rule is part of the intermediate *sanctions* regime, which is somewhat akin to the private foundation self-dealing rules (see Chapter 5).) A grant, loan, compensation, or other similar payment (such as an expense reimbursement) by any type of supporting organization to a substantial contributor or a person related to a substantial contributor, as well as a loan provided by a supporting organization to certain disqualified persons with respect to the supporting organization, is automatically an excess benefit transaction. Thus, the entire amount paid to the substantial contributor, disqualified persons, and related parties is an excess benefit.

A supporting organization must annually demonstrate that one or more of its disqualified persons (other than its managers and supported organization(s)) do not, directly or indirectly, control it. This is done by means of a certification on its annual information return.

Supporting organizations are among the most versatile planning options in the realm of public charities. They can be used, for example, as a home for an endowment fund, a form of fundraising foundation, an entity in which programs may be conducted, a vehicle for holding title to property, an entity to receive large contributions so as to not disturb the parent's publicly supported charity status (see foregoing discussion), or the basis by which a private foundation converts to a public charity. (The law changes made in 2006, however, have substantially eroded the versatility of the supporting organization.)

(d) Planning Considerations

A charitable organization that is trying to avoid classification as a private foundation may need to do some solid financial planning, especially if the goal is to be a publicly supported organization. For organizations that desire to be regarded as publicly supported (essentially the donative and service-provider charities), however, the matter can be somewhat more complicated than for institutions or organizations that intend to be classified as supporting organizations.

An organization that can expect to receive nearly all of its support in the form of many relatively small gifts will have no trouble in achieving either donative or service-provider status. An organization that is essentially dues based will be a service provider, although not a donative entity. An organization that anticipates receiving most of its financial support as exempt function revenue must look to the category of service provider (rather than donative) organization, for relief from the private foundation rules. The reverse is probably true for an organization that is relying largely on government grants (not contracts) for support; it will look to the donative organization category.

Many organizations, during their formative years, rely on just a few sources of financial support (for example, one or more private foundations or makers of large gifts). For these entities, compliance with either the donative organization rules or the service-provider organization rules can be difficult (if not impossible). Under the service-provider organization rules, because their sources of support are likely to be substantial contributors, none of their support is eligible for treatment as public support. The outcome will be more favorable where the donative organization rules are applied: At least the amount received from each of these sources up to the 2 percent threshold can count as public support.

Compliance with either the donative organization rules or the service-provider organization rules at any time is all that is required. An organization is not locked in to one set of these rules or the other.

There is another dimension of this matter of public charity status that is sometimes overlooked. It pertains to those charities that receive (or want to receive) private foundation grants. As discussed further on, a private foundation can be taxed if it makes a *taxable expenditure*. One way to have such an expenditure is for a private foundation to make a grant to a charity that is not a public charity. If a private foundation makes a grant to a charity, thinking it is a donative organization or a service-provider organization and it is neither, there can be some serious adverse tax consequences (not to mention the termination of that private foundation's support for that grantee).

ADDITIONAL OPTIONS

A charitable organization may not be able to satisfy the requirements of the rules pertaining to institutions, publicly supported (donative or service-provider) organizations, or supporting organizations. There still remain alternatives to private foundation status, or ways to alleviate some of the stringencies of the private foundation rules.

(a) Facts-and-Circumstances Test

Some organizations generically are not private foundations, yet they come within the broad reach of that term under the federal tax law. These organizations can include museums, libraries, and other entities that have substantial endowment funds. Some of these organizations may nonetheless be able to gain nonprivate-foundation status by means of the *facts-and-circumstances* test.

To meet this test, an organization must demonstrate that

- The total amount of public support it receives is at least 10 percent of its total support.
- It has a continuous and bona fide program for the solicitation of funds from the general public, governmental units, or other public charities.
- It has other attributes of a public organization.

Among its other attributes, an organization might cite the composition of its governing board (showing how it is representative of the general public), the extent to which its facilities or programs are publicly available, its membership dues rates, and how its activities are likely to appeal to persons having some broad common interest or purpose.

The higher the percentage of public support, the easier the burden of establishing the publicly supported nature of the organization through the other factors.

A main point to be emphasized here, however, is that under this test the organization's public support need only be as little as 10 percent of its total support, rather than having to be at least one-third of the total support under the general rules.

(b) Bifurcation

An organization that is—or might be classified by the IRS as—a private foundation may be able to avoid that consequence by bifurcating (splitting) into two entities. Each of the two organizations may be able to qualify as a nonfoundation, where they could not do so if combined.

An organization may have within it a function that, if separately evaluated, would qualify as an institution, a donative publicly supported organization, or a service-provider publicly supported organization. This function could be spun off into a separate organization and qualified as a public entity. The original organization, with its remaining activities, could then become qualified as a supporting organization with respect to its offspring. In this way, one private organization becomes two public organizations.

For example, suppose an individual established a private foundation for educational purposes. Over time, the foundation begins providing direct instruction to students. The board of trustees would like the foundation to remain in existence. The trustees convert the direct-instruction part of the foundation into an operating educational institution—a school with a faculty, student body, and curricula. That organization gains classification as a public charity—one of the institutions. The remaining part of the foundation, with the original board of trustees, is converted into a supporting organization for the school. The foundation board remains in place, but the organization itself is now public in nature.

(c) Private Operating Foundation

The major program activity of a private foundation is the making of grants. The more a charitable organization engages in programs itself (rather than funding those of others), the greater the likelihood that it will be classified as something other than a private foundation.

Because of this distinction between grant making and program administration, a hybrid entity has evolved, one that has some of the characteristics of a private foundation and some of those of a public charity. It is called the *private operating foundation*, and it devotes most of its earnings and much of its assets directly for the conduct of its charitable, educational, or similar purposes.

To be a private operating foundation, the organization must meet an *income* test. Annually, it must expend directly, for the active conduct of its exempt activities, an amount equal to substantially all of the lesser of its adjusted net income or its *minimum investment return. Substantially all* means at least 85 percent. The minimum investment return is equal to 5 percent of the foundation's assets that are not used for charitable purposes. For example, to pass this test, an organization with $100,000 of investment (noncharitable) assets (such as securities) would have to expend at least $4,250 (85 percent × 5 percent × $100,000) for that year, unless an amount equal to 85 percent of its adjusted net income is less than $4,250, in which case it would have to timely expend the actual income amount.

To qualify as an operating foundation, an organization must satisfy at least one of the three other tests:

1. The *assets* test—at least 65 percent of its assets must be devoted directly to the active conduct of its charitable activities.

2. The *endowment* test—the organization must normally expend its funds directly for the active conduct of its charitable activities in an amount equal to at least two-thirds of its minimum investment return ($2/3 × 5 = 3^1/3$).

3. The *support* test—at least 85 percent of its support (other than investment income) must be normally received from the general public or at least five tax-exempt organizations (that are not disqualified persons); no more than 25 percent of its support can be derived from any one exempt organization; and no more than one-half of its support can be normally received from gross investment income.

Because of these rules, a private operating foundation is not subject to the minimum payout requirement imposed on standard private foundations. Contributions to a private operating foundation are deductible to the full extent permitted for gifts to public charities (see Chapter 11). That is, the percentage limitations that restrict the deductibility of contributions to standard private foundations do not apply to gifts to private operating foundations.

(d) Exempt Operating Foundations

Not content with the complexity introduced with the hybrid form of private foundation known as the private operating foundation, Congress created a hybrid of a hybrid. This one is known as the *exempt operating foundation. Exempt* here does not mean exempt from federal income taxes (which foundations generally are anyway).

Exempt operating foundations are presumably otherwise private operating foundations, but they enjoy two characteristics that the others do not have:

1. Grants to them are exempt from the expenditure responsibility requirements otherwise imposed on grantor foundations.

2. They do not have to pay the tax imposed on foundations' net investment income.

To be an exempt operating foundation, an organization must (in addition to satisfying the requirements to be a private operating foundation) meet three tests:

1. It must have been publicly supported (under the donative charity or service-provider charity rules) for at least ten years or have qualified as an operating foundation as of January 1, 1983.

2. It must have a board of directors that, during the year involved, consisted of individuals at least 75 percent of whom are not so-called *disqualified individuals* and was broadly representative of the general public (presumably, using the facts and circumstances test).

3. It must not have an officer who is a disqualified individual at any time during the year involved.

To be an exempt operating foundation, an organization must have a ruling from the IRS to that effect. One of the anomalies of the law in this area, however, is that an organization that is able to qualify as an exempt operating foundation often is also able to qualify under the facts-and-circumstances test—and thereby avoid all of the private foundation rules!

FACING THE INEVITABLE

If it fails to comply with any of the rules discussed so far in this chapter, a charitable organization will be classified as a *private foundation*. It becomes subject to a battery of stringent requirements that are not applicable to any other type of tax-exempt organization, charitable or otherwise.

Facts and/or the law can change. An organization may, later in its existence, shift from a private foundation to a private operating foundation (or perhaps to an exempt operating foundation). Or, a private foundation can terminate its private foundation status and become a public charity. This can be done, for example, by embarking on a fundraising program (in order to become a publicly supported charity) or restructuring into a supporting organization.

The point is that the private or public status of a charitable organization can be changed at any time. The same is true for nonprivate foundations, which can change the nature of their public charity status at any time, if the facts warrant. For example, a donative charity can switch to being a service-provider charity (or vice versa) very easily, and a supporting organization can convert itself into a publicly supported charity (or vice versa).

ONEROUS RULES

- For some pages now, we have been talking about a battery of stringent and onerous rules imposed by law on private foundations. What makes these rules worth avoiding? These rules concern self-dealing.

- Force a minimum payout (grant-making) amount.

- Limit the extent of holdings of businesses.

- Pertain to the nature of investments.

- Concern the nature and scope of programs.

- Impose a tax on net investment income.

- Make it quite unlikely that one private foundation will make a grant to another private foundation.

- Force more detailed annual reporting.

- Make charitable giving to private foundations less attractive.

The term *self-dealing* means a transaction that occurs between, directly or indirectly, a private foundation and a disqualified person. Generally, self-dealing transactions include sale or exchange of property; lease of property; lending of money or other extension of credit; furnishing of goods, services, or facilities; payment of unreasonable compensation; and transfer to, or use by or for the benefit of, disqualified persons of the income or assets of a private foundation. There are, however, many exceptions to and subtleties within the self-dealing rules.

A private foundation must annually expend for charitable purposes an amount equal to 5 percent of the value of its investment assets. This *distributable amount* is determined by calculating the foundation's *minimum investment return*. If a private foundation does not achieve at least a 5 percent return on its principal, it must use part of its assets to satisfy this minimum payout requirement. The amounts expended must constitute *qualifying distributions*, which essentially are grants for charitable purposes (including *set-asides*) and reasonable administrative expenditures. The onerous rules thus require valuation of the investment assets (which do not include assets used for charitable purposes).

Generally, a private foundation and its disqualified persons may not have combined holdings of more than 20 percent of a business enterprise. The rule applies to voting stock in a corporation, units in a partnership, and other forms of holdings in a business venture. Holdings are termed *permitted holdings* or, if not allowable, *excess business holdings*. If effective control of a business rests with unrelated parties, however, a private foundation and its disqualified persons may hold as much as 35 percent of a business enterprise. For these purposes, the term *business enterprise* does not include a *functionally related business* or a business that derives at least 95 percent of its income from passive sources.

A private foundation may not invest any amount in a manner that will jeopardize the fulfillment of any of its charitable purposes. (The law does not define jeopardizing investments, but in context it means highly speculative investments.) The rule does not apply to *program-related investments*.

A private foundation is expected to avoid making *taxable expenditures*. Generally, a taxable expenditure is an amount paid or incurred to carry on propaganda, influence legislation, promote a particular outcome of a public election, make certain grants to individuals, make certain grants to organizations where the foundation has failed to properly exercise *expenditure responsibility*, or for any other noncharitable purpose. These rules entail a range of exceptions, involving such matters as voter-registration drives; eligible scholarship and fellowship grants;

and circulation of the results of nonpartisan analysis, study, or research. (Because of these rules, most private foundations are forced to confine their grant making to public charities and cannot extend them to other types of organizations or to individuals.)

A private foundation must pay an excise tax equal to 2 percent of its net investment income for each year. *Net investment income* means interest, dividends, rents, royalties, and the like, less allowable deductions. In this tax law context (unlike most others, such as the charitable giving rules, see Chapter 8), the concept of *income* includes capital gain. As noted previously, certain operating foundations are excused from the payment of this tax.

TAXES

Part III of the book summarizes many of the instances in which ostensibly tax-exempt organizations are in fact taxable. Tax-exempt organizations that are classified as private foundations, along with their managers, are subject to many of these taxes—all considered excise (not income) taxes.

Underlying the private foundation rules are a series of sanctions, imposed in the form of these excise taxes. There are *initial* (first-tier) taxes and *additional* (second-tier) taxes. The additional taxes are payable when an offense has occurred, one or more initial taxes have been imposed, and the offense is not timely corrected.

In a case of self-dealing, the initial tax is 10 percent of the amount involved and is payable by the disqualified person who participated in the wrongful act. If that initial tax is imposed on a self-dealer, the foundation manager who participated in the act is subject to an initial tax (not to exceed $20,000) of 5 percent of the amount involved, where he or she knew the act was one of self-dealing and where the participation was willful and not due to reasonable cause. The additional tax on the self-dealer is 200 percent of the amount involved. The additional tax (not to exceed $20,000) on the participating foundation manager, who refused to agree to part or all of the correction, is 50 percent of the amount involved. Two or more individuals may be jointly and severally liable for these taxes.

If a private foundation (that is not an operating foundation) fails to satisfy the payout requirements, it must pay a tax equal to 30 percent of the undistributed income. The additional tax is 100 percent of the undistributed amount.

A private foundation must annually pay a tax equal to 10 percent of its excess business holdings. The additional tax is 200 percent of these holdings.

If a private foundation makes a jeopardizing investment, it must pay a tax equal to 10 percent of the investment. If that initial tax is imposed, a foundation manager who participated in the investment is subject to a tax (not to exceed $10,000) equal to 10 percent of the investment, where he or she knew that the investment was a jeopardizing one and where the participation was willful and not due to reasonable cause. The additional tax on the foundation is 25 percent of the amount of the investment. The additional tax (not to exceed $20,000) on the manager, who refused to agree to part or all of the removal from jeopardy, is 5 percent of the amount of the investment. Two or more individuals may be jointly and severally liable for these taxes.

The initial tax on a private foundation that makes a taxable expenditure is 20 percent of the amount involved. A 5 percent initial tax (not to exceed $10,000 per taxable expenditure) is also imposed on every foundation manager who agreed to the taxable expenditure, where he or she knew it was a taxable expenditure, where the making of the taxable expenditure was willful, and where it was not due to reasonable cause. The additional tax on the private foundation is 100 percent of the expenditure. The additional tax (not to exceed $20,000 per expenditure) on a manager of a private foundation, where he or she refused to agree to part or all of the correction, is 50 percent of the amount of the taxable expenditure. Again, two or more individuals may be jointly and severally liable for these taxes.

CONCLUSION

There is, as noted, no tax law advantage to classification as a private foundation. Private foundation status should be avoided whenever possible. This classification brings a battery of stringent rules to restrict the operations of a charitable organization and decrease the tax advantages of charitable gifts to it. A private foundation categorization means that the organization, and in many instances its directors or officers, are subject to very onerous taxes. These tax rules are technical and it is all too easy for an innocent misstep to lead to heavy taxation. Probably the most useful thing a lawyer or other tax professional can do for a charitable organization is to lead it (if at all possible) to public charity status.

Checklist

❏ Is the (charitable) organization a private foundation?
   Yes _____ No _____
❏ If yes:

   Is it a private operating foundation? Yes _____ No _____

   Is it an exempt operating foundation? Yes _____ No _____

   Has the foundation or its managers been subjected to any of the excise taxes?
      Yes _____ No _____
❏ If no:

   Is the organization publicly supported? Yes _____ No _____

   Basis for classification:
   ❏ Donative
   ❏ Service provider
   ❏ Facts-and-circumstances test
   ❏ Other

   Is the organization an institution? Yes _____ No _____

   Is the organization a supporting organization? Yes _____ No _____

FOCUS: Campaign to Clean Up America

The Campaign to Clean Up America (CCUA) is organized and will be operated to function as a charitable organization that is not a private foundation. Because of the nature of its programs, it does not qualify as one of the institutional charities. Lacking any formal relationship to another nonprofit organization, it does not qualify as a supporting organization.

Because of its funding—principally, grants and contributions—the CCUA is to be qualified as a donative publicly supported charity. This status will be under the general rules—that is, the facts and circumstances test will be unnecessary.

CHAPTER EIGHT

Governance: Board Duties and Liabilities

The law and practices—some of them just emerging—concerning governance principles pertaining to nonprofit organizations and the matter of potential board-member liability have quickly become some of the principal issues arising in the nonprofit law context. Scandals embroiling for-profit corporations and accounting firms—involving fraud, tax avoidance, conflicts of interests, and questionable accounting practices—led to enactment of the Sarbanes-Oxley Act in 2002. The principles embodied in that legislation are quickly being imported into the nonprofit sector, largely by means of the voluntary adoption by charitable organizations of a variety of policies and procedures.

BASICS OF GOVERNANCE PRINCIPLES

Traditionally, the law as to governance of a nonprofit organization—corporation or otherwise—has been largely confined to state rules. These principles, however, are now quickly becoming part of the federal tax law as well as organizations' practices. Although new federal law on the subject, in the form of legislation and regulations is not imminent, IRS forms and instructions are playing a major role in reshaping the charitable governance scene.

The essence of the emerging governance principles is that a charitable organization (and perhaps other types of tax-exempt entities) must be *managed* by its board of directors or board of trustees. It is becoming unacceptable for a board to meet infrequently and be merely the recipient of reports from an organization's officers and staff. The developing law is requiring the board of the nonprofit organization to become directly involved, be knowledgeable about the organization's programs and finances, understand the climate in which the entity operates, avoid conflicts of interest, place the objectives of the organization above personal desires—and *govern*.

These emerging principles are also forcing structural changes in the operations of nonprofit organizations. No longer are the operative documents confined to articles of organization and bylaws. The law is beginning to demand organizational and management policies and procedures, conflicts-of-interest policies, codes of ethics for senior officers, investment policies, and written program objectives and performance measures. Independent audit committees are becoming commonplace. Lawyers, accountants, and other consultants must be hired directly by the board, not the executive staff. Compensation arrangements for top positions must be approved at the board level. Independent auditors may have to be rotated periodically, such as every five years. Corporate executives may have to certify financial statements and perhaps annual information returns.

Even the appropriate size of the governing body is being debated. According to the law in most states, a nonprofit corporation must have at least three directors (or trustees). A few states require only one director. The appropriate number of directors for a charitable organization is a matter of some controversy. Although "one size certainly does not fit all," there is an emerging consensus among students of nonprofit governance that a charity's board should number in the range of 5–15.

EMERGING CONCEPTS

The basics as to governance principles are beginning to yield specific requirements. Board members do not, individually, have unilateral authority to make decisions about the organization's governance. Rather, the board has collective responsibilities. In 2007, Congress passed legislation that amended the congressional charter of the American National Red Cross to modernize its structure and otherwise strengthen its governance. Changes included a substantial reduction in the size of the organization's board, delegation to management of the day-to-day operations of the organization, elimination of distinctions as to how board members are elected, and transition of some board members into an advisory council.

The essence of the legislation is unique to the National Red Cross entity. Certainly some items in the following list do not apply to private foundations. Yet, it outlines the collective responsibilities for nonprofit boards in general:

- Review and approve the organization's mission statement
- Approve and oversee the organization's strategic plan and maintain strategic oversight of operational matters
- Select, evaluate, and determine the level of compensation of the organization's chief executive officer
- Evaluate the performance and establish the compensation of the senior leadership team and provide for management succession
- Oversee the financial reporting and audit process, internal controls, and legal compliance
- Ensure that the chapters of the organization are geographically and regionally diverse
- Hold management accountable for performance
- Provide oversight of the financial stability of the organization
- Ensure the inclusiveness and diversity of the organization
- Provide oversight of the protection of the brand of the organization [this is a responsibility rarely found in a list of this nature]
- Assist with fundraising on behalf of the organization.

NONPROFIT GOVERNANCE PRINCIPLES

Governance issues are dominating the nonprofit law scene. Much of this focus is on the duties and responsibilities of members of nonprofit boards and on the policies and practices they are expected to develop, implement, and maintain. Some of what is emerging is not directly applicable to private foundations, although much of it is. Three important recent developments illustrate these points: the principles of nonprofit governance promulgated by the Panel on the Nonprofit Sector established under the auspices of Independent Sector, a draft of a code of nonprofit ethics issued by the IRS, and the redesign by the IRS of the annual information return filed by most tax-exempt organizations (Form 990).

The Panel on the Nonprofit Sector, convened by Independent Sector, issued, on October 18, 2007, its principles for good governance for public and private charitable organizations. The principles are predicated on the need for a

> . . . careful balance between the two essential forms of regulation—that is, between prudent legal mandates to ensure that organizations do not abuse the privilege of their exempt status, and, for all other aspects of sound operations, well-informed self-governance and mutual awareness among nonprofit organizations.

These principles, organized under four categories, are as follows (slightly edited for brevity):

(a) Legal Compliance and Public Disclosure

- An organization must comply with applicable federal, state, and local law. If the organization conducts programs outside the United States, it must abide by applicable international laws and conventions that are legally binding on the United States.

- An organization should have a formally adopted, written code of ethics with which all of its directors, staff, and volunteers are familiar and to which they adhere.

- An organization should implement policies and procedures to ensure that all conflicts of interest, or appearance of them, within the organization and its board are appropriately managed through disclosure, recusal, or other means.

- An organization should implement policies and procedures that enable individuals to come forward with information on illegal practices or violations of organizational policies. This whistleblower policy should specify that the organization will not retaliate against, and will protect the confidentiality of, individuals who make good-faith reports.

- An organization should implement policies and procedures to preserve the organization's important documents and business records.

- An organization's board should ensure that the organization has adequate plans to protect its assets—its property, financial and human resources, programmatic content and material, and its integrity and reputation—against damage or loss. The board should regularly review the organization's need for general liability and directors' and officers' liability insurance, as well as take other actions to mitigate risk.

- An organization should make information about its operations, including its governance, finances, programs, and other activities, widely available to the public. Charitable organizations should also consider making information available on the methods they use to evaluate the outcomes of their work and sharing the results of the evaluations.

(b) Effective Governance

- An organization must have a governing body that is responsible for approving the organization's mission and strategic direction, annual budget, key financial transactions, compensation practices, and fiscal and governance policies.

- The board of an organization should meet regularly to conduct its business and fulfill its duties.

- The board of an organization should establish its size and structure and periodically review these. The board should have enough members to allow for full deliberation and diversity of thinking on organizational matters. Except for very small organizations, this generally means there should be at least five members.

- The board of an organization should include members with the diverse background (including ethnic, racial, and gender perspectives), experience, and organizational and financial skills necessary to advance the organization's mission.

- A substantial majority of the board (usually at least two-thirds) of a public charity should be independent. Independent members should not be compensated by the organization, have their compensation determined by individuals who are compensated by the organization, receive material financial benefits from the organization except as a member of a charitable class served by the organization, or be related to or reside with any person described above.

- The board should hire, oversee, and annually evaluate the performance of the chief executive of the organization and should conduct such an evaluation prior to any change in that individual's compensation, unless a multiyear contract is in force or the change consists solely of routine adjustments for inflation or cost of living.

- The board of an organization that has paid staff should ensure that separate individuals hold the positions of chief staff officer, board chair, and board treasurer. Organizations without paid staff should ensure that the position of board chair and treasurer are separately held.

- The board should establish an effective, systematic process for educating and communicating with board members to ensure that they are aware of their legal and ethical responsibilities, are knowledgeable about the programs and other activities of the organization, and can effectively carry out their oversight functions.

- Board members should evaluate their performance as a group and as individuals no less than every three years, and should have clear procedures for removing board members who are unable to fulfill their responsibilities.

- The board should establish clear policies and procedures setting the length of terms and the number of consecutive terms a board member may serve.

- The board should review the organization's governing instruments at least every five years.

- The board should regularly review the organization's mission and goals and evaluate at least every five years the organization's goals, programs, and other activities to be sure they advance its mission and make prudent use of its resources.

- Board members are generally expected to serve without compensation, other than reimbursement for expenses incurred to fulfill their board duties. An organization that provides compensation to its board members should use appropriate comparability data to determine the amount to be paid, document the decision, and provide full disclosure to anyone, on request, of the amount of and rationale for the compensation.

(c) Strong Financial Oversight

- An organization must keep complete, current, and accurate financial records. Its board should review timely reports of the organization's financial activities and have a qualified, independent financial expert audit or review these statements annually in a manner appropriate to the organization's size and scale of operations.

- The board of an organization must institute policies and procedures to ensure that the organization (and, if applicable, its subsidiaries) manages and invests its funds responsibly, in accordance with requirements of law. The full board should approve the organization's annual budget and monitor performance against the budget.

- An organization should not provide loans (or the equivalent, such as loan guarantees, purchasing or transferring ownership of a residence or office, or relieving a debt or lease obligations) to its directors or officers.

- An organization should spend a significant portion of its annual budget on programs that pursue its mission. The budget should provide sufficient resources for effective administration of the organization and, if it solicits contributions, for appropriate fundraising activities.

- An organization should establish clear, written policies for paying or reimbursing expenses incurred by anyone conducting business or traveling on behalf of the organization, including the types of expenses that can be paid or reimbursed and the documentation required. These policies should require that travel on behalf of the organization is to be undertaken in a cost-effective manner.

- An organization should neither pay for nor reimburse travel expenditures for spouses, dependents, or others who are accompanying someone conducting business for the organization unless they are also conducting the business.

(d)   Responsible Fundraising

- Solicitation materials and other communications addressed to prospective donors and the public must clearly identify the organization and must be accurate and truthful.

- Contributions must be used for purposes consistent with the donor's intent, whether as described in the solicitation materials or as directed by the donor.

- An organization must provide donors with acknowledgments of charitable contributions, in accordance with federal tax law requirements, including information to facilitate the donor's compliance with tax law requirements.

- An organization should adopt clear policies to determine whether acceptance of a gift would compromise its ethics, financial circumstances, program focus, or other interests.

- An organization should provide appropriate training and supervision of the people soliciting funds on its behalf to ensure that they understand their responsibilities and applicable law and do not employ techniques that are coercive, intimidating, or intended to harass potential donors.

- An organization should not compensate internal or external fundraisers on the basis of a commission or percentage of the amount raised.

- An organization should respect the privacy of individual donors and, except where disclosure is required by law, should not sell or otherwise make available the names and contact information of its donors without providing them an opportunity to at least annually opt out of use of their names.

IRS DRAFT OF GOOD GOVERNANCE PRINCIPLES

The IRS, in 2007, unveiled a draft of the agency's "Good Governance Practices" for charitable organizations. About one year later, the agency jettisoned this draft (see discussion following). Nonetheless, it is significant that the IRS issued this document; some of the practices are applicable to private foundations.

The IRS is of the view that governing boards of charitable organizations should be composed of persons who are informed and active in overseeing the organizations' operations and finances. If a governing board tolerates a climate of secrecy or neglect, charitable assets are more likely to be used to advance an impermissible private interest. Successful governing boards include not only individuals who are knowledgeable and passionate about the organization's programs but also those with expertise in critical areas involving accounting, finance, compensation, and ethics.

Organizations with very small or very large governing boards may be problematic: Small boards generally do not represent a public interest; large boards may be less attentive to oversight duties. If an organization's governing board is very large, it may want to establish an executive committee with delegated responsibilities or establish advisory committees.

The IRS suggested that charitable organizations review and consider the following to help ensure that directors understand their roles and responsibilities and actively promote good governance practices. While adopting a particular practice is not a requirement for tax exemption, the agency believes that an organization that adopts some or all of these practices is more likely to be successful in pursuing its exempt purposes and earning public support.

The proposed principles are discussed in the following subsections.

(a) Mission Statement

A clearly articulated mission statement that is adopted by an organization's board of directors will explain and popularize the charity's purpose and serve as a guide to the organization's work. A well-written mission statement shows why the charity exists, what it hopes to accomplish, and what activities it will undertake, where and for whom.

(b) Code of Ethics

The public expects a charity to abide by ethical standards that promote the public good. The board of directors bears the ultimate responsibility for setting ethical standards and ensuring that they permeate the organization and inform its practices. To that end, the board should consider adopting and regularly evaluating a code of ethics that describes behavior it wants to encourage and behavior it wants to discourage. The code of ethics should be a principal means of communicating to all personnel a strong culture of legal compliance and ethical integrity.

(c) Whistleblower Policy

The board of directors should adopt an effective policy for handling employee complaints and establish procedures for employees to report in confidence suspected financial impropriety or misuse of the charity's resources.

(d) Due Diligence

The directors of a charity must exercise due diligence consistent with a duty of care that requires a director to act in good faith, with the care an ordinarily prudent person in a like position would exercise under similar circumstances and in a manner the director reasonably believes to be in the charity's best interests. Directors should see to it that policies and procedures are in place to help them meet their duty of care, such as by (1) being familiar with the charity's activities and knowing whether the activities promote the charity's mission and achieve its goals, (2) being fully informed about the charity's financial status, and (3) having full and accurate information to make informed decisions.

(e) Duty of Loyalty

The directors of a charity owe it a duty of loyalty. This duty requires a director to act in the interest of the charity rather than in the personal interest of the director or some other person or organization. In particular, the duty of loyalty requires a director to avoid conflicts of interest that are detrimental to the charity. To that end, the board of directors should adopt and regularly evaluate an effective conflict-of-interest policy that (1) requires directors and staff to act solely in the interests of the charity without regard for personal interests; (2) includes written procedures for determining whether a relationship, financial interest, or business affiliation results in a conflict of interest; and (3) prescribes a certain course of action in the event a conflict of interest is identified. Directors and staff should be required to disclose annually in writing any known financial interest that the individual, or a member of the individual's family, has in any business entity that transacts business with the charity.

(f) Transparency

By making full and accurate information about its mission, activities, and finances publicly available, a charity demonstrates transparency. The board of directors should adopt and monitor procedures to ensure that the charity's Form 990, annual reports, and financial statements are complete and accurate, are posted on the organization's public website, and are made available to the public on request.

(g) Fundraising Policy

Charitable fundraising is an important source of financial support for many charities. Success at fundraising requires care and honesty. The board of directors should adopt and monitor policies to ensure that fundraising solicitations meet federal and state law requirements and that solicitation materials are accurate, truthful, and candid. Charities should keep their fundraising costs reasonable. In selecting paid fundraisers, a charity should use those that are registered with the state and that can provide good references. Performance of professional fundraisers should be continuously monitored.

(h) Financial Audits

Directors must be good stewards of a charity's financial resources. A charity should operate in accordance with an annual budget approved by the board of directors. The board should ensure that financial resources are used to further charitable purposes by regularly receiving and reading up-to-date financial statements, including Form 990, auditor's letters, and finance and audit committee reports. If the charity has substantial assets or annual revenue, the board of directors should ensure that an independent auditor conducts an annual audit. The board can establish an independent audit committee to select and oversee the independent auditor. The auditing firm should be changed periodically (e.g., every five years) to ensure a fresh look at the financial statements. For a charity with lesser assets or annual revenue, the board should ensure that an independent certified public accountant conducts an annual audit. Substitute practices for very small organizations would include using volunteers who would review financial information and practices. Trading volunteers between similarly situated organizations who would perform these tasks would also help maintain financial integrity without being too costly.

(i) Compensation Practices

A successful charity pays no more than reasonable compensation for services rendered. Charities should generally not compensate persons for service on the board of directors, except to reimburse direct expenses of such service. Director compensation should be allowed only when determined to be appropriate by a committee composed of persons who are not compensated by the charity and have no financial interest in the determination. Charities may pay reasonable compensation for services provided by officers and staff.

(j) Document Retention Policy

An effective charity will adopt a written policy establishing standards for document integrity, retention, and destruction. The document retention policy should include guidelines for handling electronic files. The policy should cover backup procedures, archiving of documents, and regular check-ups of the reliability of the system.

REDESIGNED ANNUAL INFORMATION RETURN

The IRS, in 2007, substantially revised the general annual information return (Form 990) that is filed by most tax-exempt organizations (see Chapter 9). This newly redesigned return includes a series of questions that directly reflect the agency's views as to governance principles applicable to nonprofit organizations. Indeed, this return is intended to influence and modify nonprofit organizations' behavior by in essence forcing their governing boards to adopt certain policies and procedures (so they can check "yes" rather than "no" boxes). (Almost none of these policies and procedures are required by the federal tax law.)

A nonprofit organization filing this return is required to report the total number of voting members of its governing body and the number of these members who are independent. The organization must indicate whether a trustee, director, officer, or key employee has a family relationship or a business relationship with any other trustee, director, officer, or key employee. It must report whether it has delegated control over management duties customarily performed by or under the direct supervision of trustees, directors, officers, or key employees to a management company or other person. The organization must indicate whether a copy of the annual information return was provided to each member of its governing body before it was filed. The organization is required to indicate whether it has contemporaneously documented the meetings held or written actions undertaken during the year by its governing body and/or each committee with authority to act on behalf of the governing body. The organization must describe whether and, if so, how it makes its governing documents, conflict-of-interest policy, and financial statements available to the public. This annual information return references many types of written policies or procedures that nonprofit, tax-exempt organizations may be expected to adopt (see Chapter 22).

SUBSEQUENT IRS GUIDANCE

The IRS has abandoned its draft of good governance practices for charitable organizations (see foregoing discussion), stating that current IRS positions on nonprofit governance "are best reflected in the reporting required by the revised Form 990" and the components in this document as part of the agency's Life Cycle educational tool. The IRS stated, "Good governance is important to increase the likelihood that organizations will comply with the tax law, protect their charitable assets and, thereby, best serve their charitable beneficiaries."

The contents of this document follow, albeit condensed in places, with the stated text essentially verbatim.

(a) Introduction

The IRS believes that a well-governed charity is more likely to obey the tax laws, safeguard charitable assets, and serve charitable interests than one with poor or lax governance. A charity that has clearly articulated purposes that describe its mission, a knowledgeable and committed governing body and management team, and sound management practices is more likely to operate effectively and consistent with tax law requirements. Although the tax law generally does not mandate particular management structures, operational policies, or administrative practices, it is important that each charity be thoughtful about the management practices that are most appropriate for that charity in assuring sound operations and compliance with the tax law.

(b) Mission

The IRS encourages every charity to establish and regularly review its mission. A clearly articulated mission, adopted by the board of directors, serves to explain and popularize the charity's purpose and guide its work. It also addresses why the charity exists, what it hopes to accomplish, and what activities it will undertake, where, and for whom.

(c) Organizational Documents

Regardless of whether a charity is a corporation, trust, unincorporated association, or other type of organization, it must have organizational documents that provide the framework for its governance and management. State law often prescribes the type of organizational document and its content. State law may require corporations to adopt bylaws. Organizational documents must be filed with applications for recognition of exemption.

(d) Governing Body

The IRS encourages an active and engaged board, believing that it is important to the success of a charity and to its compliance with applicable tax law requirements. Governing boards should be composed of persons who are informed and active in overseeing a charity's operations and finances. The IRS is concerned that, if a governing board tolerates a climate of secrecy or neglect, charitable assets are more likely to be diverted to benefit the private interests of insiders at the expense of public and charitable interests. Successful governing boards include individuals who not only are knowledgeable and engaged but selected with the organization's needs in mind (e.g., accounting, finance, compensation, and ethics).

Attention should also be paid to the size of the board, ensuring that it is the appropriate size to effectively make sure that the organization obeys tax laws, safeguards its charitable assets, and furthers its charitable purposes. Small boards run the risk of not representing a sufficiently broad public interest and of lacking the required skills and other resources required to effectively govern the organization. On the other hand, very large boards may have a more difficult time getting down to business and making decisions.

A governing board should include independent members and not be dominated by employees or others who are not independent individuals because of family or business relationships. The IRS reviews the board composition of charities to determine whether the board represents a broad public interest; to identify the potential for insider transactions that could result in misuse of charitable assets; to determine whether an organization has independent members, stockholders, or other persons with the authority to elect members of the board or approve or reject board decisions; and to ascertain whether the organization has delegated control or key management authority to a management company or other persons.

If an organization has local chapters, branches, or affiliates, the IRS encourages it to have procedures and policies in place to ensure that the activities and operations of these subordinates are consistent with those of the parent organization.

(e) Governance and Management Policies

Although the federal tax law does not require charities to have governance and management policies, the IRS will nonetheless review an organization's application for recognition of exemption and annual information returns to determine whether it has implemented policies relating to executive compensation, conflicts of interest, investments, fundraising, documenting governance decisions, document retention and destruction, and whistleblower claims.

Persons who are knowledgeable in compensation matters and who have no financial interest in the determination should determine a charity's executive compensation. The federal tax law does not, however, require charities to follow a particular process in ascertaining the amount of this type of compensation. Organizations that file Form 990 will find that Part VI, Section B, line 15, asks whether the process used to determine the compensation of an organization's top management official and other officers and key employees included a review and approval by independent persons, comparability data, and contemporaneous substantiation of the deliberation and decision. In addition, the Form 990 solicits compensation information for certain trustees, directors, officers, key employees, and highest compensated employees.

The IRS encourages reliance on the *rebuttable presumption*, which is part of the intermediate sanctions rules. Under this test, payments of compensation are presumed to be reasonable if the compensation arrangement is approved in advance by an authorized body composed entirely of individuals who do not have a conflict of interest with respect to the arrangement, the authorized body obtained and relied on appropriate data as to comparability prior to making its determination, and the authorized body adequately documented the basis for its determination concurrently with making the determination.

The duty of loyalty, which requires a director to act in the interest of the charity, requires a director to avoid conflicts of interest that are detrimental to the charity. The IRS encourages a charity's board of directors to adopt and regularly evaluate a written conflict-of-interest policy that requires directors and staff to act solely in the interests of the charity without regard for personal interests; includes written procedures for determining whether a relationship, financial interest, or business affiliation results in a conflict of interest; and prescribes a course of action in the event a conflict of interest is identified.

Increasingly, charities are investing in joint ventures, for-profit entities, and complicated and sophisticated financial products or investments that require financial and investment expertise and, in some instances, the advice of outside investment advisors. The IRS encourages charities that make these types of investments to adopt written policies and procedures requiring the charity to evaluate its participation in these investments, and to take steps to safeguard the organization's assets and tax-exempt status if they could be affected by the investment arrangement. The Form 990 inquires as to whether an organization has adopted this type of policy. Also, the form asks for detailed information about certain investments.

The IRS encourages charities to adopt and monitor policies to ensure that fundraising solicitations meet federal and state law requirements and that solicitation materials are accurate, truthful, and candid. Charities are encouraged to keep their fundraising costs reasonable and to provide information about fundraising costs and practices to donors and the public. The Form 990 solicits information about fundraising activities, revenues, and expenses.

The IRS encourages the governing bodies and subcommittees to take steps to ensure that minutes of their meetings and actions taken by written action or outside of meetings are contemporaneously documented. The Form 990 asks whether an organization contemporaneously documents meetings or written actions undertaken during the year by its governing body and committees with authority to act on behalf of the governing body.

The IRS encourages charities to adopt a written policy establishing standards for document integrity, retention, and destruction. This type of policy should include guidelines for handling electronic files; it should also cover backup procedures, archiving of documents, and regular check-ups of the reliability of the system. The Form 990 asks whether an organization has a written document retention and destruction policy.

The IRS also encourages a charity's board to consider adopting and regularly evaluating a code of ethics that describes behavior it wants to encourage and behavior it wants to discourage. A code of ethics will serve to communicate and further a strong culture of legal compliance and ethical integrity to all persons associated with the organization.

The IRS further encourages the board to adopt an effective policy—a whistleblower policy—for handling employee complaints and to establish procedures for employees to report in confidence any suspected financial impropriety or misuse of the charity's resources. The Form 990 asks whether the organization became aware during the year of a material diversion of its assets and whether an organization has a written whistleblower policy.

(f) Financial Statements and Form 990 Reporting

The IRS is of the view that a charity with substantial assets or revenue should consider obtaining an audit of its finances by an independent auditor. The board may establish an independent audit committee to select and oversee an auditor. The Form 990 asks whether the organization's financial statements were compiled or reviewed by an independent accountant, audited by an independent accountant, and subject to oversight by a committee within the organization. Also, the Form 990 asks whether, as the result of a federal award, the organization was required to undergo an audit.

Practices differ widely as to who sees the Form 990; when they see it (before or after its filing); and the extent of the reviewers' input, review, or approval. Some organizations provide copies of the return to the members of the board and other governance or management officials. The Form 990 asks whether the organization provides a copy of the return to its governing body and requires the organization to explain any process of review by its directors or management.

(g) Transparency and Accountability

By making full and accurate information about its mission, activities, finances, and governance publicly available, a charity encourages transparency and accountability to its constituents. The IRS encourages every charity to adopt and monitor procedures to ensure that its Form 1023, Form 990, Form 990-T, annual reports, and financial statements are complete and accurate, are posted on its public website, and are made available to the public on request.

The Form 990 asks whether and how an organization makes its returns, governing instruments, conflict-of-interest policy, and financial statements available to the public

BOARD MEMBER RESPONSIBILITIES

One of the principles that has been in the law for centuries is that trustees of charitable trusts are deemed to have the same obligation (duty of care) toward the assets of the trusts as they do toward their personal resources. Their responsibility is to act *prudently* in their handling of the nonprofit organization's income and assets. The trustees are *fiduciaries*; the law (for now, largely state law—see foregoing discussion) imposes on them standards of conduct and management that, together, comprise principles of *fiduciary responsibility*. Most state law, whether statute or court opinions, imposes the standards of fiduciary responsibility on directors of nonprofit organizations, whether or not the organizations are trusts and whether or not they are charitable.

(a) Contemporary Standards

The contemporaneous general standard is that a member of the board of a nonprofit organization is required to perform his or her duties in good faith, with the care an ordinarily prudent person in a like position would exercise under similar circumstances and in a manner the director reasonably believes to be in the best interests of the mission, goals, and purposes of the organization.

Thus, one of the main responsibilities of nonprofit board members is to maintain financial accountability and effective oversight of the organization they serve. Fiduciary duty requires board members to remain objective, unselfish, responsible, honest, trustworthy, and efficient in relation to the organization. Board members are stewards of the entity and are expected to act for the good of the organization rather than for their personal aggrandizement. They need to exercise reasonable care in all decision making, without placing the nonprofit organization at unnecessary risk.

The duties of board members of nonprofit organizations can be encapsulated in the *three Ds*: duty of care, duty of loyalty, and duty of obedience. These are the legal standards against which all actions taken by directors are tested. They are collective duties adhering to the entire board and require the active participation of all board members. Accountability can be demonstrated by a showing of the effective discharge of these duties.

(b) Duty of Care

The duty of care requires that directors of a nonprofit organization be reasonably informed about the organization's activities, participate in the making of decisions, and do so in good faith and with the care of an ordinarily prudent person in similar circumstances. This duty, therefore, requires the individual board members to pay attention to the entity's activities and operations.

This duty is carried out by the following acts:

- Attendance at meetings of the board and committees to which assigned
- Preparation for board meetings, such as by reviewing the agenda and reports
- Obtaining information, before voting, to make appropriate decisions
- Use of independent judgment
- Periodic examination of the credentials and performance of those who serve the organization
- Frequent review of the organization's finances and financial policies
- Oversight of compliance with important filing requirements, such as annual information returns (see Chapter 10).

(c) Duty of Loyalty

The duty of loyalty requires board members to exercise their power in the interest of the organization and not in their own interest or the interest of another entity, particularly one in which they have a formal relationship. When acting on behalf of the organization, board members must place the interests of the entity before their personal and professional interests.

This duty is carried out by the following acts:

- Disclosure of any conflicts of interest.
- Adherence to the organization's conflict-of-interest policy.
- Avoidance of the use of corporate opportunities for the individual's personal gain or benefit.
- Nondisclosure of confidential information about the organization.

Although conflicts of interest are not inherently illegal—in fact, they can be common because board members are often affiliated with different entities in their communities—how the board reviews and evaluates them is important. Conflict-of-interest policies can help protect the organization and board members by establishing a process for disclosure and voting when situations arise in which board members may actually or potentially derive personal benefit as a consequence of the organization's activities.

(d) Duty of Obedience

The duty of obedience requires that directors of a nonprofit organization comply with applicable federal, state, and local laws, adhere to the entity's articles of organization and bylaws, and remain guardians of the mission.

The duty of obedience is carried out by the following acts:

- Compliance with all regulatory and reporting requirements, such as overseeing filing of annual information returns (see foregoing discussion) and payment of employment taxes

- Examination and understanding of all documents governing the organization and its operation, such as the bylaws

- Making decisions that fall within the scope of the organization's mission and governing documents

(e) Personal Liability

Generally, if a director carries out his or her duties faithfully, and in adherence to the three Ds, the director will not be found personally liable for a commission or omission. Personal liability (see discussion following) can result when a trustee or director—or an officer or key employee—of a nonprofit organization breaches standards of fiduciary responsibility.

LAWSUITS AGAINST NONPROFIT ORGANIZATIONS

Nonprofit organization can be sued under federal, state, or local law. Although criminal prosecutions are rare, in the civil laws lurk many occasions for missteps leading to lawsuits. For the most part, nonprofit organization can be sued for the same reasons as for-profit organizations.

The following are the usual bases on which a nonprofit organization can be sued:

- *Nonpayment of income or property taxes.* Governments seeking unpaid taxes bring these suits. The nonprofit organization may be generally tax-exempt. but the IRS may be after one or more of the private foundation excise taxes (see Chapter 7) or unrelated business income tax (see Chapter 13), or a state may be looking for real estate tax as to a parcel of real property that allegedly is not being used for exempt (usually charitable) purposes.

- *Violation of a state's charitable solicitation act.* A charitable (or similar) organization may be raising funds in a state without complying with the registration, reporting, or other requirements. A state will not proceed directly to litigation for a violation of this nature. If, however, after a few requests, the organization refuses to obey this law, an injunction or some other form of civil (or, infrequently, criminal) litigation may be initiated.

- *Defamation.* If an organization produces a libelous publication or one of its spokespersons uses terms or makes statements that another person finds offensive, it is not uncommon for a defamation suit to erupt in response.

- *Antitrust law violation.* Membership organizations are particularly susceptible to a charge of antitrust transgressions. For example, an association may wrongfully exclude or expel a person from its membership. (This can be a form of restraint of trade.) In addition, an association may enforce a code of ethics and conclude that a member acted unethically; this finding could lead to a defamation charge (see foregoing discussion) or, if the person is expelled from membership, to an antitrust law violation complaint.

- *Employment discrimination, wrongful termination, breach of a lease or other contract, and personal injury.* These are increasingly common bases for lawsuits. As an example of a personal injury suit, recently a nonprofit swim club was sued by an individual and his spouse because of personal injuries he suffered when he fell, after swimming, in a stairway leading to the club's locker room; his spouse sued for loss of consortium.

In most of these lawsuits, the only party sued is the organization itself. There are exceptions, however, such as the liability that can be incurred by an organization as the result of something done (commission) or not done (omission) by another organization. For example, two or more nonprofit organizations may be involved in a partnership or other form of a joint venture. As a consequence of this arrangement, the conduct of one organization may bring liability to it or to another organization. Technically, the liability (if any) may be that of the venture, but this form of liability can quickly attach to the underlying parties.

Another illustration concerns national organizations and their chapters. It is possible for a chapter to incur liability and cause the national entity to be sued as well. (This is termed *ascending liability*.) The national organization may have done something or failed to do something in conjunction with the chapter. More commonly, however, the national entity is sued simply because it has the most resources. The outcome of this type of litigation often depends on whether the chapters are considered separate legal entities or are integral parts of the national organization.

DEFENDING AGAINST LAWSUITS

It probably goes without saying that a lawsuit initiated is not necessarily a lawsuit won. It is one thing to be sued; it is another to have a lawsuit ripen into a court-imposed judgment. If sued, a nonprofit organization, however, will have to defend itself against the suit (usually by filing a motion to dismiss, an answer to the complaint, or a counterclaim). The services of a lawyer are commonly required; the organization can face high legal fees and costs without having engaged in any wrongdoing.

As a case in point, a nonprofit, charitable organization annually gives an award honoring an individual in a particular field of business. One year, the organization narrowed the candidates to three and, following much deliberation, decided on a finalist. A passed-over semifinalist became so angry that he filed a lawsuit, claiming the organization violated its procedural rules. The organization was stunned to find itself a target of a lawsuit as the result of a charitable act. The matter was resolved before that case made its way to court, but the organization had to pay several thousand dollars in legal fees to end the litigation. It was not clear why the plaintiff wanted this award so badly that he sued to try to obtain it, but his action underlined the point that it does not take much these days to create a defendant, even a charitable one.

INDIVIDUALS AS DEFENDANTS

For the most part, as noted, the defendants in lawsuits involving nonprofit organizations are the organizations themselves. Seldom will the charges include other parties, such as individuals. It can happen though, and when it does, the individuals (including those acting as volunteers) that can be dragged into the fray are trustees, directors, officers, and key employees.

Conduct by employees in their role as such is generally considered conduct by the organization involved. If an employee's actions are outside the scope of his or her employment, however, they can be held responsible as individuals.

When an individual is personally sued because of something done or not done in the name of a nonprofit organization, the potential liability is termed *personal liability*. Its occurrence is rare, but when it happens it is usually for one or more of the following reasons:

- An individual had a responsibility to do something in connection with the operation of a nonprofit organization and failed to meet that responsibility.

- An individual had a responsibility to refrain from doing something in connection with a nonprofit organization and did it anyway.

- An individual failed to dissociate himself or herself from the wrongful conduct of others.

- An individual actively participated in a wrongful conduct.

For example, a nonprofit organization may have wrongfully terminated the employment of an individual on a discriminatory basis. If the termination was the result of discrimination by a manager who was an employee of the organization, the entity may be found to be the only wrongdoer. If, however, a member of the organization's board of directors actively conspired with the manager to cause the discriminatory firing, the director may be found personally liable. If another member of the board knew of the discriminatory action (and the conspiracy underlying it) and did nothing to thwart it, that board member may be found personally liable as well.

This example involves *commission*: One or more individuals committed a wrongful act and were found liable (along with the organization). But liability can also result from a failure to act. The members of a finance committee of a nonprofit organization may fail in their obligation to oversee the investment practices of the entity. Money may be lost or valuable resources may be squandered as a result. These individuals could be found personally liable for their *omissions*.

Thus, personal liability in the nonprofit (often charitable) context can result when a trustee, director, officer, or key employee of a nonprofit organization breaches the standards of fiduciary responsibility (see Chapter 8). How can an individual who is serving a nonprofit organization (or wants to serve one) avoid the ravages of personal liability? A cynic would say that the safest approach is not to participate in the good works of a nonprofit organization in the first place. That, however, is contrary to the American way (see Chapter 1). An action plan for avoiding personal liability is explored later (see Chapter 25).

CHAPTER NINE

Braving Annual Reporting

Nearly all tax-exempt organizations are required to file an *annual information return* with the IRS. This is nothing new; exempt entities have had to file these returns for decades. In late 2007, one of the most significant developments in the law affecting nonprofit organizations occurred: The IRS radically redesigned and expanded the basic annual information return. The ramifications of the revised return are enormous; what the IRS did is equivalent to the passage of a major law or the issuance of massive tax regulations.

This development has stunned the nonprofit community. Management of tax-exempt organizations have been generally appalled. Lawyers and accountants are delirious with joy. On the day after the draft of this revised return was issued, the executive director of a large public charity was heard to say: "If this is the annual return we will have to file, we don't want to be tax-exempt anymore."

By contrast, the then-Commissioner of Internal Revenue, in mid-2007, said: "The tax-exempt sector has changed markedly since the [annual information return] was last overhauled more than a quarter of a century ago. We need a [return] that reflects the way this growing sector operates in the 21st century. The new [return] aims to give both the IRS and the public an improved window into the way tax-exempt organizations go about their vital mission." In early 2008, the successor Commissioner said: "Tax-exempt organizations provide tremendous benefits to the people and the communities they serve, but their ability to do good work hinges upon the public's trust. The new Form 990 will foster this trust by greatly improving transparency and compliance in the tax-exempt sector."

The refurbished Form 990 (that organizations begin filing in 2009) is no longer an ordinary government form. This is a complex and extraordinary document. It is, in many ways, a work of art, in that it captures the requirements of a large amount of federal tax and other law, much of it recently enacted. At the same time, because of its size and complexity, many organizations will be engaging in considerable effort (time and money) to create needed documents, maintain records, and properly prepare and timely file the return.

From a law perspective, the new return has, as noted, enormous implications for tax-exempt organizations for two reasons. (1) The form in various places and ways has the effect of creating much new law. A dramatic example of this fact is the portion on governance (see Chapter 8). (2) The form is designed to induce certain behavior by the management of nonprofit, tax-exempt organizations by in essence forcing organizations to check "yes" boxes (or avoid checking "no" boxes). The import of this "shaming technique" can been seen, for example, in the requirements as to development of various policies (see Chapter 22) and dissemination to the public of various documents (see Chapter 10).

INFORMATION RETURN BASICS

As noted, nearly all nonprofit organizations that are exempt from federal income taxation must file an annual *information* return with the IRS. For most organizations, this annual return is the Form 990. This return, which is the one the IRS has so dramatically revised, calls for the provision of much information, some of it financial and some in text form. This document, being an *information return*, rather than a *tax return*, is available for public inspection (see Chapter 10).

Private foundations (see Chapter 7), however, annually file an information return that is uniquely styled for them—Form 990-PF. Small organizations (other than private foundations. supporting organizations, and certain credit counseling organizations)—that is, entities that have gross receipts that are less than $100,000 and total assets that are less than $250,000 in value at the end of the reporting year—file Form 990-EZ (as noted in Chapter 3, an example of IRS humor). Other organizations file the following returns:

- Black Lung benefit trusts file Form 990-BL.
- Cooperatives (certain types) file Form 990-C.
- Religious and apostolic organizations file Form 1065 (the partnership return).
- Very small organizations file Form 990-N (see discussion following).

Not all nonprofit organizations are freed from the requirement of filing an annual *tax* return with the IRS. Tax-exempt political organizations file Form 1120-POL (and, more frequently, Form 8872, and perhaps Form 990 as well) and homeowners' associations file Form 1120-H. Certain nonexempt trusts may file a Form 990 or a Form 1041. Nonprofit corporations that are not tax-exempt file the regular corporate tax return, which is Form 1120. Exempt organizations with unrelated business income generally file Form 990-T (see Chapter 13).

IRS GUIDING PRINCIPLES

The IRS said that its retooling of the basic annual information return (Form 990) was based on these guiding principles:

- Enhancing transparency by providing the IRS and the public with a realistic picture of the filing organization and its operations, along with the basis for comparing the organization with similar organizations
- Promoting compliance, by designing a return that accurately reflects the organization's operations and use of assets, thereby enabling the IRS to more efficiently assess the risk of any noncompliance by the organization
- Minimizing the burden on filing organizations, by asking questions in a manner that makes it relatively easy to prepare the return and not impose unwarranted recordkeeping or information-gathering burdens to obtain and substantiate the reported information

SUMMARY OF ANNUAL INFORMATION RETURN

The redesigned Form 990 includes an 11-page "core form." There is a one-page summary of the organization (Part I), followed by ten additional parts (II–XI). Part II is the signature block. This core return is accompanied by 16 schedules.

(a) Part I (Summary)

The summary requests a brief description of the organization's mission or most significant activities. It asks for the number of voting members of the organization's governing body, the number of these board members who are independent, the number of employees, and the number of volunteers. Other questions concern the amount of contributions and grants, program service revenue, investment income, other revenue, total gross unrelated business income, total revenue and expenses, grants and similar amounts paid, compensation, professional fundraising expenses, other expenses, and total assets and liabilities.

(b) Part III

Part III of the redesigned Form 990 concerns the filing organization's program service accomplishments. It is required to describe its mission, new significant program services, any significant changes in the way it conducts a program, a cessation of any activity, and the exempt purpose achievements for each of its three largest programs services by expenses. Charitable and social welfare organizations (see Chapter 4) are required to report the amount of grants and allocations to others, total; expenses, and any revenue for each program service reported.

(c) Part IV

Part IV of the redesigned Form 990 is a checklist of (potentially) required schedules. This schedule has 37 lines, with some lines containing as many as four subparts.

(d) Part V

Part V of the Form 990 pertains to a variety of activities and IRS filings. As to activities, there are questions about unrelated business income (see Chapter 13), involvement in a prohibited tax shelter transaction (see Chapter 16), use of supporting organizations (see Chapter 7), use of donor-advised funds (see Chapter 16), and payments with respect to personal benefit contracts (see Chapter 16).

(e) Part VI

Part VI of the Form 990 concerns governance, management, policies, and disclosure. As to the governing body and management (Section A), questions concern the number of the voting members of the governing body and the number of board members who are "independent." Inquiry is made as to whether the organization has conflict-of-interest, whistleblower, and document retention and destruction policies, as well as policies governing the activities of chapters, affiliates, and "branches" (Section B). Additional questions pertain to various disclosures (Section C).

(f) Part VII

Part VII of the Form 990 focuses on compensation of insiders and independent contractors. These persons currently in their positions must be listed (irrespective of compensation), along with a list of the organization's five most highly compensated employees (other than insiders) who received compensation of more than $100,000 from the organization and any related organizations during the year; the organization's former officers, key employees, or highest compensated employees who received more than $100,000 of compensation from the organization and any related organizations during the year; and the organization's former directors or trustees who received (in that capacity) more than $10,000 of compensation from the organization and any related organizations during the year.

(g) Parts VIII–XI

Part VIII of the Form 990 is a revenue statement, Part IX is a statement of expenses (including functional reporting), Part X is a balance sheet, and Part XI concerns financial statements.

(h) Schedule A

Schedule A of the Form 990 is used by charitable organizations to report their public charity status (see Chapter 7). Specific questions about supporting organizations include identification of the organization's type, a certification as to lack of control by disqualified persons, contributions from disqualified persons, and information about supported organizations.

There are separate public support schedules for the basic types of publicly supported charitable organizations. The public support computation period is five years (see Chapters 6, 7). An organization can claim public charity status on the basis of the facts-and-circumstances test on this schedule.

(i) Schedule B

Schedule B is the schedule used to report charitable contributions and grants. It is the same as the preexisting Schedule B.

(j) Schedule C

Schedule C consists of questions concerning political campaign and lobbying activities, principally by charitable organizations (see Chapters 14 and 15). Filing organizations are required to describe their direct and indirect political campaign activities, including the amounts of political expenditures and volunteer hours. There are separate parts for lobbying charitable organizations that are under the substantial part test and the expenditure test. Certain other types of tax-exempt entities must prepare additional parts of this schedule.

(k) Schedule D

Schedule D is used to report supplemental financial information, such as for investments, liabilities, conservation easements, donor-advised funds, art collections, trust accounts, and endowment funds.

(l) Schedule E

Schedule E is filed by organizations that constitute tax-exempt private schools. Most of this schedule relates to the requirement that the organization cannot, to be tax-exempt, maintain a racially discriminatory policy. One question asks whether the organization receives any financial aid or other assistance from a governmental agency.

(m) Schedule F

The essence of Schedule F is the reporting of activities outside the United States. These activities, such as program services, grant-making, and fundraising, are reported on a per-region basis. Grant-makers are required to describe their procedures for monitoring the use of grant funds. Information must be supplied if a grantee or other recipient of assistance is related to any person with an interest in the grant-making organization. Additional details are required in instances of grants or other assistance to organizations or individuals.

(n) Schedule G

Schedule G largely concerns fundraising activities. The filing organization indicates the type or types of fundraising in which it is engaged and provides information about any fundraising contracts (including those with insiders). The organization is required to list the jurisdictions in which it is authorized to solicit funds (see Chapter 12). A part of this schedule focuses on fundraising events; another part solicits details about gaming activities.

(o) Schedule H

Schedule H is filed by tax-exempt hospitals. The first part of this schedule (Part I) is a "community benefit report." The filing hospital indicates whether it provides free or discounted care to low-income individuals or those who are "medically indigent." The hospital reports on its charity care (such as care at cost, unreimbursed Medicaid services, and other unreimbursed costs in connection with government programs) and other community benefits (such as health improvement services, health professions education, subsidized health services, and research). The organization is asked whether it prepares an annual community benefit report and to describe its charity care policy.

The second part of this schedule (Part II) inquires as to the hospital's "community building" activities. These activities include physical improvements and housing, economic development, community support, environmental improvements, leadership development and training for community members, coalition-building, community health improvement advocacy, and workforce development.

Another part (Part III) pertains to bad debt, Medicare, and collection practices. A fourth part asks questions about the use of management companies and involvement in joint ventures. A fifth part (Part V) seeks information about the hospital's facilities. The schedule (Part VI) requests a description of how the organization assesses the health care needs of the communities it serves and how the organization informs patients about their eligibility for assistance under federal, state, or local government programs or under its charity care policy.

(p)   Schedule I

Schedule I is used to solicit information about the organization's domestic grant and other assistance programs. For example, the organization is asked whether it maintains records to substantiate the amount of its assistance and about the organization's selection criteria and grantees' eligibility. Information is required for grants of more than $5,000 to organizations and all grants to individuals.

(q)   Schedule J

Schedule J is used to solicit supplemental information about compensation. The organization must indicate (in Part I) whether it provides to its insiders payments or items in forms such as first-class or charter travel, a discretionary spending account, a housing allowance, or health or social club dues; it is asked whether it follows a written policy in connection with such payments (or reimbursements) or items. The organization is asked how it determines certain executive compensation and, in the case of charitable and social welfare organizations, whether it provided any form of non-fixed payments.

The organization reports information concerning compensation paid to trustees, directors, officers, key employees, and highly compensated employees (Part II). There is a breakdown as to base compensation, bonus and incentive compensation, deferred compensation, and nontaxable benefits.

(r)   Schedule K

Schedule K is used to solicit information about tax-exempt bond issues (Part I) and the use of the proceeds (Part II). There are questions about the private use rules (Part III) and arbitrage (Part IV).

(s)   Schedule L

Schedule L concerns excess benefit transactions (see Chapter 5) and loans to and from interested persons. Information sought includes the name of the debtor or creditor, original principal amount, balance due, the purpose of the loan, and whether there is a written agreement. Questions are also asked about grants or other forms of assistance benefiting, and business transactions involving, interested persons.

(t)   Schedule M

The focus of Schedule M is on non-cash contributions. Thus, information is sought about gifts of art (including fractional interests), books, clothing and household goods, automobiles, airplanes, boats, intellectual property, securities, qualified conservation property, real estate, collectibles, food inventory, drugs and medical supplies, taxidermy, historical artifacts, scientific specimens, and archeological artifacts.

This schedule inquires as to the number of Forms 8283 received by the organization for contributions for which the organization completed the donee acknowledgment portion; whether the organization received any property that it must hold for at least three years from the date of its contribution, which is not required to be used for exempt purposes during the entire holding period; whether the organization has a gift acceptance policy that requires the review of nonstandard contributions; and whether the organization used third parties or related organizations to solicit, process, or sell non-cash distributions.

(u) Schedule N

Schedule N pertains to liquidations, terminations, dissolutions, and significant dispositions of assets. Questions include a description of the assets involved, their value, the method of determining the value, the date of the distribution, and the name and address of the recipient. Other questions concern the involvement of an insider with the successor or transferee organization, notification of one or more state officials, and other compliance with state laws. Additional information is sought concerning transfers of more than 25 percent of the organization's assets.

(v) Schedule O

Filing organizations use Schedule O to provide additional information for responses to specific questions in the Form 990 and/or its schedules, and to provide additional information.

(w) Schedule R

Schedule R has as one of its purposes the identification of disregarded entities and related tax-exempt organizations. Related organizations taxable as a partnership and as a corporation or trust are also required to be identified. There is a series of questions about transactions with related organizations and unrelated organizations taxable as partnerships.

SEQUENCING GUIDELINES

The instructions accompanying the Form 990 include a *sequencing list*, to assist tax-exempt organizations in completing the return and its schedules. As is noted, "certain later parts of the form must first be completed in order to complete earlier parts." According to this list, here is the way to approach preparation of the Form 990:

1. Complete lines A–F and H(a)–M in the heading of the return.
2. Determine the organization's related organizations (see Schedule R instructions), disregarded entities, and joint ventures for which reporting will be required.
3. Complete Parts VIII, IX, and X (revenue and expense statements, and balance sheet).
4. Determine the organization's officers, directors, trustees, key employees, and five highest compensated employees (to be listed in Form 990, Part VII, section A).
5. Complete line G in the heading (gross receipts).
6. Complete Parts III, V, VII, and XI.
7. Complete Schedule L (concerning transactions with interested persons) (if required).

8. Complete Part VI.

9. Complete Part I.

10. Complete Part IV.

11. Complete remaining applicable schedules (for which "yes" boxes were checked in Part IV).

12. Complete Part II (signature block).

FILING EXCEPTIONS

The exceptions from the requirement of filing an annual information return are discussed in Chapter 10.

ELECTRONIC FILING RULES

Certain tax-exempt organizations, that have filed at least 250 returns during the calendar year, are required to electronically file their annual information returns. The basic rules are as follows:

- Tax-exempt organizations with assets of at least $100 million that are required to file annual information returns must file them electronically beginning with tax years ending on or after December 31, 2005.

- Exempt organizations with assets of at least $10 million that are required to file annual information returns must file them electronically beginning with tax years ending on or after December 31, 2006.

- Private foundations and split-interest charitable trusts (irrespective of asset size) must file their annual information returns electronically beginning with tax years ending on or after December 31, 2006.

The IRS may waive the requirements to file electronically in cases of undue economic hardship or technology issues. The IRS, however, believes that electronic filing will not impose significant burdens on filers. Thus, waivers of the electronic filing requirement are granted only in instances involving "undue hardship."

FILING REQUIREMENTS AND TAX-EXEMPT STATUS

If a tax-exempt organization that is required to file a notice with the IRS in lieu of an annual information return (see Chapter 10) fails to provide the notice for three consecutive years, the organization's exempt status is revoked by operation of law. If an exempt organization that is required to file an annual information return fails to file the return for three consecutive years, the organization's exempt status is similarly revoked. If an exempt organization fails to meet its filing obligation to the IRS for three consecutive years in instances where the organization is subject to the annual information return filing requirement in one or more years during a three-year period and also is subject to the notice requirement for one or more years during the same three-year period, the organization's exemption is likewise revoked.

A revocation under these rules is effective from the date the IRS determined was the last day the tax-exempt organization could have timely filed the third required annual information return or notice. To again be recognized as exempt, the organization must apply to the IRS for recognition of exemption irrespective of whether the organization was required to make an application for recognition of exemption in order to be exempt originally. If, on application for recognition of exemption after a revocation under these rules, the organization demonstrates to the satisfaction of the IRS reasonable cause for failing to file the required returns or notices, the organization's exempt status may, in the discretion of the IRS, be reinstated retroactively to the date of revocation.

CHAPTER TEN

Tax Exemption: Not a Paperwork Exemption

Nonprofit organizations have not escaped the burdens of governmental regulation—the returns, reports, and other paperwork demanded by federal, state, and some local governments. Two major sets of reporting obligations have been discussed – those applicable in connection with the process of applying for recognition of tax-exempt status (Chapter 6) and the requirement for most tax-exempt organizations to file an annual information return (Chapter 9).

This chapter reviews the other reporting requirements for most nonprofit organizations. This summary covers only the basics, particularly when it comes to state and local requirements. Some reporting requirements are unique to certain types of nonprofit organizations. Other nonprofit organizations (churches are the best example) may be exempt from one or more reporting requirements that most others have to face.

Some nonprofit organizations have to comply with reporting requirements that are not directly imposed by government. For example, a nonprofit organization that receives a grant usually owes a periodic report to the grantor. A supporting organization may be expected to submit information to its supported organization or organizations (see Chapter 7). A nonprofit organization that is under a group exemption (see Chapter 6) may report annually to the central organization, for the purpose of preparing combined information returns. A nonprofit organization that reports to one or more of the euphemistically termed *voluntary watchdog agencies* can expect at least annual scrutiny (see Chapter 21).

(a) Private Foundation Reporting

The annual information return for private foundations (Form 990-PF) must include

- An itemized statement of the foundation's support, expenses, assets, and liabilities

- A report of capital gains and losses

- A calculation of the excise tax on net investment income

- An information statement concerning any legislative or political campaign activities

- An information statement concerning any acts of self-dealing, mandatory payout, excess business holdings, jeopardy investments, or taxable expenditures

- A list of all directors, officers, highly paid employees, and contractors

- A list of the five persons who received the highest payment for professional services

- A computation of the minimum investment return and distributable amount

- An itemized list of all grants made or approved, showing the amount of each grant, the name and address of each recipient, any relationship between a grant recipient and the foundation's managers or substantial contributors, and a concise statement of the purpose of each grant

- The address of the principal office of the foundation and (if different) of the place where its books and records are maintained

- The names and addresses of the foundation's managers who are substantial contributors or who own 10 percent or more of the stock of any corporation of which the foundation owns 10 percent or more, or corresponding interests in partnerships or other entities

A private foundation must divulge, on Form 990-PF, a schedule of relevant statistical information regarding its principal direct charitable activities and program-related investments; organizations and other beneficiaries served, conferences convened, or research papers produced. The foundation must also provide information demonstrating conformance with the public inspection and document dissemination requirements.

(b) Exceptions

Form 990 or 990-EZ must be filed by nearly all tax-exempt organizations whose annual gross receipts are normally in excess of $25,000. The Form 990-EZ filing thresholds are discussed in Chapter 6. Supporting organizations and private foundations, however, must file annual information returns irrespective of the level of their gross receipts. However, the $25,000 filing threshold is frequently misunderstood. Generally, an organization's annual gross receipts are the total amount it received during its annual accounting period, without subtraction of any costs or expenses.

The return, however, allows an organization, in computing its *total revenue*, to net certain income items and related expenses: receipts (and associated expenses) from rents, revenue from assets sales, revenue from special fundraising events, and certain other gross sales. An organization's *gross receipts* can be more than $25,000, even though the total revenue shown on the return is less than $25,000. To add to the confusion, *normally* means a four-year average. An organization is not necessarily excused from filing an information return in any year in which its gross receipts for the year are less than $25,000. In fact, depending on its age and its particular circumstances, an organization can have more than $25,000 in gross receipts in a year and still be excused from filing an information return. An organization's gross receipts are considered to be $25,000 or less if the organization is

- Up to one year old and has received, or holds donors' pledges for, $37,500 or less during its first tax year.

- Between one and three years old and has averaged $30,000 or less in gross receipts during each of its first two tax years.

- Three or more years old and has averaged $25,000 or less in gross receipts for the immediately preceding three tax years (including the year for which the return would be filed).

In addition, the requirement to file an annual information return does not apply to:

- Churches (including interchurch organizations of local units of a church)
- Integrated auxiliaries of churches
- Conventions or associations of churches
- Financing, fund management, or retirement insurance program management organizations functioning on behalf of the foregoing organizations
- Certain other entities affiliated with a church or convention or association of churches
- Most religious orders (to the extent of their religious activities)
- State institutions
- Certain schools and mission societies
- Foreign organizations (other than private foundations) that normally do not receive more than $25,000 in gross receipts annually from sources within the United States and that do not have any significant activity (including lobbying or political activity) in the United States
- Governmental units
- Affiliates of governmental units (which can include nonprofit organizations)

Just because an organization is exempt from filing an annual information return does not always mean a return should not be filed. Preparation of the return may be a good discipline for keeping the organization's financial records up to standards, and a rehearsal for when gross receipts go over the filing threshold and a return becomes mandatory. In addition, filing the return starts the statute of limitations running—a protection against audits for years long passed.

(c) Transition Rules

At the time the IRS issued the revised Form 990, it announced a graduated three-year transition period for annual information return filings. For the 2008 tax year (returns filed in 2009), organizations with gross receipts of more than $1 million or total assets in excess of $2.5 million are required to file the Form 990. For the 2009 tax year (returns filed in 2010), organizations with gross receipts over $500,000 or total assets over $1.25 million are required to file the Form 990. Tax-exempt organizations with gross receipts or total assets below these thresholds are allowed to file the Form 990-EZ (see foregoing discussion), with the option to file the new Form 990. (The Form 990-EZ for 2008 was also released in late 2007.)

The filing threshold will be permanently set, beginning with the 2010 tax year, at $200,000 in gross receipts and $500,000 in total assets. Starting with the 2010 tax year, the filing threshold for organizations required to file the Form 990-N (the e-postcard) (see discussion following) will be increased to $50,000 (from $25,000).

(d) E-Postcard Rules

Tax-exempt organizations that are exempt from the requirement of filing an annual information return by reason of having gross receipts that are normally less than $25,000 (see foregoing discussion) must furnish to the IRS, annually and in electronic form, a notice containing the legal name of the organization, any name under which the organization operates or does business, the organization's mailing address and any website address, the organization's taxpayer identification number, the name and address of a principal officer, and evidence of the organization's continuing basis for its exemption from the annual filing requirement. Should the organization terminate its existence, notice of the termination must be provided to the IRS.

This notice is on Form 990-N; it has become known as the *e-postcard*. The requirement for filing this notice took effect for tax years beginning in 2008.

PENALTIES

Failure to file the information return in a timely way, without reasonable cause or an exception, can generally give rise to a $20-per-day penalty. The organization must pay for each day the failure continues, up to a maximum of $10,000. For larger organizations (those with annual gross receipts in excess of $1 million), the per-day penalty is $100 and the maximum penalty is $50,000. An additional penalty can be imposed, at the same rate and up to the same maximum, on the individual(s) responsible for the failure to file without reasonable cause. Other fines and imprisonment can be imposed for willfully failing to file returns or for filing fraudulent returns and statements with the IRS.

DISCLOSURE REQUIREMENTS

As a general rule, a tax-exempt organization must do the following:

- It must make its application for recognition of tax exemption available for public inspection without charge at its principal, regional, and district offices during regular business hours.

- It must make its annual information returns available for public inspection without charge in the same offices during regular business hours. Each return must be made available for a period of three years, beginning on the date the return is required to be filed or is actually filed, whichever is later.

- It must provide a copy without charge (other than a reasonable fee for reproduction and actual postage costs), of all or any part of any application or return required to be made available for public inspection to any individual who makes a request for the copy in person or in writing.

For this purpose, the term *tax-exempt organization* does not encompass organizations such as political organizations, prepaid tuition plans, and homeowners' associations.

Generally, a tax-exempt organization must provide copies of the documents, in response to an in-person request, at its principal, regional, and district offices during regular business hours. Also generally, the organization must provide the copies to a requestor on the day the request is made.

In the case of an in-person request, where unusual circumstances exist so that fulfillment of the request on the same business day places an unreasonable burden on the exempt organization, the copies must be provided on the next business day following the day on which the unusual circumstances cease to exist or the fifth business day after the date of the request, whichever occurs first. *Unusual circumstances* include receipt of a volume of requests that exceeds the organization's daily capacity to make copies, requests received shortly before the end of regular business hours that require an extensive amount of copying, and requests received on a day when the organization's managerial staff capable of fulfilling the request is conducting special duties. *Special duties* are activities such as student registration or attendance at an off-site meeting or convention, rather than regular administrative duties.

If a request for a document is made in writing, the tax-exempt organization must honor it if the request

- Is addressed to a principal, regional, or district office of the organization and is delivered by mail, electronic mail, facsimile, or a private delivery service.
- Sets forth the address to which the copy of the document should be sent.

A tax-exempt organization receiving a written request for a copy must mail it within 30 days from the date it receives the request. If, however, an exempt organization requires payment in advance, it is required only to provide the copy within 30 days from the date it receives payment. A tax-exempt organization must fulfill a request for a copy of the organization's entire application or annual information return or any specific part or schedule of its application or return.

A tax-exempt organization may charge a reasonable fee for providing copies. A fee is *reasonable* if it is no more than the per-page copying fee charged by the IRS for providing copies. It can also include postage costs. The requestor may be required to pay the fee in advance.

If a tax-exempt organization denies an individual's request for inspection or a copy of an application or return and the individual wishes to complain to the IRS, he or she may send a statement to the appropriate IRS district office, describing the reason the individual believes the denial was in violation of these requirements. (The term *complain* is not in the regulations. Reference is made to an individual who wants to "alert" the IRS "to the possible need for enforcement action.") Penalties apply for failure to comply with these rules.

A tax-exempt organization is not required to comply with requests for copies of its application for recognition of tax exemption or an annual information return if the organization has made the document widely available. The rules regarding public inspection of the documents nonetheless continue to apply.

An exempt organization can make its application or a return *widely available* by posting the document on a World Wide Web page that the organization establishes and maintains. It can also satisfy the exception if the document is posted as part of a database of similar documents with other exempt organizations on a World Wide Web page established and maintained by another entity.

The document is considered widely available only if

- The World Wide Web page through which it is available clearly informs readers that the document is available and provides instructions for downloading it.

- The document is posted in a format that, when accessed, downloaded, viewed, and printed in hard copy, exactly reproduces the image of the application or return as it was originally filed with the IRS, except for any information excluded by statute.

- Any individual with access to the Internet can access, download, view, and print the document without special computer hardware or software required for that format, and can do so without payment of a fee to the exempt organization or to another entity maintaining the World Wide Web page.

The organization maintaining the World Wide Web page must have procedures for ensuring the reliability and accuracy of the document that it posts on the page. It must take reasonable precautions to prevent alteration, destruction, or accidental loss of the document when printed on its page. In the event a posted document is altered, destroyed, or lost, the organization must correct or replace the document.

If the IRS determines that a tax-exempt organization is the subject of a *harassment campaign* and compliance with the requests that are part of the campaign would not be in the public interest, the organization is not required to fulfill a request for a copy that it reasonably believes is part of such a campaign.

A group of requests for an organization's application or returns is indicative of a harassment campaign if the requests are part of a single coordinated effort to disrupt the operations of the organization rather than to collect information about the organization. There is a facts-and-circumstances test. Factors include

- A sudden increase in the number of requests

- An extraordinary number of requests made by means of form letters or similarly worded correspondence

- Evidence of a purpose to deter significantly the organization's employees or volunteers from pursuing the organization's exempt purpose

- Requests that contain language hostile to the organization

- Direct evidence of bad faith by organizers of the purported harassment campaign

- Evidence that the organization has already provided the requested documents to a member of the purported harassment group

- A demonstration by the tax-exempt organization that it routinely provides copies of its documents upon request

A tax-exempt organization may disregard any request for copies of all or part of any document beyond the first two received within any 30-day period or the first four received within any one-year period from the same individual or the same address, irrespective of whether the IRS has determined that the organization is subject to a harassment campaign.

There is a procedure for applying to the IRS for a determination that the organization is the subject of a harassment campaign. (There is no form, however.) The organization may suspend compliance with respect to the request, as long as the application is filed within ten days after harassment is suspected, until the organization receives a response from the IRS.

Forms 990 and 990-PF are also available for public inspection and copying at the IRS. The IRS is not permitted to disclose certain portions of the returns and attachments, however, such as the list of contributors required to accompany Form 990. A request for inspection of a return must be in writing and must include the name and address of the organization that filed it. A request to inspect a return should indicate the type (number) of the return and the year(s) involved. The request should be sent to the District Director (Attention: Disclosure Officer) of the district in which the person making the request desires to inspect the return. For an inspection at the IRS National Office in Washington, D.C., the request must be sent to the Commissioner of Internal Revenue, Attention: Freedom of Information Reading Room, 1111 Constitution Avenue, NW, Washington, D.C. 20224.

There is still another dimension to the filing of annual information returns. Organizations that are eligible to receive tax-deductible contributions are listed in an IRS publication titled *Cumulative List of Organizations Described in Section 170(c) of the Internal Revenue Code* (Publication 78). This list, which the IRS periodically supplements, is frequently relied on by donors and their advisors, when they are planning charitable giving. An organization may be removed from this listing if IRS records show that the organization failed, without good cause, to file Form 990 or to advise the IRS that it was not required to file. (Even if this happens, contributions to the organization remain deductible.)

Form 990 is due on or before the fifteenth day of the fifth month following the close of the tax year. Thus, the information return for an organization with a fiscal year the same as the calendar year should be filed by May 15 of each year.

POLITICAL ORGANIZATIONS

Political organizations are subjected to unique disclosure and reporting rules. To be tax-exempt from the date of formation, these organizations must file a notice of organization (Form 8871) with the IRS within 24 hour of formation. They must file reports with the IRS (Form 8872) at least annually. Contributions in excess of $200 must be disclosed, as must expenditures in excess of $500.

This law was enacted as a result of the extensive funding of political activities by these organizations during the presidential campaign in 2000. Under prior law, when a political organization engaged solely in *issue advocacy* (that is, the organization did not advocate the election of or opposition to a candidate), it did not have to register with the Federal Election Commission. In addition, its tax returns were not made public. The controversy over the use of soft money, however, intensified to the point that Congress enacted these reporting and disclosure rules. The rules were slightly relaxed in 2002, following litigation finding a few elements of the original law unconstitutional.

UNRELATED INCOME TAX RETURNS

A tax-exempt organization with unrelated business taxable income (see Chapter 13) must file—in addition to an annual information return—a tax return, Form 990-T. On this return, the source or sources of unrelated income, and accompanying expenses, are reported, and any tax due is computed. The first $1,000 of annual net unrelated income is exempt from taxation.

Form 990-T also contains special schedules concerning rental income, unrelated debt-financed income, investment income of social clubs and certain other tax-exempt organizations, and income from controlled organizations.

This return is also due on or before the fifteenth day of the fifth month following the close of the organization's tax year. For failure to file this tax return in a timely manner, additional tax may be imposed.

The disclosure requirements discussed previously also apply with respect to the unrelated business income tax return.

MATERIAL CHANGES

A nonprofit organization that has been recognized by the IRS as a tax-exempt organization is expected, by the agency, to report to the IRS any material changes in its purposes, character, or methods of operation. This requirement enables the IRS to determine whether the change or changes may lead to revocation or alteration of the entity's tax-exempt status. A determination by the IRS that an organization is exempt is like a ruling by any other government agency—the ruling is only as valid as the facts on which it is based. If the facts materially change, the ruling may change as well.

The key word here is *materially*. An example of a material change would be a substantial alteration in the organization's statement of purpose, a major new program undertaking, or a significant structural change (such as the creation of a membership). Identifying a material change often involves a judgment, perhaps best made with the advice of a lawyer or accountant. If in doubt, the organization can send the information to the IRS. It is not always necessary to request a review of the original ruling; it may be enough simply to submit the changes and not ask for anything. In any event, all changes (such as amendments to bylaws or alterations in program activities) are to be reported to the IRS as part of the preparation and filing of the annual information return. The government should get the changes sooner or later—it is just a question of when.

DONEE RETURNS

In many instances, a charitable organization that sells, exchanges, or otherwise disposes of gift property within two years after the date of receipt of the property must file an information return with the IRS (Form 8282).

The basic purpose of this return is to enable the IRS to compare a charity's selling price of property with the value claimed by the donor in computing a charitable contribution deduction. This filing requirement is part of a package of rules concerning the need for appraisals of gift property and other aspects of the charitable deduction substantiation (including proof-of-value) rules. (See Chapter 11.)

STATE ANNUAL REPORTS

Most states require organizations created under their laws and/or operating in their jurisdictions to file annual reports with the state's appropriate governmental agency. This requirement is usually applicable to nonprofit organizations. These corporate annual reports, filed most frequently with the state's secretary of state, are not tax returns. In some states, these reports are due whether or not the entity is formally a corporation.

Some states have additional filing requirements for charitable trusts. This type of filing is usually made with the office of the state's attorney general. States may also require information and/or tax returns similar to federal Forms 990 and 990-T.

This is an area of the law where it is difficult to generalize. Each organization must, on its own or with professional assistance, determine what reports and returns may be required by the state, county, or other governmental jurisdiction in which the organization is located.

The filing requirements may be even more complex if a nonprofit organization operates in more than one state.

An organization is a *domestic* organization with respect to the state in which it is formed. In all other states, the organization is a *foreign* entity. The domestic organization may have reporting obligations under the law of the home state. The organization may also have reporting obligations under the law of the states to which it is a foreign organization *doing business* in those states. The concept of doing business is not particularly well-defined, but it includes the maintenance of an office.

An organization that is doing business in a state other than the domestic state must first obtain from that jurisdiction a *certificate of authority* to conduct operations. The organization will have to name a registered agent in that state and probably will have to file an annual report there.

A nonprofit organization that has multistate operations will likely have a registered agent and will likely file an annual report in each state in which it is operational. These requirements are in addition to those that may be required under the states' charitable solicitation acts.

CHARITABLE SOLICITATION ACTS

Most states typically regulate fundraising by charitable organizations by means of the enforcement of charitable solicitation acts. Some counties and cities are involved in this process as well.

Annual reporting is a mainstay of charitable fundraising regulation. A charitable organization that solicits contributions is generally required to file a report with every state in which it seeks funds. (A similar reporting requirement is applicable to professional fund raisers and professional solicitors.) As noted in Chapter 12, a charitable organization that is raising funds throughout the country is expected to file reports with about 46 states, not to mention the counties and towns that want reports as well.

Worse, a few states treat the process of raising funds for charitable purposes as being a form of *doing business* in the state. These states insist that the charity, in addition to complying with the states' charitable solicitation acts, obtain permission to do business there. The charity must then appoint a registered agent in each state and thereafter begin filing annual reports as a foreign corporation. If all states were to take this position, a charitable organization engaging in fundraising in each of the states would have to register and report under charitable solicitation acts and 51 (including the District of Columbia) nonprofit corporation acts!

OTHER REPORTING

Depending on state law, a nonprofit organization may have to report to a state on its exemption from or compliance with state income, sales, and/or property (tangible or intangible, personal or real) taxation.

If a nonprofit organization is an employer, it must file all of the federal and state forms concerning payment of compensation. Pertinent federal forms include Form W-2 (wage and tax statement), Form W-3 (transmittal of income and tax statements), Form W-2P (statement for recipients of annuities or pensions), Form 1096 (annual summary and transmittal of federal information returns), Form 940 (employer's annual federal unemployment tax return), Form 941 (employer's quarterly federal tax return, used to report the withholding of federal income taxes and social security taxes), and Form 5500, 5500-C, or 5500-R (reporting on employee benefit plans).

A nonprofit organization generally must file an information return (Form 1099) with the IRS when paying a person (other than an employee) more than $600 a year. Charitable organizations that make payments to individuals for information about the commission of crimes do not have to file Form 1099 for these payments.

Charitable remainder trusts, pooled income funds, and charitable lead trusts (see Chapter 11) must file Form 5227 annually. Charitable remainder trusts and charitable lead trusts whose charitable interests involve only war veterans' posts or certain cemeteries are not required to complete certain parts of this form.

FOCUS: Campaign to Clean Up America

The Campaign to Clean Up America(CCUA) fully expects to receive annual gross receipts in excess of $25,000, so it will be obligated to prepare and file with the IRS an annual information return (Form 990). The CCUA will be a publicly supported charitable organization, not a private foundation, so it will not be filing the annual return for foundations (Form 990-PF). There are no present plans to have unrelated business income, so there is no current obligation to file a tax return (Form 990-T).

The CCUA will be soliciting contributions throughout the United States, so it will be registering with each state that has a charitable solicitation act. In some of these states, the CCUA will have to obtain a certificate of authority to do business as a foreign corporation. At present, however, the CCUA does not intend to actually do business in any other state.

The state in which the CCUA is organized (Missouri) has an annual report requirement, which the CCUA will be obligated to fulfill.

At this time, the CCUA has one employee—its president. The federal and state reporting requirements associated with a payroll are therefore applicable. The CCUA will be using consultants (a lawyer, an accountant, and a fundraising professional). The compensation paid to them may have to be annually reported to the IRS (Form 1099).

CHAPTER ELEVEN

Charitable Giving Rules

The basic concept of the federal income tax deduction for a charitable contribution is this: Corporate taxpayers and individual taxpayers who itemize their deductions (for individuals, those who file a "long form") can deduct on their annual tax return, within certain limits, an amount equivalent to the amount contributed or to the value of a contribution to a qualified donee. A *charitable contribution* for income tax purposes is a gift to or for the use of one or more qualified donees.

Deductions for charitable gifts are also allowed under the federal gift tax and estate tax laws. Donors and the charitable organizations they support commonly expect gifts to be in the form of outright transfers of money or, frequently, property. For both parties (the donor and the donee), a gift is usually a unilateral transaction, in a financial sense: the donor parts with the contribution and the charity acquires it. The advantages to the donor are confined to the resulting charitable deduction and the gratification derived from making the gift.

Another type of charitable giving, referred to as *planned giving*, provides far greater financial and tax advantages to the donor. This type of giving is discussed in Chapter 19.

TYPES OF CHARITABLE GIVING

There are three categories of charitable giving: *impulse giving, interest giving*, and *integrated giving*. Each provides some form of emotional or financial satisfaction to the donor.

(a) Impulse Giving

Impulse giving is just that—the donor is responding on impulse to an appeal for a charitable gift. The gift is made in immediate response to a compelling plea (for example, children ravaged by war, hunger, or disease; suffering animals; or an impending cure for a deadly disease). A direct-mail, television, radio, telephone, Internet, door-to-door, or street-corner solicitation usually invites the response.

An impulse gift almost always is made in cash and usually is a relatively small amount. The donor may not have donated previously to the organization, probably does not intend to become involved with the organization's programs or administration, and has likely not thought about any subsequent gifts. The gift may have been prompted by the receipt of a premium (a magazine, a discount, or a token gift) and an accompanying appeal letter or other literature. Many impulse gifts are not particularly important as charitable contribution deductions because of the amounts involved. If the donor does not itemize deductions or if the donee is not a charitable entity, the deduction is not available.

(b) Interest Giving

A donor's ongoing and authentic involvement in a charitable organization's program will result in *interest giving*. Interest donors usually have some unique relationship with the charitable organization—it is the donor's church, synagogue, mosque, or other religious institution; the school, college, or university from which he or she graduated; the hospital serving his or her family or community; or a charitable organization with programs that have some special appeal to the donor's personal beliefs, background, or current interests.

Interest giving is usually done on a periodic basis (for example, weekly in church or annually in response to a yearly fund effort). Compared to an impulse gift, the typical amount of an interest gift is higher, and there is a greater possibility that the gift will consist of property—probably securities or real estate.

(c) Integrated Giving

Integrated giving is the most sophisticated form of charitable giving. Unlike the other two categories of giving, the gift is deliberately planned as part of the donor's overall financial and tax affairs or his or her estate. An integrated gift is most often from a donor who has a substantial relationship with the charitable organization. A large contribution is involved. The integrated gift is less likely to involve outright gifts of cash or property than gifts utilizing trusts, contracts, or wills. The charitable deduction is of major importance to this type of contributor, is a reason for the donation, and is an integral part of the transaction.

ACTUAL PRACTICE

In actual practice, the lines of demarcation among the three categories of charitable giving are often blurry. These somewhat arbitrary labels are not meant to suggest that an impulse donor lacks an authentic interest in the recipient charity or that an integrated donor is motivated solely by personal financial advantages. One category of charitable gift can lead to another: impulse giving can evolve into interest giving, or interest giving can give rise to integrated giving.

A good fundraising professional can bring about a progression in giving by donors. Any development (fundraising) program worthy of that name is aimed toward upgrading a donor from an impulse donor to an interest donor and perhaps to an integrated donor. For example, a direct-mail program may result in a donor's first gift (as part of a donor acquisition effort). The organization is generally interested in the donor's regular giving—that is, becoming an interest donor (as part of a donor renewal effort). Many planned giving programs (integrated gift programs) are built on the conversion of interest donors to integrated donors.

The following are the economic advantages that can result from a charitable gift:

- A federal, state, or local tax deduction for the charitable contribution

- A way of avoiding capital gains taxation

- A creation of or an increase in cash flow

- An improved tax treatment of income

- Free professional tax and investment management services

- An opportunity to transfer property between the generations of a family

- Receipt of benefits (usually services) from the charitable donee

For an impulse donor, none of these advantages may be involved, although the charitable deduction may be a possibility. For an interest donor, the charitable deduction is usually a significant amount, and avoiding capital gains tax may be important. The interest donor may receive a premium (such as a magazine, discount, or token gift in return). Only an integrated donor realizes all of the economic advantages—in addition to the satisfaction of making a major gift to a favorite charitable organization.

WHEN IS A GIFT A GIFT?

In books and articles on nonprofit organizations, much time and attention are devoted to charitable giving.

The federal tax law on charitable giving is contained in the Internal Revenue Code (IRC) and in the interpretations and expansions of it, by means of U.S. Treasury Department and IRS regulations, IRS public and private rulings, and court opinions. The IRC is rather specific on some components of the law of charitable giving—qualification of charitable donees, percentage limitations on deductibility of donations made in one year, gifts of particular types of property (such as inventory and works of art), and eligibility of various planned giving vehicles.

Despite the extent and detail of the IRC, there is a glaring omission in the rules concerning charitable giving. Oddly, this omission exists at the threshold—the law is scarce regarding the definition of the word *gift*. This omission is highly significant because there must be a *gift* in order to have a *charitable gift*.

A fundamental requirement of the charitable contribution deduction law is that the cash or property transferred to a charitable donee must be transferred as a *gift*. Just because cash is paid (or property is transferred) to a charity does not necessarily mean that the payment (or transfer) is a gift. When a university's tuition, a hospital's health care fee, or an association's dues are paid, there is no gift and thus no charitable deduction for the payment.

Most of the law on what constitutes a gift has been generated by the federal courts. The IRC and the tax regulations are essentially silent on the subject. Basically, a *gift* has two elements: it involves a transfer that is *voluntary* and is motivated by something other than *consideration* (something being received in return for a payment). Where payments are made to receive something in exchange (education, health care, and so on), the transaction is in the nature of a purchase. The law places more emphasis on what is received than on the payment given. The income tax regulations state that a transfer is not a contribution when made "with a reasonable expectation of financial return commensurate with the amount of the transfer." A single transaction can be partially a gift and partially a purchase (see discussion following); when a charity is the payee, only the gift portion is deductible.

Years ago, the U.S. Supreme Court observed that a gift is a transfer motivated by "detached or disinterested generosity." The Court also characterized a gift as a transfer stimulated "out of affection, respect, admiration, charity, or like impulses." Thus, the focus in this area for the most part has been an objective analysis, comparing what the "donor" parted with and what (if anything) the "donor" received in exchange.

Another factor, that of *donative intent* (which is hard to measure), ebbs in and out of favor. These days, the doctrine is "in." Recent tax regulations state that, for any part of a payment made in the context of a charity auction to be deductible as a charitable gift, the patron must have donative intent. More broadly, near the end of 1999, a congressional committee report was published, containing this statement: "The term 'contribution or gift' is not defined by statute, but generally is interpreted to mean a voluntary transfer of money or other property without receipt of adequate consideration *and with donative intent*. If a taxpayer receives or expects to receive a quid pro quo in exchange for a transfer to charity, the taxpayer may be able to deduct the excess of the amount transferred over the fair market value of any benefit received in return *provided the excess payment is made with the intention of making a gift*" (emphasis added).

One federal court of appeals described the matter as to what is a gift rather starkly: It is a "particularly confused issue of federal taxation." The existing IRC structure on this subject, said this court, is "cryptic," and "neither Congress nor the courts have offered any very satisfactory definition" of the terms *gift* and *contribution* (which are, for these purposes, basically synonymous).

These concepts have been revisited many times in recent years. One trouble spot has been the availability of a charitable deduction for the transfer of money to a college or university, when the transferor is then granted access to preferential seating at the institution's athletic events. The IRS refused to regard these payments as gifts, arguing that the payment results in receipt of a substantial benefit. (Congress interceded, however, and enacted a unique rule that allows 80 percent of the payment as a charitable gift.) The IRS struggled with this issue in the early 1980s, when it was popular for homes to be auctioned, with the benefits accruing to a charitable organization. In one ruling, the IRS said that those who purchase tickets from a charity are not making gifts. Various tax shelter programs involving gifts of artwork and donors' use of premiums and other items of property in response to their contributions have recently come under fire.

For years, the IRS has been advising the charitable community that, when a "donor" receives some benefit or privilege in return for a payment to charity, the payment may not, in whole or in part, constitute a deductible charitable gift. The IRS's position is that charitable organizations must advise individuals and corporations when a payment is not deductible or is only partially deductible, but the requirement lacks any sanctions. For example, suppose a charity sponsors a dinner as a fundraising event and charges $75 for a ticket. Each patron receives a dinner priced at $50 (its fair market value). The charity is supposed to advise the purchasers of the tickets that the deductible gift is $25, not $75.

Congress passed a law in 1987 requiring noncharitable organizations that solicit gifts to disclose in their fundraising literature that the contributions are not deductible. (See Chapter 12.) A report from the House Committee on Ways and Means, which accompanied the tax legislation, contained a discussion of the nondeductibility of payments to charitable organizations. The committee wrote that it "is concerned that some charitable organizations may not make sufficient disclosure, in soliciting donations, membership dues, payments for admissions or merchandise, or other support, of the extent (if any) to which the payors may be entitled to charitable deductions for such payments."

The committee's discussion focused on "memberships" in a charitable entity, typically a museum or library, where the "members" receive benefits of some monetary value, such as free admission to events for which others are charged, merchandise discounts, and free subscriptions. The committee cautioned that some or all of these membership payments are not deductible as charitable contributions.

The committee's analysis also referenced payments to a charity that are not deductible charitable gifts at all, such as the sale of raffle tickets and the auctioning of property or services. (Those who donate property to be used by a charity in an auction, however, may be entitled to a charitable deduction, within the limits described subsequently.) This legislative history states that the portion of the winning bid at a charity auction that is in excess of the fair market value of the item or service received may be deductible. The committee noted that some charities wrongfully imply that all of these payments are fully deductible, while "many other charities carefully and correctly advise their supporters of the long-standing tax rules governing the deductibility of payments made to a charitable organization in return for, or with the expectation of, a financial or economic benefit to the payor."

The committee wrote that it "anticipates" that the IRS "will monitor the extent to which taxpayers are being furnished accurate and sufficient information by charitable organizations as to the nondeductibility of payments to such organizations where benefits or privileges are received in return, so that such taxpayers can correctly compute their federal income tax liability." The committee expected the charitable community to do its part. Groups representing the community were to further "educate their members as to the applicable tax rules and provide guidance as to how charities can provide appropriate information to their supporters in this regard."

The committee fired its warning shot; six years later, it decided that the charitable community was unable to voluntarily provide the requisite disclosure to donors. In 1993, Congress included as part of major tax legislation a requirement that charitable organizations disclose to potential donors the nondeductibility (as charitable gifts) of payments to them. (Some payments of this nature are deductible as business expenses.) (See Chapter 12.)

It is thus an oddity that the statutory law can be so explicit on the consequences in tax law of making a charitable gift, yet be so skimpy in defining the threshold word *gift*.

QUALIFIED DONEES

Qualified donees are charitable organizations (including educational, religious, and scientific entities), certain fraternal organizations, certain cemetery companies, and most veterans' organizations. (These and other types of tax-exempt organizations are described in Chapter 4.) Contributions to both private and public charities are deductible, but the law favors gifts to public charities.

Federal, state, and local governmental bodies are charitable donees. State law, however, may preclude a governmental entity from accepting charitable gifts. In most jurisdictions, a charitable organization can be established to solicit deductible contributions for and make grants to governmental bodies. This is a common technique used by public schools, colleges, universities, and hospitals.

An otherwise nonqualifying organization may be allowed to receive a deductible charitable gift, where the gift property is used for charitable purposes or received by an agent for a charitable organization. An example of the former is a gift to a trade association that is earmarked for a charitable fund within the association. An example of a receiving agent would be a title-holding corporation that holds a property for charitable purposes.

GIFT PROPERTIES

Aside from the eligibility of the gift recipient, the other basic element in determining whether a charitable contribution is deductible is the nature of the property given. Basically, the distinctions are between outright giving and planned giving, and between gifts of cash and gifts of property. In many instances, the tax law differentiates between personal property and real property, and tangible property and intangible property (stocks and bonds). The value of a qualified charitable contribution of an item of property often is its fair market value.

The federal income tax treatment of gifts of property is dependent on whether the property is capital gain property. The tax law makes a distinction between *long-term capital gain* and *short-term capital gain* (although generally a net gain of the latter is taxed as ordinary income). Property that is neither long-term capital gain property nor short-term capital gain property is *ordinary income property*. These three terms are based on the tax classification of the type of revenue that would be generated upon sale of the property. Short-term capital gain property is generally treated the same as ordinary income property. Therefore, the actual distinction is between capital gain property (really long-term capital gain property) and ordinary income property.

Capital gain property is a capital asset that has appreciated in value and, if sold, would give rise to long-term capital gain. To result in long-term capital gain, property must be held for a specified period, generally 12 months. Typical forms of capital gain property are stocks, bonds, and real estate.

The charitable deduction for capital gain property is often equal to its fair market value or at least is computed using that value. Gifts of ordinary income property generally produce a deduction equivalent to the donor's cost basis in the property. The law provides exceptions to this "basis-only rule"; an example is a gift by a corporation out of its inventory.

PERCENTAGE LIMITATIONS

The extent of charitable contributions that can be deducted for a particular tax year is limited to a certain amount, which for individuals is a function of the donor's *contribution base*—essentially, the individual's adjusted gross income. This level of annual deductibility is determined by five percentage limitations. They are dependent on several factors, principally the nature of the charitable recipient and the nature of the property donated. The examples used here assume an individual donor with an annual contribution base (adjusted gross income) of $100,000.

The first three limitations apply to gifts to public charities and private operating foundations (see Chapter 7).

First, there is a percentage limitation of 50 percent of the donor's contribution base for contributions of cash and ordinary income property. A donor with a $100,000 contribution base may, in any one year, make deductible gifts up to a total of $50,000. If an individual makes contributions that exceed the 50 percent limitation, the excess generally may be carried forward and deducted in one to five subsequent years. Thus, if this donor gave $60,000 to public charities in year 1 and made no other charitable gifts, he or she would be entitled to a deduction of $50,000 in year 1 and the $10,000 would be available for deductibility in year 2.

The second percentage limitation is 30 percent of the donor's contribution base for gifts of capital gain property. A donor thus may, in any one year, contribute up to $30,000 in qualifying stocks, bonds, real estate, and like property, and receive a charitable deduction for that amount. Any excess (more than 30 percent) is subject to the carryforward rule. If a donor gave $50,000 in capital gain property in year 1 and made no other charitable gifts that year, he or she would be entitled to a charitable contribution deduction of $30,000 in year 1 and the $20,000 would be available in year 2.

A donor who makes gifts of cash and capital gain property to public charities (or private operating foundations) in any one year generally must use a blend of these percentage limitations. For example, if the donor in year 1 gives $50,000 in cash and $30,000 in appreciated capital gain property to a public charity, his or her charitable deduction in year 1 is $30,000 of capital gain property and $20,000 of cash (to keep the deduction within the overall 50 percent ceiling); the other $30,000 of cash is carried forward to year 2 (or years 2 through 5, depending on the donor's circumstances).

The third percentage limitation allows a donor of capital gain property to use the 50 percent limitation, instead of the 30 percent limitation, where the amount of the contribution is reduced by all of the unrealized appreciation in the value of the property. This election is usually made by donors who want a larger deduction in the year of the gift for an item of property that has not appreciated in value to a great extent.

The fourth and fifth percentage limitations apply to gifts to private foundations and certain other charitable donees (other than public charities and private operating foundations). These donees are generally veterans' and fraternal organizations.

Under the fourth percentage limitation, contributions of cash and ordinary income property to private foundations and other entities may not exceed 30 percent of the individual donor's contribution base. The carryover rules apply to this type of gift. If the donor gives $50,000 in cash to one or more private foundations in year 1, his or her charitable deduction for that year (assuming no other charitable gifts) is $30,000, with the balance of $20,000 carried forward into subsequent years (up to year 5).

The carryover rules blend with the first three percentage limitations. For example, if in year 1 the donor gave $65,000 to charity, of which $25,000 went to a public charity and $40,000 to private foundation, his or her charitable deduction for that year would be $50,000: $30,000 to the private foundation and $20,000 to the public charity. The remaining $10,000 of the gift to the foundation and the remaining $5,000 of the gift to the public charity would be carried forward into year 2.

The fifth percentage limitation is 20 percent of the contribution base for gifts of capital gain property to private foundations and other charitable donees. There is a carryforward for any excess deduction amount. For example, if a donor gives appreciated securities, having a value of $30,000, to a private foundation in year 1, his or her charitable deduction for year 1 (assuming no other charitable gifts) is $20,000; the remaining $10,000 may be carried forward.

Deductible charitable contributions by corporations in any tax year may not exceed 10 percent of pretax net income. Excess amounts may be carried forward and deducted in subsequent years (up to five years). For gifts by corporations, the federal tax laws do not differentiate between gifts to public charities and private foundations. As an illustration, a corporation that grosses $1 million in a year and incurs $900,000 in expenses in that year (not including charitable gifts) may generally contribute to charity and deduct in that year an amount up to $10,000 (10 percent of $100,000); in computing its taxes, this corporation would report taxable income of $90,000. If the corporation instead gave $20,000 in that year, the numbers would stay the same, except that the corporation would have a $10,000 charitable contribution carryforward.

A corporation that uses the accrual method of accounting can elect to treat a contribution as having been made in a tax year if it is actually donated during the first two-and-a-half months of the following year. Corporate gifts of property are generally subject to the deduction reduction rules, discussed next.

A business organization that is a *flow-through entity* generates a different tax result when it comes to charitable deductions. (These organizations include partnerships, other joint ventures, small business (S) corporations, and limited liability companies.) These organizations, even though they may make charitable gifts, do not claim charitable contribution deductions. Instead, the deduction is passed through to the members or other owners on an allocable basis, and they claim their share of the deduction on their tax returns.

DEDUCTION REDUCTION RULES

A donor (individual or corporation) who makes a gift of *ordinary income property* to any charity (public or private) must confine the charitable deduction to the amount of the cost basis of the property. The deduction is not based on the fair market value of the property; it must be reduced by the amount that would have been gain (ordinary income) if the property had been sold. As an example, if a donor gave to a charity an item of ordinary income property having a value of $1,000 for which he or she paid $600, the charitable deduction would be $600.

Any donor who makes a gift of *capital gain property* to a public charity generally can compute the charitable deduction using the property's fair market value at the time of the gift, regardless of the cost basis and with no taxation of the appreciation (the capital gain inherent in the property). Suppose, however, a donor makes a gift of capital gain tangible personal property (e.g., a work of art) to a public charity and the gift's use by the donee is unrelated to its tax-exempt purposes. The donor must reduce the deduction by an amount equal to all of the long-term capital gain that would have been recognized had the donor sold the property at its fair market value as of the date of the contribution.

Suppose a donee charitable organization disposes of an item of tangible personal property for which a deduction of more than $5,000 was claimed within three years of contribution of the deduction. If the disposition is in the year of the gift, the donor's charitable deduction generally is confined to the basis amount. In the case of a subsequent disposition, the donor must include as ordinary income any amount of the claimed deduction that is in excess of the donor's basis. This recapture rule includes reporting requirements and a penalty for failure to comply.

Generally, a donor who makes a gift of capital gain property to a private foundation must reduce the amount of the otherwise allowable deduction by all of the appreciation element in the gift property. An individual, however, is allowed full fair market value for a contribution to a private foundation of certain publicly traded stock.

TWICE BASIS DEDUCTIONS

As a general rule, when a corporation makes a charitable gift of property from its inventory, the resulting charitable deduction cannot exceed an amount equal to the donor's cost basis in the donated property. In most instances, this basis amount is rather small, being equal to the cost of producing the property. Under certain circumstances, however, corporate donors can receive a greater charitable deduction for gifts out of their inventory. Where the tests are satisfied, the deduction can be equal to cost basis plus one-half of the appreciated value of the property. The deduction may not, in any event, exceed an amount equal to twice the property's cost basis.

Five special requirements have to be met for this twice-basis charitable deduction to be available:

1. The donated property must be used by the charitable donee for a related use.

2. The donated property must be used solely for the care of the ill, the needy, or infants.

3. The property may not be transferred by the donee in exchange for money, other property, or services.

4. The donor must receive a written statement from the donee representing that the use and disposition of the donated property will be in conformance with these rules.

5. Where the donated property is subject to regulation under the Federal Food, Drug, and Cosmetic Act, the property must fully satisfy the Act's requirements on the date of transfer and for the previous 180 days.

For these rules to apply, the donee must be a public charity—that is, it cannot be a private foundation or a private operating foundation. An S corporation—the tax status of many businesses—cannot utilize these rules.

Similarly computed deductions are available for contributions of food and book inventory, scientific property used for research, and contributions of computer technology and equipment for educational purposes.

OTHER GIFT PROPERTIES

Congress has been busy in recent years in creating charitable giving rules for specific types of property, introducing in the process considerable complexity as to the law of charitable giving. Consider, for example, the law on charitable gifts of intellectual property (patents, copyrights, trademarks, trade names, and the like). Contributions of this type of property are initially subject to the rule where the charitable deduction is confined to the donor's basis in the property (see foregoing discussion). In this context, however, additional charitable deductions (up to 12) arise equal to various percentages of net income (from 10 to 100 percent) that flows to the charitable donee. The donee must provide certain information to the IRS and the donor.

As another illustration, special rules apply with respect to charitable gifts of vehicles, such as automobiles, boats, and airplanes. Here, the amount of the charitable deduction depends on the nature of the use of the vehicle by the donee organization. If the charitable organization sells the vehicle without any significant intervening use or material improvement of the vehicle, the amount of the deduction cannot exceed the gross proceeds received from the sale. These rules are accompanied by extensive substantiation requirements and penalties.

A donor may take a deduction for a charitable contribution of a fractional interest in tangible personal property as long as the donor satisfies the general deduction requirements and, in subsequent years, makes additional charitable contributions of interests in the same property. Recapture of the income and gift tax charitable deductions can occur under certain circumstances, such as where the donor's remaining interest in the property is not contributed to the same donee within ten years or where the donee does not timely take substantial physical possession of the property or use the property for an exempt purpose.

Generally, a charitable deduction for a gift of clothing or household items is not allowed unless the gift item is in good used condition or better. A deduction may be allowed for a charitable contribution of an item of clothing or a household item not in good used condition or better if the amount claimed for the item is more than $500 and the donor includes with the tax return a qualified appraisal with respect to the property.

There are even rules pertaining to charitable contributions of taxidermy. The amount allowed as a deduction for a charitable gift of taxidermy property that is contributed by the person who prepared, stuffed, or mounted the property is the lesser of the donor's basis in the property or its fair market value.

PARTIAL INTEREST GIFTS

Most charitable gifts are of all ownership of a property—the donor parts with all right, title, and interest in the property. A gift of a *partial interest* is also possible—a contribution of less than a donor's entire interest in the property.

As a general rule, charitable deductions for gifts of partial interests in property, including the right to use property, are not available. The exceptions, which are many, include gifts made in trust form (using a *split-interest trust*); gifts of an outright remainder interest in a personal residence or farm; gifts of an undivided portion of one's entire interest in a property; gifts of a lease on, option to purchase, or easement with respect to real property granted in perpetuity to a public charity exclusively for conservation purposes; and a remainder interest in real property granted to a public charity exclusively for conservation purposes.

Contributions of income interests in property in trust are basically confined to the use of charitable lead trusts. Aside from a charitable gift annuity and gifts of remainder interests, there is no charitable deduction for a contribution of a remainder interest in property unless it is in trust and is one of three types: a charitable remainder annuity trust, a charitable remainder unitrust, or a pooled income fund. (The concept of *partial interest* gifts, more popularly known as *planned giving*, is the subject of Chapter 19.)

Defective charitable split-interest trusts may be reformed to preserve the charitable deduction where certain requirements are satisfied.

GIFTS OF OR USING INSURANCE

One underutilized type of charitable giving involves life insurance. To secure an income tax deduction, the gift must include all rights of ownership in a life insurance policy. Thus, an individual can donate a fully paid-up life insurance policy to a charitable organization and deduct (for income tax purposes) its value. Or, an individual can acquire a life insurance policy, give it to a charity, pay the premiums, and receive a charitable deduction for each premium payment made.

For the donation of an insurance policy to be valid, the charitable organization must be able to demonstrate that it has an insurable interest in the life of the donor of the policy. From an income tax deduction standpoint, it is not enough for a donor to simply name a charitable organization as a beneficiary of a life insurance policy. There is no income tax charitable contribution deduction for this philanthropic act. Although the life insurance proceeds become part of the donor's estate, there will be an offsetting estate tax charitable deduction.

A warning: There is a use of life insurance in the charitable giving context that essentially has been outlawed and thus should be avoided. This use is embodied in the *charitable split-interest insurance plan* (see Chapter 19).

APPRAISAL RULES

The law contains requirements relating to proof when charitable deductions for contributions of property are claimed by an individual, a closely held corporation, a personal service corporation, a partnership, or an S corporation. These requirements, when applicable, must be complied with if the deduction is to be allowed.

The requirements apply to contributions of property (other than money and publicly traded securities) if the aggregate claimed or reported value of the property (and all similar items of property for which deductions for charitable contributions are claimed or reported by the same donor for the same tax year, whether or not donated to the same donee) is in excess of $5,000. The phrase *similar items of property* means property of the same generic category or type, including stamps, coins, lithographs, paintings, books, nonpublicly traded stock, land, or buildings.

For each gift of this type, the donor must obtain a *qualified appraisal* and attach an *appraisal summary* to the tax return on which the deduction is claimed. For a gift of nonpublicly traded stock, the claimed value of which does not exceed $10,000 but is greater than $5,000, the donor does not have to obtain a qualified appraisal but must attach a partially completed appraisal summary form to the tax or information return on which the deduction is claimed.

A *qualified appraisal* is an appraisal made no more than 60 days prior to the date of the contribution of the appraised property. The appraisal must be prepared, signed, and dated by a *qualified appraiser* and cannot involve a prohibited type of appraisal fee.

Certain information must be included in the qualified appraisal:

- A sufficiently detailed description of the property
- The physical condition of the property (in the case of tangible property)
- The date (or expected date) of contribution
- The terms of any agreement or understanding concerning the use or disposition of the property

- The name, address, and Social Security number of the qualified appraiser
- The qualifications of the qualified appraiser
- A statement that the appraisal was prepared for tax purposes
- The date or dates on which the property was valued
- The appraised fair market value of the property on the date (or expected date) of contribution
- The method of valuation used to determine the fair market value
- The specific basis for the valuation
- A description of the fee arrangement between the donor and the appraiser

The qualified appraisal must be received by the donor before the due date (including extensions) of the return on which the deduction for the contributed property is first claimed. If a deduction is first claimed on an amended return, the appraisal must be received before the date on which the return is filed.

One qualified appraisal for a group of similar items of property contributed in the same tax year is acceptable, as long as the appraisal includes all of the required information for each item. If a group of items has an aggregate value appraised at $100 or less, the appraiser may select these items for a group description rather than a specific description of each item.

The appraisal summary must be on IRS Form 8283, signed and dated by the donee and qualified appraiser (or appraisers), and attached to the tax return on which the donor is first claiming or reporting the deduction for the appraised property. The signature by the donee does not represent concurrence in the appraised value of the contributed property.

Certain information must be included in the appraisal summary:

- The name and taxpayer identification number of the donor
- A sufficient description of the property
- A summary of the physical condition of the property (in the case of tangible property)
- The manner and date of acquisition of the property
- The basis of the property
- The name, address, and taxpayer identification number of the donee
- The date the donee received the property
- The name, address, and taxpayer identification number of the qualified appraiser (or appraisers)
- The appraised fair market value of the property on the date of contribution
- A declaration by the qualified appraiser

The rules pertaining to separate versus group appraisals apply to appraisal summaries. A donor who contributes similar items of property to more than one charitable donee must attach a separate appraisal summary for each donee.

If the donor is a partnership or an S corporation, it must provide a copy of the appraisal summary to every partner or shareholder who is allocated a share in the deduction for a charitable contribution of property described in the appraisal summary. The partner or shareholder must attach the appraisal summary to his or her tax return.

The *qualified appraiser* declares on the appraisal summary that he or she holds himself or herself out to the public as an appraiser; because of the competencies described in the appraisal, he or she is qualified to make appraisals of the type of property being valued. The appraiser also states that he or she understands that a false or fraudulent overstatement of the value of the property described in the qualified appraisal or appraisal summary may subject the appraiser to a civil penalty for aiding and abetting an understatement of tax liability, and consequently the appraiser may have appraisals disregarded.

An individual is not a qualified appraiser if the donor had knowledge of facts that would cause a reasonable person to expect the appraiser to falsely overstate the value of the donated property. The donor, donee, or certain other related persons cannot be a qualified appraiser of the property involved in the transaction. (In formulating these rules, the government did not include in the criteria certain professional standards or the establishment of a registry of qualified appraisers.) More than one appraiser may appraise donated property, as long as each appraiser complies with the requirements.

Generally, no part of the fee arrangement for a qualified appraisal can be based on a percentage (or set of percentages) of the appraised value of the property. If a fee arrangement is based in any way on the amount of the appraised value of the property that is allowed as a charitable deduction, it is treated as a fee based on a percentage of the appraised value of the property. (In certain circumstances, this rule does not apply to appraisal fees paid to a generally recognized association that regulates appraisers.)

These rules are *directory* rather than *mandatory*. This means that the *doctrine of substantial compliance* applies. In applying this doctrine, the courts look at whether the government's requirements relate to the substance of the status. If so, strict adherence to all statutory and regulatory requirements is necessary. One court held that these appraisal substantiation requirements "do not relate to the substance or essence of whether or not a charitable contribution was actually made."

RECORDKEEPING RULES

In the case of a charitable contribution of money, irrespective of the amount, applicable recordkeeping requirements are satisfied only if the donor maintains, as a record of the contribution, a bank record or a written communication from the donee showing the name of the donee organization, the date of the contribution, and the amount of the contribution.

For this purpose, a *bank record* includes canceled checks, bank or credit union statements, and credit card statements. Contributions of *money* include those made in cash or by check, electronic funds transfer, credit card, or payroll deduction. For payroll deduction purposes, the donor should retain a pay stub, a wage statement (Form W-2), or other document furnished by the employer showing the total amount withheld for charity, along with the pledge card showing the name of the charity.

For contributions of property other than money, a corporate or individual donor must obtain a receipt from the charitable donee and a reliable written record of specified information about the donated property. The receipt must include the name of the donee, the date and location of the contribution, and a detailed description of the property (including its value). A receipt is not required where the gift is made in circumstances where it is impractical to obtain a receipt, such as when a donor drops off used clothing at a charity's receiving site after business hours.

A donor of property that has appreciated in value must maintain a *reliable written record* of the following specified information for each item of property:

- The name and address of the charitable donee

- The date and location of the contribution

- A detailed description of the property (including the value of the property) and, in the case of securities, the name of the issuing company, the type of security, and whether it is regularly traded on a stock exchange or in an over-the-counter market

- The fair market value of the property at the time of the gift, the method utilized in determining the value, and a copy of the report signed by the appraiser

- The cost or other basis of the property if it is ordinary income property or another type of property where the deduction must be reduced by the gain

- Where the gift is of a remainder interest or an income interest (see Chapter 17), the total amount claimed as a deduction for the year because of the gift, and the amount claimed as a deduction in any prior year or years for gifts of other interests in the property

- The terms of any agreement or understanding concerning the use or disposition of the property—any restriction on the charity's right to use or dispose of the property, a retention or conveyance of the right to the income from the donated property, or an earmarking of the property for a particular use.

Additional rules apply to charitable gifts of property other than money for which the donor claims a deduction in excess of $500. The donor is required to maintain additional records showing how the property was acquired and the property's cost or other basis, if it was held for less than six months prior to the date of gift. For property held for six months or more preceding the date of contribution, the cost or other basis information should be submitted by the donor if it is available.

These rules apply with respect to small gifts. They are superseded for larger gifts by the two bodies of law discussed next.

GIFT SUBSTANTIATION RULES

The federal tax law contains charitable gift substantiation rules. Under this body of law, donors who make a separate charitable contribution of $250 or more in a year, for which they claim a charitable contribution deduction, must obtain written substantiation from the donee charitable organization.

More specifically, the rule is that the charitable deduction is not allowed for a separate contribution of $250 or more unless the donor has written substantiation from the charitable donee of the contribution in the form of a contemporaneous written acknowledgment. Thus, donors cannot rely solely on a canceled check as substantiation for a gift of $250 or more. Canceled checks suffice, however, as substantiation for gifts of less than $250.

An acknowledgment meets this requirement if it includes the following information: (1) the amount of money and a description (but not value) of any property other than money that was contributed; (2) whether the donee organization provided any goods or services in consideration, in whole or in part, for any money or property contributed; and (3) a description and good-faith estimate of the value of any goods or services involved or, if the goods or services consist solely of intangible religious benefits, a statement to that effect. The phrase *intangible religious benefit* means "any intangible religious benefit which is provided by an organization organized exclusively for religious purposes and which generally is not sold in a commercial transaction outside the donative context." An acknowledgment is considered to be *contemporaneous* if the contributor obtains the acknowledgment on or before the earlier of (1) the date on which the donor filed a tax return for the taxable year in which the contribution was made or (2) the due date (including extensions) for filing the return.

There are other defined terms. The phrase *goods or services* means money, property, services, benefits, and privileges. Certain goods or services, however, are disregarded for these purposes: (1) those that have insubstantial value and (2) certain annual membership benefits offered to an individual in exchange for a payment of $75 or less per year. A charitable organization provides goods or services *in consideration* for a donor's transfer if, at the time the donor makes the payment to the charity, the donor receives or expects to receive goods or services in exchange for the payment. Goods or services a charitable organization provides in consideration for a payment by a donor include goods or services provided in a year other than the year in which the payment was made. A *good-faith estimate* means a charitable organization's estimate of the fair market value of any goods or services, without regard to the manner in which the organization in fact made the estimate.

As noted, the substantiation rule applies in respect to separate payments. Separate payments are generally treated as separate contributions and are not aggregated for the purpose of applying the $250 threshold. In cases of contributions paid by withholdings from wages, the deduction from each paycheck is treated as a separate payment. Congress has provided the IRS with authorization to issue anti-abuse rules in this area (addressing practices such as the writing of multiple checks to the same charity on the same date).

The written acknowledgment of a separate gift is not required to take any particular form. Thus, acknowledgments may be made by letter, postcard, e-mail, or computer-generated form. A donee charitable organization may prepare a separate acknowledgment for each contribution or may provide donors with periodic (e.g., annual) acknowledgments that set forth the required information for each contribution of $250 or more made by the donor during the period.

The U.S. Tax Court has made the administration of this area of the law much more difficult. This is because it held that these rules apply with respect to verbal (unwritten) *expectations* or *understandings* a donor may have of the charitable recipient when making a contribution. This court thus equated, for this purpose, expectations with goods or services. How representatives of charitable organizations are supposed to divine their donors' inner thoughts when giving is not clear.

It is the responsibility of a donor to obtain the substantiation and maintain it in his or her records. (Again, the charitable contribution deduction is dependent on compliance with these rules.) A charitable organization that knowingly provides a false written substantiation to a donor may be subject to a penalty for aiding and abetting an understatement of tax liability.

These substantiation rules do not apply to transfers of property to charitable remainder trusts or to charitable lead trusts. The requirements are, however, applicable to transfers to pooled income funds. (See Chapter 19.) In the case of these funds, the contemporaneous written acknowledgement must state that the contribution was transferred to the charitable organization's pooled fund and indicate whether any goods or services (in addition to the income interest) were provided in exchange for the transfer. The contemporaneous written acknowledgement, however, need not include a good-faith estimate of the income interest.

QUID PRO QUO CONTRIBUTIONS

Among the practices that entail payments that are partially gifts and partially payments for goods or services are special-event programs, whereby the patron receives something of value (such as a ticket to a theater performance or a dinner, the opportunity to play in a sports tournament, or participation in an auction), yet makes a payment in excess of that value amount. In these circumstances, the amount paid that is in excess of the value received by the patron is a deductible charitable gift.

The IRS also held that payments by corporate sponsors of college and university bowl games are not charitable gifts to the bowl game associations, but must be treated by the associations as forms of unrelated business income because the corporate sponsors received a valuable package of advertising services. This position led to IRS and congressional hearings, proposed regulations, and finally legislation (enacted in 1997). This legislation shields *qualified sponsorship payments* from taxation. A payment of this nature is one made by a person engaged in a trade or business, from which the person received no substantial return benefit other than the use or acknowledgment of the name or logo (or product lines) of the person's trade or business in connection with the organization's activities. This use or acknowledgment does not include advertising of the person's products or services. *Advertising* entails qualitative or comparative language, price information or other indications of savings or value, or an endorsement or other inducement to purchase, sell, or use the products or services. (See Chapter 13.)

The federal tax law imposes certain disclosure requirements on charitable organizations that receive *quid pro quo contributions*.

A quid pro quo contribution is a payment made partly as a contribution and partly in consideration for goods or services provided to the payor by the donee organization. The term does not include a payment made to an organization, operated exclusively for religious purposes, in return for which the donor receives solely an intangible religious benefit that generally is not sold in a commercial transaction outside the donative context.

Specifically, if a charitable organization (other than a state, a possession of the United States, a political subdivision of a state or possession, the United States, and the District of Columbia) receives a quid pro quo contribution in excess of $75, the organization must, in connection with the solicitation or receipt of the contribution, provide a written statement which (1) informs the donor that the amount of the contribution that is deductible for federal income tax purposes is limited to the excess of the amount of any money and the value of any property other than money contributed by the donor over the value of the goods or services provided by the organization, and (2) provides the donor with a good-faith estimate of the value of the goods or services.

In other words, this law is designed to cause a donor or patron to know that the only amount deductible in these circumstances as a charitable gift (if any) is the amount paid to the charity in excess of any benefits provided by the charity. A charitable organization may use any reasonable methodology in making this good-faith estimate as long as it applies the methodology in good faith. A good-faith estimate of the value of goods or services that are not generally available in a commercial transaction may be determined by reference to the fair market value of similar or comparable goods or services. Goods or services may be similar or comparable even though they do not have the unique qualities of the goods or services that are being valued. Of course, where the goods or services are available on a commercial basis, the commercial value is used.

For purposes of the $75 threshold, separate payments made at different times of the year with respect to fundraising events generally will not be aggregated. The IRS may, however, issue antiabuse rules in this area (addressing such practices as the writing of multiple checks for the same transaction).

These rules do not apply where only *de minimis* token goods or services (such as key chains and bumper stickers) are provided to the donor. In defining these terms, prior IRS pronouncements are followed. Nor do these rules apply to transactions that do not have a donative element (such as the charging of tuition by a school, the charging of health care fees by a hospital, or the sale of items by a museum).

The law in this area is vague on the matter of *celebrity presence*. If a celebrity is present at an event and does nothing, or does something that is different from that for which he or she is celebrated, the value of the presence is zero. (An example of the latter is a tour of a museum conducted by an artist whose works are on display.) Presumably, if the celebrity performs as such, the charitable organization must utilize the commercial value of the performance.

No part of a payment can be considered a contribution unless the payor intended to make a payment in an amount that is in excess of the fair market value of the goods or services received. This requirement of *donative intent* has particular application in the instance of auctions conducted by charitable organizations. The procedure preferred by the law is that a charity holding an auction will publish a catalog that meets the requirements for a written disclosure statement, including the charity's good-faith estimate of the value of items that will be available for bidding.

A penalty is imposed on charitable organizations that do not satisfy these disclosure requirements. For failure to make the required disclosure in connection with a quid pro quo contribution of more than $75, there is a penalty of $10 per contribution, not to exceed $5,000 per fundraising event or mailing. An organization may be able to avoid this penalty if it can show that the failure to comply was due to reasonable cause.

In general, a person can rely on a contemporaneous written acknowledgment provided in the substantiation context (described previously) or a written disclosure statement provided in the quid pro quo transaction setting. An individual may not, however, treat an estimate of the value of goods or services as their fair market value if he or she knows, or has reasons to know, that the treatment is unreasonable.

REPORTING RULES

If a charitable organization donee sells or otherwise disposes of gift property within three years after receipt of the property, it generally must file an information return (Form 8282) with the IRS. Copies of this information return must be provided to the donor and retained by the donee.

This information return must include the name, address, and taxpayer identification number of the donor and the donee; a detailed description of the property; the date of the contribution; the amount received on the disposition; and the date of the disposition.

A donee that receives from a corporation a charitable contribution valued in excess of $5,000 generally does not have to file a donee information return.

FOCUS: Campaign to Clean Up America

The Campaign to Clean Up America (CCUA), as a qualified donee, desires to be financially supported largely by charitable contributions. At the outset, these gifts are likely to be cash, in relatively small amounts. As the organization grows and its programs take hold in communities, however, larger gifts of cash should result, as well as gifts of property. The CCUA will be embarking on a gift solicitation program, relying at the beginning principally on a direct-mall effort and perhaps a telemarketing program.

The CCUA is in the process of preparing literature generally describing the deductibility of contributions of cash and property. For the larger gifts, the CCUA will generally advise donors about the appraisal, substantiation, and recordkeeping requirements.

The CCUA hopes to receive gifts from corporations out of their inventory (such as trash bags and trash collection equipment) and will be developing the requisite documentation to support the deductibility of those gifts.

The CCUA will be looking for ways to integrate its general charitable giving program with its planned giving program. (See Chapter 19.) Its fundraising activities will be registered with the pertinent states (see Chapter 12).

CHAPTER TWELVE

Government Regulation
of Fundraising

Those who manage or advise nonprofit organizations are often unaware of all of the law—federal, state, and local—that is applicable to the organizations and the individuals involved.

Nowhere are the gaps in knowledge more pronounced than in the field of fundraising regulation. The sheer magnitude of state governments' regulation of charitable gift solicitation is often underestimated, even unknown. The role of the federal government when it comes to the regulation of some aspects of nonprofit organizations' fundraising functions is a best-kept secret. Governmental regulation of fundraising is becoming so pervasive and onerous, and yet so misunderstood and even ignored despite its rapid growth, that it is next to impossible to place this body of law in some meaningful context.

FUNDRAISING REGULATION AT THE STATE LEVEL

Governmental regulation of fundraising traditionally has been at the state level. Forty-six states have some form of a *charitable solicitation act* (a statute regulating charitable fundraising). Many counties, cities, and towns compound the process with similar ordinances. As discussed further on in this chapter, the federal government has also become heavily involved in the regulation of fundraising for charity.

The scope of the laws on fundraising is grossly misunderstood. Most fundraising charitable organizations know that they must comply with the charitable solicitation act (if any) of the state in which they are principally located. They may not know, however, that these laws frequently mandate compliance by professional fundraisers, commercial co-venturers, and others who assist in fundraising endeavors, or that they are expected to adhere to the law in *each state* in which they are soliciting funds. A charitable organization that is fundraising in all the states must be in compliance annually with the laws of 46 of these states. In addition, those who aid charities in their fundraising programs must comply with these laws. Administrators of county and city ordinances on fundraising usually expect the nationwide charities to comply with them as well.

What does *compliance* with these laws mean? Compliance varies from state to state, but essentially it means that a charity must obtain permission from the appropriate regulatory authorities before a fundraising effort can begin. The permission is usually termed a *permit* or *license*, acquired as the result of filing a *registration*. Most states also require a filing fee, a bond, and the registration of professional fundraisers and others who will assist in the effort. The registration is usually updated by annually filing a report on the fundraising program, including financial information.

This process would be amply difficult if the registration and reporting requirements were uniform. The staff time and expense required to obtain, maintain, and disseminate the information throughout the states can be enormous. Historically, there has not been uniformity, although in recent years some progress has been made toward use of a uniform registration form by several states. Charities must constantly face differing registration and reporting forms, accounting methods, due dates, enforcement attitudes, and other substantial twists in the states' regulations. All of this becomes even more nightmarish when fundraising by means of the Internet is contemplated, because the charity is then (presumably) soliciting funds in every state, county, city, and town.

It is not feasible to give a brief summary of each of the states' charitable solicitation acts. Instead, what follows is an analysis of this type of law, based on the principal features of these acts as found in the majority of these statutes. This should provide some insight as to the scope of some of the fundraising regulation laws.

(a) Definitions

The typical law opens with a series of definitions. A fundraising professional is often termed a *professional fundraiser*, frequently defined as a "person who for compensation plans, manages, advises, consults, or prepares material for, or with respect to, the solicitation in this state of contributions for a charitable organization, but who does not solicit contributions and who does not employ, procure, or engage any compensated person to solicit contributions." A bona fide salaried officer, employee, or volunteer of a charitable organization is not a fundraising counsel, nor are lawyers, investment counselors, or bankers.

A *paid solicitor* is often defined as a "person who for compensation performs for a charitable organization any service in connection with which contributions are, or will be, solicited in this state by such compensated person or by any compensated person he employs, procures, or engages, directly or indirectly, to solicit." There is an exclusion from this definition for officers, employees, and volunteers of charitable organizations.

Other terms often defined in these laws are *charitable organization, solicit, solicitation, charitable purpose, contribution, commercial co-venturer,* and *charitable sales promotion.*

(b) Regulation of Charitable Organizations

Generally, every charitable organization (unless exempt) desiring to solicit contributions in the state must, in advance, file a registration statement with the appropriate state agency. This requirement applies whether the charity will solicit on its own behalf, have funds solicited for it by another organization, or be the recipient of gifts generated through the services of a commercial co-venturer or paid solicitor.

If the organization is in compliance, the state issues a certificate of registration, and the solicitation can proceed. The statement must be filed during every year in which the charitable organization is soliciting in the state. A registration fee is levied.

Unusually, a charitable organization is also required to file an annual financial report. An organization with gross support and revenue not exceeding a certain amount (the specific amount varies from state to state) is, however, often excused from filing an annual financial report. The financial information may be provided by submitting a copy of the annual information return filed with the IRS. (See Chapter 9.) Where the gross support and revenue of a charitable organization exceeds a certain amount (again, it may vary), the organization must submit audited financial statements.

Churches, other religious organizations, and charitable organizations closely affiliated with them usually are exempt from the registration requirements. (This exception, while understandable from a constitutional law standpoint, carries with it a certain amount of irony, in that many fundraising abuses are undertaken in the name of religion.) Also often exempt are organizations that engage in small annual solicitations—that is, they do not receive gifts in excess of a certain amount or do not receive gifts from more than a few persons—but sometimes only if all of their functions (including fundraising) are carried on by persons who are not paid for their services.

Under some laws, every charitable organization engaged in a solicitation in the state must disclose, at the point of solicitation, its name, address, telephone number, a "full and fair" description of the charitable program that is the subject of the campaign, and the fact that a financial statement is available upon request. Where the services of a paid solicitor are utilized, additional disclosures at the point of solicitation are required, as described subsequently.

(c) Regulation of Professional Fundraisers

Many state charitable solicitation acts go beyond the regulation of fundraising charities and impose obligations on professional fundraisers and paid solicitors (see the following section regarding the latter). The definitions of these terms vary considerably—an additional source of confusion generated by these laws.

Conceptually, a professional fundraiser is a person (often a consultant) retained by a charity who does not actually solicit gifts but rather designs and implements a fundraising program. (Employees of charitable organizations are usually excluded from professional fundraiser status for purposes of these laws.) Normally, they do not take custody of the charitable gifts. They are usually paid a fixed fee for their advice in structuring a fundraising program.

Thus, under this purist conceptualization, the actual asking for and receipt of charitable gifts is left to others. In the modern era, however, this distinction has collapsed and the functions overlap. Those who plan may also solicit. Thus, the confusion in the law mirrors reality.

The registration is annual, for a fee. The application contains such information as the state may require. The bond amount varies from state to state. Within 90 days following the completion of a solicitation campaign, and on the anniversary of the commencement of a campaign longer than one year, the professional fundraiser must account in writing to the charitable organization for all income received and expenses paid.

Often, every contract between a charitable organization and a professional fundraiser must be in writing. The professional fundraiser must file it prior to performing any material services. From the contract, the state regulator must be able to identify the services the professional fundraiser is to provide.

(d) Regulation of Paid Solicitors

A paid solicitor is often required to register annually with the state prior to any activity—using an application containing the information the state may require—and to pay a fee. At that time, the solicitor must post a bond.

Continuing with the purist conceptualization previously noted, a paid solicitor is an (perhaps the only) active participant in the gift solicitation process. He or she literally asks for gifts. This can be done by any form of communication—for example, in person (as in door-to-door or on a street corner); by telephone, letter, or other publication (such as a newsletter or journal); by fax; or through an Internet website. Again, however, this fine distinction is often abandoned in modern charitable fundraising.

In many instances, prior to a solicitation campaign, the paid solicitor must file with the state a copy of its contract with the charitable organization. In addition, the paid solicitor must file with the state a solicitation notice. In a typical requirement, this notice must include a "copy of the contract . . . , the projected dates when soliciting will commence and terminate, the location and telephone number from where the solicitation will be conducted, the name and residence address of each person responsible for directing and supervising the conduct of the campaign, a statement as to whether the paid solicitor will at any time have custody of contributions, and a full and fair description of the charitable program for which the solicitation campaign is being carried out."

Often, every contract between a paid solicitor and a charitable organization must be in writing and must "clearly state the respective obligations" of the parties. The contract must state a fixed percentage of the gross revenue (or a reasonable estimate of it) from the solicitation campaign, which is the amount the charitable organization will receive. The stated minimum percentage may not include the expenses of the solicitation paid by the charity.

Many of these laws impose a *point-of-solicitation* requirement, for which paid solicitors are responsible. Under this rule, before an oral request or within a written request for a contribution, the potential donor must be told that the solicitor is a paid solicitor and that the charitable organization will receive a percentage of gross receipts as stated in the contract. The disclosures must be "clear" and "conspicuous." In an oral solicitation (such as by telephone), a written receipt must be sent to each contributor within five days of the gift, and it must include a clear and conspicuous disclosure of the point-of-solicitation items.

Within 90 days after the completion of a solicitation campaign and on the anniversary of the start of a solicitation campaign longer than one year, the paid solicitor often is required to file with the state a financial report for the campaign.

A paid solicitor may be required to maintain certain information during each solicitation campaign and for at least three years afterward—the name and address of each contributor, the date and amount of each contribution, the name and residence of each employee or other person involved in the solicitation, and all expenses incurred in the course of the solicitation campaign.

Monies collected by a paid solicitor may have to be deposited in a bank account in a timely manner and the account must be in the name of the charitable organization involved. The charitable organization may have to have sole control over withdrawals from the account.

Special rules may be applicable to situations where paid solicitors represent that tickets to an event will be donated for use by other persons. These rules include limitations on solicitations for donated tickets and recordkeeping requirements.

(e) Regulation of Commercial Co-Venturing

Under the laws of some states, every charitable sales promotion must be the subject of a written contract, when a charitable organization hires a commercial co-venturer. A copy of the contract must be filed with the state prior to the start of the promotion.

The law defines a *commercial co-venturer* as a "person who for profit is regularly and primarily engaged in trade or commerce other than in connection with soliciting for charitable organizations or purposes and who conducts a charitable sales promotion." A *charitable sales promotion* is defined as "an advertising or sales campaign, conducted by a commercial co-venturer, which represents that the purchase or use of goods or services offered by the commercial co-venturer will benefit, in whole or in part, a charitable organization or purpose." This is also known as *embedded giving*.

The charitable sales promotion contract must include a statement of the goods or services to be offered to the public, the geographic area where the promotion will occur, the starting and concluding dates of the promotion, the manner in which the name of the charitable organization will be used (including the representation to be made to the public as to the amount or percent per unit of goods and services purchased or used that will benefit the charitable organization), a provision for a final accounting on a per-unit basis by the commercial co-venturer to the charitable organization, and the date by when and the manner in which the benefit will be conferred on the charitable organization.

The commercial co-venturer is required to disclose in each advertisement for the charitable sales promotion the amount per unit of goods or services purchased or used that will benefit the charitable organization or purpose. This amount may be expressed as a dollar amount or percentage.

The final accounting must be retained by the commercial co-venturer for three years and must be made available to the state upon request.

Commercial co-venturers (or charitable sales promotions) are becoming quite common in the United States. Often, a merchant will offer to pay a portion of proceeds from the sales of certain products (or services), during a stated period, to a charitable organization. For example, the management of a fast-food restaurant may advertise that, over the coming weekend, five cents from the sale of every cheeseburger will be contributed to a named charity. This is done both to encourage sales and to benefit a charity (thus the term *co-venture*).

(f) Other Provisions

These laws may provide that all documents required to be filed (principally registration statements, applications, and contracts) are matters of public record.

True records may have to be maintained by every charitable organization, fundraising counsel, commercial co-venturer, and paid solicitor required to register. These records, which must be retained for at least three years, must be available to the state authorities for inspection.

The law may authorize the state to enter into reciprocal agreements with other states or the federal government for the purpose of exchanging or receiving information filed by a charitable organization in another state, instead of requiring the organization to file under the particular state's law.

The state agency usually is authorized to conduct investigations and enjoin solicitations. Certain civil penalties can be imposed for failure to adhere to the law. Under various circumstances, a registration can be revoked, canceled, or suspended.

CONSTITUTIONAL LAW CONSIDERATIONS

Fundraising regulation of charitable organizations is more than the states' charitable solicitation acts and the rules governing the deductibility of charitable gifts. This aspect of the law also involves fundamental principles of constitutional law.

First, there is the doctrine of free speech, protected at the federal level by the First Amendment and at the state level by the Fourteenth Amendment. There are two forms of free speech: *pure* free speech, which may be regulated by the state by only the narrowest of means, and *commercial* free speech, which may be regulated by the state by any means that is reasonable. Fundraising by charitable organizations is a form of pure free speech.

The courts have held that, although government has legitimate interests in regulating this field, it may not do so by broad and arbitrary classifications. As the Supreme Court has written, government can regulate charitable fundraising but "must do so by narrowly drawn regulations designed to serve those interests without unnecessarily interfering with First Amendment freedoms." The Court observed in another context: "Broad prophylactic rules in the area of free expression are suspect. Precision of regulation must be the touchstone."

One of the most significant clashes between governmental police power to regulate for the benefit of its citizens and rights of free speech involves the application of percentage limitations on fundraising costs as a basis for determining whether a charity may lawfully solicit funds in a jurisdiction. Many aspects of this head-on conflict were resolved in 1980, when the Supreme Court held that a municipal ordinance was unconstitutionally overbroad and in violation of free speech rights. The ordinance had prohibited solicitation by charitable organizations that expend more than 25 percent of their receipts for fundraising and administrative expenses (known as an *absolute percentage limitation*). Subsequently, the Court addressed the *rebuttable percentage limitation* (fundraising expenses in excess of a percentage are presumed to be unreasonable, with the charity given the opportunity to rebut the presumption) and found that it too was contrary to charities' rights of free speech. These free speech rights also apply when charities obtain outside fundraising assistance.

Both the absolute percentage limitation and the rebuttable percentage limitation can initiate another constitutional law violation: denial of due process. Laws regulating the fundraising activities of charitable organizations must afford due process rights to persons subject to the laws, as prescribed in the Fifth and Fourteenth Amendments to the U.S. Constitution.

A charitable solicitation act must be in conformance with the guarantee of equal protection of the laws provided by the Fourteenth Amendment. This means that such an act may not discriminate in its classification of organizations. An equal protection argument can be raised because of exceptions from the coverage provided in a charitable fundraising regulation law.

A cardinal doctrine of administrative law is that a governmental agency may issue regulations. It must do so, however, in the context of a policy established by a legislative body that has fixed standards for the guidance of the agency in the performance of its functions. A charitable solicitation act may run afoul of this doctrine (born of the separation-of-powers principle) where the executive regulatory agency is granted such a wide range of discretionary authority that it is exercising legislative power.

STATES' POLICE POWER

How is it that the states can regulate this field the way they do, often crossing state lines (via radio and television) and involving the federal system (by using the mail)? The answer lies in the *police power* that every state and municipality inherently possesses.

Its police power enables a state or political subdivision to regulate—within the bounds of constitutional law principles—the conduct of its citizens and others, in order to protect the safety, health, and welfare of its people. A state can enact and enforce a charitable solicitation act in the exercise of its police power. It can require a charity planning on fundraising in the jurisdiction to register with the appropriate regulatory authority and to render periodic reports on the results of the solicitation.

The rationale is that charitable solicitations may be reasonably regulated in order to protect the public from deceit, fraud, unreasonable annoyance, or the unscrupulous obtaining of money under a pretense that the money is being collected for a charitable purpose. The laws that regulate charitable solicitations are by no means constitutionally deficient; they are, instead, utilizations of the states' police power. At the same time, these laws, like all legislation, must conform to certain basic legal standards or face challenges in the courts.

It is highly unlikely that a court will void a charitable solicitation act in its entirety for constitutional law deficiencies. Rather, when a court acts in this area, it does so with surgical precision, striking out only the discrete provision(s) that are overbroad—that is, that go beyond the ambit of narrowest-of-means regulation. Recently, for example, a state charitable solicitation act was found to be unconstitutional because of the burden imposed by the requirement that a professional fundraiser obtain a bond or post a letter of credit and because of too much "unbridled discretion" conferred on the state.

As noted, the biggest legal issue in this context is the attempts over the years by many states to preclude charities from fundraising in their jurisdictions if their fundraising costs are too high, as computed as a percentage of the gifts received. The Supreme Court has, to the states' dismay, repeatedly struck down laws of this nature as being unconstitutional. Nonetheless, a group of states recently tried to convince the Court that high fundraising costs are evidence of fraud, so that certain charities and their fundraisers could be prosecuted. The Court sidestepped the issue, however, holding only that fraudulent charitable fundraising cannot be protected by free speech principles—which was the state of the law before the litigation (consuming nearly 12 years) was initiated.

FEDERAL REGULATION OF FUNDRAISING

We saw in Chapter 3 (Myth 12) how the federal government is becoming greatly involved in the process of regulating fundraising for charitable purposes. Although the regulation of fundraising was once the sole province of the states, it is now also being conducted at the federal level, largely through the tax law. (Agencies such as the U.S. Postal Service, the Federal Trade Commission, and the Federal Election Commission may also be involved.) Too often, federal involvement in this area of law is ignored or, worse, unknown.

(a) Fundraising Disclosure

Congress brought the IRS into fundraising regulation when it legislated a variety of fundraising disclosure rules. These rules are in three forms. One is the package of rules requiring that most charitable gifts be *substantiated* in writing. Another set of rules are those mandating certain disclosures where there is a *quid pro quo contribution*. (These two bodies of law are discussed in Chapter 11.) The third area of disclosure is that occasioned by the requirement that copies of a tax-exempt organization's application for recognition of tax exemption and annual information returns be disclosed to the general public upon request (see Chapter 10).

(b) Exemption Application Process

To be tax-exempt as charitable entities and to be charitable donees, organizations are required to secure a letter to that effect from the IRS. The application process (see Chapter 6) requires the organization to provide considerable detail about any fundraising program(s) it may have or be contemplating (Form 1023, Part VIII, question 4). This question identifies nine types of fundraising (it missed some), which, if engaged in, must be described: mail solicitations, e-mail solicitations, personal solicitations, solicitations of vehicles, seeking of foundation grants, telephone solicitations, website-based solicitations (from the organization's own or from another organization's site), and seeking of government grants.

The application requires a description and disclosure of the organization's contracts (if any) entered into for fundraising purposes, including a recitation of the related revenue and expenses. If the organization performs fundraising for other organizations, that relationship requires discussion. The applicant must list all states and local jurisdictions in which it conducts fundraising—a tall order for an entity that solicits nationally (because it would have to list hundreds, maybe thousands, of counties, cities, towns, townships, boroughs, and the like). The organization is also asked whether it maintains "separate accounts for any contributor under which the contributor has the right to advise on the use or distribution of funds," which is a reference largely to the maintenance of donor-advised funds (see Chapter 16), and if so to describe the arrangement.

The organization will also reference its fundraising costs in the financial statement or proposed budget submitted as part of the application.

(c) Reporting Requirements

Few people realize how much regulation the federal government exercises through the annual reporting obligations it has imposed on charitable organizations. (These are discussed in Chapter 9.) The redesigned annual information return (Form 990) has substantially ratcheted up this aspect of fundraising regulation.

The annual information return requires charitable organizations (other than private foundations) to use the functional method of accounting to report their expenses

(Part IX of the return). This accounting method requires not only the identification, line by line, of expenses but an allocation of expenses by function—program services, management and general, and fundraising.

To comply with the requirements of the functional method of accounting, organizations must maintain detailed records on their fundraising (and other) expenses; the fundraising component of each line-item expenditure must be separately identified and reported. Because of this separate identification, some indirect fundraising costs may be revealed, which, when combined with direct fundraising expenses, result in considerably higher total outlays for fundraising. This amount could have adverse repercussions for the organization's status under state charitable solicitation acts, particularly those that force disclosure of total fundraising expenses. Other pertinent accounting issues are raised: What basis is to be used in making these allocations among functions? Will the state regulators accept reports containing the allocations as being in compliance with the states' reporting requirements?

The Form 990 devotes an entire schedule to the matter of fundraising (and gaming) (Schedule G). The IRS's instructions accompanying the return define the term *fundraising activities* to mean "activities undertaken to induce potential donors to contribute money, securities, services, materials, facilities, other assets, or time." Fundraising activities, according to the instructions, include publicizing and conducting fundraising campaigns; maintaining donor mailing lists; conducting fundraising events; preparing and distributing fundraising manuals, instructions, and other materials; and conducting other activities involved with the solicitation of contributions and grants from individuals, private foundations, governments, and others. Fundraising activities do not include gaming (other than gaming that is incidental to a fundraising activity) or the conduct of an unrelated business that is regularly carried on (see Chapter 13).

This definition of *fundraising activities* is far too broad. It is nonsensical to include the solicitation of *services* or *time* in the definition of *fundraising*. The fundraising community, long ago, differentiated among contributions of "time, treasure, and talent." Fundraising pertains to the solicitation of money or other property; it does not relate to solicitations of services or time. If a charitable organization's president asks an individual to serve on the charity's board of trustees, the president is not engaged in fundraising. If a charitable organization's executive director asks an individual to volunteer to assist with a particular project (even a fundraising event), the executive director is likewise not engaged in fundraising. The IRS has overlooked the fact that the concept of and the word *fundraising* not only contains the word *fund* but is predicated on it.

The IRS's instructions define *fundraising events* (or *special events*) to include "dinners/dances, door-to-door sales of merchandise, concerts, carnivals, sports events, auctions, and casino nights that are not regularly carried on." These events do not include "sales of gifts or goods or services of only nominal value, sweepstakes, lotteries or raffles where the names of contributors or other respondents are entered in a drawing for prizes, raffle[s] or lotteries where prizes have only nominal value [,] or solicitation campaigns that generate only contributions."

Special-event fundraising is somewhat unique, in that the purpose of the event often is not entirely fundraising. Community outreach or education usually also is a component of these events. (This dichotomy can sometimes be found in direct mail fundraising, where one of the reasons for the mailing is public education.) Some fundraising professionals consider special events to involve "friendraising."

The organization must indicate on the return the means of fundraising it used during the reporting year. The organization is asked whether it has a written or oral agreement with any individual (including trustees, directors, officers, or key employees) or entity in connection with professional fundraising activities. If the answer to this question is "yes," the organization must list the ten most highly paid individuals or entities where the fundraiser is to be compensated at least $5,000 in the year by the organization.

The filing organization must list all states in which it is registered or licensed to solicit funds or has been notified that it is exempt from such registration or licensing (see discussion following). The IRS's instructions state that, if the filing organization is registered, licensed, or exempted from registration or licensing "in all 50 States, it may answer 'All 50 States.'" This outcome, however, is impossible inasmuch as not all states have registration, licensing, or exemption laws.

Schedule G must be completed by organizations that reported, for the year, receipt of more than $15,000 in revenue from fundraising events. The schedule is to be completed by listing the two largest fundraising events, as measured by gross receipts; the organization also reports the total number of other events that occurred.

The contents of the annual information return pertain to how the federal government and the state regulatory agencies share the regulation of fundraising for charity. These levels of government are coordinating their respective roles. The IRS has taken a significant step toward implementation of this process by noting in the return's instructions that some states and local governments accept a copy of the annual return in place of all or part of their own financial report forms. Some states may require additional information, requiring attachments; this additional information need not be filed with the IRS. If the annual information return is amended, a copy of the revised return is to be sent to each state with which the original return was filed. More states than ever before use Form 990 for compliance with the states' charitable solicitation acts; for some reason, the IRS wants to know the states in which the return is filed and expects the organizations to report that information.

The instructions accompanying the annual information return suggest that fundraising is a form of *doing business* and therefore requires separate registration under the states' nonprofit corporation acts.

(d) Unrelated Income Rules

One of the ways in which the IRS is regulating the charitable fundraising process is through the unrelated income rules. These rules are the subject of Chapter 13 and are only briefly described here.

It would be a substantial understatement to say that charitable organizations do not regard their fundraising activities as unrelated business endeavors. Yet the fundraising practices of charities and the unrelated business rules have been enduring a precarious relationship for years. The IRS is more frequently using the unrelated income rules to characterize the receipts from certain fundraising activities as unrelated income.

Many fundraising practices possess all of the technical characteristics of an unrelated business. Reviewing the basic criteria for unrelated income taxation, some fundraising activities are indeed trades or businesses, regularly carried on, and not efforts that are substantially related to the performance of tax-exempt functions. Applying some of the tests often used by the IRS and the courts, there is no question that some fundraising endeavors have a commercial counterpart and are being undertaken in competition with that counterpart and with the objective of realizing a profit. Some fundraising activities are sheltered by law from consideration as businesses—for example, an activity in which substantially all of the work is performed for the organization by volunteers; or one that is carried on primarily for the convenience of the organization's members, students, patients, officers, or employees; or one that consists of the sale of merchandise, substantially all of which has been received by the organization as gifts.

As the functional accounting method's rules indicate, the law regards program activities and fundraising activities as separate matters. Even a simple undertaking like a car wash or a bake sale is an unrelated business. It is saved from taxation only because it is not regularly carried on or is conducted wholly by volunteers. Some fundraising activities—the mailing of greeting cards, charitable sales promotions, affinity card programs, and "membership" arrangements—are currently undergoing close scrutiny by the IRS, the courts, and Congress. The IRS is examining charities' practices of providing donors with adequate *recognition* for their gifts, as well as charity-sponsored gambling.

These rules may go beyond the question of unrelated income and may raise issues pertaining to eligibility for tax-exempt status. Fundraising charitable groups are facing a new wave of regulation, and their tax exemption or taxation of income is the federal government's leverage.

(e) Lobbying Restrictions

The Treasury Department and the IRS have written regulations that define the term *fundraising costs* and spell out rules by which to distinguish those costs from (i.e., allocate them between) the expenses of administration and program. These regulations were drawn as part of the effort to state the rules governing elective lobbying restrictions for public charities. (See Chapter 14.)

Under these lobbying rules, certain percentages are applied to the organizations' outlays for program expenditures but not most fundraising expenditures. An organization seeking to comply with these rules must distinguish between its fundraising expenses and its other costs. The amounts against which these percentages are applied are called *exempt purpose expenditures*. But exempt purpose expenditures do not include amounts paid or incurred to or for (1) a separate fundraising unit of the organization or an affiliated organization's fundraising unit or (2) one or more other organizations if the amounts are paid or incurred primarily for fundraising.

To adhere to these rules, an electing public charity must determine its direct and indirect fundraising costs, assuming that it understands the scope of the term *fundraising* in this context.

(f) Public Charity Classifications

A charitable organization is classified as either a *public* or a *private* charity. (See Chapter 17.) One of the ways to avoid private foundation status is to be a publicly supported organization, and one of the ways to be a publicly supported organization is to qualify as a *donative* charity. An organization can achieve that classification by meeting a *facts-and-circumstances* test, where the amount of public support normally received by the organization may be as low as 10 percent of its total support.

A variety of criteria may be utilized to demonstrate compliance with this test. One criterion is the extent to which the charitable organization is attracting public support: Can the organization demonstrate an active and ongoing fundraising program? The tax regulations state that an entity may satisfy this aspect of the test "if it maintains a continuous and bona fide program for solicitation of funds from the general public, community, or membership group involved, or if it carries on activities designed to attract support from governmental units or other [publicly supported] organizations."

The IRS may monitor the extent of a charitable organization's fundraising efforts, to ascertain whether the organization qualifies as an entity other than a private foundation.

(g)   Other Aspects of Federal Regulation

Federal tax law prohibits a private educational institution from qualifying as a charitable entity if it has racially discriminatory policies. Under IRS guidelines, schools must adhere to an assortment of recordkeeping requirements. Every private school must maintain, for at least three years, copies of all materials used by or on behalf of it to solicit contributions. Failure to maintain or to produce the required reports and information creates a presumption that the school has failed to comply with the guidelines and thus has a racially discriminatory policy toward its students. Loss or denial of tax-exempt status could result.

CORPORATE SPONSORSHIPS

When a for-profit corporation provides a charitable organization with a sizable amount of money to sponsor a program or event and the business corporation receives considerable favorable publicity in exchange, is the payment a (nontaxable) gift or a (taxable) payment for advertising services? Congress attempted to legislate this distinction through rules enacted in 1997. The IRS issued regulations to accompany these statutory rules pertaining to corporate sponsorships.

In general, the receipt of a qualified sponsorship payment by a tax-exempt organization is not the receipt of income that is considered unrelated business income. These rules hinge, in considerable part, on two concepts: (1) the *qualified sponsorship payment* and (2) the *substantial return benefit*.

A *qualified sponsorship payment* is any payment of money, transfer of property, or performance of services, by a person engaged in a trade or business to an exempt organization, with respect to which there is no arrangement or expectation that the person will receive any substantial return benefit. For this purpose, it is irrelevant whether the sponsored activity is related or unrelated to the recipient organization's exempt purpose. It is also irrelevant whether the sponsored activity is temporary or permanent.

A *substantial return benefit* is any benefit, other than (1) goods, services, or other benefits of insubstantial value that are disregarded or (2) certain uses and acknowledgments. A substantial return benefit includes (1) advertising, (2) the provision of facilities, services, or other privileges to the payor or persons designated by the payor (collectively, the payor) (with exceptions as noted following), and (3) granting the payor an exclusive or nonexclusive right to use an intangible asset (such as a trademark, patent, logo, or designation) of the exempt organization (see discussion following).

A substantial return benefit does not include the use or acknowledgment of the name or logo (or product lines) of the payor's trade or business in connection with the activities of the exempt organization. *Use or acknowledgment* does not include advertising (see discussion following) but may include logos and slogans that do not contain qualitative or comparative descriptions of the payor's products, services, facilities, or company; a list of the payor's locations, telephone numbers, or Internet address; value-neutral descriptions, including displays or visual depictions, of the payor's product-line or services; and the payor's brand or trade names and product or service listings.

Logos or slogans that are an established part of a payor's identity are not considered to contain qualitative or comparative descriptions. Mere display or distribution, whether for free or remuneration, of a payor's product by the payor or the exempt organization to the general public at the sponsored activity is not considered an inducement to purchase, sell, or use the payor's product and thus will not affect the determination of whether a payment is a qualified sponsorship payment.

An arrangement that acknowledges the payor as the exclusive sponsor of an exempt organization's activity, or the exclusive sponsor representing a particular trade, business, or industry, generally does not, alone, result in a substantial return benefit. For example, if in exchange for a payment, an organization announces that its event is sponsored exclusively by the payor (and does not provide any advertising or other substantial return benefit to the payor), the payor has not received a substantial return benefit.

By contrast, an arrangement that limits the sale, distribution, availability, or use of competing products, services, or facilities in connection with an exempt organization's activity generally results in a substantial return benefit. For example, if in exchange for a payment, an exempt organization agrees to allow only the payor's products to be sold in connection with an activity, the payor has received a substantial return benefit.

Thus, the regulations differentiate between an *exclusive sponsor* and an *exclusive provider*.

For these purposes, the term *advertising* means a message or other programming material which is broadcast or otherwise transmitted, published, displayed, or distributed, and which promotes or markets any trade or business, or any service, facility, or product. Advertising includes messages containing qualitative or comparative language, price information or other indications of savings or value, an endorsement, or an inducement to purchase, sell, or use any company, service, facility, or product. A single message that contains both advertising and an acknowledgment is nonetheless considered advertising. (This rule does not apply to activities conducted by a payor on its own. For example, if a payor purchases broadcast time from a television station to advertise its product during commercial breaks in a sponsored program, the exempt organization's activities are not thereby converted to advertising.)

Goods, services, or other benefits are disregarded under two sets of circumstances. One is where the benefits provided to the payor have an aggregate fair market value that is not more than 2 percent of the amount of the payment or $75 (adjusted for inflation), whichever is less. The IRS may subsequently revise these amounts or otherwise alter this test.

The other is where the only benefits provided to the payor are token items (such as bookmarks, calendars, key chains, mugs, posters, and T-shirts) bearing the exempt organization's name or logo that have an aggregate cost within the limit established for *low-cost articles*. Again, the IRS may alter this test. Token items provided to employees of a payor, or to partners of a partnership that is the payor, are disregarded if the combined total cost of the token items provided to each employee or partner does not exceed the low-cost article limit.

If the fair market value of the benefits (or, in the case of token items, the cost) exceeds the foregoing amount or limit, then (unless they constitute a use or acknowledgment) the entire fair market value of the benefits, not merely the excess amount, constitutes a substantial return benefit.

If there is an arrangement or expectation that the payor will receive a substantial return benefit with respect to a payment, then only the portion of the payment (if any) that exceeds the fair market value of the substantial return benefit is a qualified sponsorship payment. The fair market value is determined on the date the sponsorship arrangement is entered into. If, however, the exempt organization does not establish that the payment exceeds the fair market value of any substantial return benefit, then no portion of the payment constitutes a qualified sponsorship payment.

The unrelated business income tax treatment of any payment (or portion of one) that is not a qualified sponsorship payment is determined by application of the general rules in the unrelated business area. For example, payments related to the exempt organization's provision of facilities, services, or other privileges to the payor, advertising, exclusive provider arrangements, a license to use intangible assets of the exempt organization, or other substantial return benefits are evaluated separately in determining whether the exempt organization realizes unrelated business income.

To the extent necessary to prevent avoidance of this allocation rule, where the exempt organization fails to make a reasonable and good-faith valuation of any substantial return benefit, the IRS is empowered to determine the portion of a payment allocable to the substantial return benefit. The IRS can treat two or more related payments as a single payment.

Qualified sponsorship payments in the form of money or property (but not services) are treated as contributions received by the exempt organization for purposes of determining public support (see Chapter 17). This is the case irrespective of whether the *donative organization* or the *service provider organization* rules are involved.

The fact that a payment is a qualified sponsorship payment that is treated as a contribution to the payee organization is not determinative of whether the payment is deductible as a business expense or a charitable contribution.

The existence of a written sponsorship agreement does not, in itself, cause a payment to fail to be a qualified sponsorship payment. The terms of the agreement—not its existence or degree of detail—are relevant to the determination of whether a payment is a qualified sponsorship payment. Likewise, the terms of the agreement and not the title or responsibilities of the individuals negotiating the agreement determine whether a payment (or a portion of one) made pursuant to the agreement is a qualified sponsorship payment.

The term *qualified sponsorship payment* does not include any payment (the amount of which is contingent, by contract or otherwise, on the level of attendance at one or more events, broadcast ratings, or other factors indicating the degree of public exposure) to the sponsored activity. The fact that a payment is contingent on sponsored events or activities actually being conducted does not, alone, cause the payment to fail to be a qualified sponsorship payment.

These rules do not apply with respect to payments made in connection with qualified and trade show activities. These rules also do not apply to income derived from the sale of advertising or acknowledgments in exempt organization periodicals. For this purpose, the term *periodical* means regularly scheduled and printed material published by, or on behalf of, the exempt organization. A periodical is not related to, or primarily distributed in connection with, a specific event conducted by the exempt organization.

FUNDRAISING BY MEANS OF INTERNET

The Internet has greatly expanded the number of charitable organizations capable of carrying out, and actually engaged in the practice of, multistate gift solicitation activities. Essentially, to reach potential donors in all of the states, an organization needs nothing more than a computer and an account with an Internet service provider. Once established, the organization's charitable appeal can instantly be sent or made available to the entire Internet community. The large national and international charities with the resources necessary to assure compliance with the various state regulatory regimes are thus no longer the only ones affected by the state charitable solicitation laws (see foregoing discussion). Instead, even the smallest organizations are beginning to tap the national contribution market. Thus, the new technology indeed is altering the nature of communication in the charitable solicitations context—it renders these communications inexpensive.

(a) Law in General

One of the most difficult of contemporary issues in the nonprofit law setting is whether fundraising by charitable organizations by means of the Internet constitutes fundraising in every state and locality. Current thinking is that, technically, it does (see discussion following). If states asserting jurisdiction over Internet fundraising are justified in doing so, the result will be that even the smallest organizations—those too small to afford multistate solicitation efforts using any other medium—will be required to register and report under tens, maybe hundreds, of state and local charitable solicitation laws simply by virtue of utilizing the new communications technology to seek contributions. If they do not or cannot assure state law compliance, they will be forced to decide between risking adverse legal action in several states or refrain from engaging in this form of speech altogether. The question thus is whether, under this unfolding mix of facts, state laws enforced in this fashion would impermissibly restrict speech protected by free speech principles (see foregoing discussion).

There is another question that needs to be addressed. From a legal perspective, should Internet fundraising appeals be treated any differently simply because they take place via the Internet? (For federal tax purposes, the answer to this question from the IRS is no.) That is, should communication over this newest medium be regarded as anything other than communication, for which there already is a rich regulatory regime?

To determine whether the various state charitable solicitation schemes unduly intrude on the protected speech interest in this type of solicitation, the existing regulatory framework must be applied to the new set of facts. The first step in this analysis is to ascertain whether the act of an organization in placing an appeal for funds in a document on a computer in one state subjects the organization to the jurisdiction of one or more other states. There is as yet no law directly on this subject. Nonetheless, while not directly on point, a court opinion sheds some light on the matter.

A federal court of appeals had the opportunity to discuss the legal status of computer-borne communications in the First Amendment context. Two individuals operated an adult-oriented bulletin board service from their home. This site was accessible to others around the nation via modems and telephone lines.

Working with a U.S. Attorney's office in another state, a postal inspector purchased a membership in this bulletin board service and succeeded in downloading allegedly obscene images from the bulletin board. The U.S. Attorney's office filed criminal charges against these individuals for, among other reasons, transmitting obscenity over interstate telephone lines from their computer. The images involved were found by a jury to constitute obscene materials; the couple was convicted.

On appeal, this federal appellate court affirmed the convictions, holding that the crime of "knowingly us[ing] a facility or means of interstate commerce for the purpose of distributing obscene materials" did not require proof that the defendants had specific knowledge of the destination of each transmittal at the time it occurred. Of interest in the Internet setting, in determining that the crime occurred in the second state, the court placed considerable weight on its finding that "substantial evidence introduced at trial demonstrated that the . . . [bulletin board service] was set up so members located in other jurisdictions could access and order [obscene] files which would then be instantaneously transmitted in interstate commerce."

If the reasoning of this appellate court is followed by state courts, it appears that communication via computer constitutes sufficient contact with foreign states to subject the communicator to local law requirements. Applied in the charitable solicitation regulation context, then, the import of this court decision is clear: Soliciting funds by means of the Internet, where users residing in foreign jurisdictions download Web pages, in all likelihood will constitute sufficient contact to subject the organization to the jurisdiction of the foreign state or states and therefore to the foreign charitable solicitation regulatory regime or regimes.

It must next be determined whether interstate communication of this nature constitutes *solicitation* encompassed by the fundraising regulation laws of the states. Although a definite answer cannot be divined from the language of any one statute, a brief survey of some state laws strongly indicates that Internet solicitation will be held in many jurisdictions to be subject to regulation.

For example, in one state, solicitation embraced by the charitable solicitation act is defined as the making of a fundraising request "through any medium," regardless of whether any contribution is actually received. In another state, the charitable solicitation law applies to all "request[s] of any kind for a contribution." In another state, the law encompasses "each request for a contribution." The statutory scheme in another state applies to "any request, plea, entreaty, demand or invitation, or attempt thereof, to give money or property, in connection with which . . . any appeal is made for charitable purposes." In still another state, the law applies to organizations "soliciting or collecting by agents or solicitors, upon ways or in any other public places within the [state] to which the public have a right of access."

Certainly it is difficult to see how Internet fundraising is not caught by any of these strikingly broad provisions. As currently written, then, the statutes of at least five states can easily be construed to reach Internet charitable fundraising.

Indeed, it is likely that most, if not all, of the state charitable fundraising regulation regimes may be so construed and that these statutes that fail as currently written can be appropriately amended without much trouble.

(b) Charleston Principles

If the assumption is that the solicitation of funds (and perhaps other property) by charitable and other nonprofit organizations by means of the Internet constitutes, as a matter of law, fundraising in every state (and municipality), then, as suggested, the charitable community is facing an enormous burden. Many in the regulatory sector realize that, if this technically is the law, some form of relief for charities that solicit gifts by means of the Internet is warranted.

To this end, the National Association of State Charity Officials (NASCO) developed guidelines to assist state regulators, charitable organizations that solicit contributions, and their fundraisers, in deciding whether it is necessary to register fundraising efforts in one or more states when the solicitations are made by e-mail or on the organizations' websites. These guidelines are a product of discussion initiated at a NASCO conference in Charleston, South Carolina; hence the guidelines are termed the "Charleston Principles" (the Principles). The Principles are not law but rather nonbinding guidance to NASCO members.

The Principles rest on this proposition: "Existing registration statutes generally, of their own terms, encompass and apply to Internet solicitations." An unstated assumption is that it is untenable to require registration and reporting of all charities soliciting gifts solely by means of the Internet, and their fundraisers, in all of the states with reporting requirements. Thus, the scope of potential registration must be narrowed or, as the Principles put it, state charity officials should "address the issue of who has to register where."

The Principles differentiate between entities that are domiciled in a state and those that are domiciled outside the state. (An entity is *domiciled* in a state if its principal place of business is in that state.)

An entity that is domiciled in a state and uses the Internet to conduct charitable solicitations in that state must, according to the Principles, register in that state. This position reflects the prevailing view that the Internet is a form of communication and the law does not make a distinction between that type of communication and another (such as use of regular mail). The rule applies "without regard to whether the Internet solicitation methods it uses are passive or interactive, maintained by itself or another entity with which it contracts, or whether it conducts solicitations in any other manner."

Matters become more complex in situations where an entity is fundraising, using the Internet, in a state in which it is not domiciled. Registration in the state is nonetheless required if

- The organization's non-Internet activities alone are sufficient to require registration.
- It solicits contributions through an interactive website.

- The entity
  - Specifically targets persons physically located in the state for solicitation.
  - Receives contributions from donors in the state on a repeated and ongoing basis or a substantial basis through its website.
  - Solicits contributions through a site that is not interactive but either specifically invites further offline activity to complete a contribution or establishes other contacts with that state, such as sending e-mail messages or other communications that promote the website, and the entity engages in one of the foregoing two activities.

Often considerable line-drawing will be required in the application of these guidelines. The matter becomes more intricate when some definitions are factored in.

An *interactive website* is a site that "permits a contributor to make a contribution, or purchase a product in connection with a charitable solicitation, by electronically completing the transaction, such as by submitting credit card information or authorizing an electronic funds transfer." These sites include those through which a donor "may complete a transaction online through any online mechanism processing a financial transaction even if completion requires the use of linked or redirected sites." A website is considered *interactive* if it has this capacity, irrespective of whether donors actually use it.

The phrase *specifically target persons* physically *located in the state for solicitation* means to engage in one of two practices:

1. Including on the website an express or implied reference to soliciting contributions from persons in that state
2. Otherwise affirmatively appealing to residents of the state, such as by advertising or sending messages to persons located in the state (electronically or otherwise) when the entity knows, or reasonably should know, that the recipient is physically located in the state

Charities operating on a "purely local basis," or within a "limited geographic area," do not target states outside their operating area if their website makes clear in context that their fundraising focus is limited to that area, even if they receive contributions from outside that area on less than a repeated and ongoing basis or on a substantial basis.

To receive contributions from a state on a *repeated and ongoing basis* or a *substantial basis* means "receiving contributions within the entity's fiscal year, or relevant portion of a fiscal year, that are of sufficient volume to establish the regular or significant (as opposed to rare, isolated, or insubstantial) nature of these contributions."

States are encouraged to set, and communicate to the regulated entities, "numerical [sic] levels at which it [sic] will regard this criterion as satisfied." These levels should, the Principles provide, define *repeated and ongoing* in terms of a number of contributions and *substantial* in terms of a total dollar amount of contributions or percentage of total contributions received by or on behalf of the charity. The meeting of one of these thresholds would give rise to a registration requirement but would not limit an enforcement action for deceptive solicitations.

Another Principle is that an entity that solicits via e-mail in a particular state is to be treated the same as one that solicits by means of telephone or direct mail, if the soliciting party knew or reasonably should have known that the recipient was a resident of or was physically located in that state.

The Principles address the circumstance as to whether a charity is required to register in a particular state when the operator of a website, through which contributions for that charity are solicited or received, is required to register but the charity does not independently satisfy the registration criteria. If the law of the state does not universally require the registration of all charities on whose behalf contributions are solicited or received through a commercial fundraiser, commercial co-venturer, or fundraising counsel who is required to register, then the state should independently apply the criteria to each charity and only require registration by charities that independently meet the tests. If, however, the law of the state universally requires registration of all charities under these circumstances, the state should consider whether, as a matter of "prosecutorial discretion, public policy, and the prioritized use of limited resources," it would take action to enforce registration requirements as to charities that do not independently meet the criteria.

Still another Principle is that solicitations for the sale of a product or service that include a representation that some portion of the price shall be devoted to a charitable organization or charitable purpose (*commercial co-venturing*, *charitable sales promotion*, or *cause-related marketing*) (see foregoing discussion) shall be governed by the same standards as otherwise set out in the Principles governing charitable solicitations.

There are two "exclusions" from the registration requirements. One is that maintaining or operating a website that does not contain a solicitation of contributions but merely provides program services by means of the Internet does not, by itself, invoke a requirement to register. This is the case even if unsolicited contributions are received.

The other exclusion is for entities that solely provide administrative, supportive, or technical services to charities without providing substantive content or advice concerning substantive content; they are not required to register. These entities include Internet service providers and organizations that do no more than process online transactions for a separate firm that operates a website or provides similar services. This exclusion does not encompass professional fundraisers, fundraising counsel, or commercial co-venturers.

The Principles provide that state charity officials "recognize that the burden of compliance by charitable organizations and their agents, professional fundraisers, commercial co-venturers and/or professional fundraising counsel should be kept reasonable in relation to the benefits to the public achieved by registration." Projects to create "common forms," such as the unified registration statement, are "strongly encouraged."

State charity offices are also "strongly encouraged" to publish their registration and reporting forms, their laws and regulations, and other related information on the Internet to facilitate registration and reporting by charitable organizations and their agents.

The Principles encourage development of information technology infrastructure to facilitate electronic registration and reporting. Also encouraged is Internet posting by charitable organizations of their application for recognition of tax-exempt status, their IRS determination letter, their most recent annual information returns, and their state registration statement(s). (This posting practice is also encouraged by the federal tax law, which obviates the need to provide hard copies of these federal documents to requestors when they are made available on the Internet.

FOCUS: Campaign to Clean Up America

The Campaign to Clean Up America (CCUA) intends to solicit funds in nearly all of the states, principally by mail. The CCUA will register in Missouri, the state in which the fundraising will originate. Before the fundraising begins, someone representing the CCUA must review the laws of every state in which a gift solicitation will occur, determine which states require registration, obtain the necessary forms, and secure the appropriate registrations (licenses). You, as president of the CCUA, realize that this will be a very time-consuming and expensive process because of the enormous variety and sheer amount of questions that must be answered. The expense will come in diverted staff time, registration fees, bond premiums, and perhaps accounting and legal fees. The CCUA's lawyer advises that the organization has no real choice; it must comply with these state laws.

The CCUA will likely use the services of a professional fundraiser; its first project will be to develop and implement a direct-mail fundraising program. (There are no plans to hire a professional solicitor.) The lawyer for the CCUA reminds you to coordinate the organization's state registrations with those of the professional fundraiser.

This fundraising activity will principally involve outlays that are not exempt purpose expenditures under the federal tax lobbying rules. If the CCUA elects to come under the expenditure test (see Chapter 14), these fundraising expenses cannot be counted in the base against which the various percentages are applied. The CCUA does not intend to engage in any gift solicitation practices that would constitute an unrelated business.

The CCUA will have a website and will state there that contributions to it are deductible. E-mail solicitations of gifts are not contemplated at this time. The CCUA, with its lawyer's grudging consent, is taking the position (until and unless the law evolves differently) that it is not soliciting contributions in every state and local jurisdiction.

PART THREE

Tax-Exempt Organizations Can Be Taxable, and So Can Their Managers

CHAPTER THIRTEEN

Related or Unrelated?

Chapters 5 and 17 show how the tax law imposes penalties on the persons involved in law violations concerning public charities, social welfare organizations, and private foundations. This chapter deals with the taxation of income generated by activities that are unrelated to the tax-exempt functions of nonprofit organizations. The following three chapters cover taxes imposed on lobbying, political campaign activities, donor-advised funds and tax shelter activities, and more. In each situation, an organization must tread carefully. The taxes are long established and they can be heavy.

TAXES

For nearly 60 years, the law has divided the activities of tax-exempt organizations into two categories: those that are related to the performance of exempt functions and those that are not. The revenue occasioned by the latter activities, *unrelated activities*, is subject to tax. Gross revenues gained from unrelated activities are potentially taxable; however, in computing unrelated business taxable income, the organization is entitled to deduct only expenses incurred that are directly related to the conduct of the unrelated business.

For organizations that are incorporated, the net revenue from unrelated activities is subject to the regular federal corporate income tax. The federal tax on individuals applies to the unrelated activities of organizations that are not corporations (e.g., trusts). Unlike the intermediate sanctions and private foundation rules, the law on related and unrelated activities does not impose any taxes on the directors and officers of tax-exempt entities.

To decide whether any of its activities are taxable, an otherwise tax-exempt organization must first ascertain which activities are related to exempt functions and which are not. The judgments that go into assigning activities into these two categories are at the heart of one of the greatest controversies facing nonprofit organizations today. The existing legal structure is complex, intricate, and dynamic. Although the rules were enacted in 1950, it was not until the early 1970s that this body of tax law became of primary importance to nonprofit organizations.

UNRELATED INCOME RULES

The unrelated income rules were significantly rewritten by Congress in 1969. The original concept underlying these rules was that of an *outside* business owned and perhaps operated by a tax-exempt organization. In 1969, however, Congress significantly expanded the reach of these rules by authorizing the IRS to evaluate activities conducted by nonprofit organizations internally—*inside* activities. This body of law has expanded exponentially ever since.

The objective of the unrelated business income tax is to prevent unfair competition between tax-exempt organizations and for-profit, commercial enterprises. The rules are intended to place the unrelated business activities of an exempt organization on the same tax basis as those of a nonexempt business with which it competes. It is often said that the purpose of the unrelated business income tax is to "level the playing field" as between competing nonprofit and for-profit organizations. One wag suggested, however, that for-profit businesses do not even want nonprofit entities *on* the field.

To be tax-exempt, a nonprofit organization must be organized and operated primarily for exempt purposes. (See Chapter 4.) The federal tax law allows a tax-exempt organization to engage in a certain amount of income-producing activity that is unrelated to exempt purposes. Where the organization derives net income from one or more unrelated business activities, known formally as *unrelated business taxable income*, it is subject to tax on that income. An organization's tax exemption will be denied or revoked if an inappropriate portion of its activities is not promoting one or more of its exempt purposes.

Business activities may preclude the initial qualification of an otherwise tax-exempt organization. If the organization is not being operated principally for exempt purposes, it will fail the *operational test*. If its articles of organization empower it to carry on substantial activities that are not in furtherance of its exempt purpose, it will not meet the *organizational test*.

A nonprofit organization may still satisfy the operational test, even when it operates a business as a substantial part of its activities, as long as the business promotes the organization's exempt purpose. If the organization's primary purpose is carrying on a business for profit, it may be denied exemption on the grounds that it is a *feeder organization*, even if all of its profits are payable to one or more tax-exempt organizations.

Occasionally, the IRS will assume a different stance toward the tax consequences of one or more unrelated businesses when it comes to qualification for tax exemption. That is, the IRS may conclude that a business is unrelated and subject to the unrelated business income tax. Yet, the IRS may also agree that the purpose of the unrelated business is such that the activity helps further the organization's exempt function (funds are being generated for exempt purposes), even if the business activity is more than one-half of total operations. In this setting, then, the exempt organization can be in the anomalous position of having a considerable amount of taxable business activity—while still being tax-exempt.

The law in this area was, several years ago, on the brink of substantial revision. The House Subcommittee on Oversight, a unit of the House Committee on Ways and Means, held five days of hearings on the subject in 1987. Specific alterations were proposed, and they would have been sweeping. Ironically, a large part of the impetus for these hearings was the charge by the business community of unfair competition. The difference between the circumstances in the 1950s and those in the 1980s was that the competing activities of nonprofit organizations in the 1950s were of the unrelated variety; in the 1980s, the competing activities were, under existing law definitions, related to exempt functions. The drive for extensive revision of the unrelated business statutes stalled; only the IRS and the courts are currently making new law in this area.

Prior to enactment of the unrelated income rules, the law embodied a *destination of income test*. For an organization to be tax-exempt, the net profits of the organization had to be used in furtherance of tax-exempt purposes. Because the test did not consider the source of the profits, it tolerated forms of unfair competition.

In adopting these rules in 1950 and in amplifying them in 1969 and in many years since then, Congress has not prohibited commercial ventures by nonprofit organizations nor has it levied taxes only on the receipts of businesses that bear no relation to nonprofit organizations' tax-exempt purposes. Instead, it has struck a balance between, as the Supreme Court phrased it in 1986, "its two objectives of encouraging benevolent enterprise and restraining unfair competition."

Essentially, for an activity of a tax-exempt organization to be taxed, three tests must be satisfied. The activity must constitute a *trade or business*, be *regularly carried on*, and not be *substantially related* to the tax-exempt purposes of the organization. Many exceptions to these rules, however, exempt from taxation certain forms of activity and certain types of income.

The unrelated income rules are in a peculiar state of affairs these days. The courts are simultaneously developing additional and sometimes different criteria for assessing the presence of unrelated business, and from judicial decisions a doctrine of *commerciality* is emerging. This results in both considerable confusion as to what the law in this area is and extensive judgmental leeway on the part of the courts and the IRS in applying it.

(a) Affected Tax-Exempt Organizations

Nearly all types of tax-exempt organizations are subject to the unrelated income rules. They include religious organizations (including churches), educational organizations (including universities, colleges, and schools), health care organizations (including hospitals), scientific organizations, and other charitable organizations. Beyond the realm of charitable entities, the rules are applicable to social welfare organizations (including advocacy groups), labor organizations (including unions), trade and professional associations, fraternal organizations, employee benefit funds, and veterans' organizations.

Special rules tax all income not related to exempt functions (including investment income) of social clubs, homeowners' associations, and political organizations.

Certain organizations are not generally subject to the unrelated income rules, simply because they are not allowed to engage in any active business endeavors. This is the case, for example, for private foundations and title-holding organizations. The operation of an active business (externally or internally) by a private foundation would likely trigger application of the excess business holdings restrictions. (See Chapter 17.)

Instrumentalities of the United States, like nearly all governmental agencies, are exempt from the unrelated business rules. The unrelated income rules are, however, applicable to colleges and universities that are agencies or instrumentalities of a government, as well as to corporations owned by such colleges and universities.

(b) Trade or Business Defined

For the purpose of the federal tax rules, the term *trade or business* includes any activity that is carried on for the production of income from the sale of goods or the performance of services. Most activities that would constitute a trade or business under basic tax law principles are considered a trade or business for purposes of the unrelated income rules.

This definition of the term *trade or business* embraces nearly every activity of a tax-exempt organization; only passive investment activities generally escape this classification. In this sense, every tax-exempt organization should be viewed as a bundle of activities, each of which is a trade or business. (It must be emphasized that this definition has nothing to do with whether a particular activity is related or unrelated; there are related businesses and unrelated businesses.)

The IRS is empowered to examine each of an organization's activities in search of unrelated business. Each activity can be examined as though it existed wholly independently of the others; an unrelated activity cannot, as a matter of law, be hidden from scrutiny by tucking it in among a cluster of related activities. As Congress chose to state the principle, an "activity does not lose identity as a trade or business merely because it is carried on within a larger aggregate of similar activities or within a larger complex of other endeavors which may, or may not, be related to the exempt purposes of the organization." This is known, in the jargon of tax law professionals, as the *fragmentation rule*. For example, the fragmentation rule allows the IRS to treat the income from the sale of advertising space in an exempt organization's magazine as revenue derived from an unrelated business, even though otherwise the publication of the magazine is a related business.

The federal tax law also states that, "[w]here an activity carried on for profit constitutes an unrelated trade or business, no part of such trade or business shall be excluded from such classification merely because it does not result in profit." In other words, just because an activity results in a loss in a particular year, that is insufficient basis for failing to treat the activity as an unrelated one (including reporting it as such to the IRS). Conversely, because the fact that an activity generates a profit is not alone supposed to lead to the conclusion that the activity is unrelated (although there are many in the IRS and on court benches who are likely to leap to that conclusion).

There is a problem here, nonetheless. An activity that consistently (over several consecutive years) results in losses will not be regarded as a *business*. If that is the only unrelated activity, that characterization is good news, because then it cannot be an *unrelated business*. Some tax-exempt organizations, however, have more than one unrelated business. They can offset the losses generated by one business against the gains enjoyed by another business in calculating unrelated business taxable income. But, if the loss activity is not a business to begin with, its losses cannot be credited against unrelated gain.

Just as *profits* are not built into the formal definition of the term *trade or business*, so too is the element of *unfair competition* missing from that definition. Yet, unfair competition is the driving force behind the unrelated income rules, and the IRS and the courts sometimes use the factor of competition in assessing whether an activity is related or unrelated to exempt functions.

Another absent term in the tax law definition of *trade or business* is *commerciality*. Nothing in the statutory law generally authorizes the IRS and judges to conclude that an activity is unrelated solely because it is conducted in a commercial manner, which basically means it is conducted the way a comparable activity is carried on by for-profit businesses. But the IRS does it anyway.

(c) Regularly Carried On

To be considered an unrelated business, an activity must be *regularly carried on* by a tax-exempt organization.

Income from an activity is considered taxable only when (assuming the other criteria are satisfied) the activity is regularly carried on, as distinguished from sporadic or infrequent transactions. The factors that determine whether an activity is regularly carried on are the frequency and continuity of the activities, and the manner in which the activities are pursued. (In this context, the statutory law comes the closest to using a doctrine of *commerciality*.)

These factors must be evaluated in light of the purpose of the unrelated business income tax, which is to place tax-exempt organizations' business activities on the same tax basis as those of their nonexempt business competitors. Specific business activities of a tax-exempt organization will generally be deemed to be regularly carried on if they are frequent and continuous and are pursued in a manner that is generally similar to comparable commercial activities of nonexempt organizations.

Where an organization duplicates income-producing activities performed by commercial organizations year-round, but performs those activities for a period of only a few weeks, they do not constitute the regular carrying on of a trade or business. Similarly, occasional or annual income-producing activities, such as fundraising events, do not amount to a business that is regularly carried on. The conduct of year-round business activities, such as the operation of a parking lot for one day each week, however, constitutes the regular carrying on of a business. Where commercial entities normally undertake income-producing activities on a seasonal basis, the conduct of the activities by an exempt organization during a significant portion of the season is deemed the regular conduct of that activity. For this purpose, a *season* may be a portion of the year (such as the summer) or a holiday period.

There are two problem areas to watch out for. Generally, the law, in ascertaining regularity, looks only at the time consumed in the actual conduct of the activity. The IRS, however, is of the view (not unreasonably) that time expended *preparing* for the event (*preparatory time*) should also be taken into account. This can convert what appears to be an exempted activity into a taxable business.

Outsourcing is a popular management tool these days. Tax-exempt organizations often try to outsource unrelated activities (and try to bring these profits in as nontaxable income, usually as royalties—see discussion following). This arrangement often entails a contract that sometimes casts the party with whom the exempt organization is contracting as the organization's *agent*. This is a bad idea. Under the law of *principal* and *agent*, the activities of the agent are attributed to the principal. Here, the exempt organization is the principal. To attribute the "agent's" activities to the exempt organization destroys any tax planning reasons for the relationship.

In summary, a trade or business is regularly carried on by a tax-exempt organization where the attributes of the activity are similar to the commercial activities of nonexempt organizations.

(d) Unrelated Trade or Business

The term *unrelated trade or business* is defined to mean "any trade or business the conduct of which [by a tax-exempt organization] is not substantially related (aside from the need of such organization for income or funds or the use it makes of the profits derived) to the exercise or performance by such organization of its charitable, educational, or other purpose or function constituting the basis for its exemption." The parenthetical clause means that an activity is not related simply because the organization uses the net revenue from the activity for exempt purposes.

The revenue from a regularly conducted trade or business is subject to tax, unless the business activity is substantially related to the accomplishment of the organization's exempt purpose. The key to taxation or nontaxation in this area is the meaning of the words *substantially related*. Yet the law tells us merely that to be substantially related, the activity must have a *substantial causal relationship* to the accomplishment of an exempt purpose.

The fact that an asset is essential to the conduct of an organization's exempt activities does not shield from taxation the unrelated income produced by that asset. The income-producing activities must still meet the causal relationship test if the income is not to be subject to tax. This issue arises when a tax-exempt organization owns a facility or other assets that are put to a dual use. For example, the operation of an auditorium as a motion picture theater for public entertainment in the evenings is treated as an unrelated activity even though the theater is used exclusively for exempt purposes during the daytime hours. The fragmentation rule allows this type of use of a single asset to be split into two businesses.

Activities should not be conducted on a scale larger than is reasonably necessary for the performance of exempt functions. Activities in excess of the needs of exempt functions constitute unrelated businesses.

There is a host of court cases and IRS rulings providing illustrations of related and unrelated activities. Colleges and universities operate dormitories and bookstores as related activities but can be taxed on travel tours and sports camps. Hospitals may operate gift shops, snack bars, and parking lots as related activities but may be taxable on sales of pharmaceuticals to the public and on performance of routine laboratory tests for physicians. Museums may, without taxation, sell items reflective of their collections but are supposed to be taxable on the sale of souvenirs and furniture. Trade associations may find themselves taxable on sales of items and particular services to members, whereas dues and subscription revenue are nontaxable. Fundraising events may be characterized as unrelated activities, particularly when compensation is paid or when the activity is regularly carried on (see Chapter 12).

(e) Unrelated Business Taxable Income

As noted earlier, to be subject to the unrelated income rules, an activity must satisfy (or, depending on one's point of view, fail) three tests. These tests are built into the definition of the term *unrelated business taxable income*: the "gross income derived by any [exempt] organization from any unrelated trade or business . . . regularly carried on by it, less the deductions allowed . . . [under federal tax law in general] which are directly connected with the carrying on of such trade or business."

Both this gross income and allowable deductions are computed in conformance with the *modifications* (see discussion following).

When the organization covered by the unrelated income rules is a foreign organization, its unrelated business taxable income is "its unrelated business taxable income which is derived from sources within the United States and which is not effectively connected with the conduct of a trade or business within the United

States" and "its unrelated business taxable income which is effectively connected with the conduct of a trade or business within the United States."

Some tax-exempt organizations are members of partnerships (see Chapter 18). If a trade or business regularly carried on by the partnership is an unrelated trade or business, the organization has special reporting requirements. In computing its unrelated business taxable income, it must (subject to the modifications) include its share (whether or not distributed) of the partnership's gross income from the unrelated business and its share of the partnership deductions directly connected with the gross income. (This is an application of what the tax law terms the *look-through rule*.) A tax-exempt organization's share (whether or not distributed) of the gross income of a *publicly traded partnership* must be treated as gross income derived from an unrelated business, and its share of the partnership deductions is allowed in computing unrelated business taxable income.

A tax-exempt organization may own *debt-financed property*, and the use of the property may be unrelated to the organization's exempt function. When the organization computes its unrelated business taxable income, any income from the property has to be included as gross income derived from an unrelated business. The income is subject to tax in the same proportion that the property is financed by debt. The debt involved must be what the tax law terms *acquisition indebtedness*. The most common example is a mortgage.

(f) Exempted Activities

Despite the foregoing general rules, certain businesses conducted by tax-exempt organizations are exempted from taxation. A frequent exemption from taxation is a business "in which substantially all the work is performed for the organization without compensation." If a tax-exempt organization conducts an unrelated business using services substantially provided by volunteers, the net revenue from that business is not taxable. This exemption protects from taxation many ongoing charitable fundraising activities. Caution must be exercised, however, because *compensation* is not confined to a salary, wage, or fee; the slightest amount of remuneration (such as tips) can nullify an individual's status as a *volunteer*.

Also exempted is a trade or business carried on by the organization "primarily for the convenience of its members, students, patients, officers, or employees." This exception is available, however, only to organizations that are charitable, educational, and the like, or are governmental colleges and universities.

A further exemption is given to a trade or business "which is the selling of merchandise, substantially all of which has been received by the organization as gifts or contributions." This exemption shelters the work of exempt thrift stores from taxation. Its use, though, is not confined to thrift shops. For example, it can protect auction revenue from taxation—even if auctions are regularly carried on. Similarly, the exception prevents charities that receive donated vehicles and then sell them (see Chapter 11), from being considered in the unrelated business of dealing in automobiles, boats, and the like.

The term *unrelated trade or business* does not include *qualified public entertainment activities*. A public entertainment activity is any entertainment or recreational activity traditionally conducted at fairs or expositions promoting agricultural and educational purposes. Typically, these activities attract the public to fairs or expositions or promote the breeding of animals or the development of products or equipment.

To be *qualified*, a public entertainment activity must be conducted

- In conjunction with an international, national, state, regional, or local fair or exposition
- In accordance with the provisions of state law which permit the activity to be operated or conducted solely by a qualifying organization or by a governmental agency
- In accordance with the provisions of state law, which permit a qualifying organization to be granted a license to conduct no more than 20 days of the activity, on payment to the state of a lower percentage of the revenue from the licensed activity than the state requires from nonqualifying organizations

To earn the public entertainment activities exception, a *qualifying organization* must be a tax-exempt charitable, social welfare, or labor organization that regularly conducts, as one of its substantial exempt purposes, an agricultural and educational fair or exposition.

The term *unrelated trade or business* also does not include qualified convention and trade show activities. These activities, traditionally conducted at conventions, annual meetings, or trade shows, are designed to attract attention from persons in an industry. There is no requirement for those persons to be members of the sponsoring organization. The shows' purposes are to display industry products; to stimulate interest in, and demand for, industry products or services; or to educate persons within the industry in the development of new products and services or new rules and regulations affecting industry practices.

To be *qualified*, a convention and trade show activity must be carried out by a qualifying organization in conjunction with an international, national, state, regional, or local convention, annual meeting, or show that the organization is conducting. One of the purposes of the organization in sponsoring the activity must be the promotion and stimulation of interest in, and demand for, the products and services of that industry in general, or the education of attendees regarding new developments or products and services related to the exempt activities of the organization. The show must be designed to achieve its purpose through the character of the exhibits and the extent of the industry products displayed.

A *qualifying organization* is a charitable, social welfare, or labor organization or a trade association that regularly conducts a show as one of its substantial exempt purposes. The show must be aimed toward stimulating interest in and demand for the products of a particular industry or a segment of an industry, or toward educating attendees on new developments of products and services related to the exempt activities of the organization.

The concept of unrelated trade or business does not include situations where cooperative hospital service organizations furnish services to one or more other tax-exempt hospitals. The services, however, (1) must be furnished solely to hospitals that have facilities for no more than 100 inpatients; (2) if performed on its own behalf by the recipient hospital, must constitute exempt activities of that institution; and (3) must be provided for at a fee or cost that does not exceed the actual cost of providing the services. The cost must include straight-line depreciation and a reasonable amount for return on capital goods used to provide the services.

The concept of unrelated trade or business also does not include bingo games. The game must be (1) of a type in which usually the wagers are placed, the winners are determined, and the prizes or other property are distributed in the presence of all persons placing wagers in the game; (2) not an activity ordinarily carried out on a commercial basis; and (3) not in violation of any state or local law.

For a charitable, veterans', or other organization to which contributions are deductible, the term *unrelated trade or business* does not include activities relating to a distribution of low-cost articles that is incidental to the solicitation of charitable contributions. A *low-cost article* is one that has a maximum cost of $5.00 (indexed for inflation) to the organization that distributes the item (directly or indirectly). A *distribution* qualifies under this rule if it is not made at the request of the recipients, if it is made without their express consent, and if the articles that are distributed are accompanied by a request for a charitable contribution to the organization and a statement that the recipients may retain the article whether or not a contribution is made.

For a charitable, veterans', or other organization to which contributions are deductible, the term *trade or business* does not include exchanging with another like organization the names and addresses of donors to or members of the organization, or the renting of these lists to another like organization.

Other exemption rules apply to certain local organizations of employees, the conduct of certain games of chance, and the rental of poles by mutual or cooperative telephone or electric companies.

(g) Exempted Income

Certain types of passive income and income derived from research are exempt from the unrelated income tax.

Because the unrelated income tax applies to active businesses conducted by tax-exempt organizations, most types of passive income are exempt from taxation. This exemption generally covers dividends, interest, securities, loan payments, annuities, royalties, rent, capital gains, and gains on the lapse or termination of options written by exempt organizations.

There are, however, important exceptions to this exemption for passive income:

- Income in the form of rent, royalties, and the like from an active business undertaking is taxable—that is, merely labeling an income flow as rent, royalties, and so forth does not make it tax-free.

- The unrelated debt-financed income rules override the general exemption for passive income.

- Interest, annuities, royalties, and rents from a controlled corporation may be taxable.

The following exemptions pertain to the conduct of research:

- Income derived from research for the United States or any of its agencies or instrumentalities, or for any state or political subdivision of a state

- Income derived from research performed for any person at a college, university, or hospital

- Income derived from research performed for any person at an organization operated primarily for purposes of carrying on fundamental research, the results of which are freely available to the general public

This exemption for research income is under strain. Some organizations do not engage in research at all; rather, they are merely testing products for public use just prior to marketing. Other organizations, principally universities and scientific research institutions, are engaging in research, but their discoveries are licensed or otherwise transferred to business organizations for exploitation in the public marketplace. This closeness between businesses and nonprofit organizations— known as *technology transfer*—is raising questions as to how much commercial activity is being sheltered from tax by the research exceptions.

For the most part, the tax law is clear regarding what constitutes *dividends, interest*, an *annuity, rent*, and *capital gain*. There is, however, considerable controversy (reflected in many recent court opinions) concerning what constitutes a *royalty*. The term, not defined by statute or regulation, is being defined by the courts.

Generally, a *royalty* is a payment for the use of one or more valuable intangible property rights. In the tax-exempt organizations setting, this is likely to mean payment for the use of an organization's name and logo. The core issue usually is the extent to which the exempt organization receiving the (ostensible) royalty can provide services in an attempt to increase the amount of royalty income paid to it. This issue was the subject of extensive litigation spanning many years, principally involving revenue from the rental of mailing lists and revenue derived from affinity card programs. The resulting rule is that these services are permissible as long as they are insubstantial. Beyond that, the IRS may argue that the exempt organization is in a *joint venture*, which is an active business undertaking that defeats the exclusion.

There is a specific deduction of $1,000. This means that the first $1,000 of unrelated income is spared taxation.

(h) Use of Subsidiaries

As discussed more fully in Chapter 17, some tax-exempt organizations elect to spin off their unrelated activities to related taxable subsidiaries. The tax on the net income of the unrelated activity is then not borne directly by the exempt organization. The managers of the tax-exempt organization may be averse to reporting any unrelated income or the unrelated activity may be too large in relation to related activity.

If funds are transferred from a taxable subsidiary to an exempt parent, that income will be taxable as unrelated income to the parent if it is interest, rents, royalties, or annuities, where the parent has, directly or indirectly, more than 50 percent control of the subsidiary. If, however, the subsidiary pays dividends to the tax-exempt parent, the dividends are not taxable to the parent because they are not deductible by the subsidiary.

Congress created, for the 2006–2009 period, a carve-out for preexisting arrangements, to spare exempt organizations this tax where the amount paid to the exempt parent is reasonable. Although this special provision is set to expire, efforts will be made to extend it or make it permanent.

INTERNET ACTIVITIES

Recently, the IRS came up with this salient statement: "The use of the Internet to accomplish a particular task does not change the way the tax laws apply to that task. Advertising is still advertising and fundraising is still fundraising." That was in reflection of the enormous use now of the Internet by nonprofit organizations and a pertinent reminder that the IRS is scrutinizing these activities. Still, there are those who think that an activity engaged in through the Internet is somehow different for tax law purposes.

As the quotation indicates, one use of the Internet by charitable organizations is for fundraising (see Chapter 12). The IRS discussed the matter of making charitable gifts of money using the Internet. (Non-cash gifts are not discussed because they generally are not made directly over the Internet.) It is still necessary to be certain that the recipient of the contribution is a charity. If the donee is a charity, the gift may not be earmarked for a specific individual or for an organization that is not entitled to receive charitable contributions.

Again, the substantiation requirements apply, as do the rules for quid pro quo contributions and appraisals (see Chapter 11). Disclosure rules for noncharitable contributions are also applicable to solicitations over the Internet.

Many charities solicit charitable contributions by means of their Web page. As the IRS has pointed out, this activity does not raise any "novel tax issues." (Again, as noted, donors need to be certain that the gifts are to qualifying organizations and for qualified purposes.) Then, however, there is a marvelous understatement: "For the charities themselves, a greater concern may be the applicability of state and local laws requiring registration before soliciting contributions. There is some concern that states and local governments will argue that if any resident of their jurisdiction can access a Web site and thus see a solicitation, the charity must register." (See Chapter 12.) Think of the time and financial burdens were that to happen!

The IRS has had something to say about "third-party sites." These are for-profit companies that post a list of charitable organizations. The mission statements are provided, along with a link to charities' own websites if they have one. Gifts are made by credit card. Some time may pass (such as a month) before the company remits the net gifts to the charities. The company retains a portion of the gift (such as 15 percent) as an administrative fee.

Issues arise here, even assuming the donee is a bona fide charity. Is the third-party entity an agent of the charity? (The gift is made to it first.) Is this one of those situations where there is a deductible gift, even though the initial recipient is not a charity, since the funds are earmarked for a charity? The little law there is on the point suggests that, for deductibility to be available, the funds must be transferred to the charity frequently (e.g., weekly). A holding of the funds for a month may preclude deductibility. Moreover, are these third parties functioning as professional fundraisers, requiring registration and reporting under some states' laws?

Regarding marketing, merchandising, advertising, and the like, the IRS has yet to consider many of the questions raised by these activities. (Considering the recent extent and growth of these activities, it is surprising that some guidance has not been forthcoming—see discussion following.) Again, however, the IRS has stated that "it is reasonable to assume that as the Service position develops it will remain consistent with our position with respect to advertising and merchandising and publishing in the off-line world."

The IRS has gingerly broached the subject of charity website HyperText links to related or recommended sites. Link exchanges may cause activities of a linked organization to be attributed to a tax-exempt organization. Compensation for a linkage may be unrelated business income. The purpose of the link may be determinative: Is its purpose furtherance of exempt purposes (a referral of the site visitor to additional educational information) or is it part of an unrelated activity (including advertising)?

Also involved are corporate sponsorships, inasmuch as exempt organizations may seek corporate support to underwrite the production of all or a portion of the organization's website (see Chapter 11). These relationships may be short-term or continue on a long-term basis. The financial support may be acknowledged by means of display of a corporate logo, notation of the sponsor's Web address and/or 800 number, a "moving banner" (defined as a graphic advertisement, usually a moving image, measured in pixels), or a link. The issue here is: Is the support a *qualified sponsorship payment*, in which case the revenue is not taxable, or is it advertising income, which generally is taxable as unrelated business income?

A tax-exempt organization may provide a link to a corporate sponsor and still preserve its treatment of the revenue as a nontaxable corporate sponsorship. Even with a link, the organization's public statement of appreciation for the payment can retain its character as a mere acknowledgment. That is, without more, the presence of a link is not considered a substantial return benefit. A moving banner is more likely to be considered advertising.

Another problem relates to the rule that qualified sponsorship payments do not include payments that entitle the sponsors to acknowledgments to regularly scheduled printed material published by or on behalf of the tax-exempt organization. Here, the issue is the characterization of website materials. The IRS has written: "Most of the materials made available on exempt organization Web sites are clearly prepared in a manner that is distinguishable from the methodology used in the preparation of periodicals."

Nonetheless, the IRS recognizes that there can be an online publication that is treated as a periodical. (When this is the case, the special rules by which unrelated business income from periodical advertising is computed become available.) Some periodicals have online editions and some print publications are reproduced online, sometimes on a subscription basis or in a member-only access portion of a website. The IRS has observed that these "materials should be and generally are sufficiently segregated from the other traditional Web site materials so that the methodology employed in the production and distribution methods are clearly ascertainable and the periodical income and costs can be independently and appropriately determined." The IRS adds that presumably "genuine" periodicals have an editorial staff, marketing program, and budget independent of the organization's Webmaster.

Then there is the matter of the *virtual trade show*, which generates income for trade associations and other exempt entities from *virtual exhibitors*. This brings into play the rules by which traditional trade show income is excluded from the unrelated business income tax (see previous discussion). The IRS has written that the extent to which the traditional rules will apply to virtual trade show income "will most likely depend in large part on whether the qualifying organization is able to demonstrate that its exhibits or displays are substantially similar to those traditionally carried on at a trade show."

The IRS has hinted that the tax exclusion is not available for a mere listing of links to industry suppliers' websites. In addition, it is "highly questionable" whether income from a year-round virtual trade show is excludable from unrelated business income. Conversely, virtual trade shows with displays including educational information related to issues of interest to industry members, or those that are timed to coincide with the sponsoring organization's annual meeting or regular trade show may qualify for the exclusion.

What about online storefronts, complete with virtual shopping carts, on exempt organizations' websites? Again, the IRS expects to be using the same analysis that it applies in sales made through stores, catalogs, and other traditional vehicles. Reference has been made to the comparable treatment of museum gift shop sales. In deciding whether the unrelated business income tax applies, the IRS looks to the nature, scope, and motivation for the particular sales activities. Merchandise is evaluated on an item-by-item basis (applying the previously noted *fragmentation rule*) to determine whether the sales activity furthers the accomplishment of the organization's exempt purposes or is simply a way to increase revenue.

As to online auctions, the IRS is particularly concerned with charities' use of "outside auction service providers." The IRS has recognized that utilization of these providers may provide a larger audience for the auction and enable the organization to avoid credit card problems, but it cautions that the relationship "might have tax implications."

Again, as is the case with respect to subsidiaries (see Chapter 17) and joint ventures (see Chapter 18), the focus is on *control*. The IRS will consider how much control the charity exercises over the marketing and conduct of the auction. The IRS wants the charity to have "primary responsibility" in this regard. Otherwise, the IRS "may be more likely to view income from such auction activities as income from classified advertising rather than as income derived from the conduct of a fundraising event." A warning: The IRS stated that these service providers are "essentially professional fundraisers" (with implications concerning state charitable solicitation acts), and thus their functions and fees should be scrutinized using the doctrines of private inurement and private benefit.

Finally, the IRS is concerned about affiliate and other co-venture programs with merchants. Of particular note are arrangements with large, online booksellers. Some exempt organizations make book recommendations that are displayed on their website; others have a link to the bookseller. The exempt organization earns a percentage of sales from recommended materials and perhaps also a commission on purchases sold through the referring link. The principal issue here is whether the resulting income is a tax-excludable royalty.

On this point, the IRS analogizes to the litigation involving the tax treatment mailing list and affinity card income. The IRS again stated its view that the marketing of a credit card by an exempt organization constitutes services typically provided by a commercial company. The IRS has ruefully noted that (as discussed previously) this view has not prevailed in the many cases contested in the courts.

(a) Gaming

The IRS is concerned about gaming—or, if you prefer, gambling—by nonprofit, tax-exempt organizations. Yet, aside from an exception in the unrelated business rules for bingo games (see Chapter), there is no formal federal tax law on the point.

Nonetheless, the views of the IRS on the subject are found in its examination guidelines (see Chapter 24) and forms and instructions accompanying the new annual information return (see Chapter 9). As to the latter, nonprofit organizations with any appreciable amount of gaming activity must report it on a schedule.

The instructions accompanying the new annual information return state that the term *gaming* includes "bingo, pull tabs/instant bingo (including satellite and progressive bingo), Texas Hold-Em Poker and other card games, raffles, scratch-offs, [use of] charitable gaming tickets, break-opens, hard cards, banded tickets, jar tickets, pickle cards, Lucky Seven cards, Nevada Club tickets, casino nights, Las Vegas nights, and coin-operated gambling devices." *Coin-operated gambling devices* include "slot machines, electronic video slot or line games, video poker, video blackjack, video keno, video bingo, [and] video pull tab games."

The main focus of the IRS in this regard, principally in the contexts of examinations, is on bingo and pull-tab games. Bingo games are, as noted, generally excluded from the definition of unrelated business. Nonetheless, however, the regular operation by a tax-exempt organization of gaming activities (including instant bingo, pull-tab games, and the like) is likely to be the conduct of an unrelated business, particularly where the activities involve the public. A gaming activity conducted entirely by volunteers may be exempt from unrelated business taxation.

In some instances, gaming activities can be substantially related activities, such as when conducted by a tax-exempt organization for social or recreational purposes for its members and their bona fide guests. These exempt organizations include social clubs, fraternal beneficiary societies, domestic fraternal societies, and veterans' organizations. Gaming activities involving only members and their guests directly furthers exempt purposes in these instances.

A *nonmember*, in this context, is defined in the annual return instructions as an "individual who is not a member of the organization but who participates in recreational activities sponsored by the organization or receives services or goods from the organization and pays for the services or goods received." These instructions continue, "Such an individual, even when accompanied by a member, is generally considered to be the principal in a business transaction with the organization. Gaming open to the general public may result in unrelated business income tax (UBIT) or adversely affect exempt status."

Many states have gaming laws that identify the types of organizations that are allowed to conduct gaming activities and the conditions pursuant to which the games may be conducted (such as a requirement that volunteers be utilized or a limit on the number of nights in a week a tax-exempt organization can conduct gaming activity). If there is an IRS examination of an exempt organization as to gaming, it should be expected that the examining agent(s) will be aware of the state's agency in charge of gaming activities enforcement, policy memoranda, and reporting requirements.

CHARITABLE REMAINDER TRUSTS

For many years a charitable remainder trust (see Chapter 19) could not be tax-exempt for any year in which the trust had any unrelated business taxable income. A trust in this circumstance was taxed on all of its income for the year. Today, however, the good news is that charitable remainder trusts that have unrelated business taxable income remain exempt from federal income tax. The bad news is that the trust will be assessed a 100 percent excise tax on that income.

CONCLUSION

The unrelated income rules represent an attempt by Congress to prevent tax-exempt organizations from unfairly competing with for-profit businesses. These rules generally equalize the tax treatment of unrelated business activities by segregating them, for tax purposes, from the other activities of tax-exempt organizations and taxing them as though they were free-standing business undertakings.

For an activity to be taxable under these rules, it must be a trade or business that is regularly carried on and is not substantially related to the performance of tax-exempt functions. If a tax-exempt organization uses the net revenue from an unrelated business to fund related activities, that use is not enough to convert the unrelated activity into a related one.

The law provides a variety of exemptions that allow certain activities and certain forms of income to be tax-free. The most important of these exemptions is for passive income.

In computing taxable unrelated income, a tax-exempt organization may utilize all business expense deductions, as long as the expenses are directly related to the conduct of the unrelated business.

As tax-exempt organizations struggle to generate additional income in these days of declining governmental support, proposed adverse tax reform, more sophisticated management, and greater pressure for more services, they are increasingly drawn to service-provider activities, some of which may be unrelated to their exempt purposes.

The growth of service-provider activities, the increasing tendencies of the courts to find activities unrelated because they are *commercial*, and the unrest over *unfair competition* between tax-exempt organizations and for-profit entities—all of these are clear evidence that this aspect of the law of tax-exempt organizations is constantly evolving and will be reshaped. Indeed, the IRS has been concentrating its audit force on universities, colleges, and hospitals, hoping to tap unrelated business income as one of the main areas for new revenue.

This subject is among the most fast-paced of any topics covered by federal tax law. All indications are that this trend will continue.

Checklist

❏ Does the organization have one or more unrelated businesses?
Yes _____ No_____

❏ If yes, identify them:

_____

_____

_____

If yes and if applicable, check one or more of the following:

The organization does not pay any unrelated business income tax because:

❑ The activity is not regularly carried on.

❑ The income from the activity is considered passive income.

❑ The business is conducted substantially by volunteers.

❑ The convenience exception is used.

❑ The items sold were donated.

❑ The activity is a qualified public entertainment activity.

❑ The activity is an exempted game of chance.

❑ The standard deduction applies.

❑ The expenses are equal to or exceed the unrelated income.

❑ One or more other reasons are applicable.

❑ Does the organization have any unrelated debt-financed income?
Yes _____ No _____

FOCUS: Campaign to Clean Up America

The Campaign to Clean Up America (CCUA) does not initially intend to conduct any unrelated business activities. Its service-provider revenue will be insubstantial and is expected to come from related businesses (such as seminars and the sale of publications).

As the CCUA grows and becomes known, however, it may find that it can profitably engage in one or more unrelated businesses. For example, it could sell trash bags and similar supplies and equipment. It could provide property maintenance services for individuals or communities. It could consult with government agencies in the development and maintenance of large-scale beautification programs.

Some of these unrelated activities could be conducted within the organization. Others could be undertaken by means of one or more for-profit subsidiaries.

CHAPTER FOURTEEN

Lobbying Constraints—And Taxes

Congress has long been concerned with attempts to influence legislation—lobbying—by nonprofit organizations. This concern is particularly evident in the federal tax law pertaining to charitable organizations and trade, business, and professional associations. The Treasury Department and the IRS have promulgated extremely stringent regulations and rules in an attempt to restrict lobbying by nonprofit organizations—most notably, charitable groups. The federal courts are upholding the government in its efforts to enforce these constraints.

Regulation in this area is currently active. Congress, in 1987, introduced rules in an effort to further limit lobbying by charitable organizations and, to some extent, other nonprofit organizations. The Treasury Department and the IRS issued sweeping regulations in an effort to curb lobbying by public charities and related organizations. (The tax law generally prohibits lobbying by private foundations.)

In addition to the tax law, other federal law imposes meaningful constraints on lobbying by nonprofit organizations. For example, the U.S. Postal Service will not allow the use of the nonprofit mailing rates by nonprofit groups whose primary purpose is lobbying. Under authority of the Federal Regulation of Lobbying Act, lobbying organizations or individual lobbyists are required to register with the clerks of the House of Representatives and the Senate. Still other laws may have an impact in this area; among them are the law requiring registration and reporting by lobbyists for foreign governments and the laws restricting the use of federal funds for lobbying (such as various rules of the Office of Management and Budget and the Byrd Amendment). Also, most states have laws regulating lobbying by nonprofit and other organizations.

The principal laws regulating lobbying by nonprofit organizations, however, are the federal tax laws. They are explored in this chapter.

LOBBYING RESTRICTIONS ON CHARITABLE ORGANIZATIONS

Organizations that are tax-exempt because they are charitable in nature (this classification includes educational, religious, scientific, and similar entities) must, to preserve the exemption, adhere to a variety of requirements. One of these is that "no substantial part of the activities" of the organization may constitute "carrying on propaganda, or otherwise attempting, to influence legislation." Because of the considerable and continuing uncertainty as to the meaning and scope of this rule, many nonprofit organizations have experienced much anguish in attempting to fathom this *substantial part test*.

The difficulties of compliance with this limitation on legislative activities have been manifold. In reaction to an increasingly intolerable situation, Congress, in 1976, tried to clarify compliance but failed, due in no small part to the insistence of the IRS in proposing broad rules in interpretation of the statutory law. As is so often the case with "tax reform," the law ends up being much more complicated than it was before.

The law in this area has three sets of rules. One set of rules applies to private foundations (essentially, no lobbying). The other two sets of rules are available for other types of charitable organizations (public charities). (For the distinctions between public and private charities, see Chapter 17.) One of these sets of rules, which is available to most public charities, must be elected by them. This is called the *expenditure test*. The third set of rules, called the *substantial part test*, is applicable to those public charities that have not (or cannot) come within the elective rules.

Why, as a matter of policy, is it inappropriate for a charitable organization to engage in lobbying in pursuit of its exempt purposes? The law on this subject was originally enacted in 1934, without benefit of congressional hearings, in an effort to stop the activities of a particular organization that had antagonized some members of the U.S. Senate. Case law prior to that date suggests that lobbying may be a legitimate way for a charitable organization to pursue its exempt goals; there is nothing in the common law of charitable trusts (on which the tax law of charities is based) that specifies that lobbying by charitable groups is contrary to their status as charities. One clue to the rationale for the prohibition was offered by the U.S. Supreme Court in 1983, when it observed that Congress, in enacting the substantial part test, "was concerned that exempt [charitable] organizations might use tax-deductible contributions to lobby to promote the private interests of their members." The Treasury Department has expressed opposition to any relaxation of the limitation on lobbying by charitable organizations. Liberalization of the rules, said the Treasury, would enable more nonprofit entities to become classified as charitable ones, therefore becoming eligible to attract deductible gifts and in turn helping to aggravate the federal deficit by increasing the use of the charitable contribution deduction!

Philosophical or policy considerations aside, the law is the law. Lobbying by public charities is restricted under either set of rules. If a charitable organization, relying on the expenditure test, loses its tax exemption because of lobbying activities, it may not convert to a tax-exempt social welfare organization (see discussion following).

(a) Lobbying

The general rules pertaining to lobbying by public charities are found in the Treasury regulations, IRS rulings, and court opinions that comprise the body of law consisting of the substantial part test. These rules label a charitable organization that has lobbying as a substantial activity an *action* organization—and, needless to say, action organizations are not tax-exempt as charities.

Legislative activities can take many forms. Some amount to *direct* lobbying, which occurs when one or more representatives of an organization make contact with a legislator or his or her staff or the staff of legislative committees. Direct lobbying includes office visits, presentation of testimony at hearings, correspondence, publication and dissemination of material, e-mail and other Internet communications, and entertainment.

Grass-roots (or indirect) lobbying is another form. This type of lobbying occurs when the organization urges the public, or a segment of the public, to contact members of a legislative body or their staffs for the purpose of proposing, supporting, or opposing legislation.

Generally, the federal tax rules concerning lobbying and political campaign activities (see Chapter 15) are separate, discrete bodies of law. If, however, a nonprofit organization engages in grass-roots lobbying, doing so in the context of a political campaign, so that the advocacy of the issue(s) involved can be tied to the political fortunes of a candidate, the lobbying activity can also be regarded as political campaign activity. Undertakings of this nature are said to have a *dual character*.

The law, under the substantial part test, does not differentiate between lobbying that is related to an organization's exempt purposes and lobbying that is not. The function is still lobbying, and both types are subject to the proscription. A charitable organization, however, that does not initiate any action with respect to pending legislation but merely responds to a request from a legislative committee to testify is not, solely because of that activity, considered an action organization. Also, a charitable organization can engage in nonpartisan analysis, study, and research and can publish its results. Even where some of the plans and policies formulated can be carried out only through legislative enactments, as long as the organization does not advocate the adoption of legislation or legislative action to implement its findings, it escapes being an action organization. In both of these instances, the organization is advancing education, not engaging in advocacy activities.

There can be a fine line between nonpartisan analysis, study, or research, and lobbying. An organization may evaluate proposed or pending legislation and present to the public an objective analysis of it, as long as it does not participate in the presentation of suggested bills to a legislature and does not engage in any campaign to secure enactment of the legislation. If the organization's primary objective can be attained only by legislative action, however, it is an action organization.

For example, a nonprofit organization was formed to study alternatives to federal tax reform; it had an affiliated fundraising fund. The organization did not conclude its work with a report summarizing tax reform options, such as a value-added tax, a national sales tax, or retention of the present system. Instead, it recommended only one choice—a flat tax system. Inasmuch as that outcome can be accomplished only by legislative action, the courts held that the affiliated fund was an action organization and thus not eligible for tax-exempt status. In general, then, promoting activism instead of promoting educational activities can deny an organization classification as a charitable entity.

(b) Legislation

Because these rules obviously apply to legislative activities—activities undertaken in connection with the championing or opposing of legislation—it is necessary to know what does and does not constitute *legislation*. The term *legislation* refers principally to action by the U.S. Congress, a state legislative body, a local council or similar governing body, and by the general public in a referendum, initiative, constitutional amendment, or similar procedure. In the view of the IRS, congressional action on cabinet and judicial nominees constitutes *legislating*. Legislation does not generally include action by the executive branch, such as the promulgation of rules and regulations, nor does it include action by the independent regulatory agencies. Charitable organizations can lobby executive branch and independent agencies in support of or opposition to the agencies' rules, and the lobbying will not endanger their tax-exempt status.

(c) Substantiality

The most important concept under the general rules is the meaning of the word *substantial*. As noted earlier, the law offers no formula for computing *substantial* or *insubstantial* legislative undertakings.

There are at least three ways to measure *substantial* in this context:

1. Determine what percentage of an organization's annual expenditures are devoted to efforts to influence legislation

2. Apply a percentage to the legislative activities themselves, in relation to total activities

3. Ascertain (usually with hindsight) whether an organization has had a substantial impact on the legislative process simply by virtue of its prestige and influence

Case law and IRS practice support the use of all three practices.

The IRS being the IRS, substantiality is usually measured in terms of money. Because of the way the term *substantial* is used in other tax contexts, it is likely that a public charity's annual outlays for lobbying can constitute up to 15 percent of its total expenditures without causing loss of tax-exempt status. (It must be emphasized strongly, however, that this is merely a guideline, based on practical experience, and should not be regarded as a rule of law.)

The true measure of substantiality remains elusive. In reports accompanying tax legislation over the years, the Senate Finance Committee has characterized the state of affairs well. In 1969, the Committee wrote that the "standards as to the permissible level of [legislative] activities under the present law are so vague as to encourage subjective application of the sanction." Later, in 1976, the Finance Committee portrayed the dilemma this way: "Many believe that the standards as to the permissible level of [legislative] activities under present law are too vague and thereby tend to encourage subjective and selective enforcement."

The confusion and frustration with the substantial part test of the general rules led to enactment of the expenditure test, discussed in the following section. The chafing under the restrictions also led to litigation challenging the general rule on constitutional law grounds. Essentially, the courts have upheld the limitation in the face of charges that it violates free speech and equal protection rights. The rationale is that the tax law does not prohibit organizations from engaging in substantial efforts to influence legislation; it merely refrains from allowing the federal treasury to subsidize the lobbying efforts. As the U.S. Supreme Court stated in 1983, the constraints pass constitutional muster and "Congress has merely refused to pay for the lobbying out of public moneys."

(d) Lobbying Taxes

Lobbying by charitable organizations, or on their behalf by related nonprofit organizations, was the subject of congressional hearings in 1987. The result was enactment of even more legislation, designed to give the general rules more strength.

The 1987 legislation, which is applicable to most public charities, introduced a system of excise taxes on excess lobbying outlays. Under these rules, if a charitable organization loses its tax exemption because of attempts to influence legislation, a tax of 5 percent of the *lobbying expenditures* is imposed on the organization. (This tax *does not apply* to any organization that is under the expenditure test described below or that is ineligible to make that election.) A lobbying expenditure is any amount paid or incurred by a charitable organization in carrying on propaganda or otherwise attempting to influence legislation.

A separate 5 percent tax is applicable to each of the organization's managers (its officers, directors, and key employees) who agreed to the lobbying expenditures (knowing they were likely to result in revocation of its exemption), unless the agreement was not willful and was due to reasonable cause. The burden of proof for whether a manager knowingly participated in the lobbying expenditure is on the IRS. The imposition of an excise tax on an organization does not itself establish that any manager of the organization is subject to the excise tax.

(e) Expenditure Test

The expenditure test regarding permissible lobbying by charitable organizations arose from a desire to clarify the law that had been made unclear by the substantial part test. In other words, the purpose of this test is to offer charitable groups some certainty on how much lobbying they can undertake without endangering their tax-exempt status. This purpose has not been fulfilled: The IRS has made the rules sweeping and complex, and few organizations have elected to use the rules. (Some day, Congress may make the expenditure test rules mandatory, as a definition of the substantial part standard.)

The expenditure test utilizes a tax system as well, although none of the taxes falls on individuals involved. These rules are not a substitute for the general rules (embodied in the substantial part test) but serve as a "safe harbor" guideline, so that a charitable organization that is in compliance with the expenditure test is deemed to be in conformance with the general rules.

These rules are termed *elective* because charitable organizations must elect to come under these standards. Organizations that choose not to make the election are governed by the substantial part test, with all of its uncertainties. Churches, conventions or associations of churches, integrated auxiliaries of churches, certain supporting organizations, and (of course) private foundations may not elect to come under the expenditure test.

The expenditure test rules provide a definition of terms such as *legislation, influencing legislation, direct lobbying,* and *grass-roots lobbying.* These terms are essentially the same as those used in connection with the substantial part test. In an attempt to define when the legislative process begins (and, therefore, when a lobbying process begins), however, the expenditure test offers a definition of legislative *action:* the "introduction, amendment, enactment, defeat, or repeal of Acts, bills, resolutions, or similar items."

The expenditure test measures permissible and impermissible legislative activities of charitable organizations in terms of sets of declining percentages of total exempt purpose expenditures. (These do not include fundraising expenses.) The basic permitted annual level of expenditures for legislative efforts (termed the *lobbying nontaxable amount*) is 20 percent of the first $500,000 of an organization's expenditures for an exempt purpose (including legislative activities), plus 15 percent of the next $500,000, 10 percent of the next $500,000, and 5 percent of any remaining expenditures. The total amount spent for legislative activities in any one year by an electing charitable organization may not exceed $1 million. A separate limitation—amounting to one-fourth of the foregoing amounts—is imposed on grass-roots lobbying expenditures.

Here is where some other taxes come in. A charitable organization that has elected these limitations and exceeds either the general lobbying ceiling amount or the grass-roots lobbying ceiling amount becomes subject to an excise tax of 25 percent of the excess lobbying expenditures. The tax falls on the greater of the two excesses. If an electing organization's lobbying expenditures normally (an average over a four-year period) exceed 150 percent of either limitation, it will lose its tax-exempt status as a charitable organization.

The expenditure test rules contain exemptions for five categories of activities. The term *influencing legislation* does not include

1. Making available the results of nonpartisan analysis, study, or research.

2. Providing technical advice or assistance in response to a written request by a governmental body.

3. Appearances before, or communications to, any legislative body in connection with a possible decision of that body that might affect the existence of the organization, its powers and duties, its tax-exempt status, or the deductibility of contributions to it.

4. Communications between the organization and its bona fide members regarding legislation or proposed legislation that is of direct interest to them, unless the communications directly encourage the members to influence legislation or to urge nonmembers to influence legislation.

5. Routine communications with government officials or employees.

The third of these exemptions is an underutilized one; it is known as the *self-defense exception*. Sheltered by this exception is *all* lobbying by a qualified public charity, as long as it can be reasonably rationalized in regard to one or more of the allowable purposes.

The expenditure test contains a method of aggregating the expenditures of related organizations. The intent is to forestall the creation of numerous organizations for the purpose of avoiding the expenditure test.

Where two or more charitable organizations are members of an *affiliated group* and at least one of the members has elected coverage under these provisions, the calculations of lobbying and exempt purpose expenditures must take into account the expenditures of the group. If these expenditures exceed the permitted limits, each of the electing member organizations must pay a proportionate share of the penalty excise tax. The nonelecting members are treated under the substantial part test.

Generally, two organizations are *affiliated* where (1) one organization is bound by decisions of the other on legislative issues as stated in its governing instrument or (2) the governing board of one organization includes enough representatives of the other (that is, there is an interlocking directorate) to cause or prevent action on legislative issues by the first organization. Where a number of organizations are affiliated, even in chain fashion, all of them are treated as one group of affiliated organizations. If a group of autonomous organizations controls an organization but no one member of the group has exclusive control of the organization, however, the group is not considered an affiliated group by reason of the interlocking directorates rule.

Special reporting requirements are imposed on charitable organizations that engage in lobbying. One set of obligations is for those under the substantial part test; the other set is for organizations that have elected the expenditure test. The record-keeping and reporting requirements are more onerous for charitable organizations that are under the expenditure test, although the IRS is working to bring approximately equal reporting burdens to groups under the substantial part test.

(f) Should the Election Be Made?

There is some controversy as to whether, or when, a charitable organization should elect to come under the expenditure test. The IRS strenuously advocates the election (so it can obtain the additional information on lobbying that must be reported). The biggest advantages to the election are that

- The test can offer greater certainty on the amount of permissible lobbying.
- The tax rules enacted in 1987 are not applicable.
- Various statutory exceptions apply.
- The time of volunteers is excluded from the computation of lobbying time.
- The method used for computing and reporting lobbying expenditures can be used in complying with the Federal Regulation of Lobbying Act (see discussion following).

The biggest disadvantages are that

- Recordkeeping and reporting requirements are more extensive.
- Assessment of permissible lobbying is still sometimes uncertain.
- The election can be particularly onerous for grass-roots lobbying organizations.
- The rules concerning affiliated organizations apply.
- The organization cannot convert to a social welfare organization.

(g) Where Are We?

These rules concerning lobbying and charities seemed, until recently, relatively clear: Charitable organizations may not make substantial expenditures for the purpose of influencing legislation. A federal court of appeals, however, wrote (having held that a charitable organization was not tax-exempt because of undue lobbying): "We are not holding that any organization which studies an issue touching on legislation, reaches a conclusion with respect to that issue, and then argues the merits of that conclusion must necessarily be characterized as an 'action' organization." What does that mean? Since when does pre-lobbying "study" immunize the activity from being cast as lobbying?

The court then further muddied these waters. It added: "We are simply holding that an organization which assumes a conclusion with respect to a highly public and controversial legislative issue and then goes into the business of selling that conclusion may properly be designated an 'action' organization." Again, what does that mean? What is the difference between arguing the merits of a conclusion in a legislative setting and attempting to "sell" a conclusion? It looks like more lawsuits will be needed to resolve this issue.

LOBBYING RESTRICTIONS ON OTHER NONPROFIT ORGANIZATIONS

The federal law pertaining to tax-exempt status imposes lobbying restrictions only on charitable organizations, not on other nonprofit organizations. The only constraint (if it can even be called that) is that the organization must pursue its exempt functions (whatever they may be) as its primary purpose and that any lobbying it may do must not interfere with that principal requirement. Basically, entities such as social welfare organizations, labor organizations, business and professional associations (business leagues), and veterans' organizations may lobby without restriction.

Indeed, this stark contrast in the law between charitable organizations and other types of tax-exempt organizations (even those to which deductible gifts can be made) gave rise to challenges to the general rules on equal protection grounds. But the U.S. Supreme Court ruled that "[l]egislatures have especially broad latitude in creating classifications and distinctions in tax statutes."

Because of these distinctions, charitable organizations are afforded a major opportunity to sidestep the rigorous rules regulating lobbying by them: A charitable organization can create a related social welfare organization and use it as a lobbying arm. Some Justices of the U.S. Supreme Court believe that the easy availability of tax-exempt lobbying arms of charitable organizations is the feature of the tax law that prevents the lobbying restrictions on charities from being unconstitutional.

A few other aspects of the federal tax laws bear on this matter. These are described next.

(a) Associations

Nonprofit membership associations are generally tax-exempt. Most of these are trade, business, or professional associations (business leagues) or charitable organizations. Others are labor organizations or social welfare organizations. The pertinent common element is that all of these associations receive dues revenue and, in many cases, the dues are deductible as business expenses.

Associations are not restricted as to lobbying by the rules governing their tax-exempt status. Generally, however, since there is no business expense deduction for an amount paid in connection with influencing legislation, lobbying by an association can reduce the deductibility of its members' dues. The amount of an association's total annual expenditures is compared with its lobbying outlays for the year, and that ratio is applied to the dues amount for purposes of determining the extent to which the dues are deductible as a business expense. For example, if an association spends 25 percent of its funds in a year for lobbying and the annual dues are $100, a member of the association can deduct only $75 of the dues. This is a *flow-through rule.*

An association, in this circumstance, must disclose in its annual information return (see Chapter 9) the total amount of its lobbying expenditures and the amount of dues allocable to these expenditures. The association also must notify its members regarding the portion of the dues the organization reasonably estimates will be allocable to its lobbying expenditures during the year. If an association's lobbying expenditures for a year exceed this estimate, the organization may have to pay a *proxy tax* on the excess amount. This tax may also be applicable if the association failed to provide its members with the requisite notice.

There are many exceptions to these rules. For example, the disclosure and notice requirements are not applicable to an association where substantially all of its members are not entitled to deduct their dues. Some organizations, such as labor unions, are completely exempted from these rules.

Not surprisingly, the association community is unhappy with this dues deduction reduction and proxy tax scheme. Litigation challenging the constitutionality of these rules, basically on free speech claims, has failed. The courts are finding the rules rational, as part of Congress's decision to eliminate a tax subsidy for lobbying. As one court stated the matter, this law "does not discriminate against [associations] if they seek to influence legislation; the [law] simply advances Congress's purpose that such speech not be paid for with pretax dollars."

(b) Political Organizations

One type of tax-exempt organization is the *political organization*. A political organization, such as a political action committee (PAC), is unlikely to engage in lobbying. Legislative activities are not *exempt functions* for a political organization and may cause taxation if they are undertaken.

To qualify for exemption, a political organization must be organized and operated primarily for the purpose of directly or indirectly accepting contributions and making expenditures for an exempt function. In this context, an exempt function is influencing or attempting to influence the selection, nomination, election, or appointment of any individual to any federal, state, or local public office. Lobbying, then, is not an exempt function for a political committee. If lobbying is done in an insubstantial amount by a political committee, the outcome from a tax law viewpoint would be the payment of some tax; if done in violation of the primary purpose standard, the outcome would be loss of tax-exempt status.

(c) Other Organizations

As observed previously, nearly all forms of tax-exempt organizations may engage in lobbying without endangering their tax exemption under federal law. The exceptions, in varying degrees, are charitable organizations, membership associations, and political organizations.

There are a few instances where lobbying activities are inconsistent with tax-exempt status. One example is the title-holding corporation—either single-parent or multiparent (see Chapter 4)—which must be operated for the exclusive purpose of holding title to property and paying over the income from the property to its parent. Lobbying by such an entity would be contrary to the exclusivity requirement and inconsistent with the passive nature of the organization. Some governmental units may operate under restrictions that preclude lobbying. No type of tax-exempt organization, however, other than the charitable one, is expressly prohibited from engaging in activities to influence legislation.

NONTAX RULES

There are bodies of law, other than federal taxation, that may pertain to lobbying done by or for nonprofit organizations. The principal law outside the federal tax context is the Federal Regulation of Lobbying Act. Most individuals who lobby for compensation must register with and report to the Clerk of the House of Representatives and the Secretary of the Senate.

There are other rules. The Byrd Amendment prohibits the use of federal funds received as grants, contracts, loans, or pursuant to cooperative agreements for attempts to influence an officer or employee of a governmental agency in connection with the awarding, obtaining, or making of any federal contract, grant, loan, or cooperative agreement. Regulations published by the U.S. Office of Management and Budget provide that costs associated with most forms of lobbying activities do not qualify for reimbursement by the federal government.

Most states have laws regulating lobbying by nonprofit and other organizations.

Checklist

- ❏ Does the organization engage in legislative activities?
  Yes _____ No _____

- ❏ If yes, how much money was expended for legislative activities over the past year? $ _____

- ❏ What percentage of total annual expenditures is this amount? _____ %

- ❏ If yes:

- ❏ How much was spent for direct lobbying? $ _____

- ❏ How much was spent for grass-roots lobbying? $ _____

- ❏ What was the total value of volunteer time? $ _____

- ❏ If a charitable organization, has it elected the expenditure test?
  Yes _____ No _____

- ❏ Does the organization keep its board of directors informed as to its legislative activities? Yes _____ No _____

- ❏ Does the organization have a related and/or affiliated organization that engages in lobbying? Yes _____ No _____

FOCUS: Campaign to Clean Up America

The Campaign to Clean Up America (CCUA) has exempt purposes that clearly can be furthered by lobbying. Its primary purposes—volunteer clean-up programs and public education—enable it to qualify as a charitable organization. Still, the CCUA would like to press for federal, state, and local law changes, such as tougher penalties for those who litter and incentive programs for those who collect and dispose of trash found in public places.

You, as president, and your CCUA managers have a decision to make: Should you elect to bring the CCUA under the expenditure test for public charities? After consulting with legal counsel, you and your managers choose not to make the election at this time, because the amount of lobbying that is contemplated is less than 10 percent of total activities. Also, a substantial portion of the lobbying that is to be done may be grass-roots lobbying, and the CCUA would like to avoid the narrower range of percentages that the elective rules impose on that type of lobbying. Besides, because of this decision, the CCUA is not subject to the detailed IRS regulations that accompany the expenditure test, and it need not annually report its legislative activities to the IRS in the detailed form required of electing organizations.

Indeed, you and the management of the CCUA have decided to seriously consider organizing and operating a related social welfare organization for the purpose of conducting lobbying activities, should the level of lobbying increase beyond the 10 to 15 percent range.

CHAPTER FIFTEEN

Political Campaign Activities— And More Taxes

Congress and the IRS, as troubled as they are about nonprofit entities' lobbying activities, are even more concerned about political campaign activities by nonprofit organizations, particularly charitable ones. There are vagaries and uncertainties associated with federal constraints on lobbying activities, but the federal tax law regulating political campaign activities is relatively clear.

An extensive federal statute—the Federal Election Campaign Act—regulates political campaign activity, and a federal agency—the Federal Election Commission—enforces the law in this area. This area of the law was substantially revised by enactment of the Bipartisan Campaign Reform Act, which the Supreme Court, in 2003, pronounced constitutional. The election laws and the tax laws are clearly separate sets of requirements, yet there is interplay between them. Nonprofit organizations are very much subject to the federal election laws and thus should arrange their activities to conform with those laws as well as the tax laws. State laws operate to regulate intrastate political campaign activity.

POLITICAL ACTIVITIES BY CHARITABLE ORGANIZATIONS

Congress has decreed –flatly—that tax-exempt charitable organizations may not engage in political campaign activity. There may be no other provision in federal or state law concerning nonprofit organizations that has been so repeatedly and conspicuously violated.

(a) General Rules

The prohibition states that charitable organizations must "not participate in, or intervene in (including the publishing or distributing of statements), any political campaign on behalf of or in opposition to any candidate for public office." Coincidentally, this restriction originated in the U.S. Senate, as did the lobbying limitations on charitable organizations (see Chapter 14).

There were no hearings on the restriction, and its enactment can be traced to one senator's interest in preventing campaign activity (against him) by a particular organization. (As described in Chapter 7, there are separate rules against electioneering that are applicable only to private foundations.)

The prohibition on charitable organizations' involvement in political campaigns is said by the IRS to be absolute; the rules do not use a substantiality test. As a practical matter, a minor involvement in a political campaign may not trigger loss of exemption because, as one court put it, a "slight and comparatively unimportant deviation from the narrow furrow of tax approved activity is not fatal."

The concept of an *action organization* (see Chapter 14) is used in the political campaign context. An action organization is one that participates or intervenes, directly or indirectly, in any political campaign on behalf of or in opposition to any candidate for public office. An action organization cannot qualify as a charitable organization. No charitable organization may make a contribution to a political candidate's campaign, endorse or oppose a candidate, or otherwise support a political candidacy.

A dramatic illustration of the applicability of this law occurred in mid-1999. Earlier, the IRS had revoked the tax-exempt status of a church as the result of its involvement in the 1992 presidential campaign. The church, in full-page newspaper advertisements, expressed its concern about the moral character of one of the candidates. The matter was litigated, and two federal courts upheld the revocation. This development surprised many, in that the IRS did not do what it often does in cases of first violation of this rule: either simply to warn the offending organization or to impose the tax on political expenditures (see discussion following).

Most of the law amplifying the political campaign proscription for charitable groups is in IRS rulings. These rulings, over the years, have been uniformly rigid in their finding that nearly any activity relating to the political process will prevent charitable organizations from being tax-exempt. For example, the evaluation of candidates, the administration of a fair campaign practices code, and assistance to individuals after they have been elected have been found to be prohibited activities.

In recent years, the IRS has relented somewhat, conceding that voter education activities are permissible for charitable organizations. As an illustration, a charitable organization can prepare and disseminate a compilation of the voting records of legislators on a variety of subjects, as long as there is no editorial comment and no approval or disapproval of the voting records is implied. A charitable organization may also conduct public forums where there is a fair and impartial treatment of political candidates. In practice, some charitable organizations have disseminated information about candidates' voting records and positions on issues in formats that clearly reflect approval and disapproval, but the IRS has not acted to stop them. While this practice remains risky, it is less so where the opinionated material is not widely distributed to the general public or not timed to be disseminated on the eve of an election.

Despite the stringent prohibition on their political campaign activities, the law permits charitable organizations to engage in educational undertakings, such as instruction of the public on matters useful to individuals and beneficial to communities. There is an inherent tension between political campaign activities and educational activities—just as there is within the constraints on legislative activities.

Some charitable organizations have cautiously entered the political milieu, as part of the process of advancing education. For example, charitable organizations have been permitted to assemble and donate to libraries the campaign speeches, interviews, and other materials of a candidate for a historically important elective office and to conduct public forums at which debates and lectures on social, political, and international questions are considered.

In performing this type of educational activity, however, charitable organizations are expected to present a balanced view of the pertinent facts. Members of the public must be permitted to form their own opinion or conclusion independent of any presented by the organization. The organization may advocate a particular position or viewpoint, but not a particular candidate. A charitable organization may seek to educate the public on patriotic, political, and civic matters, but it may not do so by using disparaging terms, insinuations, innuendos, or suggested implications drawn from incomplete facts. In a sense, this aspect of the prohibition on political activity is not unlike the prohibition on propagandizing that is part of the constraints on lobbying by charitable groups.

Until recently, the IRS generally did little to enforce this law, notwithstanding innumerable well-publicized incidents of transgression of it. In 2004, the agency abruptly changed course and began closely monitoring the involvement of churches and other public charities in political campaigns. This effort continued with the 2006 and 2008 elections, and is expected to remain an IRS audit priority (see Chapter 24). Indeed, the IRS now expects, because of its strenuous examination undertakings in this area, to face challenges (most likely on free speech grounds) in the courts. (Prediction: The IRS will not lose these cases.)

(b) Taxation of Political Expenditures

Once, the only legal sanction for charitable organizations' violation of the political campaign activities proscription was revocation of their tax-exempt status. Congress came to see that sanction as somewhat ineffective. The IRS had little revenue incentive to take such drastic action. The organizations involved, as well as those who managed them, had little incentive to strictly adhere to the rules: They could simply start anew with a successor organization. The enactment of a law in 1987 dramatically changed the rules of this game.

The federal tax law levies taxes in situations where a charitable organization makes a *political expenditure*. Generally, a political expenditure is any amount paid or incurred by a charitable organization in any participation or intervention (including the publication or distribution of statements) in any political campaign, on behalf of or in opposition to any candidate for public office.

In an effort to discourage ostensibly educational organizations from operating in tandem with political campaigns, the term *political expenditure* also applies with respect to "an organization which is formed primarily for purposes of promoting the candidacy (or prospective candidacy) of an individual for public office (or which is effectively controlled by a candidate or prospective candidate and which is availed of primarily for such purposes)." In these circumstances, a political expenditure includes any of the following:

- Amounts paid to or incurred by the individual for speeches or other services
- The travel expenses of the individual
- The expenses of conducting polls, surveys, or other studies, or the preparation of papers or other materials, for use by the individual
- The expenses of advertising, publicity, and fundraising for the individual
- Any other expense "which has the primary effect of promoting public recognition, or otherwise primarily accruing to the benefit of" the individual

Initial taxes and additional taxes similar to the private foundation taxes are applicable in the political activities context. A political expenditure triggers an initial tax, payable by the organization, of 10 percent of the amount of the expenditure. An initial tax of 2.5 percent of the expenditure is also imposed on each of the organization's managers (such as directors and officers), where these individuals knew it was a political expenditure, unless the agreement to make the expenditure was not willful or was due to reasonable cause. The IRS has the discretionary authority to abate these initial taxes where the organization is able to establish that the violation was due to reasonable cause and not to willful neglect and timely corrects the violation.

An additional tax is levied on a charitable organization, at a rate of 100 percent of the political expenditure, where the initial tax was imposed and the expenditure was not timely corrected. An additional tax is levied on the organization's manager, at a rate of 50 percent of the expenditure, where the additional tax was imposed on the organization and the manager refused to agree to part or all of the correction.

An organization that loses its status as a charitable organization because of political campaign activities is precluded from becoming tax-exempt as a social welfare organization. (This rule is identical to the rule concerning a charity's inability to convert to social welfare status after engaging in substantial lobbying.)

Under certain circumstances, the IRS is empowered to commence an action in federal district court to enjoin a charitable organization from making further political expenditures and for other relief to ensure that the assets of the organization are preserved for charitable purposes.

If the IRS finds that a charitable organization has flagrantly violated the prohibition against political expenditures, the IRS is required to immediately determine and assess any income or excise tax(es) due, by terminating the organization's taxable year.

The discussion to this point has been deliberately written to refer only to *political campaign activity*. Let's turn now to *political activity*. Essentially, there are two types.

The first type is *activism*. This term embraces a wide range of political undertakings constitutionally protected as free speech. These activities have a variety of forms—writings, demonstrations, boycotts, strikes, picketing, and litigation. These activities frequently give the IRS pause, but, unless the activities can be fairly characterized as being lobbying or electioneering, the IRS has no basis in the tax law for denying tax-exempt status to organizations that engage in them or for revoking the organizations' tax-exempt status.

Activist activities are usually a permissible method for furthering a charitable organization's tax-exempt purposes. These activities often are not inherently exempt functions but are viewed by the law as being means to further the end result of achieving exempt purposes. As the U.S. Tax Court once wrote, "the purpose towards which an organization's activities are directed, and not the activities themselves, is ultimately dispositive of the organization's right to be classified as a . . . [charitable] organization." These activities will jeopardize tax exemption, however, where they are illegal or are otherwise contrary to public policy.

The second type of political activity is tax-triggering activity. The taxes involved are by-products of the rules defining the tax-exempt *political organization*.

(c) Political Organization Taxes

The law defines political organizations' *exempt function* as, essentially, engagement in political activity. This exempt function involves actions of influencing or attempting to influence the selection, nomination, election, or appointment of any individual to any federal, state, or local public office. The wording of this definition makes the term *political activity* considerably broader than *political campaign activity*. *Political activity* includes words such as *selection* and *appointment*, which can mean processes other than electioneering. For example, if a representative of a charitable organization testifies for or against a presidential appointment to a cabinet position or a judgeship, the organization is not engaging in political campaign activity (because there is no campaign and no election) but it is engaging in political activity.

When a charitable organization engages in a political activity that is not a political campaign activity, it will presumably not forfeit its tax-exempt status but will have to pay a tax. The tax is determined by computing an amount equal to the lesser of the organization's net investment income for the year involved or the amount expended for the political activity. This amount, characterized as *political organization taxable income*, is taxed at the highest corporate rates.

Unlike the restrictions on lobbying by charitable organizations, which allow a charitable entity to operate a related lobbying organization, a charitable organization is not permitted to operate a related political campaign organization—namely, a political action committee (PAC). Under present law, the activity of the PAC is attributable to the parent charity and it will lose its tax exemption. Individuals who are involved with a charitable organization may, however, be able to establish and utilize an "independent" PAC. The IRS has not addressed the matter, but the Federal Election Commission issued guidelines according to which the type of a committee—technically termed a *nonconnected political committee*—may be created and used. A charitable or other tax-exempt organization may operate a PAC for the purpose of conducting political activities that are not political campaign activities.

(d) Is the IRS Biased?

Some accuse the IRS of bias in this area, particularly when it comes to the political activity of churches and other religious organizations. This argument essentially is as follows: The IRS is quick to pounce when religious organizations on the right of the political spectrum engage in political campaign activity and is equally adept at looking the other way when religious organizations on the left do the same.

In truth, there is at least some superficial evidence that this argument has merit. The case mentioned previously, where the church lost its tax exemption for participating in the 1992 presidential campaign, involved a conservative church. There have been countless instances in which political campaign activity took place in other churches, with the IRS doing nothing about the violations (many of which occurred just a few blocks away from the IRS's national office). During recent presidential campaigns, for example, there have been Sunday mornings where candidates spoke from the pulpit during church services and received endorsements from the clergy. Political fundraising currently takes place in churches and temples.

The matter became so obvious that the staff of the Joint Committee on Taxation undertook a study to determine whether the IRS is institutionally biased in this area—that is, whether it engages in *selective prosecution*. In a report issued in early 2000, however, the Committee's staff fully exonerated the IRS, finding no conclusive evidence to support any of the allegations of bias.

POLITICAL ACTIVITIES BY OTHER NONPROFIT ORGANIZATIONS

Federal tax law does not completely impede political campaign activities by tax-exempt organizations other than charitable ones. Federal and state campaign finance laws, however, limit the extent to which nonprofit organizations can directly participate in the political campaign process. For example, the Federal Election Campaign Act makes it unlawful for a corporation—including a nonprofit corporation—to make a contribution or expenditure for a political candidate in a federal election.

Because of the campaign law restrictions, most nonprofit organizations do not directly engage in political campaign activities; instead, they use PACs. The nonprofit organizations that most commonly use PACs are trade, business, and professional associations and labor organizations; some social welfare organizations maintain PACs as well.

The federal election laws term these adjunct political committees *separate segregated funds* and permit the "establishment, administration, and solicitation of contributions to a separate segregated fund to be utilized for political purposes by a . . . membership organization." The costs of establishing and administering a separate segregated fund (political action committee), however, are not contributions or expenditures that are prohibited under the federal election laws. These costs, termed *soft-dollar expenditures*, are contrasted with *hard-dollar expenditures*, which are direct outlays for political purposes (monies given by the membership and expended for the benefit of candidates).

The tax laws get confused with the federal election laws on these points because of the double meaning given the term *exempt function*. As described in the tax laws, the exempt function of a political organization basically is the funding of campaigns (put another way, the making of hard-dollar expenditures). (See Chapter 4.) That exempt function is also recognized by the federal election laws. A nonprofit organization that has (without endangering its exemption) a PAC may make soft-dollar political expenditures but may not, because of the federal election laws, make hard-dollar political expenditures. Yet, under the tax laws, if a nonprofit organization (other than a political organization) engages in an *exempt function* (as that term is defined in the federal election laws context), it is subject to tax (or, perhaps, loss of exemption), even though it may also be engaging in an *exempt function* (as that term is defined in the law pertaining to its tax-exempt status).

The dichotomy between political campaign activities and political activities carries over to nonprofit organizations other than charitable ones. Even though the federal campaign laws prohibit a social welfare, labor, trade, business, or professional organization from making a political campaign contribution (hard-dollar expenditure), that type of organization may make a political expenditure under the tax laws. In this setting, a political activity includes the function of influencing or attempting to influence the selection, nomination, election, or appointment of an individual to any federal, state, or local public office (an *exempt function*). These types of membership organizations may, for example, support or oppose a presidential nominee for a cabinet position or judgeship—a political activity and not a political campaign activity. Therefore, the federal election laws are not a factor, but the tax laws may force the payment of a tax (but not loss of tax exemption) as the result of participation in that type of activity. For example, if an organization that is primarily engaged in social welfare functions also carries on activities involving participation and intervention in political campaigns on behalf of or in opposition to candidates for public office, it will not lose its tax-exempt status, but it may have to pay a political activities tax.

Another tricky area is the matter of *advocacy communications*, relating to public policy issues, by noncharitable tax-exempt organizations. If this type of communication explicitly advocates the election or defeat of an individual to public office, the expenditure for the communication is, of course, for a (political) exempt function. Otherwise, the IRS looks at the facts and circumstances in determining whether the expenditure is for an exempt function. Two factors involved are whether the timing of the communication coincides with a political campaign and whether the communication identifies the position of a political candidate on a public policy issue. In some instances, what appears to be only legislative activity (see Chapter 14) also becomes political activity—and thus is taxable.

Checklist

- ❑ Does your organization engage in political campaign activities?
  Yes _____ No _____

- ❑ If yes: How much money was expended for political campaign activities over the past year? $_____

- ❑ Is the organization certain that the Federal Election Campaign Act was not violated? Yes _____ No _____

- ❑ If the organization has engaged in political activities that are not political campaign activities, describe them: _____

- ❑ Does the organization have a political action committee (PAC)?
  Yes _____ No _____

- ❑ Does the organization have any other related or affiliated organization that engages in political activities? Yes _____ No _____

- ❑ Does the organization keep its board of directors informed as to its political activities? Yes _____ No _____

FOCUS: Campaign to Clean Up America

The Campaign to Clean Up America (CCUA) has no plans to engage in political campaign activities. As with lobbying activities, the exempt purposes of the CCUA can clearly be furthered by involvement in political campaigns. Its purposes can be advanced by those in government who agree with its principles and programs, so the CCUA is rightfully concerned about those who are elected and appointed to public office.

Yet, at this stage in its formation, the CCUA cannot afford to jeopardize its eligibility for deductible charitable gifts. It will not participate in any campaigns for candidates for public office.

The management of the CCUA remains well aware of the relationship between the success of its programs and those who hold public office. It is seriously considering undertaking political activities that are not political campaign activities and are in advancement of its program objectives of a litter-free America.

CHAPTER SIXTEEN

Donor-Advised Funds, Tax Shelters, Insurance Schemes—And Still More Taxes

One of the most significant trends in nonprofit law at the federal level is the imposition of taxes on ostensibly "tax-exempt" organizations and, in some instance, on their managers. Congress's appetite in this regard was whetted when it enacted the unrelated business income tax rules (see Chapter 13), followed by the private foundation rules (see Chapter 7), followed again by taxes on public charities for engaging in unwarranted amounts of advocacy (see Chapters 14 and 15), and followed once again by taxes on management (and others) for involvement in excess benefit transactions (see Chapter 5).

This trend is continuing, with more taxes on nonprofit entities and management being recently added. The following sections discuss three more of these instances.

DONOR-ADVISED FUNDS

The donor-advised fund has long been a legitimate, albeit controversial, alternative to the private foundation (see Chapter 7). Until recently, this type of fund had not been defined in the law. Generally, however, a donor-advised fund is a segregated fund or account maintained by a public charity for contributions received from a donor (or donors) as to which there is an understanding that the donor (or the donor's designee) may advise the charity regarding the distribution of any amounts held in the fund.

(a) Controversies

There are several reasons why donor-advised funds are controversial. Some contend that the organization that maintains them is not *charitable* at all (and thus is not tax-exempt). It is seen as no more than a commercial bank's holding accounts for the private benefit of depositors. This argument has no merit, in that once the donated funds are placed in the accounts, they belong to the sponsoring charity; no interest accrues to any "depositor," and the monies cannot be withdrawn. Not surprisingly, the argument has been generally rejected by courts.

Another contention is that these transfers are not *gifts* (and thus are not deductible). The ostensible reason is that the "donor" has not, by reason of this *understanding*, parted with all of his or her (or sometimes its) right, title, and interest in the gift money or other property. To assess this, the IRS has applied a set of *material restrictions* rules that have been promulgated in the private foundation setting to test whether a private foundation has properly terminated its status by granting its assets to one or more private charities. This argument is not supported by the law either.

Another (ostensible) issue is whether charities that maintain these funds are really public charities. In fact, however, the gifts (and that is what they are) to the charity (and that is what it is) are forms of public support for purposes of publicly supported charity status. Almost always, these entities are *donative type* publicly supported charities (see Chapter 7). Then, when a grant is made from an account within the public charity to another charity, it can be public support for the ultimate grantee. Some in the IRS are pained at the thought that a gift (or a portion of it) can constitute public support twice. Private letter rulings from the IRS, however, reveal that in actual practice the agency is not pursuing this line of argument.

(b) Statutory Criteria

Legislation that generally took effect for tax years beginning after August 17, 2006, introduced a statutory definition of the term *donor-advised fund*. Essentially, it is a fund or account (1) that is separately identified by reference to contributions of one or more donors, (2) that is owned and controlled by a sponsoring organization, and (3) as to which a donor or a donor advisor (a person appointed or designated by a donor) has, or reasonably expects to have, advisory privileges with respect to the distribution or investment of amounts held in the fund or account by reason of the donor's status as a donor. A *sponsoring organization* is a public charity that maintains one or more donor-advised funds.

A donor-advised fund does not include funds that make distributions only to a single identified organization or governmental entity, nor does it include certain funds where a donor or donor advisor provides advice as to which individuals receive grants for travel, study, or similar purposes. The IRS has the authority to exempt a fund from treatment as a donor-advised fund under certain circumstances. Exercising this authority, the IRS announced that employer-sponsored disaster relief assistance funds do not constitute donor-advised funds.

A distribution from a donor-advised fund is taxable if it is to (1) a "natural person" (that is, a human being) or (2) any other person for a noncharitable purpose unless expenditure responsibility (see Chapter 7) is exercised with respect to the distribution. A tax, of 20 percent of the amount involved, is imposed on the sponsoring organization for making a taxable distribution. Another tax, in the amount of 5 percent, is imposed on the agreement of a fund manager (i.e., the trustees, directors, officers, and executive employees of a sponsoring organization) to the making of a taxable distribution, where the manager knew that the distribution was a taxable one. The tax on fund management, which is generally confined to $10,000 per transaction, is subject to a joint and several liability requirement. This tax does not apply to a distribution from a donor-advised fund to most public charities (but not including a Type III nonfunctionally integrated supporting organization), the fund's sponsoring organization, or another donor-advised fund.

If a donor, donor advisor, or a person related to a donor or donor advisor with respect to a donor-advised fund provides advice as to a distribution that results in any of those persons receiving, directly or indirectly, a benefit that is more than incidental, an excise tax equal to 125 percent of the amount of the benefit is imposed on the person who advised as to the distribution and on the recipient of the benefit. Also, if a manager of the sponsoring organization agreed to the making of the distribution, knowing that the distribution would confer more than an incidental benefit on a donor, donor advisor, or related person, the manager is subject to an excise tax equal to 10 percent of the amount of the benefit. These taxes are subject to a joint and several liability requirement.

A grant, loan, compensation, or other similar payment (such as reimbursement of expenses) from a donor-advised fund to a person that, with respect to the fund, is a donor, donor advisor, or related person automatically is treated as an excess benefit transaction for intermediate sanctions law purposes. This means that the entire amount paid to any of these persons is an excess benefit. Donors and donor advisors with respect to a donor-advised fund and related persons are disqualified persons for intermediate sanctions law purposes with respect to transactions with the donor-advised fund (although not necessarily with respect to transactions with the sponsoring organization).

The private foundation excess business holdings rules (see Chapter 7) apply to donor-advised funds. For this purpose, the term *disqualified person* means, with respect to a donor-advised fund, a donor, a donor advisor, a member of the family of either, or a 35-percent controlled entity of any such person.

Contributions to a sponsoring organization for maintenance in a donor-advised fund are not eligible for a charitable deduction for federal income tax purposes if the sponsoring organization is a fraternal society, a cemetery company, or a veterans' organization. Contributions to a sponsoring organization for such maintenance are not eligible for a charitable deduction for federal estate or gift tax purposes if the sponsoring organization is a fraternal society or a veterans' organization. Contributions to a sponsoring organization for such maintenance are not eligible for a charitable deduction for income, estate, or gift tax purposes if the sponsoring organization is a Type III supporting organization (other than a functionally integrated Type III supporting organization). A donor must obtain, with respect to each charitable contribution to a sponsoring organization to be maintained in a donor-advised fund, a contemporaneous written acknowledgment from the sponsoring organization that the organization has exclusive legal control over the funds or assets contributed.

A sponsoring organization is required to disclose on its annual information return (see Chapter 9) the number of donor-advised funds it owns, the aggregate value of assets held in the funds at the end of the organization's tax year involved, and the aggregate contributions to and grants made from these funds during the year. When seeking recognition of tax-exempt status, a sponsoring organization must disclose whether it intends to maintain donor-advised funds. As to this latter rule, the organization must provide information regarding its planned operation of these funds, including a description of procedures it intends to use to

- Communicate to donors and donor advisors that assets held in the funds are the property of the sponsoring organization.
- Ensure that distributions from donor-advised funds do not result in more than incidental benefit to any person.

The Department of the Treasury has been directed by Congress to undertake a study regarding the organization and operation of donor-advised funds, to consider

- Whether the deductions allowed for income, estate, or gift taxes for charitable contributions to sponsoring organizations of donor-advised funds are appropriate in consideration of the use of contributed assets or the use of the assets of such organizations for the benefit of the person making the charitable contribution.

- Whether donor-advised funds should be required to distribute for charitable purposes a specified amount in order to ensure that the sponsoring organization with respect to the donor-advised fund is operating in a manner consistent with its tax exemption or public charity status.

- Whether the retention by donors to donor-advised funds of "rights or privileges" with respect to amounts transferred to such organizations (including advisory rights or privileges with respect to the making of grants or the investment of assets) is consistent with the treatment of these transfers as completed gifts.

- Whether these issues are also issues with respect to other forms of charitable organizations or charitable contributions.

TAX SHELTERS

In 2005, Congress enacted a complex body of law intended to discourage nonprofit organizations from participating in tax-shelter transactions. Pursuant to these rules, an excise tax is imposed on most tax-exempt entities and/or entity managers that participate in prohibited tax shelter transactions as accommodation parties. This tax can be imposed in three instances:

1. An exempt organization is liable for the tax in the year it becomes a party to the transaction and any subsequent year or years in which it is such a party.

2. An exempt organization is liable for the tax in any year it is a party to a subsequently listed transaction.

3. An entity manager is liable for the tax if the manager caused the exempt organization to be a party to a prohibited tax shelter transaction at any time and knew or had reason to know that the transaction is such a transaction.

For this purpose, the term *tax-exempt entity* includes most types of exempt organizations. The term *entity manager* means, with respect to a tax-exempt entity, (1) an individual with authority or responsibility similar to that exercised by a trustee, director, or officer of the exempt organization; and (2) with respect to any act, the person having authority or responsibility with respect to that act.

A *prohibited reportable transaction* is any confidential transaction or any transaction with *contractual protection* (an as-yet undefined term) that is a reportable transaction. A *subsequently listed transaction* is a transaction to which a tax-exempt entity is a party and is determined by the IRS to be a listed transaction at any time after the entity has become a party to the transaction.

In the case of a tax-exempt entity, the amount of the excise tax imposed with respect to a transaction for a year generally is an amount equal to the product of the highest rate of corporate income tax and the greater of the entity's net income for the year, which (a) in the case of a prohibited tax shelter transaction (other than a subsequently listed transaction) is attributable to the transaction, or which (b) in the case of a subsequently listed transaction is attributable to the transaction and is properly allocated to the period as previously described.

This tax is increased in instances where the tax-exempt organization knew, or had reason to know, that a transaction was a prohibited tax-shelter transaction at the time the entity became a party to the transaction. The excise tax on an entity manager is $20,000 for each approval of, or other act causing the entity's participation in, a prohibited tax shelter transaction.

In addition to this excise-tax regime, disclosure obligations are imposed on tax-exempt entities. They must disclose the fact of being a party to a prohibited tax shelter transaction and the identity of other parties to the transaction. A taxable organization that is a party to a prohibited tax-shelter transaction must disclose to a tax-exempt entity that is a party to the transaction that the transaction is a prohibited tax-shelter transaction. Penalties apply for violation of these disclosure rules.

These rules are generally applicable with respect to tax years ending after May 17, 2006, with respect to transactions before, on, or after that date. This excise tax, however, did not apply with respect to income or proceeds that are properly allocable to any period ending on or before August 15, 2006. Nonprofit organizations that are limited partners in a partnership that has one or more investments that may entail a reportable transaction may be a party to a prohibited tax shelter transaction.

The IRS issued temporary and proposed regulations providing guidance relating to entity-level and manager-level excise taxes with respect to prohibited tax-shelter transactions to which tax-exempt organizations are parties, to certain disclosure obligations with respect to these transactions, and to the requirement of a return and time for filing with respect to these taxes. These regulations, in addition to addressing the definition of the term *tax-exempt entity*, coordinate the term *prohibited tax-shelter transaction* with the term *reportable transaction* and define the term *subsequently listed transaction* as a transaction (other than a reportable transaction) to which an exempt entity becomes a party before the transaction becomes a listed transaction. The most significant element of these regulations is the threshold definition of *party* to a prohibited tax-shelter transaction, which (1) means an exempt entity that facilitates a prohibited tax-shelter transaction by reason of its exempt (or tax-indifferent or tax-favored) status and (2) includes an exempt entity that enters into a listed transaction and reflects on its tax return a reduction or elimination of its liability for federal employment, excise, or unrelated business income taxes that is derived directly or indirectly from tax consequences or tax strategy described in the published guidance that lists the transaction. These proposed regulations also clarify the definition of the term *entity manager*, *net income*, and *proceeds*; provide rules regarding the manner and timing of the requisite disclosures; and specify the tax forms used to pay the taxes under this regime.

Thereafter, the IRS issued final regulations on the matter of reportable transactions, including a new category of arrangements that must be disclosed, known as *transactions of interest*. The identification of a transaction (or a transaction similar to the identified one) as a transaction of interest alerts persons involved with these transactions to "certain responsibilities" that may arise from their involvement with the transaction. The first transaction of interest announced by the IRS concerns a transaction in which a taxpayer directly or indirectly holds real property, transfers the rights more than one year after the acquisition to a charitable organization, and claims a charitable contribution deduction that is significantly higher than the amount that the taxpayer paid to acquire the rights.

INSURANCE SCHEMES

Charitable split-dollar insurance plans, whereby life insurance has become the basis for a form of endowment-building investment vehicle for charitable organizations, is effectively outlawed by the federal tax law. That is, the federal tax law denies an income tax charitable contribution deduction for, and imposes excise tax penalties on, transfers associated with the use of these plans.

Thus, there is no federal charitable contribution deduction for a transfer to or for the use of a charitable organization, if, in connection with the transfer (1) the organization directly or indirectly pays, or has previously paid, any premium on any personal benefit contract with respect to the transferor; or (2) there is an understanding or expectation that any person will directly or indirectly pay any premium on this type of a contract with respect to the transferor. A *personal benefit contract* with respect to a transferor is any life insurance, annuity, or endowment contract, if any direct or indirect beneficiary under the contract is the transferor, any member of the transferor's family, or any other person (other than a charitable organization) designated by the transferor.

Checklist

❏ Does the organization maintain one or more donor-advised funds?
    Yes _____ No _____

❏ If so, is the organization in compliance with the post-2006 statutory law?
    Yes _____ No _____

❏ Is the organization a party to a prohibited tax-shelter transaction?
    Yes _____ No _____

❏ If so, is the organization in compliance with the post-2005 statutory law?
    Yes _____ No _____

❏ Is the organization a participant in a charitable split-dollar insurance plan?
    Yes _____ No _____

❏ Is the organization a party to a personal benefit contract?
    Yes _____ No _____

PART FOUR

Helpful Hints and Successful Techniques

CHAPTER SEVENTEEN

Subsidiaries: For-Profit and Nonprofit

It is becoming commonplace—and frequently essential—for a tax-exempt organization to utilize a for-profit, taxable subsidiary.

The reasons include situations where

- The activity to be housed in the subsidiary is an unrelated one (see Chapter 13) and is too extensive to be conducted within the tax-exempt organization.

- The management of an exempt organization does not want to report the receipt of any unrelated income and so shifts it to a separate subsidiary.

- The management of an exempt organization is enamored with the idea of using a for-profit subsidiary.

In most instances, the first reason is the true reason, if not the only one. An unrelated business may be operated as an activity within an exempt organization, as long as the primary purpose of the organization is to carry out one or more exempt functions (see Chapter 4). Generally, there is no fixed percentage of permissible unrelated activity—that is, unrelated business that may be engaged in by a tax-exempt organization without loss of tax exemption. (Title-holding companies have a 10 percent limit, but that limitation is too small for exempt organizations in general.) In one instance, the IRS allowed a charitable organization to remain tax-exempt, even though 95 percent of its income was derived from unrelated (albeit passive) sources, because about 40 percent of the organization's time was devoted to charitable ends.

Therefore, if a tax-exempt organization wants to engage in one or more unrelated activities and the activities will be *substantial* in relation to its exempt activities (e.g., constituting more than half of its total activities), the use of a for-profit subsidiary is unavoidable.

Considerations are not that much different when it comes to a nonprofit subsidiary. Usually, both entities are tax-exempt, yet the exempt functions often differ. Thus, a public charity may have a lobbying arm, or a social welfare organization or business league will have a charitable foundation. A charitable organization, however, may have a charitable subsidiary, such as a fundraising or endowment entity. Where the subsidiary is a charitable organization, it may well be a supporting organization (see discussion following and Chapter 7).

ESTABLISHING A FOR-PROFIT SUBSIDIARY

When should a particular activity be housed in a tax-exempt organization or a for-profit organization? The factors to be considered are the same as those weighed at the start-up of a business, when deciding whether it will be conducted in a tax-exempt or a for-profit form:

- The value of or need for tax exemption

- The true motives of those involved in the enterprise (e.g., profit)

- The desirability of creating an asset (such as stock that is appreciating in value) for equity owners (shareholders) of the enterprise

- The compensatory arrangements contemplated for the employees

The law is clear: A tax-exempt organization can have one or more for-profit subsidiaries. In a ruling, the IRS succinctly stated the overarching rule of law in this setting: "An [exempt] organization can organize, capitalize and own, provide services and assets (real and personal, tangible and intangible) to a taxable entity without violating the requirements for exemption, regardless of whether the taxable entity is wholly or partially owned." The tax-exempt parent organization can own some or all of the equity (usually, stock) of the for-profit subsidiary (unless the parent is a private foundation, in which case special rules apply).

If an activity of a tax-exempt organization is unrelated to its exempt purpose or functions but is not a principal activity, it may be conducted within the exempt organization without impairment of its tax-exempt status (although taxes would have to be paid on the net income generated by the activity).

STRUCTURAL CONSIDERATIONS

Several matters of structure should be taken into account when contemplating the use of a for-profit subsidiary by a tax-exempt organization. These include choice of form and the control mechanism.

(a) Choice of Form

Just as in forming nonprofit organizations, the choice of organizational form is important when establishing for-profit subsidiaries. Most will be regular corporations (known as C corporations)—the most common business form and one that enables the exempt parent to own the subsidiary by holding all or at least a majority of its stock.

Although a few taxable businesses are sole proprietorships, this form is of no avail in the exempt-organization context. A business activity operating as a sole proprietorship is an undertaking conducted directly by the exempt organization and does not lead to the desired goal of having an unrelated activity in a separate entity.

There are three other business forms. One is the partnership, where the exempt organization can be involved as a general partner or a limited partner (or perhaps both). An exempt organization's participation in a partnership may involve some unique legal difficulties (see Chapter 18). Limited liability companies (LLCs) are popular currently; a tax-exempt organization can be a member of an LLC, which is not a taxable entity. If, however, the exempt organization is the sole member, the LLC will be disregarded for tax purposes; consequently, the activities of the LLC will be considered those of the exempt organization (including annual information return reporting). The third alternative (available only to charitable organizations) is the small business corporation (known as the S corporation) which is treated, for federal tax purposes, the same as a partnership. There is a major caution here, however: Income (actual or allocated) of a charity from an S corporation is automatically treated as unrelated business income, as is any gain on the sale of S corporation stock.

Because several states allow businesses to be conducted by means of business trusts, this approach may be available to a nonprofit organization. Before this approach (or any other approach other than forming a corporation) is used, however, those involved must be absolutely certain that the corporate form is not the most beneficial. One important consideration must be stock ownership: A share of stock in and of itself is an asset that can appreciate in value and can be sold in whole or in part.

A potential compromise is to house the business activity within a taxable nonprofit organization. This approach is a product of the distinction between a nonprofit organization (a state law concept) and a tax-exempt organization (a federal tax law concept). Assuming state law permits (an activity may be *nonprofit* yet still be *unrelated* to the parent's exempt functions), a business activity may be placed in a nonprofit yet taxable organization.

(b) Control

Presumably, a tax-exempt organization, when it forms a taxable subsidiary, intends to maintain control over the subsidiary. After capitalizing the enterprise, nurturing its growth and success, and desiring enjoyment of some profits from the business, the exempt organization parent would not want to give up its control.

Where the taxable subsidiary is structured as a business corporation, the tax-exempt organization parent can own the entity and ultimately control it simply by owning the stock (received in exchange for the capital contributed). The exempt organization parent, as the stockholder, can thereafter select the board of directors of the corporation and, if desired, its officers.

If the taxable subsidiary is structured as a nonprofit corporation, two choices are available. The entity can be structured as a conventional nonprofit organization; the exempt organization parent would then control the subsidiary by means of interlocking directorates. Alternatively, the entity can be structured as a nonprofit organization that can issue stock; the exempt organization parent would then control the subsidiary by holding its stock. If the latter structure is chosen and if the nonprofit subsidiary is to be headquartered in a state where stock-based nonprofits are not authorized, the subsidiary can be incorporated in a state that allows nonprofits to issue stock and thereafter to be qualified to do business in the home state.

(c) Attribution Considerations

For federal income tax purposes, a parent corporation and its subsidiary are respected as separate entities as long as the purpose for which the subsidiary is formed is reflective of true business activities. Where an organization is established with the bona fide intention that it will have some real and substantial business function, its existence will generally not be disregarded for tax purposes. This calls for corporate niceties such as separate bank accounts, separate sets of board minutes, and a separate board of directors (although not necessarily separate individuals, as discussed subsequently).

There is a second element of the law that must be satisfied—the matter of day-to-day control of the subsidiary. Where the parent exempt organization so controls the affairs of the subsidiary that it is merely an extension or instrumentality of the parent, the subsidiary will not be regarded, for tax purposes, as a separate legal entity. This factor of control usually is manifested by an identity of directors and/or officers, so it is a good practice for at least a majority of the officers and directors of the subsidiary to be individuals who are not officers or directors of the parent or who are not otherwise formally associated with the parent. In an extreme situation, the establishment of an ostensibly separate entity will, by reason of undue control by its parent, be regarded as a sham.

The IRS generally will respect the separateness of closely related entities, even in situations where the tax-exempt parent wholly owns the for-profit subsidiary.

FINANCIAL CONSIDERATIONS

The principal financial considerations that a tax-exempt organization should keep in mind, when contemplating the establishment of a for-profit subsidiary, are capitalization, individuals' compensation, and liquidation. Finally, as discussed in the following section, a fourth consideration is the tax treatment of any revenue flowing from the subsidiary to the parent.

(a) Capitalization

Assets that are currently being used in an unrelated activity (if any) may be spun off into a related, for-profit organization. The extent to which a for-profit corporation can be capitalized using exempt assets, however, is far less clear.

A tax-exempt organization can invest a portion of its assets and engage in a certain amount of unrelated activities. At the same time, the governing board of a tax-exempt organization must act in conformance with basic fiduciary responsibilities, and the organization cannot operate for the benefit of private interests.

IRS private letter rulings suggest that perhaps only a very small percentage of an organization's resources should be transferred to controlled subsidiaries. The percentages approved by the IRS are usually unduly low and probably pertain only to money. A specific asset may be best utilized—in some cases, it must be utilized—in an unrelated activity, even though its value represents a meaningful portion of the organization's total resources.

The best guiding standard in capitalizing a subsidiary is that of the prudent investor (also known as the *prudent person rule*). A tax-exempt organization should only part with an amount of resources that is reasonable under the circumstances and can be rationalized in relation to amounts devoted to programs and invested in other ways. Relevant to this decision is the projected return on the investment, in terms of both income and capital appreciation. If a contribution to a subsidiary's capital seems unwise, the parent-to-be should consider a loan bearing a fair rate of interest and accompanied by adequate security.

(b) Compensation

The structure of a tax-exempt parent and a taxable subsidiary may generate questions and issues regarding compensation of employees.

The compensation of employees of a taxable subsidiary is subject to an overall requirement that the amounts paid may not exceed a reasonable salary or wage. To be deductible, all business expenses must be *ordinary and necessary*. The compensation of the employees of the parent exempt organization is subject to a similar limitation, under the private inurement doctrine (see Chapter 5).

The employees of the tax-exempt parent can participate in deferred compensation plans or tax-sheltered annuity programs. The subsidiary may also use deferred salary plans or qualified pension plans. The plans that are used by the parent exempt organization may be the same as or different from those used by the for-profit subsidiary.

Use of a taxable subsidiary may facilitate an offering of stock options to employees, to enable them to share in the growth of the corporation. Another possibility may be an employee stock ownership plan—a plan that invests in the stock of the sponsoring company. The subsidiary may issue unqualified options to buy stock or qualified incentive stock options.

Tax-exempt organizations must annually report to the IRS the amount of compensation received by an individual from both the exempt organization and a related organization where the total amount of compensation is at least $100,000 and the amount of compensation from the related organization is at least $10,000.

(c) Liquidation

A corporation must recognize its gain or loss on a liquidating distribution of its assets (as if the corporation had sold the assets to the distributee at fair market value) and on liquidating sales. There is a nonrecognition exception for liquidating transfers within an affiliated group (which is regarded as a single economic unit), so that the distributee's basis in the property is carried over.

This nonrecognition exception is modified for eligible liquidations in which an 80 percent corporate shareholder receives property with a carryover basis. Nonrecognition of gain or loss is allowed on any property actually distributed to that shareholder. This exception for 80 percent corporate shareholders is generally not available, however, where the shareholder is a tax-exempt organization. Translated, this means that, when the decision is made to liquidate the subsidiary by transferring assets to the exempt parent, there may be taxation of the gain inherent in the assets (if any).

Whether or not there is taxation of this sort is dependent on the subsequent use of the assets by the tax-exempt parent. If the property distributed out of the subsidiary is used by the exempt organization in an unrelated business immediately after the distribution, the gain is not taxed. Conversely, if the property is used in a related business, there will be taxation. If the property is first used in an unrelated business and is then used in a related business, the gain will be taxed at that time. (This is the only area of the law that encourages unrelated activity!)

There are two traps here. One is that the IRS has promulgated regulations that make these rules applicable to liquidations (asset transfers) by taxable entities into tax-exempt organizations, even where the relationship is not that of parent–

subsidiary. The other is that a liquidation is deemed to occur where a taxable entity converts to an exempt organization, such as where (when state law permits) the articles of organization are amended to cause the change.

TREATMENT OF REVENUE FROM SUBSIDIARY

Most tax-exempt organizations develop an unrelated activity in anticipation of its serving as a source of revenue (as well as preserving exempt status). When the unrelated business is developed into or shifted to a taxable subsidiary, it should be done in such a way that the flow of income from the subsidiary to the parent is not slowed down or stopped.

The staff and other resources of an affiliated business are usually those of the exempt organization parent; the headquarters used are likely to be the parent's. This means that the taxable subsidiary will have to reimburse the parent for the subsidiary's occupancy costs, share of employees' time, and use of the parent's equipment and supplies. Dollars can flow from the subsidiary to the parent in the form of reimbursement, which would include rent.

A lender–borrower relationship may exist between an exempt organization parent and its taxable subsidiary—that is, in addition to funding its subsidiary by means of a capital contribution (with the parent holding the equity), the parent may lend money to its subsidiary. Because a no-interest loan to a for-profit subsidiary by an exempt organization parent may endanger the parent's tax-exempt status and trigger problems under the imputed interest rules, the loan should bear a fair market rate of interest. Interest is another way for dollars to flow from the subsidiary to the parent.

The business activities of a for-profit subsidiary may be marketing and selling a product or service. When done in conformance with its tax-exempt status, the parent can license the use of its name, logo, acronym, or some other feature that would enhance the sale of the product or service provided by the subsidiary. For this license, the subsidiary would pay the parent a royalty—another way of transferring dollars from subsidiary to parent.

A conventional way of transferring money from a corporation to its stockholders is for the corporation to distribute its earnings and profits to them. These distributions, or dividends, represent still another way in which a taxable subsidiary can transfer dollars to its tax-exempt parent.

As discussed (see Chapter 13), certain types of income are exempted from taxation as unrelated income—principally, the various forms of passive income, such as dividends, interest, rent, and royalties. Were it not for a special rule of federal tax law, a tax-exempt organization could have it both ways: It could avoid taxation on unrelated income by housing the activity in a subsidiary and receive passive, nontaxable income thereafter from the subsidiary.

Congress was mindful of this potential double benefit and legislated an exception to the general rule that exempts passive income from taxation: Otherwise passive nontaxable income that is derived from a controlled taxable subsidiary is taxed as unrelated income. When an exempt organization parent receives rents, interest, or most other forms of passive income from a controlled taxable subsidiary, those revenues will generally be taxable. In this instance, *control* means an ownership interest of any type that is more than 50 percent of the total ownership; there are also constructive ownership rules. (As discussed in Chapter 13, however, there is a limited exception to this rule.)

As is typical of the tax laws, there is an exception to the exception—a rule predicated on the fact that the payment of rents, interest, or royalties creates a tax deduction for the payor corporation. So, for example, when a for-profit subsidiary pays interest to its exempt organization parent in connection with a loan, the interest payments are deductible by the subsidiary (and taxable to the parent).

There is, however, no tax deduction for the payment of dividends. When a for-profit subsidiary pays dividends to its exempt organization parent, the dividend payments are not deductible by the subsidiary. Congress determined that it would not be appropriate to tax revenue to an exempt organization parent where it is not deductible by the taxable subsidiary.

The following general principle has developed and it has eased tax planning regarding which entity, if any, is to be taxed: If the income paid to an exempt organization parent is deductible by the subsidiary, it is unrelated income to the parent. If the income paid is not deductible by the subsidiary, it is not taxable to the parent. The exception to the exception is for dividend income: It is not taxable to an exempt organization parent even when it is derived from a controlled taxable subsidiary.

SUBSIDIARIES IN PARTNERSHIPS

In the discussion of exempt organizations in partnerships in Chapter 18, there is allusion to another use of a taxable subsidiary by a tax-exempt organization parent. A charitable organization, which would endanger its tax-exempt status if it were a general partner in a partnership, can cause its taxable subsidiary to be the general partner instead.

This can be an effective strategy as long as all the laws are satisfied, including the requirement that the subsidiary must be an authentic business entity. If the exempt organization parent is too intimately involved in the day-to-day management of the subsidiary, however, the IRS may impute the activities of the subsidiary to the parent and treat it as if it were directly involved as the general partner of the partnership. Its tax-exempt status would be at high risk.

In the federal tax law concerning the depreciation deduction, there are rules that reduce the deduction in situations where otherwise depreciable property is being used for the benefit of tax-exempt organizations. These rules are the *tax-exempt entity leasing rules*. They force investors to compute their depreciation deduction over a longer recovery period where the property is *tax-exempt use property*. The tax-exempt entity leasing rules can cause property to be tax-exempt use property where the property is owned by a partnership in which a tax-exempt organization is a partner or where the property is owned by a partnership in which a for-profit subsidiary owned by a tax-exempt organization is a partner.

Suppose a property that would not otherwise be tax-exempt use property is owned by a partnership that has both a tax-exempt organization and a nonexempt entity as partners. An amount equal to the tax-exempt organization's proportionate share of the property is treated as tax-exempt use property, unless there is a *qualified allocation* of the partnership items (such as gains and losses). In an attempt to prevent property from becoming tax-exempt use property, some exempt organizations did not enter into partnership arrangements directly but used for-profit subsidiaries as the partners instead. Congress reacted to thwart this technique by causing taxable subsidiaries to be considered tax-exempt organizations for purposes of the tax-exempt entity leasing rules. These subsidiaries are termed *tax-exempt controlled entities*.

TITLE-HOLDING CORPORATIONS

This discussion of the use of subsidiaries by tax-exempt organizations has been confined to this point to the use of for-profit subsidiaries. There has not been a direct focus on situations where a subsidiary also is a tax-exempt organization, such as a membership organization utilizing a related foundation, or a charitable organization utilizing a related advocacy organization.

One type of subsidiary related to an exempt organization parent warrants mention—the *title-holding corporation*, which is somewhat of a hybrid. This entity's activities are generally in the business context, yet it is tax-exempt by reason of a relationship with a tax-exempt parent.

Essentially, the function of a title-holding corporation is a passive one: to hold title to property, to pay expenses associated with maintenance of the property, and, at least annually, to remit any net revenue to the parent organization. A title-holding corporation cannot be engaged in an active business undertaking, although, under certain circumstances, it can serve two or more tax-exempt parent organizations. This type of subsidiary can be useful in the administration of property and perhaps as a device for limiting liability.

SUPPORTING ORGANIZATIONS

The best example of a subsidiary of a nonprofit organization, where the subsidiary is also a nonprofit organization, is the *supporting organization*. These are entities that are related, structurally or operationally, to their tax-exempt nonprofit parent(s). The Type I supporting organization is involved in a typical parent-subsidiary relationship. As noted (see Chapter 7), supporting organizations can be used to house an endowment fund, as a fundraising vehicle, as an entity in which programs can be conducted, and for other purposes. The largest detriment to the use of supporting organizations is the various rules, enacted in 2006, which have severely damaged the flexibility and versatility that used to be associated with them as a wonderful tax-planning strategy.

OTHER NONPROFIT SUBSIDIARIES

Charitable organizations are by *no* means the only type of nonprofit organizations that can usefully deploy nonprofit subsidiaries. Social welfare organizations, trade and business associations, and labor organizations frequently have related charitable subsidiaries by which they conduct educational and similar programs and fundraising; these subsidiaries are often supporting organizations. Other types of tax-exempt, nonprofit entities that are likely to have charitable subsidiaries are social clubs, fraternal organizations, and veterans' organizations. In addition, not all subsidiaries are charitable; an association or labor organization may have a political action committee.

Indeed, many types of employees' funds underlying nonprofit organizations' retirement and similar funds can be thought of as subsidiaries.

Back to this matter of charities as parents: Not all subsidiaries are charitable organizations. A public charity, for example, may have a lobbying arm, structured as a social welfare organization (see Chapter 14). Likewise, a charitable entity with a membership of individuals may have a body that accredits these individuals, established as a business league.

Checklist

❏ If the organization has any of the following, identify each entity:

For-profit subsidiary _____

For-profit subsidiary in a partnership _____

For-profit subsidiary in a joint venture _____

Title-holding corporation _____

Supporting organization _____

Lobbying arm _____

Fundraising entity _____

Other nonprofit subsidiary _____

❏ Describe any existing compensation arrangements where an individual is being paid by both a tax-exempt organization and a for-profit subsidiary.

FOCUS: Campaign to Clean Up America

At present, the Campaign to Clean Up America (CCUA) does not have any plans to utilize a for-profit subsidiary. As discussed in the unrelated income context (see Chapter 13), there are potential unrelated businesses for the CCUA. Some of these may ultimately be housed in a subsidiary.

As the CCUA grows, and if federal tax laws allow, the organization may find it productive to utilize one or more for-profit subsidiaries in advancement of businesses selling supplies, equipment, and/or consulting services.

CHAPTER EIGHTEEN

Joint Venturing and Other Partnering

One of the most important current phenomena involving tax-exempt organizations is their use of related organizations. There is nothing particularly revolutionary about this technique; Chapter 17 explains how tax-exempt organizations use subsidiaries. What is fairly new and different is the willingness of tax-exempt organizations to simultaneously use so many different forms of related entities—for-profit or non-profit, trust or corporation, taxable or nontaxable.

Some observers ascribe this development to the economic pressures on tax-exempt organizations that have resulted from the decline in government funding. Others trace it to tax law revision. There is ample cause in both of these sources, but they do not explain, for example, the trade association surrounded by a charitable foundation, a political action committee, and two for-profit business subsidiaries, one of which is a general partner in a real estate limited partnership. This typical cast of characters was not born of the mother-of-invention theory. It is attributable to another factor—sophistication. Tax-exempt organizations are better managed and better advised than ever before.

This improvement in management is due in part to the transfer of chief executive officers from the for-profit business sector to the nonprofit sector. An article in the April 9, *New York Times* concerning this importation of management talent to a particular public charity, stated that an individual's appointment as president of the charity "exemplifies a trend in the nonprofit sector to recruit successful business executives in the hope that their expertise will instill greater professionalism and financial acumen in the sector."

Exempt organizations have discovered that partnerships or limited liability companies are available to facilitate almost anything they would like to do. A partnership, an LLC, is often a financing technique.

REAL ESTATE ACQUISITIONS

Managers of tax-exempt organizations are more frequently concluding that their organizations should own real estate, usually for purposes of housing their offices. These are the financial advantages:

- A preferable position economically if occupancy costs are fixed rather than subject to the vagaries of the rental market

- A stronger portfolio if real property is among the assets of an organization

- An opportunity to conduct program activities at an organization's own location or to utilize the property to generate additional revenue

- An improved image to the membership, contributors, or perhaps the general public, because of the prestige associated with owning the organization's headquarters

For some nonprofit organizations, ownership of real property has a long history. Many churches, universities, colleges, schools, hospitals, country clubs, and some major charities and associations were founded on the land on which they are still operating. Real estate ownership—particularly for office headquarters purposes—is becoming more commonplace, however, for a wide variety of newer charitable, educational, religious, scientific, trade, business, professional, veterans', and other nonprofit organizations.

There are several aspects of real estate ownership by nonprofit organizations. As a general proposition, it is clear that a nonprofit organization will not jeopardize its tax exemption because of acquisition, ownership, and maintenance of real property. In some states, real property owned by a nonprofit organization will be exempt from property tax. As a general rule, there is no likelihood that tax exemption will be impaired where a nonprofit organization leases space in property it owns, whether to other nonprofit entities or to the general public.

Still, a variety of potential unrelated income tax considerations are associated with the acquisition, ownership, and maintenance of real property by nonprofit organizations.

In the simplest of circumstances, where a nonprofit organization acquires real property with no financing and uses the property wholly for its tax-exempt purposes, there would be no adverse consequences to its tax-exempt status and no unrelated income taxation. Federal tax considerations come into play where the property is acquired with the assistance of others (such as by means of a partnership or other joint venture), rental or other income is involved, financing is utilized, or the property is put to an unrelated use.

In the property acquisition phase, tax considerations can be prominent, and the issue is likely to be whether tax-exempt status would be jeopardized. Unrelated income taxation is a much smaller threat.

A common way for an organization (nonprofit or not) to acquire real property, where the organization is unable or unwilling to do so using only its own resources, is to utilize a partnership. The partnership may well be composed of the organization, the person(s) providing the financing, and the construction company. In many instances, there will be a limited partnership, with the tax-exempt organization being the general partner or one of the general partners. The partnership is the entity that acquires the property, develops it (if necessary), and sometimes continues to operate and maintain it. Subsequently, the nonprofit organization involved may acquire the property from the partnership, by purchase or (if the organization is a charitable one) by being the recipient of gifts of the partnership interests.

Not all partnerships utilized by tax-exempt organizations involve the acquisition and maintenance of real estate. (Others are used to acquire and operate capital equipment.) Because most of these partnerships are employed in the real estate context, however, this use is appropriate for examining the underlying rationale for this technique.

Assume that a charitable organization has decided that it no longer wishes to pay rent for its office space. Instead, it wants to own a building for its own use. These are its options for deriving the necessary funds:

- Using money it has saved and held for investment
- Embarking on a capital campaign and raise the money from gifts and grants
- Utilizing tax-exempt bonds
- Acquiring the property by means of a real estate partnership
- Combining two or more of the foregoing approaches

The drawbacks for most of these options are that the tax-exempt organization usually does not have or cannot acquire the money or lacks the time or other resources to attract the funding. The pluses of the partnership approach include the ability of the organization to acquire the building using the funds of others. As observed previously, a partnership is a financing mechanism—a means to an end.

SOME LAW BASICS ABOUT PARTNERSHIPS

A partnership is a business form that is recognized as an entity under the law just as is a corporation or a trust. Its formal document is a partnership agreement. The agreement is between persons who are the partners; the persons may be individuals, corporations, or other partnerships. Each partner owns one or more interests, called *units*, in the partnership.

Partners are of two types: general and limited. Every partnership must have at least one general partner. Where there is more than one general partner, one of them is often designated the managing general partner.

Many partnerships have only general partners, and they contribute cash, property, or services. The interests of the general partners may or may not be equal. This type of partnership is essentially a joint venture: Generally, all of the partners are equally liable for satisfaction of the obligations of the partnership and can be called on to make additional capital contributions to the partnership.

Some partnerships need or want to attract capital from sources other than the general partners. This capital can come from investors, called *limited partners*. Their interest in the partnership is limited in the sense that their liability is limited. The liability of a limited partner is confined to the amount of the capital contributed—the investment. General liability for the acts of the partnership rests with the general partner or partners. A partnership with both general and limited partners is a *limited partnership*.

When the partners decide to buy real estate, the partnership acquires the property, develops it (if necessary), and sometimes continues to operate and maintain it. Where a tax-exempt organization is a general partner, it is not the owner of the property (the partnership is) but it can enjoy many of the perquisites of ownership, such as participation in the cash flow generated by the property, a preferential leasing arrangement, and the general perception by the outside world that the property is owned by the tax-exempt organization (often furthered by giving the building the organization's name). The tax-exempt organization leases space in the property owned by the partnership; often, the organization will have an option to purchase the property from the partnership after the passage of a few years.

Partnerships do not pay taxes. They are merely conduits of net revenue to the partners, who bear the responsibility for paying tax on their share of the net income. Partnerships are also conduits of the tax advantages of the ownership of property; they pass through preference items such as depreciation and interest deductions.

As a general rule, a partnership is a very useful and beneficial way for one or more individuals or organizations to acquire, own, and operate a property. Tax-exempt organizations can, however, face problems with this approach.

TAX EXEMPTION ISSUE

The IRS is not thrilled with the presence of nonprofit organizations in partnerships, unless they are limited partners in a prudent investment vehicle. To date, all of the controversy concerning partnerships in this setting has focused on charitable organizations, although some or all of the principles of law being developed may become applicable to other tax-exempt organizations, such as social welfare organizations and membership associations.

In the view of the IRS, substantial benefits can be provided to the for-profit participants in a partnership (usually the limited partners) where a tax-exempt organization is a general partner. This concern has its origin in arrangements involving hospitals and physicians. An example would be a partnership formed to build and manage a medical office building, with a hospital as the general partner and investing physicians as limited partners. Where these substantial benefits are present, the IRS—upon discovering them—will not be hesitant to assert private inurement and private benefit.

The IRS's current position is that a charitable organization will lose its federal income tax exemption if it is a general partner in a partnership, unless the principal purpose of the partnership itself is to further charitable purposes. Even where the partnership can so qualify, the exemption is revoked if the charitable organization/general partner is not adequately insulated from the day-to-day management responsibilities of the partnership or if the limited partners are receiving an unwarranted return.

The IRS's position on tax-exempt organizations in partnerships is questionable, somewhat unfair, and in conflict with basic legal principles. Still, its present view is far more enlightened than its original position. The IRS now concedes that a charitable organization can (as required) be operated exclusively for exempt purposes and simultaneously be a general partner and satisfy its fiduciary responsibilities to the other partners. (The IRS's original view was predicated on the private inurement doctrine.)

The courts have forced the IRS to relax its stance on participation of tax-exempt organizations in partnerships. The IRS's lawyers have opined that it is possible for a charitable organization to participate as a general partner in a limited partnership without jeopardizing its tax exemption. The lawyers have advised that two aspects of the arrangement should be particularly reviewed:

1. Was the participation in conflict with the goals and purposes of the charitable organization?

2. Did the terms of the partnership agreement contain provisions that *insulated* the charitable organization from certain obligations imposed on a general partner?

This position of the IRS's legal counsel opened the way for many favorable private letter rulings concerning charitable organizations in partnerships. Each of these partnerships, however, has been held to be in furtherance of charitable objectives—for example, the construction and operation of a medical office building on the grounds of a hospital, the purchase and operation of medical equipment at a hospital, and the initiation of low-income housing projects. To date, the IRS has yet to issue a private letter ruling denying a charitable organization tax-exempt status because of its involvement as a general partner in a limited partnership.

In summary, the current position of the IRS on whether a charitable organization will have its tax-exempt status revoked (or recognition denied) if it functions as a general partner in a limited partnership is the subject of a *two-part test* (really a three-part test). The IRS first looks to determine whether the charitable organization/general partner is serving a charitable purpose by means of the partnership. If the partnership is serving a charitable purpose, the IRS applies the second portion of the test. If the partnership fails to adhere to the charitability standard, however, the charitable organization/general partner will be deprived of its tax-exempt status.

The second part of the two-part test is designed to ascertain whether the charity's role as general partner inhibits its charitable purposes. Here, the IRS looks to means by which the organization may, under particular facts and circumstances, be insulated from the day-to-day responsibilities as general partner and (the true third part of the test) whether limited partners are receiving an undue economic benefit from the partnership. In the view of the IRS, there is an inherent tension between the ability of a charitable organization to function exclusively in furtherance of its exempt functions and the obligation of a general partner to operate the partnership for the benefit of the limited partners. This tension is the same perceived phenomenon that the IRS, at the outset, chose to characterize as a conflict of interest.

DANGEROUS JOINT VENTURES

Until recently, partnerships and other joint ventures involving tax-exempt organizations (almost always, charitable ones) were used only to facilitate specific projects or programs. Matters have evolved to the point, however, where the *entirety* of the exempt organization is placed in the venture. Like so many innovations in the nonprofit legal arena, this approach originated in the health care field. These arrangements are termed *whole hospital joint ventures*.

In a typical venture of this type (used to provide additional financing for the hospital), the hospital and a for-profit corporation (the financier) form a limited liability company (LLC). All of the operating assets of the hospital are transferred to the LLC. The LLC has a governing board that consists of individuals selected by the hospital and the for-profit entity. The LLC receives day-to-day management services from a management company. In some instances, the hospital is obligated to use its distributions from the LLC to fund grants to support activities that promote the health of the hospital's community and to help the indigent obtain health care.

Superficially, this structure looks great. But there are serious traps lurking, where a misstep can lead to loss of the tax status of the exempt organization involved (here, a hospital). Overall, there must be certainty that any undue benefits to the for-profit partner are incidental (see Chapter 5).

Trap one concerns the composition of the board of directors of the LLC. If the for-profit entity controls that board, the hospital's activities and assets are considered to have come under the domain of that entity; that constitutes more than incidental private inurement, and the hospital will lose its exemption.

Trap two pertains to the management company. If that company is controlled by the for-profit partner and the management contract is long-term and its terms otherwise make leaving the contractual obligation difficult for the exempt organization, the nonprofit partner will be considered to have forfeited control over its resources. Again, this is considered meaningful private benefit, and the hospital will have its tax exemption revoked.

Trap three is a blend of the other two traps—control. If the for-profit has unwarranted control over the exempt organization's activities and assets and the hospital cannot initiate programs within the LLC to serve new health needs in the hospital's community without the consent of the for-profit, excessive private benefit arises again. (One court characterized this outcome as one where the hospital "ceded its authority" to the for-profit co-venturer.) This is a basis for revocation of tax exemption.

To date, these ventures have been seen only in the health care setting. But the fundamental principles cut across the operations of all public charities (and perhaps other nonprofit organizations). The lesson is clear. The nonprofit organization will be deprived of its tax exemption if the partnership or other joint venture arrangement allows nonexempt partners undue dominion over the exempt organization's programs and operating assets.

It is the view of the IRS that the tax law principles of whole entity joint ventures also apply where the charitable organization places only a portion of its resources in a joint venture. These are known as *ancillary joint ventures*.

ALTERNATIVES TO PARTNERSHIPS

Until or unless the IRS revises its rules in this area, charitable organizations must avoid participation in partnerships where the purpose of the partnership is not itself charitable (or else it must be prepared to test the government's position in court).

One way for a charitable organization to avoid the dilemma is to establish a wholly owned organization, usually a for-profit corporation, that would serve as the general partner in the partnership. This approach has been upheld by the IRS in private letter rulings. The tax-exempt entity leasing rules have been revised to make this approach somewhat less attractive.

Limited liability companies (LLCs) are rapidly growing in popularity, and they can have a major role in this area. LLCs are (like partnerships) not taxed, although they offer some of the limitations on personal liability that corporations do (see Chapter 2). Tax-exempt organizations can be members of LLCs. (If they are used as joint venture vehicles, the problems discussed above must be avoided.) Creative uses of LLCs abound. Some examples follow:

- Two private foundations invested in a partnership, the general partner of which was an LLC controlled by charitable organizations; the IRS ruled that the investment was a charitable undertaking (a program-related investment).

- Revenue generated by an LLC, owned by exempt health care providers, from transplant and other medical activities was found by the IRS to be related business income.

- A group of health care organizations in the United States used an LLC to partner with public hospitals in a foreign country to establish and operate a charitable hospital in that country; the hospital is operated by the LLC.

- A tax-exempt health care system and a group of physicians formed an LLC for the purpose of owning and operating an ambulatory surgery center.

- A hospital formed a cardiac catheterization laboratory as an outpatient facility by creating an LLC, consisting of its supporting organization and a group of physicians.

- Private colleges and universities formed an LLC for the purpose of housing a collective qualified prepaid tuition plan.

- Three trade associations used an LLC to conduct a single trade show.

Some charitable organizations are using a pooled income fund (discussed in the following chapter). Donors transfer cash or property to a pooled income fund and receive a charitable contribution deduction. The assets of the fund are used to purchase and maintain real property; the depreciation deduction flows through the fund and to the income beneficiaries for their use in computing income tax liability. Under some circumstances, the tax-exempt entity leasing rules will be applicable in determining the depreciation deduction. Sometimes, these benefits will be reduced because of the recent insistence by the IRS that pooled income funds holding depreciable property must establish depreciation reserve funds.

Another approach is to avoid partnerships or other *pass-through* entities altogether and set up a leasing arrangement. This works best where a tax-exempt organization acquires unimproved land and subsequently desires to have it improved (often, for its offices). The organization can acquire land and enter into a long-term ground lease with a developer or development group. The developer would construct the building, perhaps giving it the organization's name and otherwise providing all external appearances that the structure is the organization's own building. The developer or development group is in the position of fully utilizing all of the tax benefits. The nonprofit organization leases space in the building, perhaps pursuant to a "sweetheart" lease, and may be accorded an option to purchase the building after the passage of a few years.'

OTHER FORMS OF "PARTNERING"

In the world of nonprofit organizations, the word *partnership* (or *partnering*) is tossed around a lot, to mean far more than its connotation in the law. In this sense, a partnership is nearly any type of in-tandem relationship with another nonprofit or for-profit organization. Usually, when this type of partnership is used, the purpose is the conduct of a money-making business (related or unrelated (see Chapter 13)); it may also be the basis for advancement of a program of a nonprofit organization. Where the venture is between a nonprofit and a for-profit entity, it frequently is for fundraising purposes (termed a *commercial co-venturer* or a *charitable sales promotion*) (see Chapter 12). Indeed, in a few instances, this type of partnership rises to the level of a true (in the law sense) partnership, with the parties failing to treat it as a separate legal entity and thus not complying with federal tax reporting requirements.

Checklist

❏ If the organization has any of the following, identify those in each category:

Participation in partnership as general partner _____

Participation in partnership as limited partner _____

Membership in a limited liability company _____

Participation in other joint venture _____

Use of pooled income fund _____

Other leasing arrangements _____

FOCUS: Campaign to Clean Up America

The Campaign to Clean Up America (CCUA) is not ready, at this stage in its development, for participation in a joint venture or other type of partnership.

There will be opportunities in the future for advancement of the programs of the CCUA by means of one or more joint ventures with other nonprofit organizations. Perhaps a general partnership with a for-profit entity will prove advantageous, or a limited partnership may become available as a financing vehicle. Part of this depends on the success of the CCUA itself and part depends on forthcoming developments in the law of tax-exempt organizations.

CHAPTER NINETEEN

Wonderful World
of Planned Giving

One of the great mysteries in the world of charity is why so few nonprofit organizations take advantage of the most remunerative fundraising technique there is— planned giving. Those that do venture into the realm of planned giving are inevitably successful if they have given the attempt even half a chance. The managers of nonprofit organizations, of course, talk to one another. Why then is planned giving not commonplace throughout the charitable community?

One reason is that over the years, planned giving has been seen as mysterious and complicated. Management, at many organizations, has grown fearful of it. The other reason is a consequence of the nonprofit mentality—the frequent tendency of the management of nonprofit organizations to think small and to see short sightedly. These two reasons are actually tightly interwoven. Most organizations think about planned giving from time to time but put off implementing a planned giving program to another day—a tomorrow that never comes. Perhaps this is why the old term— *deferred giving*—is more accurate!

APPRECIATED PROPERTY GIFTS—A REPRISE

One of the chief principles undergirding the advantages of charitable gifts of securities, real estate, and other property is that the deductible amount is generally equal to the full fair market value of the property at the time of the gift (see Chapter 11). The amount of appreciation in the property (the amount exceeding the donor's basis), which would be taxed if sold, escapes income taxation. For this favorable result to occur, the property must constitute long-term capital gain property.

Consequently, the key to wise charitable giving is to give property that is long-term capital gain property and has substantially appreciated in value. The greater the appreciation, the greater the charitable deduction and other income tax savings. The appreciated property gift is, therefore, a core concept of planned giving.

PLANNED GIFTS—AN INTRODUCTION

There are two basic types of planned gifts. One type is a legacy: under a will, a gift comes out of a decedent's estate (as a bequest or devise). The other type is a gift made during a donor's lifetime, using a trust or other agreement.

These gifts once were termed *deferred gifts* because the actual receipt of the contribution by the charity is deferred until the happening of some event (usually the donor's death). But the term *deferred giving* has fallen out of favor. Some donors (to the chagrin of the gift-seeking charities) gained the impression that it was their tax benefits that were being deferred.

A planned gift usually is a contribution of a donor's interest in money or an item of property, rather than an outright gift of the money or property in its entirety. (The word *usually* is used because gifts using insurance do not neatly fit this definition and because an outright gift of property, in some circumstances, is treated as a planned gift.) Technically, this type of gift is a conveyance of a partial interest in property; planned giving is (usually) partial interest giving.

An item of property conceptually has within it two interests: an *income interest* and a *remainder interest*.

The income interest within an item of property is a function of the income generated by the property. A person may be entitled to all of the income from a property or to some portion of the income—for example, income equal to 6 percent of the fair market value of the property, even though the property is producing income at the rate of 9 percent. This person is said to have the (or an) income interest in the property. Two or more persons (such as husband and wife) may have income interests in the same property; these interests may be held concurrently or consecutively.

The remainder interest within an item of property is the projected value of the property, or the property produced by reinvestments, at some future date. Put another way, the remainder interest in property is an amount equal to the present value of the property (or its offspring) when it is to be received at a subsequent point in time.

These interests are measured by the value of the property, the age of the donor(s), and the period of time that the income interest(s) will exist. The actual computation is made by means of actuarial tables, usually those promulgated by the Department of the Treasury.

An income interest or a remainder interest in property may be contributed to charity, but a deduction is almost never available for a charitable gift of an income interest in property. By contrast, the charitable contribution of a remainder interest in an item of property will—assuming all of the technical requirements are met—give rise to a (frequently sizable) charitable deduction.

When a gift of a remainder interest in property is made to a charity, the charity will not acquire that interest until the income interest(s) have expired. The donor receives the charitable deduction for the tax year in which the recipient charity's remainder interest in the property is established. When a gift of an income interest in property is made to a charity, the charity acquires that interest immediately and retains it until such time (sometimes measured by a term of years) as the remainder interest commences. Again, any resulting charitable deduction is available for the tax year in which the charity's income interest in the property is established.

Basically, under the federal tax law, a planned gift must be made by means of a trust if a charitable deduction is to be available. The trust used to facilitate a planned gift is known as a *split-interest trust*, because it is the mechanism for satisfying the requirements involving the income and remainder interests. In other words, the trust is the medium for splitting the property into its two component types of interests. Split-interest trusts are charitable remainder trusts, pooled income funds, and charitable lead trusts (explained later).

There are some exceptions to the general requirements on using a split-interest trust in planned giving. The principal exception is the charitable gift annuity, which uses a contract rather than a trust. Individuals may give a remainder interest in their personal residence or farm to charity and receive a charitable deduction without utilizing a trust. A trust is also not required for a deductible gift of a remainder interest in real property when the gift is granted to a public charity or certain operating foundations exclusively for conservation purposes. Similarly, a donor may contribute a lease on, an option to purchase, or an easement with respect to real property, granted in perpetuity to a public charity or certain foundations exclusively for conservation purposes, and receive a charitable contribution deduction without a trust. A contribution of an undivided portion of one's entire interest in property is not regarded as a contribution of a partial interest in property.

A donor, although wishing to support a particular charity, may be unwilling or unable to fully part with property, either because of a present or perceived need for the income that the property provides or because of the capital gains taxes that would be experienced if the property were sold. The planned gift is likely to be the answer in this situation: The donor may satisfy his or her charitable desires and yet continue to receive income from the property. The donor also receives a charitable deduction for the gift of the remainder interest, which will reduce or eliminate the tax on the income from the gift property. There is no income tax imposed on the capital gain inherent in the property. If the gift property is not throwing off sufficient income, the trustee of the split-interest trust may dispose of the property and reinvest the proceeds in more productive property. The donor may then receive more income from the property in the trust than was received prior to the making of the gift.

The various planned giving vehicles are explored next.

CHARITABLE REMAINDER TRUSTS

The most widespread form of planned giving involves a split-interest trust known as the *charitable remainder trust*. The term is nearly self-explanatory: The entity is a trust by which a remainder interest destined for charity has been created. Each charitable remainder trust is designed specifically for the particular circumstances of the donor(s), with the remainder interest in the gift property being designated for one or more charities.

A qualified charitable remainder trust must provide for a specified distribution of income, at least annually, to or for the use of one or more beneficiaries (at least one of which is not a charity). The flow of income must be for life or for a term of no more than 20 years, with an irrevocable remainder interest to be held for the benefit of the charity or paid over to it. The beneficiaries are the holders of the income interests, and the charity has the remainder interest.

How the income interests in a charitable remainder trust are ascertained depends on whether the trust is a *charitable remainder annuity trust* (income payments are in the form of a fixed amount, an *annuity*) or a *charitable remainder unitrust* (income payments are in the form of an amount equal to a percentage of the fair market value of the assets in the trust).

The income payout of both of these trusts is subject to a 5 percent minimum. That is, the annuity must be an amount equal to at least 5 percent of the value of the property initially placed in the trust. Likewise, the unitrust amount must be an amount equal to at least 5 percent of the value of the trust property, determined annually. These percentages may not be more than 50 percent. Also, the value of the remainder interest in the property must be at least 10 percent of the value of the property contributed to the trust.

All categories of charitable organizations—both public charities and private foundations—are eligible to be remainder beneficiaries of as many charitable remainder trusts as they can muster. The amount of the charitable deduction will vary for different types of charitable organizations, however, because of the percentage limitations (see Chapter 11).

Often, a bank or similar financial institution serves as the trustee of a charitable remainder trust. The financial institution should have the capacity to administer the trust, make appropriate investments, and timely adhere to all income distribution and reporting requirements. It is not unusual, however, for the charitable organization that is the remainder beneficiary to act as trustee. If the donor or a related person is named the trustee, the *grantor trust* rules may apply: The gain from the trust's sale of appreciated property is taxed to the donor.

Conventionally, once the income interest expires, the assets in a charitable remainder trust are distributed to the charitable organization that is the remainder beneficiary. If the assets (or a portion of them) are retained in the trust, the trust will be classified as a private foundation, unless it can qualify as a public charity (most likely a supporting organization) (see Chapter 7).

Unfortunately, there have been some abuses in this area in recent years. One problem has been the use of short-term (such as a term of two years) charitable remainder trusts to manipulate the use of assets and payout arrangements for the tax benefit of the donors. Certain of these abuses were stymied by legislation enacted in 1997. Regulations which took effect in the fall of 1999 are designed to prevent transactions by which a charitable remainder trust is used to convert appreciated property into money while avoiding tax on the gain from the sale of the assets. (Some of these arrangements were so audacious that the vehicles garnered the informal name *chutzpah trust*.)

POOLED INCOME FUNDS

Another planned giving technique involves gifts to a *pooled income fund*. Like a charitable remainder trust, a pooled income fund is a form of split-interest trust.

A donor to a qualified pooled income fund receives a charitable deduction for giving the remainder interest in the donated property to charity. The gift creates income interests in one or more noncharitable beneficiaries; the remainder interest in the gift property is designated for the charity that maintains the fund.

The pooled income fund's basic instrument (a trust agreement or a declaration of trust) is written to facilitate gifts from an unlimited number of donors, so the essential terms of the transactions must be established in advance for all participants. The terms of the transfer cannot be tailored to fit any one donor's particular circumstances (as they can with the charitable remainder trust). The pooled income fund is, literally, a pooling of gifts.

Contributions to a pooled income fund may be considerably smaller amounts than those to a charitable remainder trust. Gifts to pooled income funds are generally confined to cash and readily marketable securities (other than tax-exempt bonds).

Each donor to a pooled income fund contributes an irrevocable remainder interest in the gift property to (or for the use of) an eligible charity. Each donor creates an income interest for the life of one or more beneficiaries, who must be living at the time of the transfer. The properties transferred by the donors must be commingled in the fund (to create the necessary pool of gifts).

Each income interest beneficiary must receive income at least once each year. The pool amount is determined by the rate of return earned by the fund for the year. Beneficiaries receive their proportionate share of the fund's income. The dollar amount of the income share is based on the number of units owned by the beneficiary, and each unit must be based on the fair market value of the assets when transferred.

A pooled income fund is essentially an investment vehicle whose funding is motivated by charitable intents.

A pooled income fund must be maintained by one or more charitable organizations. The charity must exercise control over the fund; it does not have to be the trustee of the fund (although it can be), but it must have the power to remove and replace the trustee. A donor or an income beneficiary of the fund may not be a trustee. A donor may be a trustee or officer of the charitable organization that maintains the fund, however, as long as he or she does not have the general responsibilities toward the fund that are ordinarily exercised by a trustee.

Unlike other forms of planned giving, a pooled income fund is restricted to certain categories of charitable organizations. Most types of public charities can maintain a pooled income fund; private foundations and some nonprivate foundations cannot. (The distinctions between public and private charities are summarized in Chapter 7.)

The same general tax advantages that are available as the result of gifts to charitable remainder trusts are available for gifts to pooled income funds. The advantages are particularly solid when the gift consists of fully marketable and appreciated securities. A pooled income fund transfer may accommodate a smaller amount (value) of securities than a transfer to a remainder trust. If fixed income is an important consideration, however, a charitable remainder annuity trust (see foregoing discussion) or a charitable gift annuity (see discussion following) will be preferable to a gift to a charitable remainder unitrust or pooled income fund.

A qualified charitable organization can have as many pooled income funds as it wishes. One or more funds may be for general fundraising purposes, and one or more for use in lieu of a partnership (see Chapter 18).

Pooled income funds currently are somewhat out of favor due to declines in interest rates and bond yields. This is causing a reduction in the investment return of these funds and, thus, a reduction in the amount of income paid to the income beneficiaries. Donors are avoiding pooled funds, thereby increasing the costs of maintaining them. Some charities have terminated their pooled income funds, although many funds at the larger institutions are performing adequately.

CHARITABLE LEAD TRUSTS

Most forms of planned giving have a common element: The donor transfers to a charitable organization the remainder interest in a property, and one or more noncharitable beneficiaries retain the income interest. A reverse sequence may occur, however, and that is the essence of the *charitable lead trust*.

The property transferred to a charitable lead trust is apportioned into an income interest and a remainder interest. Like the charitable remainder trust and the pooled income fund, this is a split-interest trust. An income interest in property is contributed to a charitable organization, either for a term of years or for the life of one individual (or the lives of more than one individual). The remainder interest in the property is reserved to return, at the expiration of the income interest (the *lead period*), to the donor or pass to some other noncharitable beneficiary or beneficiaries; often, the property passes from one generation (the donor's) to another.

Recent regulations limit the types of individuals whose lives can be used as *measuring lives* for determining the period of time the charity will receive the income flow from a charitable lead trust. The only individuals whose lives can be used as measuring ones are those of the donor, the donor's spouse, or a lineal ancestor of all the remaining beneficiaries. This regulation project is designed to shut down the practice of using the lives of seriously ill individuals to move assets and income away from charitable beneficiaries prematurely and, instead, to private beneficiaries. These trusts are sometimes referred to as *vulture trusts* or *ghoul trusts*.

The charitable lead trust can be used to accelerate into one year a series of charitable contributions that would otherwise be made annually. There can be a corresponding single-year deduction for the "bunched" amount of charitable gifts.

In some circumstances, a charitable deduction is available for the transfer of an income interest in property to a charitable organization. There are stringent limitations, however, on the deductible amount of charitable contributions of these income interests.

CHARITABLE GIFT ANNUITIES

Still another form of planned giving is the *charitable gift annuity*. It is not based on use of a split-interest trust. Instead, the annuity is arranged in an agreement between the donor and donee. The donor agrees to make a gift and the donee agrees, in return, to provide the donor (or someone else) with an annuity.

With one payment, the donor is engaging in two transactions: the purchase of an annuity and the making of a charitable gift. The gift gives rise to the charitable deduction. One sum is transferred; the money in excess of the amount necessary to purchase the annuity is the charitable gift portion. Because of the dual nature of the transaction, the charitable gift annuity transfer constitutes a *bargain sale*.

The annuity resulting from the creation of a charitable gift annuity arrangement is a fixed amount paid at regular intervals. The exact amount paid depends on the age of the beneficiary, which is determined at the time the contribution is made.

A portion of the annuity paid is tax-free because it is a return of capital. Where appreciated securities are given, there will be capital gain on the appreciation that is attributable to the value of the annuity. If the donor is the annuitant, the capital gain can be reported ratably over the individual's life expectancy. The tax savings occasioned by the charitable contribution deduction may, however, shelter the capital gain (resulting from the creation of a charitable gift annuity) from taxation.

Because the arrangement is by contract between the donor and donee, all of the assets of the charitable organization are on the line for ongoing payment of the annuities. (With most planned giving techniques, the resources for payment of income are confined to those in a split-interest trust.) That is why some states impose a requirement that charities must establish a reserve for the payment of gift annuities—and why many charitable organizations are reluctant to embark on a gift annuity program. This outcome is unfortunate; millions of dollars are lost annually by charitable organizations that fail to use charitable gift annuities. Even those that are reluctant to commit to the ongoing payment of annuities can eliminate the risk by reinsuring them.

LIFE INSURANCE

An underutilized form of planned giving is the donation of individual (not group) life insurance. A gift of life insurance is an excellent way for a person who has a relatively small amount of present resources to make a major contribution to a charitable organization. Gifts of life insurance are particularly attractive for younger donors.

If the life insurance policy is fully paid up, the donor will receive a charitable deduction for the cash surrender value or the replacement value of the policy. If the premiums are still being paid, the donor receives a deduction on his or her annual tax return for the premium payments made during the taxable year. For the deduction to be available, however, the donee charity must be both the beneficiary and the owner of the insurance policy.

There is some uncertainty in legal circles as to whether a gift of life insurance is valid (and thus deductible), because of the necessity of *insurable interest*—the owner and beneficiary of the policy must be more economically advantaged with the insured alive rather than dead. (Examples of relationships where insurable interests exist are healthy marriages and employment of key individuals.) In many instances, a charitable organization is advantaged by having a donor of a life insurance policy alive: He or she may be a key volunteer (such as a trustee or officer) or a potential donor of other, larger gifts.

CHARITABLE SPLIT-DOLLAR PLANS

Notwithstanding the foregoing, there is one type of giving involving life insurance that charities must avoid: *charitable split-dollar insurance plans*. These plans are complex, and there are several variations of them. Irrespective of the plan, charities are taxed if they participate in them.

The typical charitable split-dollar insurance transaction involves a transfer of funds by an individual to a charitable organization, with the "understanding" that the charity will use the funds to pay premiums on a cash value life insurance policy that benefits both the charity and the individual's family. Generally, the charity or an irrevocable life insurance trust formed by the individual (or a related person) purchases the insurance policy. The designated beneficiaries of the policy include the charity and the trust. Members of the individual's family (and perhaps the individual) are beneficiaries of the trust.

In a related transaction, the charity enters into a split-dollar arrangement with the trust. The agreement specifies the portion of the insurance policy premiums to be paid by the trust and the portion to be paid by the charity. The agreement states the extent to which each party can exercise standard policyholder rights, such as the right to borrow against the cash value of the policy, to partially or completely surrender the policy for money, and to designate beneficiaries for specified portions of the death benefit.

The agreement also specifies the manner in which it may be terminated and the consequences of the termination. Although the terms of these split-dollar arrangements vary, the feature that upsets the IRS is that commonly, over the life of the agreement, the trust has access to a "disproportionately high percentage" of the cash surrender value and death benefit under the policy, compared to the percentage of premiums paid by the trust.

As part of the charitable split-dollar insurance transaction, the individual (or a related person) who transfers funds to the charity treats the payment as a gift. Although there may not be a legally binding obligation expressly requiring the individual to transfer the funds to assist the charity in making premium payments, as the IRS puts it, "both parties understand that this will occur."

Basically, as noted, the tax law denies any charitable contribution deduction for these transfers (see Chapter 16). (These arrangements are cast as *personal benefit contracts*.) Also, there is an excise tax imposed on a charitable organization, with the tax equal to the amount of the premiums paid by the organization on any life insurance, annuity, or endowment contract if the premiums are paid in connection with a transfer for which the charitable deduction is not available.

STARTING A PROGRAM

Knowing something about the various planned giving techniques is only a start. A planned giving program must be implemented, and that takes more than knowing about income and remainder interests.

Some tips on how to launch a planned giving program are found in the next chapter.

Checklist

❏ If the organization has any of the following, identify those in each category:

One or more charitable remainder annuity trusts _____

One or more charitable remainder unitrusts _____

One or more pooled income funds _____

One or more charitable gift annuity contracts _____

One or more charitable lead trusts _____

One or more donated life insurance contracts _____

Other forms of a planned gift _____

FOCUS: Campaign to Clean Up America

The Campaign to Clean Up America (CCUA) is implementing a planned giving program at the very outset of its operations. The CCUA does not have a defined constituency (like a church's parish or a university's graduates), but it will be able, over time, to identify sources of planned gifts from its developing donor base.

The CCUA is presently prepared to accept gifts by means of charitable remainder trusts, charitable lead trusts, and life insurance. The CCUA is holding off on implementing a full-scale effort to secure charitable gift annuities until it can satisfy the various state laws on this form of giving.

CHAPTER TWENTY

Putting Ideas into Action

It is one thing to have an idea; putting the idea into actual practice is something else. The chapters in this part of the book are offered to stimulate ideas rather than to pre-scribe firm solutions for particular problems. Starting and operating a nonprofit orga-nization is a relatively common undertaking. Planned giving, subsidiaries, joint ventures, and partnerships are not so common, however, and not all of these possibil-ities are suitable for all nonprofit organizations at all times. The intent is not to over-look a possibility that can prove useful for a particular organization.

When approaching key decisions of this sort, professional guidance is a must. Fees for lawyers, accountants, or management or fundraising consultants may seem unaffordable at first, but the money is usually well spent.

JOINT VENTURES

A *joint venture* basically is any undertaking involving two (or more) organizations. In the context of nonprofit organizations, the venturers can both be nonprofits, or one can be a nonprofit and one a for-profit organization.

Most joint ventures are the products of decisions that two heads are better than one. A pooling of resources occurs. Partnerships, more so than other forms of joint ventures, pool financial resources. Most often, a joint venture is an aggregation of programs: One organization has a program resource and the other organization has another program resource, and the purpose of the joint venture can only be accom-plished (or can be better accomplished) through a blending of the two.

From the standpoint of a nonprofit organization, two general outcomes are possible:

1. It will be approached by another organization that is seeking access to one of its resources.

2. It will seek out a resource of another organization, to carry out one of its own desired programs.

The management of a nonprofit organization should always have an ongoing business plan that includes an inventory of what the organization is doing or wishes to do. From the inventory, management may discover that the organization lacks the resources to undertake a particular project. Some nonprofit managers might give up at this point. Others may expend the effort needed to purchase the personnel, equip-ment, or other resources necessary to tackle the project.

A third option is possible: use of the existing resources of another organization. Despite the effort and ingenuity required, this alternative can be preferable to the others. When one nonprofit organization joins with another organization to advance a particular undertaking, a joint venture results.

Besides being a medium for furthering program objectives, a joint venture can be a way to further management objectives. If one nonprofit organization is merely providing management services to another, however, the provision of services may be an unrelated business of the provider (see Chapter 13).

A joint venture can be used to advance fundraising objectives. This is often done with another nonprofit organization, but it can also be done with a for-profit organization—for example, in a *commercial co-venture*. This is an unfortunate term, because of the connotation (usually inaccurate) that the nonprofit organization involved is engaged in some activity that is commercial. Often, a commercial co-venture is not really a venture—although it can be (and increasingly is).

A commercial co-venture is an arrangement between a business and a charitable organization whereby the business agrees to make a contribution to the charity. The gift's amount is related to the volume of sales of the company's service or product during a particular period of time. That is, the company agrees to donate to the charity an amount equal to a percentage of sales during the time of the promotion, and the fact of the prospective gift is advertised to the consuming public. The charity benefits because of the gift, and the business benefits because of the positive marketing and (it hopes) an increase in the sales volume. The relationship can turn into a true joint venture if the charity itself becomes involved in the promotional aspects of the sales campaign. A word of caution: As the charity becomes more involved in this type of joint venture, the likelihood increases that the business's payments to the charity will be treated as a taxable payment for services rendered rather than a charitable contribution.

PARTNERSHIPS

The concept of a partnership is described in Chapter 18. A partnership can be general or limited.

As a practical matter, there is little difference between a general partnership and a joint venture. Both involve a pooling of resources, often programmatic ones. Astute managers of nonprofit organizations will always be alert to opportunities to achieve something by using the resources of others. This is not a selfish or unilateral approach; the other party to the venture, by definition, also will be entering into the arrangement for the purpose of achieving some desired end.

Whenever programs and objectives are reviewed, nonprofit management should determine whether something can be better accomplished (or just plain accomplished) working in tandem with one or more other organizations.

Sometimes, because of the nature of the relationship, one or more of the partners is bringing to the arrangement something other than programmatic resources. The resource brought may be money, and in this context a partnership is used as a financing device. As noted in Chapter 18, when a limited partnership is utilized, the limited partners are investors and the resource they bring to the arrangement is money. When a nonprofit organization is involved, the limited partners will most likely be strong supporters of the organization—people who are particularly interested in its programs and objectives and who are then acting in a dual capacity. They desire to make an investment and receive an economic return, and they wish to assist the organization. These limited partners tend to be directors, trustees, or officers of the organization, or its substantial contributors. Nonprofit organizations have unique opportunities in limited partnerships.

The management of a nonprofit organization should approach the possibility of a partnership, particularly a limited partnership, as a search for funding, perhaps blended with a fundraising program. Limited partners and donors can be drawn from the same constituency. For example, an individual can become a limited partner in a partnership where a charitable organization is a general partner and then subsequently donate his or her limited partnership interest to the organization.

When considering the possibilities of a limited partnership, the management of a nonprofit organization should do the following:

- Review all program, administrative, and fundraising objectives, with a view to the best way of funding them.

- Develop a schedule of priority for financing each of the objectives.

- Identify those that may be clearly fundable with contributions (in the case of charitable organizations), those that may be funded with service-provider revenue, those that may be funded with membership fees (assuming a membership), and those that may be funded with investment income (funded out of an endowment).

- Earmark any programs or functions that cannot be fully funded using one or more of these approaches (or cannot be funded at all) as possibilities for a limited partnership.

- Make certain that the organization, in entering into the partnership, is not transgressing any of the principles generated by the law created as the result of whole hospital joint ventures (see Chapter 18).

Does the organization need or want its own building? A new computer system? Other major equipment or capital assets? What about a facility to further its programs, such as a research center or conference facility? A limited partnership can be used as a financing mechanism to accomplish these ends.

The process of deciding whether to utilize a partnership or joint venture is really one of matching means to ends. It requires the management of a nonprofit organization to take an expansive view of its objectives and opportunities and to seek the fullest available exploitation of the organization's potential.

As an illustration, some nonprofit organizations' management only dream of having their own building for their offices. They fear a conventional fundraising program to that end, believing (in some instances, correctly) that they lack the donor base to accumulate the necessary funds through gifts and grants. Others take a broader view. They assemble board members and other supporters and persuade them to become limited partners in a partnership. Using the capital thus acquired or borrowed by the partnership, the partnership acquires the property, creates the offices, leases them (presumably on some favorable basis) to the organization, and passes along to the limited partners all or some of the cash flow of the property and the tax advantages of owning property. In the meantime, the organization can (particularly if a charitable one) raise funds to ultimately purchase the property from the partnership. When the process is completed, the organization has done a remarkable thing: It has acquired its own headquarters, which it can now occupy rent free, solely using the funds of others.

Some programs of nonprofit organizations can be enhanced by administering them by means of a general partnership. Some functions of nonprofit organizations can be best financed using a limited partnership, but that choice must be weighed against and integrated with other financing techniques. Without intending to be too opportunistic, a limited partnership is a legitimate way of utilizing the money of others to achieve one's own ends. That ability can be doubly enhanced when coupled with the charitable deduction.

PLANNED GIVING

In Chapter 19, it was observed that charitable organizations are underutilizing planned giving, often because of an aura of mystery that surrounds it. Many managers perceive planned giving as far too complex for their organizations, or as not dynamic enough to generate badly needed current dollars. The implementation of a planned giving program usually gets deferred to another day—one that never seems to come.

There is also an erroneous belief that planned giving is only for the larger charities, those that have been in existence for some time and have an existing constituency. Finally, the initial process of establishing a planned giving program is thought to be too expensive.

None of these reasons for delaying a planned gift is truly valid. Nearly every charitable organization, no matter how small or how new, should have a planned giving program.

The very term *planned giving* usually causes some uncertainty. The pairing of these two words does not mean that all other gifts are unplanned. As noted in Chapter 8, a far better term would be *integrated giving*. The concept of planned giving means that a gift is of sufficient magnitude that the transfer of it is integrated with the donor's personal financial plan or estate plan. A planned gift is not an impulse gift; its consequences (other than to the charity) relate, for example, to the donor's family or business and are taken into account before the gift is made, when determining the type of gift that it will be.

Probably the simplest of planned gifts is a bequest in a will. The larger the gift or the more complicated the terms (one or more trusts may be included), the greater the extent of the planning. Writing a will or setting up a trust means formulating a plan.

Usually, an outright gift of cash or property is not regarded as a planned gift, although sometimes an outright contribution of property can be, if it is a gift of a business or a partnership interest. A mere gift of an insurance policy may not be regarded by some as a planned gift, but the process of deliberately selecting a particular policy for donation to charity and the circumstances of giving it can easily entail some serious planning.

Most planned gifts are based on the fundamental principle that property consists of two interests; an income interest and a remainder interest. Planned gifts usually involve the donation to charity of either an income interest or a remainder interest.

A gift of an income interest is made by means of a charitable lead trust. Most remainder interest gifts are made using a charitable remainder trust, a pooled income fund, or a charitable gift annuity.

A knowledgeable fundraiser can do more in the planned giving field than ask for gifts and collect them. He or she can simultaneously render to the donor valuable services that can have the following beneficial effects:

- The donor may end up with more income as the result of the gift.

- The donor's earnings may be shifted from taxable income to nontaxable income.

- The donor becomes enabled to dispose of property without paying taxes—in many cases, property that he or she did not really need.

- The donor may be able to pass property to other family members without incurring estate taxes.

Planned giving can yield professional money and property management without cost to the income beneficiaries. It can be the foundation for retirement plans, tuition payments, and memorial gifts. The list goes on and on.

(a) How to Start a Planned Giving Program

If planned giving is so great, why is every charity not using it? The principal reasons have already been stated. Another reason, however, may be that the organization simply does not quite know how to begin. Here are the ten easy steps to implementation of a successful planned giving program.

(i) Step 1. The members of the organization's board of directors *must* be involved. At this point, *being involved* does not mean as donors—that comes later. It means involved in the launching of the program.

The best way to start this process is to have the board pass a *planned giving launch resolution*. This resolution should state that there is to be such a program, who on the staff and among the officers is principally responsible for it, and, most importantly, what planned giving methods are going to be used. The resolution should expressly identify the vehicles: wills, charitable remainder trusts, insurance, pooled income fund, and the like.

(ii) Step 2. Most of the board members will not have heard of these vehicles. At a board meeting, some time should be set aside for a brief presentation on the basics of planned giving. The presentation should be made by an outsider—a lawyer, professional development counselor, or bank trust officer, for example. The board members should be given some written material to peruse at their leisure.

(iii) Step 3. Once the board has received its initial training and has adopted the launch resolution, some prototype instruments should be developed—documents, with the organization's name in the appropriate places, that can be shown to interested parties. These documents may be will clauses, charitable remainder trust models (both annuity trust and unitrust, and one-life and two-lives versions), stock powers, pooled income fund transfer agreements, or charitable gift annuity contracts.

Although donors will rarely be interested in these prototype documents, some of the board members may be. Those who are going to be asking for planned gifts should, however, have some basic familiarity with them. The greatest use of these instruments will be to provide them to a potential donor's professional counselor, whether a lawyer, accountant, financial planner, insurance agent, or securities broker. These persons may be unfamiliar with planned giving and will find actual documents very helpful.

(iv) Step 4. Government regulation of planned giving programs is unavoidable, so this step is to adhere to the requirements of the law. Asking for a planned gift is still asking for a gift, and it is important to register in each of the states that have charitable solicitation acts, if the charity has not already done so (see Chapter 9). State securities laws may be invoked if a charity is seeking gifts by means of charitable remainder trusts or a pooled income fund. If charitable gift annuities are to be used, state insurance law requirements must be complied with. Where gifts of insurance policies are involved, it may be necessary to be able to establish that the charity has an insurable interest in the lives of the donors.

(v) Step 5. The marketing phase begins here. This step may involve many alternatives, but the first concern must be acquisition of some easy-to-understand brochures on the concept and methods of planned giving, to be distributed to prospective donors. Having separate brochures on each of the techniques is far preferable to having one large booklet. The organization can either write and print its own brochures or have brochures prepared commercially.

Back to the board of directors, who have now been provided copies of the literature. The process of getting some (preferably all) of the directors to commit to some form of planned gift begins here and should be concluded without hedging or postponements. How can others be expected to give when the organization's own leadership has not (or worse, will not)?

(vi) Step 6. Start the process of building a network or cadre of volunteers who will be planned giving advocates to the outside world. This group should be composed in part of members of the organization's board of directors; other possibilities include individuals from the organization's prior leadership, active members, community leaders, and volunteer professionals (such as lawyers and accountants). These individuals will assist in procuring planned gifts by making them themselves, by asking others, and by influencing others who will do the asking.

The volunteers will need some training before they are sent out looking for planned gifts. Special sessions with someone knowledgeable about planned giving are essential, as are comprehensible printed materials. The intent is not to make these persons instant planned giving experts or even expect them to procure the gift. Their job is to become sufficiently familiar with the concept and techniques of planned giving that they know the basics of each method and how to correlate these basics with the facts and circumstances of each prospect's situation. The actual "ask" will probably be done by a staff person or a professional planned giving consultant.

(vii) Step 7. Identify prospective planned gift donors. This step is actually an ongoing process. If the organization has a membership, those individuals form the base with which to begin. The giving history of donors (frequency and amount of gifts) should be reviewed to identify planned giving prospects. Others who are interested in the organization's programs are prospects as well. Even new organizations have dedicated supporters who are thus potential planned givers.

(viii) Step 8. Once the prospective donors have been identified, they must be contacted. This is the essence of the marketing phase, and how it is done will vary from group to group. One tried-and-true approach is to send letters to the prospects explaining the planned giving program and inviting them to request additional information; those who respond are sent the appropriate brochures. Another approach is to concentrate on one vehicle, such as the charitable remainder trust or insurance, and market just that method by sending a brochure with the introductory letter. Some organizations like to lead with a wills program; others have had success opening with a pooled income fund program.

There are many marketing techniques. Some organizations have had success with financial planning seminars, where planned giving is stressed. Others hold seminars for those in the community who advise donors—lawyers, financial planners, accountants, and so on. If the organization has a magazine or newsletter, it should regularly publish items on planned giving. If the organization has an annual meeting or convention, a presentation on planned giving should be on the agenda. One favorite technique at the annual membership meeting is to have a planned giving booth among the other displays in the exhibit hall as part of the trade show.

The marketing aspects of planned giving must be ongoing practices. Some organizations can use all of the techniques just described. For launching a planned giving program, a combination of a special mailing, a seminar, and coverage in the organization's regular publications can be powerful.

(ix) Step 9. The next process is to obtain the gift once a bona fide prospect has signaled some interest. Advice here is hard to generalize. For organizations with an emerging planned giving program, the best way to proceed is to have a staff person or a volunteer meet with the prospective donor and work out a general plan, and then have a subsequent session with a planned giving professional who can advise the parties as to the specific method that is best for all concerned. A lawyer can prepare the specific instrument. As the organization matures, it can build planned giving expertise into its in-house operations.

Here is an example of the acquisition of a typical planned gift. An individual has been contacted about a charitable organization's planned giving program. Having coincidentally received a large amount of money as the result of a sale of property, he or she is looking for some tax relief. The prospective donor has an interest in the programs of the organization, so he or she and a staff person meet and work out these general guidelines: the donor needs a charitable deduction of X amount and annual income of Y amount. The parties subsequently meet with a lawyer, the numbers are run on a computer, the deduction and income amounts for each planned giving method are reviewed, and a specific arrangement (in this case, perhaps a charitable remainder annuity trust) is developed and subsequently executed.

One thing is clear: The organization's staff and volunteers will learn only by doing. As the gifts come in and the various processes that lead to the gifts are experienced, the parties involved will gain greater confidence and will need to rely less on the outside professional. It is advisable to have a planned giving professional on call at the outset and available thereafter as circumstances warrant.

(x) Step 10. This step may have occurred much earlier in the process—the selection of legal counsel or another professional who can work with the organization in the launching and ongoing administration of the program.

(b) Excuses and Misunderstandings

One of the excuses frequently given for postponing the inauguration of a planned giving program (or altogether ignoring the idea of such a program) is that it is not suitable for a new organization. There is no question that a university with decades of graduations has a larger and more solid donor base than a community service group incorporated last week. But the service group's relative disadvantage is not an arguable reason for doing nothing. Every organization has a support base or it would not exist. It may be that, on day 1, there is only one planned gift prospect, yet that is no reason not to approach that one prospect. The largest planned giving program started with one gift.

Another excuse for not implementing a planned giving program is that the organization must channel all of its fundraising energies into the generation of current dollars. Of all the excuses for not beginning, this is the most plausible. Still, it is an excuse, not a reason.

Two aspects of planned giving are misunderstood when it comes to the need for current support. There *are* some forms of planned giving that produce current dollars; planned giving is not simply waiting 30 years for someone to die. The planned giving methods that yield current dollars are

- The charitable lead trust, where the charity is provided immediate income out of the trust, rather than a deferred remainder interest

- The charitable remainder trust, where the donor (in addition to giving the remainder interest) gives the portion that is income interest to charity

- Gifts of life insurance (or gifts based on life insurance), where the policy can be surrendered if necessary for its cash value, or the charity can borrow money using the policy's cash value as collateral

The other fact that is often misunderstood is that planned gifts generate usable support much more quickly than is usually realized. Without becoming too morbid or grasping about it, individuals can die sooner than expected. Or, to state the matter more charitably, not everyone reaches his or her life expectancy. The odds being what they are, the larger the portfolio of planned gifts, the greater the likelihood of a speedy return.

The planned gift is ideal for an organization that is amassing a general endowment, scholarship, memorial, research, building, or similar fund. Everyone likes current gift dollars, but once a base of investment assets (principal) is established, the investment income can nicely complement the gift support, and the organization has the security of knowing that the assets remain in place.

The more it is understood that planned giving means service to the donors and receipt of large gifts, the more appreciated it will be. Some money will have to be expended at the outset, but it will be minimal in relation to the gifts received. The hurdle is simply getting started—taking the *deferral* out of this form of giving. Once the program is launched, the mystery will fall away and planned giving will become the most enjoyable and remunerative component of the fundraising and development program.

FINDING THE BEST BLEND

Innovative and energetic management of nonprofit organizations may well utilize all of these ideas—and more. A contemporary nonprofit organization may have subsidiaries, be involved in a partnership, and have a successful planned giving program.

Once again, it cannot be sufficiently stressed that all of these techniques are means to ends. They are ways for an organization to acquire what it wants and needs. Usually, the need is for money, and all of these suggestions are fundraising techniques.

The place to begin is the organization's wish list. What does it want? A building? A computer? An endowment? Thereafter, the technique is matched with the wish, and the sky is the limit.

These techniques can be blended. A partnership may be the best way to acquire the organization's offices; an ongoing fundraising program (including planned giving) can be used to buy out partnership interests so as to own the property directly someday. A conventional fundraising program may be used to acquire a computer system, but an endowment fund (fueled in part by planned giving) may secure future upgrades and replacements of equipment. A subsidiary or other separate organization may be appropriate to house a particular activity, but, as the organization grows, it may be able to absorb the activity within its basic operations, and an ongoing fundraising program can provide the wherewithal to buy out shareholders or otherwise acquire the assets supporting the activity.

Fundraising programs are not the only option. A joint venture or subsidiary may be preferable to any fundraising.

Generalizations are difficult here. There are many opportunities and many techniques. All an organization has to do is match its wants and needs to these techniques, and the rest is relatively simple.

PART FIVE

Sidestepping Traps

CHAPTER TWENTY-ONE

Watchdogs on the Prowl

For public charities and certain other nonprofit organizations, worrying about federal, state, and local law is not enough. They have to fret about the machinations of the several *watchdog agencies*. These groups are themselves nonprofit, tax-exempt, charitable organizations, established to tell other nonprofit, tax-exempt (usually), charitable entities how to operate and punish them if they do not adhere to the watchdogs' dictates (which are often inconsistent).

These organizations have been around for years, albeit in a variety of incarnations. Recently, it seemed that the influence of these organizations was waning, largely because information about charitable organizations is widely available to the public. Disclosure rules, for example, have made documents such as the application for recognition of exemption and the annual information return easily publicly accessible (see Chapter 10). This information and much more is available on the Internet; some organizations post their key documents on their websites or find that they are published elsewhere, such as on the Guidestar site (www.guidestar.org).

But, counterintuitively, the Internet has fostered a proliferation of these watchdog agencies. Regulation by these groups is on the rise, fueled in part by the contemporary surge in interest in governance of charitable organizations and the increase in the number of watchdog organizations.

WATCHDOG GROUPS: AN OVERVIEW

These watchdog groups are self-appointed bodies that call themselves *voluntary* agencies. This term is used to differentiate themselves from government regulatory bodies, but it is misleading. In fact, they are the antithesis of voluntarism; a charitable or other organization that dares spurn one of these agencies soon becomes publicly pilloried and financially damaged. Consequently, most organizations are forced to comply with these agencies' standards and demands. This is far from voluntary behavior.

At its most benign, the typical watchdog group serves as a source of information about nonprofit organizations, principally those that engage in fundraising, for the media, researchers, legislators, government regulators, and the public. They promulgate and apply standards, prepare and disseminate reports on nonprofit organizations, and distribute lists identifying the entities that do and do not meet the standards. The public, including donors and grantors and the media typically gives these ratings and reports considerable credibility; donors act (give or not give) accordingly. This lack of challenge and fawning acceptance of watchdog agencies' determinations gives these groups a substantial degree of clout and leverage. The public charity that stands up to one of these voluntary agencies does so at great peril to its reputation and finances. Watchdog agencies can have a powerful impact on the public perception of a charitable organization and its ability to successfully attract contributions and grants.

This fact was amply illustrated when the American Institute of Philanthropy (AIP) (see discussion following), in 1994, assigned a well-known public charity a grade of F. This lowest grade was given because this charity had assets, most of which were held in a separate foundation, representing funding of operations for about five years (an endowment). This rating was reported (but not explained) in an AIP charity guide, accompanied by an article about "corrupt and wasteful" practices by charitable organizations. The charity received a barrage of mail from outraged donors, who correlated the F grade with corrupt conduct and thus announced they would never contribute to the organization again because of its "fraudulent," "rip-off," and "shameful" operations. The charitable organization sued AIP for defamation and sought damages; the litigation was eventually settled out of court.

The reasons for the positive and accepting image these agencies have managed to create for themselves is not clear. Often, they are operated by individuals who, not to put too fine a point on the matter, do not know what they are doing and have an antiphilanthropic mindset. Reports are usually factually inaccurate, out-of-date, and sometimes unfairly written. The standards can be nonsensical, arbitrary, and inconsistent; they can be contrary to legal requirements. The rating process is often unfair; organizations that operate in a lawful manner and have meaningful programs find themselves on a widely distributed list of organizations that "fail to meet standards." The damage inflicted on a charitable organization can be devastating; the public comes to believe that the organization is poorly run and directs its support elsewhere. Yet, these agencies function with a nearly godlike aura, with members of Congress, funders, and others believing every word they publish. It is astonishing that the media, so fond of investigating charities, leaves these agencies alone and instead reports their findings as if they are pure fact.

At the present, there are several of these voluntary watchdog agencies. Let's take a look at them and how they operate.

(a) Wise Giving Alliance

Perhaps the best-known of these watchdog groups is the Wise Giving Alliance of the Council of Better Business Bureaus (CBBB). This Alliance is the successor to a division of the CBBB, which began operation in 1971, known as the Philanthropic Advisory Service (PAS). The Alliance was formed in 2001, the product of a merger of the National Charities Information Bureau (another of the early watchdog agencies) with the CBBB Foundation.

According to its website, the Alliance "collects and distributes information on hundreds of nonprofit organizations that solicit [contributions] nationally or have national or international program services." It "routinely asks such organizations for information about their programs, governance, fund raising practices, and finances when the charities have been the subject of inquiries." The Alliance "selects charities for evaluation based on the volume of donor inquiries about individual organizations." The organization serves "donors' information needs" and helps donors "make their own decisions regarding charitable giving."

The Alliance developed its "Standards for Charity Accountability" to "assist donors in making sound giving decisions and to foster public confidence in charitable organizations." One of the purposes of these standards is to "promote ethical conduct" by charitable organizations. The Alliance prepares reports about charitable organizations and publicly disseminates ratings of charities based on its standards.

(b) Evangelical Council for Financial Accountability

Religious organizations have established watchdog agencies that focus only on religious entities. Among them is the Evangelical Council for Financial Accountability (ECFA), which states on its website that it is an "accreditation agency dedicated to helping Christian ministries earn the public's trust through adherence to seven Standards of Responsible Stewardship." ECFA states that these standards, "drawn from Scripture, are fundamental to operating with integrity." In addition to these standards, ECFA has developed a series of best practices that are intended to "encourage [its] members to strive for the highest levels of excellence." Founded in 1979, ECFA states that its constituency comprises more than 2,000 evangelical Christian organizations. An organization that cannot comply with one or more of the standards is ineligible for membership in ECFA.

(c) Standards for Excellence Institute

The Standards for Excellence Institute (Institute) is a membership organization of charitable entities that claims, in its marketing material, to uphold standards that are higher "than the minimal requirements imposed by local, state and federal laws and regulations." This program was launched to "strengthen nonprofit governance and management, while also enhancing the public's trust in the nonprofit sector." This organization "promotes widespread application of a comprehensive system of self-regulation in the nonprofit sector." These standards are based on "fundamental values" such as "honesty, integrity, fairness, respect, trust, compassion, responsibility and accountability," and provide guidelines for how nonprofit organizations should act to be "ethical and accountable in their programs operations, governance, human resources, financial management and fundraising."

(d) Charity Navigator

Charity Navigator, billed (on its website) as "America's premier independent charity evaluator," endeavors to "advance a more efficient and responsible philanthropic marketplace." This watchdog group rates public charities on the basis of their *organizational efficiency* and *organizational capacity*. As to organizational efficiency, this rating process analyzes four categories of performance: program expenses, administrative expenses, fundraising expenses, and fundraising efficiency. (A charity that spends less than one-third of its annual revenue on program is automatically given an organizational efficiency score of zero.) Organizational capacity is rated on the basis of primary revenue growth, program expenses growth, and working capital ratio. Charities that are rated by Charity Navigator receive zero (exceptionally poor) to four (exceptional) stars.

(e) Ministry Watch

Ministry Watch endeavors, according to statements on its website, to provide pro-spective donors with an insight into ministries' "commitment to transparency" and attempts to help donors "search out those nonprofit Christian ministries that excel in the area of Transparency." To this end, the watchdog group has Guidelines for Trans-parency, with transparency assessed on the basis of timeliness of communication of information, availability of financial information, clarity of information (description and abundance), and level of cooperation (with the group). A score is assigned be-tween 0 (worst practice) and 100 (best practice). This group also has a "5 Star Ratings System" (0 percent to 100 percent) based on fund acquisition (fundraising), resource allocation (spending), and asset utilization.

(f) American Institute of Philanthropy

The American Institute of Philanthropy (AIP) is, according to its web site, a "nation-ally prominent charity watchdog service whose purpose is to help donors make informed giving decisions." In testimony before a congressional committee in 2007, the founder of AIP testified that the organization is "America's toughest and most independent watchdog of the accountability, finances, governance and promotional practices of charities." AIP, which is essentially a one-person operation, is generally considered one of the most extreme of the watchdogs, an outlier in this context.

AIP analyzes charitable organizations using three criteria: the percentage of total revenue that the charity spends on program services, the charity's fundraising costs, and the amount of assets that the charity has available to it. If AIP does not agree with the methodology used by a charitable organization (or a charity's accounting firm) in computing fundraising costs or in allocating fundraising and program expenses, it will propose a reallocation of the charity's expenses (and do so without any detailed analytical justification or third-party review for the reallocation). AIP publishes its analyses in its charity guides, distributed three times annually. Charities that AIP rates are given letter grades of A through F.

ISSUES ADDRESSED BY WATCHDOGS

These watchdog agencies address a multitude of issues involving charitable organiza-tions. Some of these issues are discussed elsewhere in this book—namely, board member duties and responsibilities (see Chapter 8) and good governance principles and policies (see Chapter 22). Watchdog standards, however, go considerably beyond these two important categories of issues.

(a) Expenditures for Program and Fundraising

One aspect of charities' operations that the watchdog agencies simply cannot shake is the idea that it is appropriate to impose percentage minimums as to expenditures for program and percentage maximums as to expenditures for fundraising. It has been shown repeatedly that one size cannot fit all in this regard. The U.S. Supreme Court has repeatedly held that percentage limitations of this nature are unconstitutional when made a part of state law. Yet the watchdogs persist.

This all started with the PAS. The PAS standards required that a charity spend a "reasonable percentage" of total income on programs, as well as a "reasonable percentage" of contributions on activities that are in accordance with donor expectations. In this context, PAS defined a "reasonable percentage" to mean at least 50 percent. Charities were also expected to ensure that their fundraising costs are "reasonable." In this context, fundraising costs were reasonable if those costs did not exceed 35 percent of related contributions. In the area of total fundraising and administrative costs, PAS standards also required that these costs be "reasonable." In this latter context, these costs were reasonable if they did not exceed 50 percent of total income. A charity was expected to establish and exercise "adequate controls" over its disbursements.

The Wise Giving Alliance standards require that an organization "[s]pend at least 65% of its total expenses on program activities" and "[s]pend no more than 35% of related contributions on fund raising." (An organization, however, does not spend expenses.)

The AIP believes fundraising costs should be reasonable. In this organization's view, this means that a charity should expend at least 60 percent of its outlays for charitable purposes. The balance, of course, is to be allocated to fundraising and administration. Fundraising expenses should not exceed 35 percent. These percentages are based on related contributions, not total income (thereby usually making the fundraising cost ratio higher). AIP sometimes takes it on itself to adjust an organization's fundraising expense ratio, such as where it is allocating expenses to program in the context of direct mail fundraising.

(b) Board Composition

The PAS standard concerning "adequate governance" required that there be an "independent governing body." Organizations did not meet this standard if "directly and/or indirectly compensated board members constitute more than one-fifth (20%) of the total voting membership of the board or of the executive committee." (The ordained clergy of a "publicly soliciting church," however, were excepted from this 20 percent limitation.) Organizations failed to meet this third standard if board members had material conflicting interests resulting from any relationship or business affiliation.

The Wise Giving Alliance standards require that the governing board of a soliciting charitable organization be a "volunteer" and "independent" group. A board is to be composed of a "minimum of five voting members." The standards provide that no more than one or 10 percent (whichever is greater) "directly or indirectly compensated person(s) [may] serv[e] as voting member(s) of the board." Further, "[c]ompensated members shall not serve as the board's chair or treasurer." The standards forbid "transaction(s) in which any board or staff members have material conflicting interests with the charity resulting from any relationship or business affiliation." Factors that are considered in determining whether a transaction entails a *conflict of interest*, and if so whether the conflict is *material*, include "any arm's length procedures established by the charity; the size of the transaction relative to like expenses of the charity; whether the interested party participated in the board vote on the transaction; if competitive bids were sought [;] and whether the transaction is one-time, recurring or ongoing."

The standards of the Evangelical Council for Financial Accountability (ECFA) also stipulate a board of at least five individuals, a majority of whom must be "independent." Likewise, according to the Institute, an organization's governing board should have at least five unrelated directors; seven or more directors are preferable. Where an employee of the organization is a voting member of the board, there must be assurance that that individual will "not be in a position to exercise undue influence." Indeed, the Institute's standards state that the governing board of an organization "should be composed of individuals who are personally committed to the mission of the organization and possess the specific skills needed to accomplish the mission."

As to this matter of board composition, it may be noted that the staff of the Senate Finance Committee issued a paper, in 2004, that included the proposal that boards of charitable organizations be required to be comprised of at least three members, with a maximum of 15 members. No more than one board member could be directly or indirectly compensated by the organization. A compensated board member could not serve as the chair of the board or treasurer of the organization. In the case of public charities, at least one board member or one-fifth of the board would have to be independent; a "higher number of independent board members might be required in limited cases. An *independent* board member would be defined as "free of any relationship with the corporation or its management that may impair or appear to impair the director's ability to make independent judgments."

Pursuant to the proposed "best practices" of the Committee for Purchase, (1) a nonprofit organization's board of directors should be composed of individuals who are "personally committed to the mission of the organization and possess the specific skills needed to accomplish the mission"; (2) where an employee of the organization is a voting member of the board, the "circumstances must [e]nsure that the employee will not be in a position to exercise 'undue influence'"; (3) the board should have at least five unrelated directors; (4) the chair of the board should not simultaneously be serving as the entity's CEO or president; (5) there should be term limits for board members; (6) board membership should reflect the "diversity of the communities" served by the organization; and (7) the board should have at least one "financial expert" among its membership.

The Panel on the Nonprofit Sector recommended that the federal tax regulations be amended to generally require that tax-exempt charitable organizations have a minimum of three members on their governing boards. Generally, at least one-third of the members of the board of a public charity would have to be independent. *Independent* board members would be individuals (1) who have not been compensated as an employee or independent contractor by the organization within the past 12 months, except for reasonable compensation for board service; (2) whose compensation, except for board service, is not determined by individuals who are compensated by the organization; (3) who do not receive, directly or indirectly, material financial benefits from the organization, except as a member of the charitable class served by the organization; and (4) who are not related to any of the foregoing individuals.

Another recommendation of this panel was to prohibit individuals, who are barred from service on boards of publicly traded companies or convicted of crimes directly related to breaches of fiduciary duty in their service as an employee or board member of a charitable organization, from serving on the board of a charitable organization for five years following their removal or conviction.

This panel observed that experts in the realm of nonprofit board governance "are not of one mind as to the ideal maximum size of nonprofit boards." They note that board size "may depend upon such factors as the age of the organization, the nature and geographic scope of its mission and activities, and its funding needs." Some experts believe that a "larger board may be necessary to ensure the range of perspectives and expertise required for some organizations or to share in fundraising responsibilities." Others argue that "effective governance is best achieved by a smaller board, which then demands more active participation from each board member." The panel concluded that "each charitable organization must determine the most appropriate size for its board and the appropriate number and responsibilities of board committees to ensure that the board is able to fulfill its fiduciary and other governance duties responsibly and effectively."

As to the recommendation concerning independent board members of public charities, the panel wrote that "it is important that at least one-third of their board members be free of the conflicts of interest that can arise when they have a personal interest in the financial transactions of the charity." It concluded that the "effort to find independent members is important to the long-term success and accountability of the organization and should be a legal requirement for public charities that are eligible to receive tax-deductible contributions on the most favorable terms."

In its draft of good governance recommendations, the IRS expressed its view that governing boards of charitable organizations "should be composed of persons who are informed and active in overseeing a charity's operations and finances." If a governing board "tolerates a climate of secrecy or neglect, charitable assets are more likely to be used to advance an impermissible private interest." Successful governing boards "include individuals [who are] not only knowledgeable and passionate about the organization's programs, but also those with expertise in critical areas involving accounting, finance, compensation, and ethics." Organizations with "very small or very large governing boards may be problematic: Small boards generally do not represent a public interest and large boards may be less attentive to oversight duties." If an organization's governing board is "very large, it may want to establish an executive committee with delegated responsibilities or establish advisory committees."

The Panel on the Nonprofit Sector stated that the board of an organization "should establish its own size and structure and review these periodically." The board "should have enough members to allow for full deliberation and diversity of thinking on governance and other organizational matters." Except for very small organizations, "this generally means that the board should have at least five members." Nonetheless, the Panel noted that the "ideal size of a board depends on many factors, such as the age of the organization, the nature and geographic scope of its mission and activities, and its funding needs."

The board of an organization should, wrote the Panel, include members with the "diverse background (including, but not limited to, ethnic, racial and gender perspectives), experience, and organizational and financial skills necessary to advance the organization's mission." Boards of charitable organizations "generally strive to include members with expertise in budget and financial management, investments, personnel, fundraising, public relations and marketing, governance, advocacy, and leadership, as well as some members who are knowledgeable about the charitable organization's area of expertise or programs, or who have a special connection to its constituency." Some organizations "seek to maintain a board that respects the culture of and reflects the community served by the organization." An organization should "make every effort" to ensure that at least one member of the board has "financial literacy."

A "substantial majority of the board of a public charity, usually meaning at least two-thirds of the members, should be independent." "Independent" members are those who are not compensated by the organization, do not have their compensation determined by individuals who are compensated by the organization, do not receive material financial benefits from the organization (except as a member of the charitable class served by the organization), or are not related to or reside with any of the foregoing persons. An individual who is not independent is, in the view of the Panel, potentially in violation of the directors' duty of loyalty (see Chapter 8), that requires the directors to "put the interests of the organization above their personal interests and to make decisions they believe are in the best interest of the nonprofit." The Panel declared that it is "important to the long-term success and accountability of the organization that a sizeable majority of the individuals on the board be free of financial conflicts of interest."

(c) Financial Oversight

The ECFA standards require an organization's board to "understand the organization's financial health." In "linking budgeting to strategic planning," the board "should approve the annual budget and key financial transactions, such as major asset acquisitions, that can be realistically financed with existing or attainable resources." The board should "utilize a committee, whose members have financial expertise, totally comprised of independent members to annually review the financial statements." This committee should "[c]onduct at least a portion of the committee meeting to review the financial statements with the accounting firm in the absence of staff"; if the board "handles the financial review function, staff should be recused from a portion of the meeting with the representative(s) from the accounting firm." The board should "[r]equest the periodic rotation of the lead or review partners, if this is feasible for the accounting firm." The board should obtain "competitive fee quotes every few years." If, however, the accountants are "independent, providing quality service at competitive fees, it is generally wise to continue with the current accounting firm."

Every organization that is an accredited member of ECFA must obtain an annual audit performed by an independent certified public accounting firm, including a financial statement prepared in accordance with generally accepted accounting principles. ECFA may provide for an alternative category of membership that does not require audited financial statements, in which case the organization must have financial statements that are compiled or reviewed by an independent certified public accounting firm. An ECFA best practice has the organization assuring that "all material related-party transactions are disclosed in the financial statements."

(d) Asset Reserves

The Wise Giving Alliance standards admonish organizations to avoid unwarranted accumulations of funds. In the view of the AIP, a reserve of assets to enable an organization to function without fundraising for less than three years is reasonable. Organizations with "years of available assets" of more than five years are considered the "least needy." (This fact earns an organization the grade of "F" irrespective of other considerations.)

(e) Law Compliance

Organizations must, according to the Institute, be "aware of and comply with all applicable Federal, state, and local laws." These laws include those pertaining to fundraising, licensing, financial accountability, document retention and destruction, human resources, lobbying and political advocacy, and taxation.

The Panel on the Nonprofit Sector's first principle in its statement of good governance practices is that an organization "must comply with all applicable federal laws and regulations, as well as applicable laws and regulations of the states and the local jurisdictions in which it is based or operates." If the organization conducts programs outside the United States, it must abide by applicable international laws and conventions that are legally binding on the United States. The Panel observed that an organization's governing board is "ultimately responsible for overseeing and ensuring that the organization complies with all its legal obligations and for detecting and remedying wrongdoing by management." The Panel added that, "[w]hile board members are not required to have specialized legal knowledge, they should be familiar with the basic rules and requirements with which their organization must comply and should secure the necessary legal advice and assistance to structure appropriate monitoring and oversight mechanisms."

(f) Organization and Board Performance

The Wise Giving Alliance standards provide that an organization "should regularly assess its effectiveness in achieving its mission." An organization should have "defined, measurable goals and objectives in place and a defined process in place to evaluate the success and impact of its program(s) in fulfilling the goals and objectives of the organization" and a process that "identifies ways to address any deficiencies." An organization should "[h]ave a board policy of assessing, no less than every two years, the organization's performance and effectiveness and of determining future actions required to achieve the mission." There should be a submission to the board, "for its approval, a written report that outlines the results of the aforementioned performance and effectiveness assessment and recommendations for future actions."

A nonprofit organization should, according to the Institute, have "defined, cost-effective procedures for evaluating, both qualitatively and quantitatively, its programs and projects in relation to its mission." These procedures "should address programmatic efficiency and effectiveness, the relationship of these impacts to the cost of achieving them, and the outcomes for program participants." Evaluations, which "should include input from program participants," should be "candid, be used to strengthen the effectiveness of the organization and, when necessary, be used to make programmatic changes." The board of an organization "should engage in short-term and long-term planning activities as necessary to determine the mission of the organization, to define specific goals and objectives related to the mission, and to evaluate the success of the organization's programs toward achieving the mission."

The Panel on the Nonprofit Sector advised that the board of a charitable organization "should establish and review regularly the organization's mission and goals and should evaluate, no less frequently than every five years, the organization's programs, goals and [other] activities to be sure they advance its mission and make prudent use of its resources." Every board should "set strategic goals and review them annually." The Panel noted that, "[b]ecause organizations and their purposes differ, it is incumbent on each organization to develop its own process for evaluating effectiveness." At a minimum, "interim benchmarks can be identified to assess whether the work is moving in the right direction."

WATCHDOG STANDARDS AND CHARITIES' RIGHTS

For the most part, any rights charitable organizations have against the abuses of watchdog groups cannot rise to the level of constitutional law protections, such as those accorded pursuant to the principles of due process enunciated in the Fifth and Fourteenth Amendments to the U.S. Constitution and in comparable provisions in the constitutions of the states. This is because due process rights are generally granted only with respect to actions by a government. The *state action doctrine*, however, can mandate the adherence to due process requirements by a nongovernmental organization when there is sufficient entanglement between government and the nongovernmental group, such as in the form of support or activities in tandem.

Nonetheless, where a nongovernmental organization promulgates and enforces standards, there are two situations where the law requires that the standards and the application of them be *fair*.

The first of these situations is the presence of a significant economic factor. That is, where the power of the standards enforcement agency becomes so great as to cause adverse economic consequences to the charity that is ranked as not meeting standards, the courts can intervene to rectify the application of unfair standards or the unfair application of standards. The test in either circumstance is whether the standards and/or the administration of them are *fair* or *reasonable*. There should be no question that the ratings of and reports on charitable organizations by watchdog agencies have economic consequences to the affected charities (see foregoing discussion): individual and corporate donors rely on the listings in determining which organizations are to receive their gifts; private foundations and other grantors similarly rely on these listings in determining their grantees; state governmental agencies take the status of charities in relation to the independent agencies' standards into account in determining the status of charities under the states' charitable solicitation acts; and the IRS from time to time relies on the rankings of these agencies. Moreover, the watchdog agencies readily provide information to the media, and the resulting publicity can cause one or more of the same three results to occur.

The second of these situations arises when the agency's ratings power is in an area of public concern. Again, there is little doubt that these agencies envision themselves as operating in the public interest, forcing disclosure of information to the public and otherwise acting for the benefit of prospective donors. Public reliance on the watchdog agencies' pronouncements has become so great as to make a national organization's fundraising success significantly dependent on a favorable rating, or to divert gifts from a national organization that receives a negative rating. A positive rating accorded a charity by a watchdog agency may well confer on the charity a significant "competitive" advantage in relation to one or more organizations that receive an adverse rating.

The foregoing two principles have been succinctly stated in a treatise on the antitrust law: "Self regulation programs should be based on clearly defined standards that plainly indicate what is considered proper and improper. Vague standards invite arbitrary action," and "[s]tandards once set also should be administered in a reasonable manner."

The setting and application of standards by the watchdog agencies are squarely subject to both of these threshold tests, and fundamental fairness dictates that their enforcement of standards be on the basis of processes that are reasonable.

WATCHDOGS: A CLOSING PERSPECTIVE

Those who manage and represent charitable and other nonprofit organizations, particularly those who engage in fundraising, should be apprehensive about these watchdog agencies. The preferable position, of course, is to stay below their sight. Once tagged, however, the organization has some decisions to make. The first, obviously, is whether to comply with the demands for information and compliance. It is the rare (and brave) charity that desists here. If the decision is made to comply, the organization will face a series of other decisions, some with financial impact, as it attempts to meet the standards. For example, expansion of a board of directors from three to five can mean a significant increase in travel, lodging, meals, and similar costs.

The believability of these watchdog groups has evolved to the point that few charitable organizations possess the fortitude to challenge them. In a recent congressional hearing, members of Congress were lambasting charitable organizations largely on the basis of AIP reports, even though the organizations in question adhered to generally accepted accounting principles and satisfied applicable legal requirements. Charities meekly—and, again, involuntarily—struggle to conform with the standards because of the immense power, including the ability to swiftly decrease giving to targeted charitable organizations, the watchdog agencies have amassed. The rating processes are frequently unfair and otherwise flawed. (A lawyer who complained about the absence of a fair process in a watchdog agency's rating procedure received a letter from the agency's president dismissing these concerns as being nothing more than "lawyerly sounding" phraseology and "high-falutin'" language.)

In the meantime, these standards-setting and rating "voluntary" agencies seize on the perception (which they assiduously foment) that much wrongdoing is occurring in charitable fundraising, governance, and other operations. Their reports and ratings continue to flow. Some day, some court, it may be hoped, will intercede and expose these groups for what they are and trim the scope of what they do. Perhaps that is the only way to shake the public's and the media's erroneous view that these agencies are objective and performing useful functions.

Or, there may come a time when an enterprising journalist will see through the watchdog agencies' skein of standards and ratings and make manifest the misleading rationale for the existence of these groups and the often harmful and counterproductive outcomes they thrust on the charitable sector. The closest we have come in this regard was in 2005, when a "rating the raters" report, published by the National Council of Nonprofit Associations and the National Human Services Assembly, observed that these watchdog agencies "serve a noble purpose, *in concept*: helping donors make responsible choices" when considering contributing to a charitable organization (emphasis added). This report noted that how a charitable organization is rated or ranked by the watchdog organizations "can have a significant impact" on the charity's level of contributions and, thus, on the charity's ability to fulfill its mission.

This analysis concluded that charitable organizations "are not easily measured or compared based on simplistic criteria and/or benchmarks." The "programmatic, mission-based work" of charities is "complex." Thus, "[s]imple financial ratios and/or measures that apply in some circumstances may not apply at all in others." Also, "financial efficiency remains the primary focus in most third-party ratings/rankings," rather than the effectiveness of charitable organizations in providing services.

The denouement: "There is great potential for these ratings to be misinterpreted and misused, which would cause more harm than good to both donors and [charitable organizations]. In the worst case scenario, donors could withhold vital contributions from a worthy organization based on inaccurate, incomplete or misunderstood information they received from an evaluator."

Meanwhile, the reach of the watchdog agencies continues to expand. Managers of charitable organizations, and lawyers, accountants, and fundraisers for them should be forewarned. The watchdogs are on the prowl.

Checklist

❑ Is the organization currently rated by a watchdog agency?
    Yes _____ No _____

❑ If so, which one(s)? _____

❑ What percentage of the organization's annual expenditures is for program?
    _____

❑ What percentage of the organization's annual expenditures is for fundraising?
    _____

❑ Does the organization allocate a portion of direct mail costs to program?
    Yes _____ No _____

❑ Is the organization satisfied that its fundraising costs are reasonable?
    Yes _____ No _____

❑ How many voting members are on the board? _____

❑ Is the organization satisfied that this is a sufficient number?
    Yes _____ No _____

❑ How many board members are "independent"? _____

❑ Are any board members compensated for board service?
    Yes _____ No _____

❑ Is the organization satisfied that this compensation is reasonable?
    Yes _____ No _____

❑ Does the organization have an audit committee?
    Yes _____ No _____

❑ Is an annual audited financial statement prepared?
    Yes _____ No _____

❑ Is the organization in compliance with all applicable federal, state, and local laws?[1] Yes _____ No _____

❑ Does the organization have a process for regularly assessing achievement of its mission? Yes _____ No _____

❑ Does the organization's board have a process for regularly reviewing its goals? Yes _____ No _____

Focus: Campaign to Clean Up America

The Campaign to Clean Up America (CCUA), with its program expenditures at 66 percent and its fundraising costs at 32 percent, has been favorably rated by the two watchdog agencies whose attention it has attracted (the Wise Giving Alliance and Charity Navigator). The CCUA has a board of five individuals, none of whom are compensated by the organization. The CCUA, however, is concerned that it may be adversely rated by the AIP (namely, receive an F), and thus have the flow of contributions and grants to it substantially negatively impacted, because (1) it allocates a portion of its fundraising expenses to program and (2) it is developing an endowment (assets reserve) that may grow to the point where it covers more than five years of operations.

---

[1] This question is posed with tongue largely in cheek.

CHAPTER TWENTY-TWO

Potpourri of Policies and Procedures

The matter of *governance* has become, for a variety of reasons, the hottest topic in the realm of nonprofit organizations, primarily public charities (see Chapter 8). The forces driving this development include both congressional investigations into the operations and finances of public charities and other tax-exempt organizations and the leadership of the component of the IRS that is responsible for overseeing the nonprofit sector.

As to the latter, the technical name for this portion of the IRS is the Tax Exempt and Government Entities Division (see Chapter 24). An IRS commissioner, known as the *TE/GE Commissioner*, is the head of this division. The current occupant of that position, Steven T. Miller, has been quite outspoken on the matter of governance of nonprofit organizations and on the IRS' role in formulating and enforcing good-governance practices. An analysis of and quotations from some of his recent speeches on the subject are provided subsequently. But first it is important to note the state of the federal tax law on this subject of nonprofit governance.

FEDERAL TAX LAW AND GOVERNANCE

The federal tax law is, of course, predicated on the Internal Revenue Code. The word *governance*, along with nearly all aspects of governance of nonprofit organizations, does not appear in this code. The tax regulations are likewise silent on the subject. IRS public rulings and federal tax law court opinions do not address the subject. What "law" there is (and this really is not law) is found in the annual information return (see Chapter 9) and the accompanying instructions. Indeed, this matter of governance, at least until recently, has been confined to state law, where the focus is on trustees' and directors' fiduciary responsibility (see Chapter 25).

Thus, this question may be posed: Is regulation of the governance of public charities and other nonprofit organizations within the ambit of the IRS's jurisdiction? For three reasons, the answer to that question must be "no." First, as is clear from the IRS website, the agency's mission is to "provide America's taxpayers with top quality service by helping them understand and meet their *tax* responsibilities and by applying the *tax law* with integrity and fairness to all" (emphasis added). This phraseology is repeated in each issue of the IRS's *Internal Revenue Bulletin*. The mission of the TE/GE Division is, according to the IRS website, the "uniform interpretation and application of the *Federal tax laws* on matters pertaining to the Division's customer base" (emphasis added). Thus, at least on the face of things, the mission of the IRS generally and of the Division in particular does not extend to the administration of non-tax laws, including principles (meritorious as they may be), pronouncements, and examinations in the area of good-governance as that subject applies (ostensibly or otherwise) to nonprofit organizations.

Throughout the course of the Charles Dickens novel *A Tale of Two Cities*, Madame Defarge knits; she indefatigably knits. One can say with confidence that she sticks to her knitting. (Surely, dear reader, you can see this one coming.) According to the second edition of the Dictionary of American Slang, the phrase *stick to one's knitting* means to "attend strictly to one's own affairs; not interfere with others; be single-minded." To bring this back to the subject at hand, one can say that the IRS should attend strictly to its own affairs, which is to administer the federal tax laws (the name of the outfit is, after all, the Internal *Revenue* Service), and not interfere with others (such as the states' attorneys general). The IRS, according to this view, should stick to its knitting.

The second reason that nonprofit governance is properly outside the scope of the responsibilities of the IRS is that it is not competent to regulate in this area. Two developments amply evidence this point. One is a draft of good-governance principles published by the IRS (and mercifully later jettisoned) in early 2007. This code contained nothing innovative; the elements of governance contained in it have been hashed and rehashed by others (see Chapter 8 and below), in many instances in a far better fashion. Some of the elements in this IRS package were unrealistic; a few were silly. Here are some examples:

- The IRS draft governance policies required that the directors of nonprofit organizations be passionate about the organization's programs. Would the IRS start examining nonprofit organizations and interviewing board members to assess whether they are sufficiently passionate?

- The policies called for nonprofit boards to include an individual who is an expert on ethics. Whose ethics? Are there enough ethicists to go around? (The IRS rules did not call for a lawyer on every nonprofit board, even though the draft principles would have required a board "culture of legal compliance.")

- Nonprofit boards were to have an expert on compensation. Aside from lack of clarity as to what that means, surely there are few such experts.

- Boards of nonprofit charitable organizations would have had to represent a public interest. What does that mean? Whatever it means, the law does not require it.

- This code stated that "success at fundraising requires care and honesty." Most likely there are state attorneys general that disagree with that view.

- Mission statements of nonprofit organizations would have had to be clearly articulated and well-written. Organizations were fearful that the IRS word police would be out, examining the phraseology, punctuation, and grammar of these statements.

- The IRS proposed that charitable organizations periodically trade their volunteers to other organizations. This wacky idea overlooked the fact that these individuals are not tradable at will and ignored why individuals volunteer in the first place. Perhaps a picture of each volunteer could be packaged with a slab of bubble gum, and traded about on the basis of the volunteers' skills and popularity.

The second item of evidence proving why the IRS is not competent to regulate nonprofit governance lies in the actions of its personnel, when processing applications for recognition of exemption or auditing tax-exempt organizations. They are not trained in governance law. They try to impose their personal views as to what nonprofit board members and organizations *should* do. They read the emerging governance principles (see Chapter 8) and immediately arrive at the conclusion that they apply as a matter of law; agents are insisting that boards be larger and be void of related individuals, that organizations adopt conflict-of-interest policies, and that nonprofit entities adopt and adhere to all manner of other policies and procedures, none of which is required by law as a condition of tax exemption.

The third reason why the IRS ought not be bogged down in governance regulation is that, as to nonprofit law over which it clearly has jurisdiction, it is woefully behind in its work. Regulation projects are stagnated, there are dozens of topics that cry out for rulings and other guidance, and the agency can barely handle the flow of applications for recognition of exemption that annually come its way (about 90,000). The IRS lacks the resources to timely respond to rulings and technical advice requests.

CURRENT VIEW OF IRS

When the TE/GE Commissioner first began talking about the IRS's role in nonprofit governance, in an April 2007 speech, he conceded that, for the IRS to propound and enforce good-governance principles, the agency would have to go "beyond its traditional spheres of activity." (This was certainly a more elegant way of phrasing the matter than not sticking to one's own knitting.) The Commissioner on that occasion revealed that he was pondering the question of "whether it would benefit the public and the tax-exempt sector to require [by the IRS] organizations to adopt and follow recognized principles of good-governance." He asserted that there is a "vacuum" that needs to be filled in the realm of *education* on "basic standards and practices of good-governance and accountability." (As noted in Chapter 8 and below, there are no uniform or generally "recognized principles of good-governance," and IRS agents are quickly moving beyond a function of educating to mandating.)

The TE/GE Commissioner, that memorable day, made the best case that can be asserted for the intertwining of the matter of governance and nonprofit, tax-exempt organizations' compliance with the federal tax law. He said that a "well-governed organization is more likely to be compliant, while poor governance can easily lead an exempt organization into trouble." He spoke, for example, of an "engaged, informed, and independent board of directors accountable to the community [that the exempt organization] serves." (This type of board, under any circumstances, is not appropriate for all nonprofit entities, such as social clubs, veterans' organizations, and family private foundations.)

By the time the TE/GE Commissioner returned to this subject, in a November 2007 speech, his attitude and tone had dramatically changed. No more pondering, musing, and speculating. Rather, the Commissioner stated that, "[w]hile a few continue to argue that governance is outside our jurisdiction, most now support an active IRS that is engaged in this area." (No evidence was cited for this massive surge in support for an "active IRS" in the area of nonprofit governance.) He expressed his view that the IRS "contributes to a compliant, healthy charitable sector by expecting the tax-exempt community to adhere to commonly accepted standards of good-governance." He said that IRS involvement in this area is "not new"; the agency has been "quietly but steadily promoting good-governance for a long time." He noted that "[o]ur determination agents ask governance-related questions" and "our agents assess an organization's internal controls as the agents decide how to pursue an examination." He continued: "We are comfortable that we are well within our authority to act in these areas." And: "To more clearly put our weight behind good-governance may represent a small step beyond our traditional sphere of influence, but we believe the subject is well within our core responsibilities."

When April 2008 rolled around, the TE/GE Commissioner had once again significantly evolved in his thinking on these points. In two speeches, he made his view quite clear: (1) the IRS has a "robust role" to play in the realm of charitable governance, (2) the IRS does not even entertain the thought that involvement in governance matters is beyond the sphere of the agency's jurisdiction, and (3) he cannot be convinced that, "outside of very very small organizations and perhaps family foundations, the gold standard should not be to have an active, independent and engaged board of directors overseeing the organization." Thus, the "question is no longer whether the IRS has a role to play in this area, but rather, what that role will be." That role, he said, will be primarily dictated by the governance section of the new annual information return.

SOURCES OF POLICIES

One of the products of the emergence and evolution of nonprofit governance principles is the increase in the importance of a multitude of written policies, processes, and procedures. Traceable to enactment of the Sarbanes-Oxley Act in 2002, many of these policies have been developed, in one form or another, by various entities that are in the business, in whole or in part, of formulating governance principles, largely for public charities.

These entities fall into three categories. The first category consists of components of the federal government—namely, the investigatory staff of the Senate Finance Committee, the Department of the Treasury, the Committee for Purchase from People Who Are Blind or Severely Disabled, the U.S. Congress, and the IRS. The Finance Committee staff in 2004 developed a paper that referenced some nonprofit governance policies. The Treasury Department in 2005 promulgated voluntary best practices in the form of anti-terrorist financing guidelines. The Committee for Purchase issued, in late 2005, a draft of criteria and tests that it believes are "widely considered as benchmarks of good nonprofit agency governance practices." Congress legislated (in addition to the Sarbanes-Oxley Act) the American National Red Cross Governance Modernization Act (in 2007) and criteria for tax-exempt credit counseling agencies (in 2006). The IRS (as discussed previously) published a draft of good-governance principles (early 2007), the redesigned annual information return (late 2007), and then jettisoned these principles and substituted an educational document predicated on the return (early 2008). (So far, only California with its Nonprofit Integrity Act has enacted this type of governance legislation.)

The second category of these entities consists of nonprofit organizations, or appendages of them, formed to study and promulgate nonprofit governance principles. The principal organization in this category is Independent Sector, which convened a Panel on the Nonprofit Sector that formulated a package of good-governance principles for nonprofit entities (the best of the lot), termed "Principles for Good Governance and Ethical Practice" (for charitable organizations). The Standards for Excellence Institute (the Institute) has also published useful good-governance principles.

The third category of these organizations consists of the watchdog agencies, for whom adoption and enforcement of governance principles is a principal mainstay. These entities are the Better Business Bureau (BBB) (by means of the Wise Giving Alliance), the Evangelical Council for Financial Accountability (ECFA), Charity Navigator, Ministry Watch, the Philanthropy Group, and the American Institute of Philanthropy (see Chapter 21).

POLICIES OVERVIEW

Thus, whether the nonprofit world likes it or not, the IRS is becoming extremely active in pushing good-governance policies for public charities and other tax-exempt organizations. This attention to nonprofit governance will, unless checked by the judicial system, continue unabated and quickly move beyond the education and outreach approach and become rooted in IRS demands as conditions of tax exemption.

What, then, should nonprofit organizations do to stay out of the IRS's line of fire? (A few hardy souls may contest these IRS initiatives in court.) The answer to this question lies in the redesigned Form 990 (see Chapter 9), particularly in what the TE/GE Commissioner has labeled the "crown jewel" of the return, which is its section on governance.

One of the principal features of the new return is the structuring of the form so that pointed questions are answered by checking a "yes" box or a "no" box, with a check in a "no" box often plummeting the nonprofit organization into a morass of difficult and uncomfortable questions. Consequently, the organization is not so subtly encouraged to look good in the eyes of the IRS, the public, and the media by having checked only "yes" boxes. This phenomenon is termed, by psychologists, as *shaming*.

The Form 990, however, is signed under penalties of perjury, so an organization preparing it is well-advised to be truthful when checking a box "yes." What does it take to check all these "yes" boxes? The answer: adoption of a battery of policies, processes, and procedures, all picked up by the IRS from the efforts of the many undertakings, referenced previously, to formulate good-governance principles:

- A conflict-of-interest policy (Form 990, Part VI, Section B, line 12)
- A whistleblower policy (id., line 13)
- A document retention and destruction policy (id., line 14)
- A process for determining executive compensation (id., line 15)
- A policy or procedure concerning participation in a joint venture arrangement (id., line 16)

- A policy regarding documentation of meetings (Part VI, Section A, line 8)
- A policy or procedure concerning activities of affiliates (id., line 9)
- A process used to review the Form 990 (id., line 10)
- A gift acceptance policy (Schedule M, line 31)
- A policy concerning the acceptance and maintenance of conservation easements (Schedule D, Part II, line 5)
- Procedures regarding international grantmaking (Schedule F, Part I)
- If a hospital, a policy as to charity care (Schedule H)
- If a hospital, a policy on debt collections (id.)

Although it is not reflected in the Form 990, the IRS also encourages an investment policy and a fundraising policy. Many of the good-governance principles advocate adoption of a code of ethics and an expense reimbursement policy.

(a) Mission Statement Policy

Many aspects of a nonprofit organization's operations can be the subject of a policy (or a procedure or process). Take, for example, the matter of an entity's mission statement. In the summary portion of the annual information return (see Chapter 9), which is Part I of the return, an organization can describe either its mission or its most significant activity for the year. (A *mission statement*, as defined by the IRS, is a statement of why the organization exists, what it hopes to accomplish, who it intends to serve, and what activities it will undertake and where.) An organization *must*, however, describe its mission in Part III of the return, but it can do this only if it has a mission statement that has been adopted by its governing body. Thus, an organization may consider it important to adopt a policy of having a mission statement that has been approved and periodically reviewed by its board.

(b) Conflict-of-Interest Policy

The most venerable of the policies in the bundle of emerging good-governance practices involving nonprofit organizations (and the one most heartily insisted on by the IRS) is the *conflict-of-interest policy*. There has long been inherent tension in this area, between the view that conflicts of interest should be prohibited (a wholly unrealistic notion) and the approach that calls for disclosure (and, if necessary, resolution) of one or more conflicts of interest. The conflict-of-interest policy is a manifestation of the latter view.

The BBB standards reflect the first of these views, in that they forbid "transaction(s) in which any board or staff members have material conflicting interests with the charity resulting from any relationship or business affiliation." Factors that are considered in determining whether a transaction entails a *conflict of interest*, and if so whether the conflict is *material*, include "any arm's length procedures established by the charity; the size of the transaction relative to like expenses of the charity; whether the interested party participated in the board vote on the transaction; if competitive bids were sought [;] and whether the transaction is one-time, recurring or ongoing." These standards, however, hint at the utility of a conflict-of-interest policy in the reference to "arm's length procedures established by the charity."

By contrast, the ECFA opts for the other approach. One of its best practices requires the organization's members to "avoid conflicts of interest." Having said that, members are allowed to engage in transactions with related parties if (1) a material transaction is fully disclosed in the audited financial statements of the organization, (2) the related party is excluded from the discussion and approval of the transaction, (3) a competitive bid or comparable valuation exists, and (4) the organization's board has demonstrated that the transaction is in the best interest of the entity. The ECFA best practices include (1) adoption of a conflict-of-interest policy covering the governing board and key executives, (2) annual documentation of any potential related-party transactions, and (3) initial approval by the board of all significant related-party transactions and, if continuing, annual reapproval.

Similarly, the standards of the Standards for Excellence Institute state that a nonprofit organization should have a conflict-of-interest policy applicable to "all board members and staff, and to volunteers who have significant independent decision making authority regarding the resources of the organization." This policy "should identify the types of conduct or transactions that raise conflict of interest concerns, should set forth procedures for disclosure of actual or potential conflicts, and should provide for review of individual transactions by the uninvolved members of the board of directors." The policy should include a statement that provides "space for the board member, employee, or volunteer to disclose any known interest that the individual, or a member of the individual's immediate family, has in any business entity, which transacts business with the organization." This statement should be signed by board members, staff, and volunteers, "both at the time of the individual's initial affiliation with the organization and at least annually thereafter."

The IRS, in a draft of good-governance principles, stated that the duty of loyalty imposed on directors of charitable organizations "requires a director to avoid conflicts of interest that are detrimental to the charity." According to these principles, the board of a charitable organization "should adopt and regularly evaluate an effective conflict of interest policy" that "requires directors and staff to act solely in the interests of the charity without regard for personal interests," includes "written procedures for determining whether a relationship, financial interest, or business affiliation" results in a conflict of interest, and prescribes a "certain course of action in the event a conflict of interest is identified." Directors and staff "should be required to disclose annually in writing any known financial interest that the individual or a member of the individual's family has in any business entity that transacts business with the charity."

The Panel on the Nonprofit Sector stated in its principles for good governance and ethical practices for charitable organizations that an organization should "adopt and implement policies and procedures to ensure that all conflicts of interest, or the appearance thereof, within the organization and the board are appropriately managed though disclosure, recusal, or other means." A conflicts-of-interest policy "must be consistent with the laws of the state in which the nonprofit is organized and should be tailored to specific organizational needs and characteristics." This policy "should require full disclosure of all potential conflicts of interest within the organization" and "should apply to every person who has the ability to influence decisions of the organization, including board and staff members and parties related to them."

(c) Whistleblower Policy

The ECFA best practices include adoption of a whistleblower policy. The IRS, in its draft of good-governance principles, stated that the board of directors of a charitable organization "should adopt an effective policy for handling employee complaints and establish procedures for employees to report in confidence suspected financial impropriety or misuse of the charity's resources."

The Panel on the Nonprofit Sector stated that an organization "should establish and implement policies and procedures that enable individuals to come forward with information on illegal practices or violations of organizational policies." This whistleblower policy "should specify that the organization will not retaliate against, and will protect the confidentiality of, individuals who make good-faith reports." The Panel recommended that "[i]nformation on these policies . . . be widely distributed to staff, volunteers and clients, and should be incorporated both in new employee orientations and ongoing training programs for employees and volunteers." These policies "can help boards and senior managers become aware of and address problems before serious harm is done to the organization" and "can also assist in complying with legal provisions that protect individuals working in charitable organizations from retaliation for engaging in certain whistle-blowing activities."

(d) Document Retention and Destruction Policy

The ECFA best practices include adoption of a record retention policy. The IRS's draft of good-governance principles stated that an "effective charity" will "adopt a written policy establishing standards for document integrity, retention, and destruction." (A charitable organization, however, can be effective, presumably programmatically, in the absence of a document retention and destruction policy.) According to the IRS, this type of policy, which "should include guidelines for handling electronic files," should "cover backup procedures, archiving of documents, and regular check-ups of the reliability of the system."

The Panel on the Nonprofit Sector stated that an organization should "establish and implement policies and procedures to protect and preserve the organization's important documents and business records." The Panel observed that a document-retention policy "is essential for protecting the organization's records of its governance and administration, as well as business records that are required to demonstrate legal compliance." This type of policy "also helps to protect against allegations of wrongdoing by the organization or its directors and managers."

(e) Executive Compensation Policy

The ECFA best practices include adoption of an "executive compensation philosophy statement." According to the Standards for Excellence Institute, the board or a committee of it "should hire the executive director, set the executive's compensation," and "periodically review the appropriateness of the overall compensation structure of the organization."

The IRS's draft of good-governance principles stated that a "successful charity pays no more than reasonable compensation for services rendered." (Again, however, there is no correlation between the success of a charitable organization, presumably from a program standpoint, and whether the compensation it pays is reasonable—for example, a charity can pay excessive compensation to its chief executive and nonetheless be a successful organization in terms of program outcomes.) Charities, said the IRS, "may pay reasonable compensation for services provided by officers and staff."

The Panel on the Nonprofit Sector stated that the board of a charitable organization should "hire, oversee, and annually evaluate the performance of the chief executive officer of the organization, and should conduct such an evaluation prior to any change in that officer's compensation," unless a multiyear contract is in force or the change consists solely of routine adjustments for inflation or the cost of living. The Panel stated that "[o]ne of the most important responsibilities of the board . . . is to select, supervise, and determine a compensation package that will attract and retain a qualified chief executive." The organization's governing documents should require the full board to evaluate the executive's performance and approve his or her compensation.

(f) Joint-Venture Policy

None of the entities that have written good-governance principles have addressed the matter of a joint-venture policy. This policy is solely the subject of federal tax law considerations. An organization in this position is to evaluate its participation in joint-venture arrangements and take the requisite steps to safeguard its tax-exempt status. This policy requirement is targeted at public charities.

The essence of the law in this area is found in applicable elements of the private benefit doctrine (see Chapter 5). The organization should develop a policy that states, in general, that it will not lose control of its facilities and programs to a for-profit participant in the program. This policy will take account of relationships reflected in management agreements, leases, fundraising contracts, as well as partnership, limited liability company, or other joint-venture agreements.

(g) Meetings Documentation Policy

The ECFA best practices include the standard that the organization should "properly document the proceedings of all board and board committee meetings in order to protect the organization" and board minutes "should identify all voting board members as present or absent to clearly document a quorum."

From the perspective of the IRS, the agency will be looking to see whether the meetings of the governing board and any committee with authority to act on behalf of the board are the subject of minutes or a written unanimous consent document. The IRS will also inquire as to whether this documentation is *contemporaneous*.

(h) Policy Concerning Affiliates

The IRS, in connection with the annual information return, asks organizations that have chapters, branches, or affiliates whether they have a policy or procedure governing the activities of these affiliated organizations, to ensure that their operations are "consistent" with those of the principal organization. Some organizations have formal agreements with their chapters, which encompass this aspect of the affiliation; many organizations, however, do not. This new requirement is likely to provide an incentive for organizations that have chapters or the like to implement this type of policy.

(i) Annual Information Return Review Policy

The IRS requires an organization to describe, in its annual information return, the process, if any, it uses to have the return reviewed (presumably before it is filed). This review may be by one or more members of the board, one or more officers, one or more staff members, and/or the organization's lawyer. A question on the annual return inquires as to whether a copy of the return was provided to the organization's governing body in advance of its filing.

(j) Gift Acceptance Policy

The standards of the Institute state that a charitable organization should have policies governing the acceptance and disposition of charitable gifts, including procedures to determine any limits on individuals or entities from which the organization will accept a gift, the purposes for which contributions will be accepted, the type of property that will be accepted, and whether an "unusual or unanticipated" gift will be accepted in view of the organization's mission and "organizational capacity."

The IRS has launched an examination program pertaining to charitable contributions of certain successor member interests, involving the questionable use of limited liability companies, ostensibly done to inflate the value of contributed property for deduction purposes. The agency has developed a prototype document that it is sending to various charities, asking pointed questions that charitable organizations should ponder when considering whether to accept an "unconventional" charitable contribution. These questions include a request for a summary of the economic rights the charity anticipates, the nature of the legal advice obtained in connection with the gift, whether the organization has "guidelines" for accepting "unusual" gifts, and whether the gift transaction was reviewed by the organization's board.

(k) Conservation Easements Policy

Few charitable organizations have the need for a policy as to conservation easements, simply because it is not common for entities to receive this type of property by gift. For a charitable contribution of a conservation easement (or certain other conservation properties) to be deductible, however, the charitable donee must be *qualified* to receive and maintain the property. A policy in this context, therefore, will focus on the organization's ability to properly maintain the conservation property and enforce the terms of the easement (and perhaps other restrictions) placed on it.

(l) International Grantmaking Policy

If an organization engages in international grantmaking activities, it should consider adoption of a procedure summarizing the substance of these activities and the grantees involved, including their location. *Grantmaking* includes awards, prizes, cash allocations, stipends, scholarships, fellowships, and research grants. Grantees can be foreign organizations, governments, or individuals. Program services in this context include the provision of assistance, such as food, shelter, clothing, medical assistance, or supplies. This policy should be formulated taking into account the concerns of the federal government that U.S. charitable dollars may be funneled to terrorist organizations.

(m) Charity Care Policy

The only type of nonprofit organization that needs to concern itself with a charity care policy is a tax-exempt hospital. This policy should describe how the organization will provide *charity care,* a controversial topic that generally means free or discounted health services made available to individuals who meet the organization's criteria for assistance and are thereby deemed unable to pay for all or a portion of the services. It is the view of the IRS that the concept of charity care does not include (1) bad debt or uncollectible charges that the hospital recorded as revenue but wrote off due to failure to pay by patients who did not qualify for charity care, or the cost of providing that care; (2) the difference between the cost of care provided under Medicaid or other means-tested government programs or under Medicare and the revenue derived from the programs; or (3) contractual adjustments with third-party payors.

(n) Debt Collection Policy

Similarly, only exempt hospitals need be concerned with a debt collection policy; this policy pertains to the collection of amounts owed by patients. The policy may contain provisions for collecting amounts due from patients who would likely qualify under the organization's charity care or financial assistance policies. These include provisions such as procedures for internal review of accounts prior to initiation of legal action or prior to initiating or continuing a collection action undertaken by an outside agency.

(o) Investment Policy

Oddly, none of the organizations that promulgate good-governance principles have focused on the terms of a nonprofit organization's investment policy. The closest in this regard is the Panel on the Nonprofit Sector standards, which state that the board of a charitable organization "must institute policies and procedures to ensure that the organization (and, if applicable, its subsidiaries) manages and invests its funds responsibly, in accordance with all legal requirements." This two-part admonition is not particularly helpful.

An investment policy should primarily address two elements. One concerns the nature of the organization's portfolio, stating the vehicles and properties in which the organization will invest (or, in some instances, will not invest). This includes stocks, bonds, real estate, partnerships, and investment funds. The other element is the general balance of the portfolio, stipulating the percentages of investments in equities, interest-bearing instruments, foreign investment property, and the like.

(p) Fundraising Policy

The ECFA best practices standards require that, in fundraising materials, representations of fact, descriptions of the organization's financial condition, and narrative about events be "current, complete, and accurate." "Material omissions or exaggerations of fact" are not permitted. Member organizations are exhorted to "not create unrealistic donor expectations of what a donor's gift will accomplish." Organizations are asked to make efforts to "avoid accepting a gift from or entering into a contract with a prospective donor which would knowingly place a hardship on the donor, or place the donor's wellbeing in jeopardy." The ECFA practices address the compensation paid to outside fundraisers, require the organization to honor statements made in fundraising appeals, and include adoption of a policy concerning donor confidentiality.

Along these lines, the Institute's standards state that solicitation materials should be "accurate and truthful and should correctly identify the organization, its mission, and the intended use of the solicited funds." All statements made by a charitable organization in its fundraising appeals "about the use of a contribution should be honored." A charitable organization "must honor the known intention of a donor regarding the use of donated funds." Charitable organizations should respect the privacy of donors and "safeguard the confidentiality of information that a donor reasonably would expect to be private." These standards likewise address the topic of fundraisers' compensation, including a prohibition on compensation on the basis of a "percentage of the amount raised or other commission formula," and mandate that a charitable organization should contract only with those persons who are "properly registered with applicable regulatory authorities."

The IRS' draft of good-governance principles, which observed that "success at fundraising requires care and honesty" (regrettably, a dubious assumption), stated that the board of directors of a charitable organization "should adopt and monitor policies to ensure that fundraising solicitations meet federal and state law requirements and [that] solicitation materials are accurate, truthful, and candid." Charities "should keep their fundraising costs reasonable." In selecting paid fundraisers, a charity "should use those that are registered with the state and that can provide good references." Performance of professional fundraisers "should be continuously monitored."

The position of the Panel on the Nonprofit Sector is that solicitation materials and other communications addressed to prospective donors and the public "must clearly identify the organization and be accurate and truthful." The Panel stated that a prospective donor "has the right to know the name of anyone soliciting contributions, the name and location of the organization that will receive the contribution, a clear description of its activities, the intended use of the funds to be raised, a contact for obtaining additional information, and whether the individual requesting the contribution is acting as a volunteer, employee of the organization, or hired solicitor." (The derivation of this right, ostensibly possessed by prospective contributors, to know the names of everyone soliciting contributions is not clear.)

The Panel's view is that contributions "must be used for purposes consistent with the donor's intent, whether as described in the relevant solicitation materials or as specifically directed by the donor." The Panel stated that solicitations should "indicate whether the funds they generate will be used to further the general programs and operations of the organization or to support specific programs or types of programs." The Panel advised charitable organizations to "carefully review the terms of any contract or grant agreement before accepting a donation."

An organization must, according to the Panel, "provide donors with specific acknowledgments of charitable contributions, in accordance with [federal tax law] requirements, as well as information to facilitate the donor's compliance with tax law requirements." The Panel noted that, not only is this type of acknowledgment generally required by law, "it also helps in building donors' confidence in and support for the activities they help to fund."

(q) Expense Reimbursement Policy

The ECFA best practices include the standard that the organization should adopt a policy with respect to "accountable expense reimbursements."

It is prudent for a nonprofit organization to adopt an accountable plan in this context. Expenses paid or incurred by an employee under a reimbursement or other expense allowance arrangement with an employer are excludable from the employee's gross income if the arrangement meets the requirements of an *accountable plan*. A reimbursement or other expense allowance arrangement qualifies as an accountable plan by meeting certain requirements as to business connection, substantiation, and returning amounts in excess of substantiated expenses.

An arrangement meets the *business connection* requirement if it provides advances, allowances (including per diem allowances, allowances only for meals and incidental expenses, and mileage allowances), or reimbursements only for deductible business expenses. These allowances and the like must be paid or incurred by the employee in connection with the performance of services as an employee of the employer. The payment may include amounts charged directly or indirectly to the payor through credit card systems or otherwise.

A *substantiation* requirement covers reimbursements for travel, entertainment, use of a passenger automobile, and certain other business expenses. Substantiation of the amount of a business expense in accordance with rules of certain other federal tax rules is treated as substantiation of the amount of an expense for purposes of the accountable plan rules. For example, for business expenses other than travel, entertainment, use of a personal vehicle, gifts, and certain property, an employee must submit information sufficient to enable an employer to identify the specific nature of each expense and to conclude that the expense is attributable to the employer's business activities. For expenses relating to travel and entertainment, an employee must substantiate the amount, time, place, business purpose, and (with respect to entertainment) the business relationship to the persons entertained.

The rules concerning *return of excess amounts* are satisfied if the employee is required to return to the payor, within a reasonable period of time, any amount paid under the arrangement in excess of the substantiated expenses. The accountable plan rules state that an expense substantiated to the payor within 60 days after it is paid or incurred, or an amount returned to the payor within 120 days after an expense is paid or incurred, will be treated as having occurred within a reasonable period of time.

The treatment of reimbursements is different under a nonaccountable plan. If a plan does not qualify as an accountable plan, all amounts reimbursed to an employee, even business expenses, are includible in an employee's gross income, must be reported as wages or other compensation, and are subject to withholding and employment taxes. The employee can then deduct, as a business expense, the amounts that are properly treated as business expenses, provided the employee can substantiate the expenses, but the employee can deduct them only as miscellaneous itemized deductions subject to the appropriate limitations (such as the limitations on the deduction of expenses attributable to meals and entertainment, and the two-percent floor for miscellaneous itemized deductions). If an employer provides a nonaccountable plan, an employee who receives payments under the plan cannot compel the payor to treat the payments as paid under an accountable plan by voluntarily substantiating the expenses and returning any excess to the payor.

The IRS treats expenses incurred by an employee through charges to a corporate credit card consistently with the above rules. If an employer has an accountable plan, personal expenses paid on behalf of an employee are taxable and should be included in wages. If employees are not required to substantiate that expenses charged to a corporate credit card were for business expenses, the reimbursement is considered to have been made under a nonaccountable plan and the entire reimbursement is taxable to the employee, and is treated as wages.

The intermediate sanctions rules (see Chapter 5) address accountable and nonaccountable plans. If an arrangement constitutes an accountable plan, reimbursements of expenses incurred by a disqualified person that are paid by a tax-exempt organization to the disqualified person are disregarded as compensation under the intermediate sanctions rules. If, however, a plan is not an accountable plan, all amounts paid by an exempt organization to a disqualified person may be subject to the intermediate sanctions rules. Furthermore, if amounts are paid under a nonaccountable plan and are not contemporaneously substantiated as an employee's compensation, the reimbursed amounts result in an automatic excess benefit transaction regardless of whether the reimbursements are reasonable, any other compensation the disqualified person receives is reasonable, and the aggregate of the reimbursements and any other compensation the disqualified person may have received is reasonable.

(r) Code of Ethics

The ECFA best practices standards include a requirement that the organization adopt a "stewardship philosophy statement." The IRS, in its draft of good-governance principles, stated that the public "expects a charity to abide by ethical standards that promote the public good." According to the IRS, the board of directors of a charitable organization "bears the ultimate responsibility for setting ethical standards and ensuring [that] they permeate the organization and inform its practices." To that end, the board "should consider adopting and regularly evaluating a code of ethics that describes behavior it wants to encourage and behavior it wants to discourage." This code of ethics "should be a principal means of communicating to all personnel a strong culture of legal compliance and ethical integrity."

The Panel on the Nonprofit Sector, in its good-governance principles for charitable organizations, stated that an organization should have a "formally adopted, written code of ethics with which all of its directors or trustees, staff and volunteers are familiar and to which they adhere." This principle is predicated on the thought that "[a]dherence to the law provides a minimum standard for an organization's behavior" (see below). The adoption of a code of ethics "helps demonstrate the organization's commitment to carry out its responsibilities ethically and effectively." The code should be "built on the values that the organization embraces, and should highlight expectations of how those who work with the organization will conduct themselves in a number of areas, such as the confidentiality and respect that should be accorded to clients, consumers, donors, and fellow volunteers and board and staff members."

(s) Other Policies

The ECFA standards include adoption of policies concerning board confidentiality and ownership of intellectual property. Some sets of good-governance principles provide that a nonprofit organization have a policy of compliance with all applicable federal, state, and local laws. This latter type of policy can be problematic, even if the organization is aware of all applicable law. For example, it is doubtful that a charitable organization that engages in nationwide fundraising is registered in compliance with the solicitation ordinance of every county in the land.

The Panel on the Nonprofit Sector, as part of its battery of proposed policies, stated that a charitable organization's board "should ensure that the organization has adequate plans to protect its assets – its property, financial and human resources, programmatic content and material, and its integrity and reputation – against damage or loss." The board "should review regularly the organization's need for general liability and directors' and officers' liability insurance, as well as take other actions necessary to mitigate risks." The Panel noted that the board is "responsible for understanding the major risks to which the organization is exposed, reviewing those risks on a periodic basis, and ensuring that systems have been established to manage them." It was observed that the "level of risk to which the organization is exposed and the extent of the review and risk management process will vary considerably based on the size, programmatic focus, geographic location, and complexity of the organization's operations."

POLICIES FOR TYPICAL NONPROFIT

An organization is highly unlikely to need all of these policies. The typical nonprofit entity, particularly if it is a public charity, should consider having, at a minimum, the following policies in place: policy as to creation and review of the entity's mission statement, a conflict-of-interest policy, a whistleblower policy, a document retention and destruction policy, and an expense reimbursement policy. Other policies to consider are a meetings documentation policy, a gift acceptance policy, an investment policy, a fundraising policy, and an annual information return review policy.

Checklist

❑ Does the organization have a conflict-of-interest policy?
Yes _____ No _____

❑ Does the organization have a whistleblower policy?
Yes _____ No _____

❑ Does the organization have a document retention and destruction policy?
Yes _____ No _____

❑ Does the organization have a process for determining executive compensation?
Yes _____ No _____

❑ Does the organization have a policy concerning participation in a joint venture? Yes _____ No _____

❑ Does the organization have a policy concerning documentation of meetings?
Yes _____ No _____

❑ Does the organization have a policy concerning the activities of its affiliates (if any)? Yes _____ No _____

❏ Does the organization have a process for review of annual information returns? Yes _____ No _____

❏ Does the organization have a gift acceptance policy?
Yes _____ No _____

❏ Does the organization have a policy concerning conservation easements?
Yes _____ No _____

❏ Does the organization have a policy concerning international grantmaking?
Yes _____ No _____

❏ Does the organization have a policy as to charity care?
Yes _____ No _____

❏ Does the organization have a policy as to debt collections?
Yes _____ No _____

❏ Does the organization have an investment policy?
Yes _____ No _____

❏ Does the organization have a fundraising policy? Yes _____ No _____

❏ Does the organization have an expense reimbursement policy?
Yes _____ No _____

❏ Does the organization have a mission statement policy?
Yes _____ No _____

❏ Does the organization have a code of ethics? Yes _____ No _____

❏ Of the applicable policies referenced in the organization's annual information return, how many are the subject of checked "yes" boxes? _____ of _____

Focus: Campaign to Clean Up America

The board of directors of the Campaign to Clean Up America (CCUA), desiring to have the best-looking annual information return it can muster, has adopted policies concerning conflicts of interest, whistleblower protection, document retention and destruction, executive compensation, meetings documentation, annual information return review, investments, fundraising, and expense reimbursement. The organization has adopted a code of ethics for its directors, officers, and other executive staff. Because they are not applicable, the CCUA has not adopted policies concerning joint venture arrangements, affiliates, gift acceptance (because of no non-standard gifts), conservation easements, international grantmaking, charity care, or debt collection.

CHAPTER
TWENTY-THREE

Commerciality, Competition, Commensurateness

Three bodies of law concerning nonprofit organizations have one thing in common: they are vague. These groupings of law are the commerciality doctrine, the rules concerning competition with for-profit businesses, and the commensurate test. There is almost nothing in the statutory law or the tax regulations on these points. The federal courts are developing most of the law in these areas, although state courts have also had something to say about the competition issue.

COMMERCIALITY DOCTRINE

The commerciality doctrine, to date, has been applied by the courts only with respect to public charities. (The IRS occasionally asserts that the doctrine is applicable to tax-exempt social welfare organizations.) The general concept is that a charitable organization that operates in a commercial manner is an organization that is not entitled to tax exemption. The IRS, however, is showing a propensity to apply the doctrine also when assessing whether an exempt organization is engaged in an unrelated business (see Chapter 13).

(a) Nature of the Doctrine

The commerciality doctrine, while not crisply defined, is essentially this: A nonprofit organization is involved in an inappropriate activity (a nonexempt activity in the case of a tax-exempt organization) when that activity is engaged in in a manner that is considered to be *commercial* in nature. An activity is a commercial one if it has a direct counterpart in, or is conducted in the same manner as is the case in, the realm of for-profit organizations. As discussed subsequently, one court has developed criteria for determining commerciality in this setting.

The commerciality doctrine is born of the fact that U.S. society, being a democracy (see Chapter 1), is composed of three sectors: the business (for-profit) sector, the governmental sector, and the nonprofit sector. The United States is essentially a capitalist society; thus, the business sector is, in several ways, the preferred sector. While the courts see entities in the business sector as being operated for private ends (e.g., profits to shareholders), with the overall result an economy beneficial to society, the nonprofit sector is seen as being operated for public ends (the general good of society).

Many today, in and out of government, still perceive of nonprofit organizations as entities that do not and should not earn a profit, are operated largely by volunteers, and are not to be "run like a business."

Out of these precepts (some of which are false) is the view that organizations in the nonprofit sector should not compete with organizations in the business sector (see discussion following). Thus, over recent years, the nonprofit community has been hearing much about competition between for-profit organizations (usually, small business) and nonprofit organizations—with the word *competition* almost always preceded by the word *unfair* (see Chapter 13).

The commerciality doctrine thus involves a *counterpart* (or *analog*) test. When a court sees an activity being conducted by a member of the business sector and the same activity being conducted by a member of the nonprofit sector, often, motivated by some form of intuitive offense at the thought that a nonprofit organization is doing something *commercial*, the court concludes that the nonprofit organization is engaged in an inappropriate (nonexempt) activity. There is an unstated presumption that a commercial function ought be undertaken only by a for-profit business. This is a tough rule, inasmuch as the tax exemption of charitable organizations is on the line.

Congress has been leery about writing the commerciality doctrine into the tax law. In fact, it has done so only once, legislating on situations where charitable or social welfare organizations issue *commercial-type insurance*. (This means nearly all types of insurance that is provided by for-profit insurance companies.)

(b) Tax Regulations

As noted, the tax regulations are nearly silent on this matter of commerciality and nonprofit organizations. The term *commercial* is, however, used in the regulations as part of the means for determining whether or not a business is regularly carried on (see Chapter 13). Thus, the regulations provide that business activities of a tax-exempt, nonprofit organization are ordinarily deemed to be regularly carried on if they "manifest a frequency and continuity, and are pursued in a manner, generally similar to comparable *commercial* activities of nonexempt organizations" (emphasis added).

To determine whether an activity is substantially related to an organization's exempt purposes, it is necessary, according to these regulations, to examine the "relationship between the business activities which generate the particular income in question (i.e., the activities of producing or distributing the goods or performing the services involved) and the accomplishment of the organization's exempt purposes."

A business is related to exempt purposes where the conduct of the business activity has a *causal relationship* to the achievement of exempt purposes, and it is substantially related where the causal relationship is a substantial one. For a business to be substantially related to exempt purposes, the production or distribution of the goods or the performance of the services from which the gross income is derived must, in the words of the regulations, "contribute importantly to the accomplishment of those purposes." Whether activities productive of gross income contribute importantly to the accomplishment of one or more exempt purposes "depends in each case upon the facts and circumstances involved."

Thus, this regulatory definition of relatedness does not make any reference to the commerciality doctrine. Rather, this definition is predicated on a causal relationship test. Thus, under the tax regulations, a business may be regularly carried on (that is, be commercial in nature) and not be taxed, where there is a substantial causal relationship between the activity and the accomplishment of exempt purposes. In other words, the regulations promulgated by the IRS contemplate (or at least tolerate) a nontaxable, related business that is commercially carried on.

(c) Beginnings of the Doctrine

No doctrine formulated by the judiciary has humbler beginnings than the commerciality doctrine. This doctrine is not the consequence of some grand pronouncement by the U.S. Supreme Court—or, for that matter, by any court. The doctrine has just evolved, starting with loose language in court opinions; it is the product of what is known in the law as *dictum*: a gratuitous remark by a judge that need not have been uttered to resolve the case.

The idea of commerciality is traceable to a mention of it in a 1924 Supreme Court opinion. The case concerned a tax-exempt religious order that engaged in activities that the government alleged destroyed the basis for its exemption: extensive investments in real estate and securities, and incidental sales of wine, chocolate, and other articles. The Supreme Court found that the order continued to be exempt as a religious entity, justifying its investment and business efforts by writing that "such [religious] activities cannot be carried on without money." In its opinion, the Court characterized the government's argument as being that the order was "operated also for business and commercial purposes." Consequently, by merely using the word in describing the government's position, the Court inadvertently gave birth to the commerciality doctrine.

The Court edged up to articulation of a commerciality doctrine in 1945, when reviewing a case concerning an organization that was seeking tax-exempt status as an educational organization. Considering the rule that an organization must be *exclusively* engaged in exempt functions, the Court wrote that this requirement "plainly means that the presence of a single non-educational purpose, if substantial in nature, will destroy the exemption regardless of the number or importance of truly educational purposes." In its opinion holding the organization ineligible for exemption, the Court came the closest that it has come to identification of a commerciality doctrine, writing that the organization has a "commercial hue" and that its activities are "largely animated by this commercial purpose."

During the 1960s, the commerciality doctrine flourished, as the courts considered the tax status of a number of nonprofit publishing organizations. A court wrote that the sheer existence of profits is "at least some evidence indicative of a commercial character." Stating the matter another way, a court said that "consistent nonprofitability is evidence of the absence of commercial purposes." Another court wrote that a nonprofit entity was "in competition with other commercial organizations providing similar services." A publisher of religious materials was denied exemption because it was "clearly engaged primarily in a business activity, and it conducted its operations, although on a small scale, in the same way as any commercial publisher of religious books for profit would have done."

Thereafter, the commerciality doctrine was repeatedly invoked. The IRS lost a case concerning an organization with the purpose of helping disadvantaged artisans in poverty-stricken countries to subsist and preserve their craft; the IRS characterized the organization as a "commercial import firm." By contrast, an organization that derived most of its income from the leasing of oil well drilling equipment was held to be operating in a commercial manner, as was an entity conducting a "highly efficient business venture" and an ostensibly religious organization engaged in "tax avoidance" counseling, providing services "no different from that furnished by a commercial tax service." A nonprofit adoption agency was denied exemption because it was operating in a manner not "distinguishable from a commercial adoption agency," because it generated substantial profits, accumulated capital, was funded entirely by fees, did not solicit contributions, and had a paid staff. A court proclaimed that, if a nonprofit organization's "management decisions replicate those of commercial enterprises, it is a fair inference that at least one purpose is commercial."

(d) Contemporary Application of the Doctrine

The adoption agency case (decided in 1988) was the principal precursor to the contemporary explication of the commerciality doctrine. Despite a rather compelling set of facts, involving a religious organization affiliated with a mainstream church that operated (in advancement of church doctrine) vegetarian restaurants and health food stores, the courts declared it to not warrant tax-exempt status. A court wrote that the organization's activity was "conducted as a business and was in direct competition with" other restaurants and health food stores, adding that "competition with commercial firms is strong evidence of a substantial nonexempt purpose."

The appellate court decision in this case (1991) remains the most significant of the commerciality doctrine decisions because the court stated the elements to review in assessing the presence of commerciality. The fact that an organization sells goods and services to the public was said to cause these operations to be "presumptively commercial." Commerciality is also present, according to this court, where there is "direct competition" with counterpart for-profit businesses. Another factor is the prices set by the organization; if they are based on pricing formulas common in the business involved, commerciality is present. (The court stated that the organization's "profit-making price structure loom[ed] large" in its analysis and criticized the organization for lacking "below-cost pricing.") The other elements cited by the court in proving commercial operations were the use of promotional materials and "commercial catch-phrases," advertising, hours of operation, a requirement that management have training and business ability," use of employees (rather than volunteers), and the absence of charitable contributions.

Another court, in denying an organization tax-exempt status that operated a conference center, closely applied these elements (2003). The IRS enthusiastically embraces the commerciality doctrine, employing its precepts in a variety of settings. The doctrine is widely accepted in the courts, often employed, in addition to exemption cases, in conjunction with application of the unrelated business rules (see Chapter 13), the private benefit doctrine (see Chapter 5), and the commensurate test (see below).

(e) What to Do?

Some of the elements of the commerciality doctrine are understandable. Direct competition with for-profit entities, the extent and degree of low-cost services provided, and pricing policies are legitimate factors to consider. Overall, however, the doctrine is troublesome and worrisome. For example, many nonprofit, tax-exempt organizations sell goods and services to the public (colleges, universities, schools, museums, hospitals, theaters, orchestras, operas, and many more). Other public charities sell services such as conferences, publications, and consulting, which have analogs in the for-profit sector. And that fact is said to give rise to a *presumption* that an organization is substantially commercial.

How many nonprofit organizations engage in advertising? Obviously, those listed in the preceding paragraph. (One court was disturbed inasmuch as an organization had a "jingle.") How many nonprofit organizations have employees? (A court faulted an organization for having employees that were *trained*.) The fact that an organization does not receive charitable contributions is irrelevant. (See the discussion of *service provides publicly supported charities* in Chapter 7.) After all, the Supreme Court back in 1924 recognized that an organization cannot carry out its nonprofit purposes "without money." So, some aspects of the commerciality doctrine are clearly nonsensical. If the doctrine were applied evenly throughout the nonprofit sector—which it is not—there would be few tax-exempt organizations.

There are two aspects of the commerciality doctrine criteria that can be summarily dismissed, since they are so preposterous. One is whether an organization has employees. That one, being so silly, does not even merit discussion. The other is whether an organization charges fees for its goods or services; the law is crystal clear that an entity can have that type of financial support and be charitable. (Similarly, there is no requirement that an organization, to be charitable, must receive contributions and grants.) Many tax-exempt organizations charge fees for the services they provide; where the business generating this revenue is a related one, the receipts are characterized as *related business income* (see Chapter 13) or *exempt function revenue* (see Chapter 7).

Universities, hospitals, and other entities in the foregoing list generate exempt function revenue without adverse impact as to their exempt status. Nonprofit organizations such as medical clinics, homes for the aged, and blood banks impose charges for their services and are not thereby deprived of exemption (or subjected to unrelated income taxation). Indeed, the IRS, in a ruling discussing the tax status of homes for the aged as charitable organizations, observed that the "operating funds [of these homes] are derived principally from fees charged for residence in the home." Other nonprofit entities that have received similar rulings from the IRS are theaters, hospices, and organizations providing housing for the disabled. Several categories of nonprofit, exempt organizations, such as alumni associations, trade and business associations, professional societies, unions, social clubs, fraternal groups, and veterans' organizations, are dues-based (fee-for-service) entities.

Despite the formal elements of the law, however, this controversy festers. For example, in 2007, the TE/GE Commissioner (see Chapter 22) spoke of the "increasingly blurred line between the tax-exempt and the commercial sectors," bemoaning unfair competition and the potential for undermining the "precious good will" possessed by most charitable organizations. This matter of the commerciality doctrine is not, by the way, confined to law books and rarified policy discussions in Washington, D.C. The front page main article in the *New York Times*, on Memorial Day 2008, proclaimed that "[a]uthorities from the local tax assessor to members of Congress are increasingly challenging the tax-exempt status of nonprofit institutions . . . questioning whether they deserve special treatment." One issue in this regard, according to the article, is the "growing confusion over what constitutes a charity at a time when nonprofit groups look more like businesses, charging fees and selling products and services to raise money."

Consequently, most nonprofit, tax-exempt organizations should be concerned (albeit mildly) about the potentiality of application of the commerciality doctrine to them. They should evaluate each of their program activities and assess whether any of them could reasonably be considered conducted in a commercial manner. Probably, using the foregoing criteria, most of them will be deemed commercial in nature. But that does not mean that the organization should cease engaging in them. The likelihood of the commerciality doctrine being applied is remote. Yet, interest in the doctrine is continuing to grow and, as noted, the IRS is enamored of the doctrine. Thus, about all a nonprofit organization can do (pre-audit, anyway) is assess its facts and be vigilant.

COMPETITION

As the discussion of the commerciality doctrine indicates, an important factor in its application is the element of competition in a field between nonprofit and for-profit entities. This issue of nonprofit/for-profit competition, however, transcends the commerciality doctrine. The issue has been around since the dawn of the concept of tax exemption (1913). For example, concern about competition between exempt and for-profit organizations is the principal reason for and underpinning of the unrelated business rules (enacted in 1950—see Chapter 13). (Oddly, though, the presence or absence of competition is not among the criteria, in any statute or regulation, applied in assessing whether an activity of an exempt organization is an unrelated business.)

This matter of competition is a hot issue in three areas today. The outcomes in these areas could dramatically affect the state of nonprofit law concerning commerciality and competition.

The first area is health care, where there is great controversy as to the criteria for tax-exempt hospitals or whether nonprofit hospitals should be exempt at all. There are, of course, exempt and for-profit hospitals. What is the difference between them? Some legislators and other government officials are struggling with that question. (An IRS commissioner once said he could not see any distinction between the two types of institutions.) Part of the present controversy is whether to keep the existing criterion for tax exemption for hospitals (the *community benefit standard*) in place or to replace it with a requirement that charitable hospitals provide services without charge to the poor (the *charity care standard*). Another aspect of the controversy is the disagreement as to what constitutes *charity care* in the first instance.

The second area is tax-exempt status for nonprofit credit unions. These institutions have been exempt for decades, on the rationale that, by operating in a cooperative manner they encourage thrift and self-reliance among their members (where there is the requisite *common bond*) by creating a source of credit at a fair and reasonable rate of interest in order to improve the economic and social conditions of their members. Today, however, commercial banks and other for-profit financial institutions are calling for repeal of this tax exemption, on the ground that nonprofit credit unions are providing financial services to the public far beyond their constituencies. The IRS has weighed in on the side of the banks, ruling that various insurance products and other financial services provided by exempt credit unions to the public constitute unrelated businesses.

The third area concerns the tax status of insurance activities of nonprofit fraternal beneficiary societies. Here again, the issue is the distinction between these insurance activities and those of for-profit commercial insurers. A 1993 report from the Department of the Treasury found these activities to be similar and serving the same markets (although the report stopped short of recommending taxation of the societies' insurance activities). This issue, like the other two discussed previously, still simmers.

The pattern that may unfold in one or more of these settings is exemplified by the fate of the Blue Cross and Blue Shield organizations. At their beginning, they were deemed worthy of tax exemption; they were novel entities and seen as providers of health care to those who could not otherwise afford it. As the decades went by, however, the Blues broadened the base of their subscribers and began charging more competitive rates. As the nation's health care system changed (such as with the advent of Medicare and Medicaid), these organizations found themselves competing with for-profit health insurance providers. The latter eventually prevailed, and in 1986, Congress removed the Blues organizations from the rolls of tax-exempt organizations.

As noted, the United States is generally a capitalist society; nonprofit organizations are likely to be secondary as a matter of policy and practice, to for-profit ones when it comes to similar activities. The management of nonprofit organizations should do here what they should do in the face of the commerciality doctrine: evaluate each of their program activities and assess whether any of them could reasonably be considered competitive with one or more for-profit entities. Just because the answer is yes does not mean that the activity should be discontinued. The organization needs to be aware of the issue and, once again, be vigilant.

COMMENSURATE TEST

There is no element of the law of nonprofit, tax-exempt organizations that is more obscure than the *commensurate test*. (This state of affairs is about to change.) Indeed, this aspect of the law barely exists, found only in one court opinion and a few IRS rulings. To date, the test has been applied only with respect to the tax-exempt status of charitable organizations.

The commensurate test is a form of rough justice. When used, the fact-finder assesses whether a charitable organization is maintaining program activities to a sufficient extent in relation to, or commensurate in scope with, its financial resources. This test can help or hurt a charity. The first time the IRS applied this test (in 1964) a charity was helped; the organization derived most of its income from rents, yet its tax-exempt status was preserved because it was engaging in an adequate amount of charitable functions.

After nearly 30 years had passed, the commensurate test popped up again. In a well-publicized and quite controversial move, the IRS revoked the tax-exempt status of a charitable organization on a variety of rationales, including the ground that its fundraising costs were too high (allegedly 98 percent) and thus it violated the commensurate test. (This argument was dropped in the course of litigation.) The IRS's lawyers on this occasion (1991) wrote that the commensurate test "does not lend itself to a rigid numerical distribution formula—there is no fixed percentage of income that an organization must pay out for charitable purposes." (This is not true in the case of private foundations—see Chapter 7.) This is a facts-and-circumstances test; in each case, these lawyers said, "it should be ascertained whether the failure to make real and substantial contributions for charitable purposes is due to reasonable cause." They added that the "financial resources of any organization may be affected by such factors as startup costs, overhead, scale of operations, whether labor is voluntary or salaried, [and/or] phone or postal costs."

Nonetheless, continuing with these lawyers' observations, "distribution levels that are low invite close scrutiny." The commensurate test "requires that organizations have a charitable program that is both real and, taking the organization's circumstances and financial resources into account, substantial." Therefore, they asserted, an organization that "raises funds for charitable purposes but consistently uses virtually all of its income for administrative and promotional expenses with little or no direct charitable accomplishments cannot reasonably argue that its charitable program is commensurate with its financial resources and capabilities." The current controversy over the level of university tuition and accessibility to higher education by the indigent, in relation to the size and payouts from university endowment funds, is a manifestation of the commensurate test.

The commensurate test and the primary purpose test (see Chapter 4) have an awkward coexistence. For example, a charitable organization was allowed to retain its tax-exempt status while receiving 98 percent of its financial support in the form of unrelated business income, inasmuch as 41 percent of the organization's activities were charitable programs. In another instance, a charitable organization remained exempt, despite the conclusion of the IRS that two-thirds of its operations constituted unrelated businesses, because the net income from these businesses was used to advance charitable ends.

Despite its long-standing obscurity, however, the commensurate test may be coming into its own. In a speech in early 2007, the TE/GE Commissioner startled a roomful of conference attendees by announcing that the IRS would place more emphasis on use of the test. Defining the test as a "comparison between what a charity ought to be able to do, given its resources, and what it actually does," he asked whether "providing a peppercorn of public benefit [is] enough?" Indeed, the Commissioner invoked the notion of an "annual payout or spending rate" for charitable organizations. Whatever the test will be, he said, it will reflect an effort to "create and enforce a standard that ensures [that] exempt organizations are spending in line with their resources."

Once again, what is a nonprofit, tax-exempt organization to do? The answer is the same as with the commerciality test and the matter of competition: assess the organization's operations from the perspective of the test and become knowledgeable and vigilant. Aside from its traditional criteria for assessing whether a nonprofit organization warrants tax exemption, particularly as a charitable entity, it may be anticipated that the IRS will be looking to the presence and extent of commerciality, competition, and commensurateness.

Checklist

- ❏ Does the organization conduct activities in a manner that may reasonably be considered commercial? Yes _____ No _____
- ❏ Does the organization conduct activities that compete with the business activities of for-profit entities? Yes _____ No _____
- ❏ Does the organization satisfy the commensurate test?
  Yes _____ No _____

Focus: Campaign to Clean Up America

The Campaign to Clean Up America is not particularly concerned by these three developments in nonprofit law. None of its activities are commercial in nature, it does not compete with for-profit businesses, and it is amply in compliance with any emerging version of a commensurate test.

IRS Audits of Nonprofit Organizations

The IRS, of course, has the authority to examine (i.e., audit) nonprofit, tax-exempt organizations. Until recently, this has not been a priority for the IRS. With more appropriations from Congress, considerable prodding from members of Congress, and an energetic Commissioner of Internal Revenue, IRS audits of exempt organizations have been steadily increasing. Today, IRS audit activity involving exempt organizations is at an all-time high. Thus, managers of nonprofit organizations are on notice that the chance of their organization getting audited, while inherently slight, is statistically greater than ever.

ORGANIZATION OF IRS

The leadership of nonprofit organizations, and those who represent these entities, should understand the organization of the IRS. Among the many reasons for this is to gain a perspective on the IRS audit function. Generally, an IRS audit is less traumatic if the overall process is understood. It helps with the coping.

The IRS is an agency (bureau) of the U.S. Department of the Treasury. One of the functions of the Treasury Department is assessment and collection of federal income and other taxes. Congress has authorized the Secretary of the Treasury to, in the language of the Internal Revenue Code, undertake what is necessary for "detecting and bringing to trial and punishment persons guilty of violating the internal revenue laws or conniving at the same." This tax assessment and collection function has largely been assigned to the IRS.

The IRS website proclaims that the agency's mission is to "provide America's taxpayers with top quality service by helping them understand and meet their tax responsibilities and by applying the tax law with integrity and fairness to all." (A commentator wrote: "The specific role of the Internal Revenue Service in the [federal tax] system is to both collect and protect the revenue without incidentally frustrating or terrorizing the taxpayer population.") The function of the IRS, according to its site, is to "help the large majority of compliant taxpayers with the tax law, while ensuring that the minority who are unwilling to comply pay their fair share."

The IRS is headquartered in Washington, D.C.; its operations there are housed principally in its National Office. An Internal Revenue Service Oversight Board is responsible for overseeing the agency in its administration and supervision of the execution of the nation's internal revenue laws. The chief executive of the IRS is the

Commissioner of Internal Revenue. The National Office is organized into four operating divisions; the pertinent one is the Tax Exempt and Government Entities (TE/GE) Division, headed by its Commissioner (TE/GE). Within the TE/GE Division is the Exempt Organizations Division, which develops policy concerning, and administers the law of, tax-exempt organizations. The components of this Division are Rulings and Agreements, Customer Education and Outreach, Exempt Organizations Electronic Initiatives, and Examinations.

The Examinations Office, based in Dallas, Texas, focuses on tax-exempt organizations' examination programs and review projects. This office develops the overall exempt organizations enforcement strategy and goals to enhance compliance consistent with overall TE/GE strategy, and implements and evaluates exempt organizations examination policies and procedures. Two important elements of the Examinations function are the Exempt Organizations Compliance Unit (see discussion following) and the Data Analysis Unit.

REASONS FOR IRS AUDITS

The reasons for an IRS examination of a nonprofit, tax-exempt organization are manifold. Traditionally, the agency has focused on particular categories of major exempt entities, such as health care institutions, colleges and universities, political organizations, community foundations, and private foundations. Recent years have brought more targeted examinations, such as those involving credit counseling entities and down payment assistance organizations.

An examination of a tax-exempt organization may be initiated on the basis of the size of the organization or the length of time that has elapsed since a prior audit. An examination may be undertaken following the filing of an annual information return (see Chapter 9) or a tax return, inasmuch as one of the functions of the IRS is to ascertain the correctness of returns. An examination may be based on a discrete issue, such as compensation practices (see Chapter 5) or political campaign activity (see Chapter 15). Other reasons for the development of an examination include media reports, a state attorney general's inquiry, or other third-party reports of alleged wrongdoing. The IRS has a form that can be used to file a complaint about an exempt organization (Form 13909).

IRS AUDIT ISSUES

The audit of a nonprofit, tax-exempt organization is likely to entail one or more of the following issues:

- The organization's ongoing eligibility for exempt status (see Chapter 4)
- Public charity/private foundation classification (see Chapter 7)
- Unrelated business activity (see Chapter 13)
- Extensive advocacy undertakings (see Chapters 14, 15)
- One or more excise tax issues
- Whether the organization filed required returns and reports (see Chapter 9)
- Payment of employment taxes
- Involvement in a form of joint venture (see Chapter 18)

TYPES OF IRS EXAMINATIONS

There are four basic types of IRS examinations of nonprofit, tax-exempt organizations. (As discussed subsequently, a compliance check is not technically an audit. In addition, there are special procedures for inquiries and examinations of churches.)

(a) Field Examinations

Common among the types of IRS examinations of tax-exempt organizations are *field examinations*, in which one or more revenue agents (typically only one) review the books, records, and other documents and information of the exempt organization under examination, on the premises of the organization or at the office of its representative. IRS procedures require the examiner to establish the scope of the examination, state the documentation requirements, and summarize the examination techniques (including interviews and tours of facilities).

(b) Office and Correspondence Examinations

The IRS's office/correspondence examination program entails examinations of tax-exempt organizations by means of office interviews and/or correspondence. An *office interview* case is one where the examiner requests an exempt organization's records and reviews them in an IRS office; this may include a conference with a representative of the organization. This type of examination is likely to be of a smaller exempt organization, where the records are not extensive and the issues not particularly complex. A *correspondence examination* involves an IRS request for information from an exempt organization by letter, fax, or e-mail communication.

Office or correspondence examinations generally are limited in scope, usually focusing on no more than three issues, conducted by lower-grade examiners. The import of these examinations should not be minimized, however. A correspondence examination can be converted to an office examination. Worse, an office examination can be upgraded to a field examination.

(c) Team Examinations

For years, one of the mainstays of the IRS tax-exempt organizations examination effort was the *coordinated examination program* (CEP), which focused not only on exempt organizations but also on affiliated entities and arrangements (such as subsidiaries, partnerships, and other joint ventures) and collateral areas of the law (such as employment tax compliance and tax-exempt bond financing). The CEP approach (which was much dreaded), involving relatively sizeable teams of revenue agents, was concentrated on large, complex exempt organizations, such as colleges, universities, and health care institutions. Exempt organizations management could expect the CEP exercise to span about three years, with the IRS agents decamping in offices at the exempt organization, to which they would daily directly commute.

The CEP approach was abandoned in 2003 and replaced by the *team examination program* (TEP). Both the CEP and TEP initiatives nonetheless share the same objective, which is to avoid a fragmenting of the exempt organization examination process by using multiple agents. The essential characteristics of the TEP approach that differentiates it from the CEP approach are that the team examinations are being utilized in connection with a wider array of exempt organizations, the number of revenue agents involved in an examination is somewhat smaller, and the revenue agents are less likely to semipermanently carve out office space in which to live at the exempt organization undergoing the examination. The TEP agents, however, are still likely to want an office for occasional visits and storage of computers and documents.

A TEP case generally is one where the annual information return (see Chapter 9) of the tax-exempt organization involved reflects either total revenue or assets greater than $100 million (or, in the case of a private foundation, $500 million—see Chapter 7). Nonetheless, the IRS may initiate a team examination where the case would benefit (from the government's perspective) from the TEP approach or where there is no annual information return filing requirement. IRS examination procedures include a presumption that the team examination approach will be utilized in all cases that satisfy the TEP criteria.

In a TEP case, the examination will proceed under the direction of a case manager. One or more tax-exempt organizations revenue agents will be accompanied by others, such as employee plans specialists, actuarial examiners, engineers, excise tax agents, international examiners, computer audit specialists, income tax revenue agents, or economists. These examinations may last about two years; a post-examination critique may lead to a cycling of the examination into subsequent years. The IRS examination procedures stipulate the planning that case managers, assisted by team coordinators, should engage in when launching a team examination; these procedures also provide for the exempt organization's involvement in this planning process. It is all quite an event. Long-standing friendships (even marriages) as well as sustained battles can emerge.

(d) Criminal Investigations

The foregoing types of IRS audits are those normally used to examine nonprofit, tax-exempt organizations. The IRS, however, has within it a Criminal Investigation Division (CID), the agents of which occasionally are involved in exempt organizations examinations. The management of an exempt organization under audit is free to decide whether to involve legal counsel in the process. Some organizations elect (foolishly) to save the costs of lawyers and weather examinations on their own. Other organizations are content to have an accountant provide the representation. When the IRS agent or agents arrive, management of the exempt organization should be quick to read their badges or business cards. If the initials CID appear, the decision as to whether to involve a lawyer has been made for the organization.

COMPLIANCE CHECKS

An overlay to the IRS program of examinations of tax-exempt organizations is the agency's *compliance check projects*, which focus on specific compliance issues. These projects, orchestrated by the Exempt Organizations Compliance Unit, are a recent invention of the IRS; they are designed to maximize the agency's return (gaining data and assessing compliance) on its investigation efforts. In a pronouncement issued in early 2008, the IRS stated that its exempt organizations examination and compliance-check processes are among the "variety of tools at [the agency's] disposal to make certain that tax-exempt organizations comply with federal tax law designed to ensure they are entitled to any tax exemption they may claim."

Usually, in the commencement of these projects, the IRS contacts exempt organizations only by mail to obtain information pertaining to the particular issue. An exempt organization has a greater chance of being a compliance check target than the subject of a conventional audit. A compliance check, however, can blossom into an examination.

At the present, nine compliance check projects are in play, with varying levels of intensity.

(a) Executive Compensation

In 2004, the IRS announced its formation of an Executive Compensation Compliance Initiative. The agency then stated that it was going to "identify and halt" the practice of some tax-exempt organizations of paying excessive compensation and other benefits to insiders (see Chapter 5). This program entailed contact (compliance check letters) with 1,223 public charities and private foundations. More than 100 of these organizations became the target of formal examinations.

As it turned out, the IRS found less wrongdoing (unreasonable compensation) than initially contemplated. Thus, in a preliminary report on its findings (2007), the agency wrote that "examinations to date do not evidence widespread concerns other than reporting." (Over 30 percent of these compliance check recipients were required to amend their annual information returns.) Cryptically, the IRS concluded that, "although high compensation amounts were found in many cases, generally they were substantiated based on appropriate comparability data." (Translation: *high* compensation is not necessarily *excessive* compensation.) Twenty-five examinations resulted in proposed excise tax assessments pursuant to the intermediate sanctions rules (over $4 million) and the self-dealing rules (over $16 million).

These compliance checks continue. Inquiries into compensation levels are part of other compliance checks and usually are embedded in every examination of a tax-exempt organization.

(b) Political Campaign Activities

The IRS began a Political Activities Compliance Initiative, starting with the 2004 election campaign, in response to various allegations of participation by charities, including churches, in political campaigns in violation of the tax law (see Chapter 15). This initiative continued with the 2006 and 2008 election cycles and may be anticipated to remain in place.

The effort with respect to the 2004 campaign caused the IRS to review 166 cases. For the most part, either no violations were found or the IRS helped organizations correct their activities by issuing *written advisories*. Revocation of exemption was proposed in three instances. There were 237 cases in connection with the 2006 elections. No exemption revocations have been reported as a result of these cases, although the IRS uncovered about $300,000 in inappropriate campaign contributions (about one-half of which have been refunded). The IRS is doing its best to monitor exempt organizations' involvement in the 2008 campaign.

(c) Hospitals

In 2006, the IRS initiated a Hospital Compliance Project, the purpose of which is to study tax-exempt hospitals and assess how these institutions believe they are providing a community benefit, as well as to determine how exempt hospitals establish and report executive compensation. This massive effort, involving 487 hospitals, was commenced with the mailing of a nine-page questionnaire containing 81 questions. Information was requested regarding the type of hospital and patient demographics, governance, medical staff privileges, billing and collection practices, and categories of programs that might constitute community benefit, such as uncompensated care, medical education and training, medical research, and other community programs conducted by hospitals.

The IRS is still processing the data gathered from these questionnaires. In a preliminary report (2007), the agency observed that "there is variation in the level of expenditures hospitals report in furtherance of community benefit." (The report did not address the point that the law does not include a uniform definition of *community benefit*.) This report also noted that "there is considerable variation in how hospitals report uncompensated care." (The term *uncompensated care* was deliberately not defined in the questionnaire because the IRS wanted to learn how the exempt hospital community is applying it.) Hospitals, according to the report, also "vary in how they measure and incorporate bad debt expense and shortfalls between actual costs and Medicare or Medicaid reimbursements into their measures, and whether they use charges or costs in their measures." The IRS's analysis of exempt hospitals is continuing and will spill over into data-gathering efforts that will be the result of reporting on the redesigned annual information return (see Chapter 9). The IRS has not released any data concerning compensation paid by exempt hospitals.

(d) Excess Benefit Reporting

Another of the ongoing IRS compliance initiatives, one that is relatively low key these days, is a project concerning compliance with the intermediate sanctions reporting rules (see Chapter 5). The annual information return asks questions about exempt organizations' participation in excess benefit transactions. When one of these returns, lacking answers to these questions, is received by the IRS, an exempt organizations law specialist in the National Office may contact the organization, seeking the response(s).

(e) Fundraising Costs Reporting

Another low-key ongoing IRS compliance initiative is a project concerning the reporting of fundraising costs. From time to time, IRS reviewers of annual information returns will come across a return that reflects a considerable amount of gifts and grants and little or no fundraising expense. This anomaly is likely to perplex the reviewer, who may contact the organization for an explanation. The IRS may also advise the organization that its subsequent annual information returns may be reviewed, from this perspective, by personnel in the Exempt Organizations Compliance Unit.

(f) Tax-Exempt Bonds Recordkeeping

The IRS, in 2007, undertook a compliance check initiative, this one targeting charitable organizations that are engaged in tax-exempt bond financing. The agency has concluded (based on about 40 audits during fiscal year 2006) that there is a lack of compliance with certain record-retention rules. The IRS is currently surveying about 500 charitable organizations in this regard.

(g) Charitable Giving Scam

The IRS has embarked on a project inquiring as to charitable contributions of interests in limited liability companies, involving questionable transactions concerning successor member interests in these companies. This program is unique in that, instead of a mailing of letters or questionnaires, the IRS developed and is sending (starting in late 2007) a prototype information document request (see discussion following). This IDR (11 single-spaced pages) includes some pointed questions. Management of charitable organizations, even if not involved in this successor-member interest scheme, should ponder these questions in the context of considering whether to accept an unconventional charitable gift.

(h) Community Foundations

The IRS has launched a compliance check project, by the mailing of questionnaires, to the nation's community foundations. Concerned that these foundations may be wandering outside of their legal bounds, the IRS is asking detailed questions about these foundations' "area of service" (in that they are, after all, *community* foundations), revenues, assets, investments, grantmaking, business relationships, fees paid, and staff.

(i) Colleges and Universities

In the works is a compliance initiative targeting tax-exempt colleges and universities. By means of dissemination of a compliance check questionnaire, the IRS will look at how institutions of higher education (1) report income and expenses on their annual information returns, (2) calculate and report losses on their unrelated business income tax returns, (3) allocate income and expenses in calculating their unrelated business taxable income, (4) invest and use their endowment funds, and (5) (once again) determine executive compensation.

HARDENING THE TARGET

There are 13 steps a nonprofit, tax-exempt organization can take to improve and maximally enhance its "public face" in advance of any IRS examination that may reduce the chances of an examination or, failing that, move the examination to its conclusion quickly, efficiently, and with minimal costs.

(a) Review Governing Instruments

A nonprofit organization should, from time to time, review its governing instruments. These are the *articles of organization* (articles of incorporation, constitution, declaration of trust, and the like) and *bylaws*. The purpose of this exercise is to ensure that these documents accurately describe the organization's purposes and do not contain words or phrases that are inconsistent with its tax-exempt status. The IRS examiner will definitely review these instruments.

(b) Review Operations

The IRS will certainly inquire into the tax-exempt organization's programs and other activities. The organization should have sufficient documentation about each of its programs (including annual reports, grant requests, and fundraising literature), and the relationship between them and achievement of its exempt purposes. Documentation of this nature that is in the organization's files when the IRS arrives is far more potent than materials assembled after the agency has initiated contact.

(c) Review Books and Records

The organization should attend to its financial, operational (e.g., grant files), and governance (e.g., minutes) records. Of all of the types of documents that will be read by an IRS examiner, only board and committee minutes have the ability to be created specifically in anticipation of (and in an attempt to influence the outcome of) an IRS (or other government agency) review of the organization's operations. The organization should be certain that it knows where these records are located and that they contain what is required. A document-retention policy will impress the IRS revenue agent.

(d) Review Publications

The organization should review its publications that are disseminated to the public. Examples of these are magazines, journals, newsletters, mission statements, and federal or state lobbying disclosure reports. These materials should be reviewed to identify any statements that may be harmful in relation to the organization's tax-exempt status. (Recently, a nonprofit organization claiming to promote safety in flying, principally through publication of a magazine, was audited. Perusing issues of the magazine, the IRS agent found little material about flying safety but came upon this disclaimer in each issue: "This publication is strictly for your entertainment value." The IRS revoked the organization's exempt status.) Usually, this text cannot be amended, but at least the organization and its professional representatives can become aware of any problematic language and prepare accordingly.

(e) Review Correspondence

Reviewing correspondence (including e-mail) is a tedious exercise, but it must be done because an IRS examiner is likely to do so. There may be documents that adversely (at least potentially) impact public charity status or the merits of a tax-exempt activity (such as a scholarship or fellowship program).

(f) Review Federal Returns

The principal returns that will be examined are the annual information return and any unrelated business income tax return (see Chapter 9). In addition to their proper preparation and timely filing, these returns should be reviewed from time to time in anticipation of a possible audit. The IRS examination procedures instruct agents to look for "gaps or incongruities" and "entries [not] credible on their face."

(g) Review Contracts

In anticipation of the IRS's doing so, a nonprofit organization should review its contracts (including letter agreements and perhaps signed informal memoranda). Of particular interest to the IRS are employment contracts, severance agreements, management agreements, fundraising contracts, and leases.

(h)   Other Documents

Documents that please IRS revenue agents are properly prepared codes of ethics, conflict-of-interest policies, document-retention and -destruction policies (as noted), whistleblower policies, insurance policies (usually), consultants' reports (particularly as to compensation), and appraisals (see Chapter 22). If the organization is a member of a partnership or other joint venture (see Chapter 18), the appropriate documentation will be reviewed. An examiner may review reports concerning an exempt organization issued by or filed with a federal, state, or local government agency.

(i)   Review Website

A nonprofit organization should periodically review its website with the federal tax law in mind. It goes without saying that this is the easiest of text to revise. If an organization is selected for an audit, it may be assumed that the IRS has visited (or certainly will visit) the site. This matter affects program, unrelated business, and fundraising.

(j)   Employment Taxes

Nonprofit organizations with employees are exposed to examination by IRS employment tax agents, in addition to exempt organizations agents. These organizations should stay current with the withholding and reporting requirements, periodically review the employee/independent contractor classification of its workers, and be certain that its files contain adequate justification for any independent contractor status.

(k)   Media Coverage

Not every nonprofit organization should have, or can afford, a media consultant. Nonetheless, an organization should do what it can to get its programs and accomplishments publicized. In addition, an organization should maintain a file of newspaper articles and other forms of media coverage about itself (particularly if the reports are favorable).

(l)   Testaments

Some nonprofit organizations operate programs that generate letters and other forms of comment about their activities from program beneficiaries and perhaps others. A file of these documents should be maintained (again, particularly if they are favorable).

(m)   Legal Audit

The foregoing pre-audit precautions are the minimum. The nonprofit organization that wants to do all it can to avoid an IRS audit or smooth the process once enmeshed in one should engage the services of a competent nonprofit lawyer to conduct a comprehensive legal audit.

WINNING THE AUDIT LOTTERY

The following steps should be anticipated by a nonprofit organization, once it has become the subject of an IRS audit, to help it get through the examination process as painlessly as possible.

(a) Telephone Call

The practice of the IRS, in connection with a typical examination of a nonprofit organization, is to commence the process with a telephone call—what the IRS terms the *initial contact*. (Many executives of nonprofit organizations find this approach unduly startling and rather unnerving, and prefer to get the bad news by letter.) The caller will, of course, announce that the organization has been selected (somewhat of a euphemism) for an IRS examination. This IRS representative will also advise the organization of the year or years that will be covered by the examination and attempt to set the date for the preexamination conference.

(b) Notice of Examination

This telephone call will be followed up with a letter from the IRS serving as formal notice of the examination, which is likely to be based on the filing of one or more annual information returns. This letter, which will undoubtedly bear the same date as the previously mentioned telephone call, will propose an initial conference about the examination. This notice will contain this bit of empathy from the IRS: "We realize some organizations may be concerned about an examination of their returns."

(c) Documents Requested

The initial information document request (IDR), which will almost certainly accompany the notice of examination, will ask for organizational documents, operational documents, and certain books and records.

This IDR will undoubtedly request copies of the tax-exempt organization's organizing document, its bylaws, the application for recognition of exemption, the determination letter recognizing its exempt status, and the minutes of the meetings of the organization's governing body for the year preceding the first year of the audit period, for the year(s) of the audit period, and for the year immediately succeeding the audit period.

The IDR will undoubtedly request copies of the exempt organization's annual information return for the year preceding the first year of the audit period, for the year(s) of the audit period, and for the year immediately succeeding the audit period; printed materials used to promote the organization's activities; and contracts to which the organization was a party during the audit period.

This IDR will probably request copies of bank statements for all accounts (checking, savings, investments), canceled checks and deposit slips, check registers, the general ledger, and documentation in support of expenses claimed.

(d) Get Organized

Having received the initial telephone call from the IRS, and the initial contact letter and IDR, the nonprofit organization should select a team that will be charged with overseeing (from the organization's standpoint) the examination. By means of this group, the organization will want to try to maintain as much control over the situation, and get through the examination process as quickly, as possible. These goals, however, may prove elusive.

(e) Contact Person

The nonprofit organization facing an IRS audit should designate an individual to be the single point of contact for the examination; the examiner will be expecting selection of this individual. All requests for documents and interviews should be to this individual, who should be responsible for timely responses. This individual should also maintain a log of IDRs from and documents provided to the IRS.

(f) Communications Strategy

The IRS may contact third parties, such as the nonprofit organization's bank or contractors as well as others with whom it does business. This can lead to media attention. The organization should be ready with a thoughtful statement for the media.

(g) Know the Cast

It is important that the nonprofit organization know who from the IRS is involved in the audit. The appropriate representative(s) of the organization should meet, greet, and record the names of the revenue agents involved, as well as of the case manager (or, at least, procure the manager's name and contact information). The organization should determine whether the office of the IRS Chief Counsel will be assisting the revenue agents. Similarly, the organization should ascertain whether one or more specialists, such as engineers, computer audit specialists, or financial analysts, are being assigned to the case.

(h) Office Facilities

The IRS may expect workspace on the nonprofit organization's premises, in the form of a workroom with locking door, desks and chairs, telephones, file cabinet (with lock), and space and power supply for a desktop computer, printer, and fax machine. The agents will want access to a photocopier. Careful consideration should be given as to the location of this workspace. The organization should endeavor to place this office as far away as possible from a dining area or kitchen where (talkative) employees congregate.

(i) Initial and Other Interviews

The initial interview is likely to be a crucial step—for both parties—in the examination process. If all goes in accordance with IRS procedures, the examiner will have carefully prepared for the meeting. Needless to say, the nonprofit organization should be prepared as well; this entails at least three elements: (1) appropriate preparation, by the lawyer or other individual who is guiding the organization through the audit, of the individuals who are to be interviewed by the examiner; (2) availability of all of the documents requested by the IRS or an explanation as to why one or more of these documents will not or cannot be provided; and (3) suitable tidying and spiffing up of the office premises and the interviewees.

   The nonprofit organization's representative should not hesitate to ask questions up front (although they may not be answered). One question is the reason for the examination, such as an event or issue. Another is whether the agent has any special areas of interest to explore. The agent may be asked whether there is an examination plan and a tentative schedule that can be shared with the organization.

Thereafter, the IRS may conduct additional interviews with the same individuals and/or interview others. All of this is likely to be done in conjunction with document reviews, more IDRs, tours, and other examination techniques. First impressions are important; everyone should endeavor to be polite. The organization should make every effort to convey the substance of the organization's governance, law compliance, programs, and other good works.

COPING WITH EXAMINERS

When an IRS examination of a nonprofit organization begins, one of the first orders of business (from the organization's standpoint) is to assess the personality of the examiner or examiners. Initially (and thus superficially), this exercise can produce great variations, such as from nice to rude, quiet to assertive. As this minuet gets underway, those representing the organization should not lose sight of the fact that the agent (1) is also positioning himself or herself, assaying the personalities of these representatives, trying to determine whether these people are going to be cooperative or disingenuous, and (2) is backed up by one of the most powerful components of the federal government.

Most often, an IRS examiner will commence the process with politeness, burnished with an air of cool assurance. This demeanor can change, of course, for better or worse, as the examiner interacts with the nonprofit organization (trustees, directors, officers, employees, maybe volunteers), its representatives (such as a lawyer or an accountant), and perhaps third parties (such as a bank or other provider of goods or services). Sometimes it's bonding; sometimes it's combat. This element of the facts interrelates with the factor of the level of knowledge of the law of tax-exempt organizations the examiner brings to the skirmish; not surprisingly, some have more than others. The less the understanding of the law, the greater the likelihood of bluster. Usually, the examiner will work, in a cooperative and courteous manner, with the nonprofit organization in developing and analyzing the applicable law. But, there is always the possibility of the type of examiner who, having (1) taken a nonsensical position, (2) asked for authority on a point of law, and (3) been told that there is nothing specific to cite (other than common sense), retorts—and this is not being made up: "If you can't provide me with some precedent, then I am the authority." (Next step: the call to the case manager.)

This is, then, a matter of group dynamics, including at least three types of interactions involving the IRS examiner: contact with other IRS personnel, with the individual(s) comprising the nonprofit organization, and with the individual(s) representing the nonprofit organization. Although it is infrequent, disagreement, animosity, and other forms of friction can be displayed by IRS personnel in the presence of those representing, in one capacity or another, the nonprofit organization. (On one memorable occasion, a lawyer, having appeared at an audit conference where the IRS representatives were confused over the schedule and thus unprepared for the meeting, watched, with equal doses of bemusement and incredulity, a tetrad of IRS employees quarrel with one another over who was at fault. Four sets of lawyers had flown in for the conference from different cities; the conference had to be rescheduled.)

The greatest amount of apprehension (from the standpoint of the nonprofit organization under examination) and tension is likely to develop between the IRS examiner and an employee, officer, or similar proxy for the nonprofit organization. The IRS makes most individuals nervous, so there is no surprise in concluding that an IRS audit is a prescription for much angst for the auditee. Moreover, most executives of nonprofit organizations are passionate about their organizations and its programs and frequently become exercised (or upset or angry) when challenged on these fronts. Thus, when it comes to interactions between an IRS examiner and such a representative of a nonprofit organization, the lawyer representing the organization (if there is one) generally will work assiduously with this individual in preparing him or her for the IRS interview or other exchange with the examiner and keep the communication between these individuals to a minimum. Conversely, in some nonprofit organizations there are executives, officers, and directors whose personality is sufficiently amiable that the lawyer wants them to spend as much time with the examiner(s) as reasonably possible. Admittedly, this is a rare phenomenon, but it can happen.

If there is to be an altercation, it probably will occur between an IRS examiner and a lawyer representing the nonprofit organization under audit. Some of these dustups may be pure personality clashes (or posturing), but far more likely is the belief, on the part of the lawyer, that the examiner either is misconstruing one or more aspects of the law of exempt organizations or is in some fashion being unreasonable. As noted, some agents are more schooled in this area than others. Disagreement over the state of the law does not always lead to a donnybrook, but it can generate frustration and tempers can flare. The lawyer in this circumstance should always strive to act in a civil manner, but there are occasions, sometimes dictated by the exigencies of advocacy, when legal counsel needs to stand up to the examiner on matters of substantive and/or procedural law.

TOURS

A particularly vexing (from the nonprofit organization's standpoint) aspect of these IRS examinations is the tour. The IRS examiner(s) quite likely will want, relatively early in the process, to tour the organization's facilities. In some instances, of course, there will not be any facilities to tour or the facilities will consist of a few offices that are not conducive to touring. The IRS representatives, by contrast, will almost certainly seek a tour of a tax-exempt organization's facilities where they house program and/or fundraising activities, such as those of a school, college, university, hospital, association, or large public charity.

These tours pose problems for nonprofit organizations; the larger the organization, the greater the headache. Management of an organization usually prefers to confine the fact of an IRS audit to as few employees as possible; a tour by the IRS widely spreads the news. These tours can depress employees' morale (or scare them); they will assume the worst when they see the IRS prowling the premises. A bigger dilemma is that one or more employees will say something to an IRS examiner that is detrimental to the cause.

The lawyer representing an audited nonprofit organization certainly should not permit one of these tours to unfold at random. The best practice is a dress rehearsal, preferably the day before the tour so that the employees involved will have the lawyer's instructions fresh in their minds and they will have minimum time to become anxious. The route of the tour should be mapped out; this needs to be carefully done, because if the tour path is obviously short, the examiner will want to explore other areas that are in plain sight. The employees whose offices are located along the tour route should be carefully counseled as to what to say and what not to say. Ideally, these individuals will be well dressed and polite (at least on tour day), will answer questions put to them by the examiner (assuming they know the answer), and will confine their responses to the scope of the questions and volunteer nothing. In short, these employees should be given a quick course in how to function as a witness. Much can go wrong on the tour; good preparation includes making the premises (and the employees) as attractive and looking as well organized and operated as possible.

Tour participants should include, in addition to the IRS examiner(s), one executive of the nonprofit organization and one lawyer representing the organization. The executive should choreograph the tour, leading the agents, pointing out the significant physical features of the premises (such as departments), and stopping at the desks of the most important (and trustworthy) of the employees. The lawyer should be poised to intervene should an employee start imparting information that is inconsistent with a favorable audit outcome. Here is where a blurt or a blunder is most likely; all involved on behalf of the organization should be cautious and on high alert (without appearing so). The plan (and hope) should be to conclude the tour as soon as reasonably possible, without providing information (if any) to the IRS that is deleterious to the organization's tax-exempt status or other tax liability, and with minimal disruption to the operation of the organization and the mood of the staff.

IRS AUDIT PROCESS

Following the fact-gathering phase (responses to IDRs, interviews, tours, conferences, and the like), the revenue agents will analyze the information and begin to discuss tentative findings, concerns, or issues that require resolution. If matters are not resolved, at some point the examination will move into a process of formal notification of issues (with attendant tax consequences), typically in the form of a *notice of proposed adjustment*.

Examination activity may uncover issues for which there is a lack of clear precedent to guide the revenue agent(s). A technical advice process is available by which the headquarters function (National Office) of the Exempt Organizations Division will become involved to establish the government's position. This procedure includes a pre-submission process pursuant to which a consultation occurs between the agents conducting the examination, the nonprofit organization involved, and headquarters personnel.

Should matters still not be resolved, the revenue agent(s) will issue a report. This is known formally as the Revenue Agent's Report and informally as the *30-day letter*. This is because, if the nonprofit organization wishes to challenge one or more findings in the RAR, it has 30 days to do so. The challenge is in the form of a written *protest*, followed by at least one conference. At this point, failing a resolution, the organization battles on, either to an administrative appeal (see below) or by receiving a *90-day letter*, which is the first formal step on the way to litigation (see discussion following).

CLOSING AGREEMENTS

An examination of a nonprofit organization may be settled. The formal way to do this is by means of a *closing agreement*. These agreements are being used with increasing frequency to resolve a variety of exempt organizations matters. This is particularly the case as use of the technical advice procedure declines (due to the length of its time and the nonprofit organization's costs involved). As two IRS officials nicely wrote, a closing agreement in the exempt organizations context is a "remedy for ambivalent conditions."

While not the solution for every disagreement with the IRS, a closing agreement can be, in the words of these officials, a "pragmatic method to resolve sensitive matters in which there are mitigating circumstances." From the standpoint of the IRS, closing agreements "promote compliance" while conserving the IRS's "scarce resources." The agency is able to resolve a compliance problem that otherwise would "consume time and resources (through the revocation or assessment process) and obtains a commitment to future compliance." The nonprofit organization "obtains both certainty that the matter is concluded once and for all and guidance on how to comply in the future."

APPEALS PROCESS

The appeals process within the IRS may take some getting used to. When one thinks of an *appeal* in the contexts of courts, it is a transfer of the dispute from one discrete court to another. With the IRS, the appeal stays within the agency; the decision of the Examination Division of the IRS is appealed to the office of Appeals within the IRS. Nonetheless, the Appeals function in practice amounts to an independent agency; it is detached from the rest of the IRS.

The mission of the Appeals component of the IRS is, in the words of IRS procedures, to "resolve tax controversies, without litigation, on a fair and impartial basis" from the standpoint of the federal government and the taxpayer, and in a manner that will enhance voluntary compliance and public confidence in the integrity and efficiency of the IRS. The Appeals office strives to be independent, and develops and implements measures that balance "customer satisfaction" and "business results." The Chief, Appeals, who reports to the Commissioner of Internal Revenue, is responsible for planning, managing, and executing nationwide activities for the Appeals function.

Arriving at Appeals is often a good development for a nonprofit organization. The difference in approach between that of an examining revenue agent and an appeals officer can be breathtakingly dramatic. An IRS appeals officer is likely to view a tax-exempt organization's circumstances far more sympathetically than did the examining agent(s). The typical pattern is that the examiner will take a hard-line position in the case, proposing revocation of exemption or imposition of a substantial penalty, with the appeals officer willing to work with the organization in preserving its exemption or reducing the penalty. An appeals officer usually will interpret the law more favorably (from the exempt organization's standpoint) and be more flexible in allowing an exempt organization to alter one or more aspects of its operations to retain (or obtain) exemption.

IRS appeals officers in general prefer to resolve tax law disputes by compromising on amounts due, such as taxes or penalties. Often the amount at issue will be halved, simply to close the case. In the tax-exempt organizations context, this mindset works when the issue is a penalty for failure to timely file an annual information return, assessment of unrelated business income tax, and the like. This approach cannot be taken, of course, when the issue is exempt status. As one appeals officer was heard to say, an organization cannot be "partially exempt."

A nonprofit organization with an appeals case involving eligibility for tax exemption may find that the appeals officer will uphold exempt status if the organization pays a certain amount of money to the IRS. This sum (which usually is negotiable) may be rather arbitrary, being the officer's determination as to what is fair recompense to the government for processing the case. This sum may be roughly equivalent to the amount of income tax the organization would have had to pay were it a taxable entity during the examination period.

One problem with Appeals is the length of time it takes to plod through the process; an appeal can easily consume three years. (There are only 12 appeals officers handling tax-exempt organizations matters.) In addition, considerable time can pass before the matter is taken up by an appeals officer. While practitioners do not want to dip into this well too often, a technique for getting some attention in Appeals is to write a letter complaining about the organization's plight to the Taxpayer Advocate Service, with a copy sent to the appeals officer.

RETROACTIVE REVOCATIONS

An outcome of an IRS audit of a nonprofit organization can be revocation of its tax-exempt status. A worse outcome is *retroactive* revocation of exempt status. An exemption ruling may be retroactively revoked if the organization omitted or misstated a material fact (such as in an application for recognition of exemption or an annual information return), operated in a manner materially different from that originally represented, or engaged in a prohibited transaction. A *prohibited transaction* is a transaction entered into for the purpose of diverting a substantial part of an organization's corpus or income from its exempt purpose.

The IRS has the discretion as to whether to revoke an organization's tax-exempt status prospectively or retroactively. This discretion is broad, reviewable by the courts only for its abuse. The IRS is rarely thwarted in this regard. The agency has been known to grant recognition of exemption to an organization, then years later change its mind, and revoke the exemption back to the date the organization was formed, setting the organization up for a huge tax liability. (Most government agencies cannot get away with behavior like this, due to a principle called *fairness*.) Sometimes, a law change triggers retroactive revocation. For example, the IRS introduced rules in 1970 prohibiting exempt schools from maintaining racially discriminatory policies; a school formed in 1959 lost its exemption in 1976 for this reason. The IRS tried to revoke the school's exemption all the way back to 1959, but a court allowed retroactivity only to 1970.

Two court opinions went against the IRS on this point. In one case (1956), the facts did not change during the period involved, the organization adequately disclosed on its annual information returns the facts that prompted the attempted revocation of exemption, there were no misrepresentations of fact, and the proposed assessment of tax was, in the words of the court, "so large as to wipe [the organization] out of existence." The court acknowledged that the IRS can change its policies but wrote that "it is quite a different matter to say that having once changed his mind the Commissioner may arbitrarily and without limit have the effect of that change go back over previous years during which the taxpayer operated under the previous ruling." The court refused to condone this "harsh result." In the second case (2008), the organization's originally stated purpose and operations did not change over the years. A court ruled that the IRS was bound by its initial determination because the organization had been operating in the manner originally represented and that the agency "abused its discretion by retroactively revoking the exempt status it originally granted" to the organization.

CHURCH AUDIT RULES

Special statutory rules apply to IRS inquiries and examinations of churches and conventions and associations of churches. A *church tax inquiry* is any inquiry by the IRS to a church (other than certain requests and a church tax examination) that serves as a basis for determining whether the church qualifies for tax exemption, is carrying any unrelated business, or otherwise is engaged in activities that may be subject to federal taxation. The term *church tax examination* means any examination, for purposes of making one or more of those three determinations, of church records at the request of the IRS or of the religious activities of any church.

The IRS may commence a church tax inquiry only when the agency has satisfied certain *reasonable belief* requirements and certain *notice* requirements. A church tax examination may be undertaken only where certain notice and conference opportunity requirements are met; even then, the examination may proceed only (1) in the case of church records, to the extent necessary to determine the liability for and the amount of any federal tax, and (2) in the case of religious activities, to the extent necessary to determine whether an organization claiming to be a church is indeed a church for any period.

In general, the IRS must complete a church tax inquiry or examination (and make a final determination as to either or both) within a two-year period beginning on the date the examination notice was issued. Also, in general, in the case of a church tax inquiry as to which there is no examination notice, the IRS must complete the inquiry (and make a final determination with respect to it) within the 90-day period beginning on the date the inquiry notice was issued. The running of these two periods may be suspended under certain circumstances.

There are limitations on the ability of the IRS to revoke the tax-exempt status of a church and on the agency's ability to send a notice of deficiency of a tax involved in a church tax examination or otherwise assess a tax underpayment in connection with an examination. Statutes of limitation apply in connection with exempt status revocations and unrelated business income tax assessments and collections. A proceeding to compel compliance with a summons issued in connection with a church tax inquiry or examination may be stayed under certain circumstances. Limitations are imposed on the ability of the IRS to conduct subsequent inquiries about or examinations of a church.

LITIGATION

When there is a federal tax issue involving a nonprofit organization that cannot be resolved administratively (that is, within the IRS), the matter may be taken to court. Again, the issue may be tax-exempt status, public charity status, or unrelated business, or the like. There are two basic pathways to the courthouse.

An organization facing loss of tax-exempt status or similar adverse treatment at the hands of the IRS may, once all administrative remedies have been exhausted, petition the U.S. Tax Court for relief following the issuance of a notice of tax deficiency, or it may pay a tax and sue for a refund in the appropriate federal district court or the U.S. Court of Federal Claims, following expiration of a statutory six-month waiting period.

A special declaratory judgment procedure is available by which to litigate the tax status of charitable organizations (exempt and/or public charity status) and farmers' cooperatives. Again, appropriate administrative remedies must be exhausted or time periods must have run out. There is no need to pay any tax to come within the jurisdiction of the court. This declaratory judgment jurisdiction is vested in the U.S. District Court for the District of Columbia, the U.S. Court of Federal Claims, and the U.S. Tax Court.

Checklist

❏ Has the organization been the subject of an IRS audit?
  Yes _____ No _____

What were the reasons for the audit? _____

What was the outcome of the audit? _____

❏ Has the organization been the subject of an IRS compliance check?
  Yes _____ No _____

What was the reason for the compliance check? _____

What was the outcome of the compliance check? _____

❏ Did the audit or compliance check result in any change in governance or other practices? Yes _____ No _____

If yes, what were these changes? _____

CHAPTER TWENTY-FIVE

Avoiding Personal Liability

Of all the labels that might be applied to U.S. society in the opening years of the twenty-first century, the Age of Litigation often seems the most appropriate. These days, it seems, anyone can sue someone else for just about any reason and for enormous amounts of money. The only restraint (which is rarely applied) is a judge's rejection of a frivolous lawsuit or a state's principles of legal ethics limiting a lawyer's ability to bring unwarranted litigation.

AVOIDING PERSONAL LIABILITY

There are six ways in which an individual who is a director (or trustee) or officer of a nonprofit organization can avoid personal liability. Five of these ways are listed subsequently, amplified with checklists and chapter references. The sixth way is this: The individual should, at all times, engage in behavior that prevents (or at least significantly minimizes) the possibility of personal liability even if the organization itself is found liable. The individual is a fiduciary and has a duty to act in a prudent manner. Constant awareness of that duty offers a measure of self-protection.

Here are the ways to avoid personal liability while fulfilling the spirit and the rules of fiduciary responsibility.

(a) Understand the Organization

Learn about the legal form of the organization and its structure. For example, if the organization is a corporation, obtain copies of its articles of incorporation and bylaws, and *read them*. Compare the organization's operating methods with the structure and procedures that are reflected in these documents. (One common problem is that an organization is operating as a membership organization even though its articles of incorporation state that it shall not have members. In an extreme example, a venerable organization was happily operating for decades, until one of its new directors happened to read the articles of incorporation. The document stated that the organization "shall cease to exist" as of 1946!)

Checklist

- ❏ Articles of incorporation and bylaws
- ❏ Application filed with the IRS to secure recognition of tax-exempt status (Chapter 6)

❏ Similar applications filed with state authorities, principally for income tax or real property tax exemptions

❏ Annual financial statements prepared by accountants, accompanying auditors' letters, and notes to the financial statements

❏ Annual information returns filed with the IRS (Chapter 7)

❏ Annual reports filed as required in some states

❏ Minutes of directors' meetings, particularly those held since the beginning of personal service or election to office

❏ Any other documents, correspondence, or memos preserved and made available by the organization's secretary or librarian

(b)   Understand the Organization's Activities

Learn how the organization operates—the purposes of its programs; their rank order of priority (as shown by budgeted allowances); their number, possible overlap, and membership support.

Checklist

❏ Review the documents that state the organization's purpose. Is each of its programs being operated in furtherance of that purpose?
Yes _____   No _____

❏ If no:

Should one or more of the organization's programs be discontinued?
Yes _____   No _____

Alternatively, should the organization's statement of purpose be expanded to accommodate the current scope of activities? Yes _____   No _____

Review the annual information returns the organization has filed with the IRS. Are the programs being accurately and adequately described?
Yes _____   No _____

Is the organization making an accurate distinction between its lobbying efforts (if any) and its other programs? (Chapter 13) Yes _____   No _____

(c)   Understand the Organization's Other Operations

Committees, subsidiaries, directors' "pet projects," members' personal interests or contacts, or community needs may have introduced activities (and budget expenditures) that were not authorized in the normal way. Some may deserve more recognition and support, while others may be innocently jeopardizing the tax-exempt status. Find out exactly what the organization is *doing*.

Checklist

❏ Are all necessary returns and reports being filed on time?
Yes _____   No _____

❏ If the organization is involved in fundraising, are all of the state laws being followed? (Chapter 9) Yes _____ No _____

❏ If you are a director, are you comfortable with all of the compensation arrangements? (Chapters 4 and 10) Yes _____ No _____

❏ Does the organization have one or more for-profit subsidiaries? (Chapter 15) Yes _____ No _____

❏ Does it participate in:

Any partnerships? (Chapter 16) Yes _____ No _____

Any other joint ventures? Yes _____ No _____

❏ Does it have:

A related lobbying organization? Yes _____ No _____

A related political action committee? Yes _____ No _____

A related fundraising foundation? Yes _____ No _____

❏ Are you comfortable with each and every one of these arrangements? Yes _____ No _____

(d) Ask Questions

Directors should never be afraid to ask about any arrangement or information that is unclear to them. An individual with fiduciary responsibility should not worry about asking "dumb questions" in front of the other directors; many of them probably have the same questions on their minds. Review the structural arrangements. Study the organization's finances. It's part of the individual's duties.

Checklist

❏ Do you understand the committee structure? Yes _____ No _____

❏ Do you fully understand the work of the committee (or committees) that you serve on? Yes _____ No _____

❏ Who is available at board meetings to answer questions?

The organization's lawyer? Yes _____ No _____

The accountant? Yes _____ No _____

The investment advisor? Yes _____ No _____

The fundraising consultant? Yes _____ No _____

(Beware of too many No answers.)

❏ In your opinion, does the organization have too many directors? Yes _____ No _____

❏ Is there a conflict-of-interest policy for directors? Yes _____ No _____

❏ Does the organization have a planned giving program? (Chapter 4) Yes _____ No _____

❑ Does the board have a "retreat" once in a while to reflect on what the organization is doing and why? Yes _____ No _____

❑ If you are a director or officer, do you contribute money or property to the organization? Yes _____ No _____

If no, why not?

❑ Are you opposed to any policy of the organization?
Yes _____ No _____

(If you were on the board when the policy was adopted, is your opposition recorded in the minutes?)

❑ If you are a director, do you miss meetings of the board?
Yes _____ No _____

(If yes, be sure that the reason for your missing a meeting is stated in the minutes.)

(e) Read Current Relevant Materials

Magazine articles and books describing the proper role for directors and officers of nonprofit organizations will help to update your knowledge of permissible and innovative practices and applicable legal opinions. Periodically, attend a seminar or conference for directors of nonprofit organizations. At almost any time, if someone were to ask you, you should be prepared to answer the questions that follow.

Checklist

❑ What is the tax-exempt status of the organization?

(IRC § _____; usually § 501(c)(_____))

❑ If the organization is a charitable one, is it *public*_____ or *private*_____?
(Chapter 11)

❑ If it is a public charity, which type is it?

❑ Donative public charity

❑ Service-provider public charity

❑ Supporting organization

❑ Other

❑ When was the last time you read the fundraising literature of the organization? Are you aware of what is currently being circulated?
Yes _____ No _____

❑ Has the organization been audited by state authorities in the past five years?
Yes _____ No _____

❑ Has the organization been audited by the IRS in the past five years?
Yes _____ No _____

❑ Has the organization recently had a *legal audit*—a thorough analysis, by a competent lawyer, of the organization's structure, operations, and law compliance?
Yes _____ No _____

❑ Are you aware of any activity (or lack of activity) within the organization that you suspect may bring liability to the organization and/or any of its directors or officers? Yes _____ No _____

❑ Can you honestly say that you are treating the assets and other resources of the organization as you are treating your own? Yes _____ No _____

(This answer has positive meaning only if you are treating your own resources in a prudent manner.)

No one can guarantee that a nonprofit organization will not be sued or that its directors and officers will not be sued. But if these techniques for achieving and maintaining fiduciary responsibility are followed, there is little possibility that personal liability will be found.

PROTECT AGAINST PERSONAL LIABILITY

As mentioned previously, self-protection, stemming from prudent behavior and fulfillment of fiduciary responsibility, can ensure that personal liability is avoided. A key source of protection is overlooked too often: Be certain that, if at all possible, the organization is incorporated. This is critical. Remember that the incorporated organization is clearly a separate legal entity, and the corporate form usually serves as a shield against personal liability. Most lawyers advise their individual clients not to sit on the board of directors of a nonprofit organization that is not incorporated. If you are an officer or director of a nonprofit organization and it is not incorporated, find out why not. Do not accept reasons for failure to incorporate lightly (see Chapter 1). In the case of the organization that was sued because an individual did not receive an award (see Chapter 8), the organization was not incorporated and its volunteer president was personally sued. (Soon afterward, the organization became incorporated, although that did not resolve the immediate problem.)

Checklist

❑ Is the organization incorporated? Yes _____ No _____

❑ If it is not incorporated, are you comfortable with that?
Yes _____ No _____

❑ Does the organization have an indemnification clause in its articles of organization? If not, why not? Yes _____ No _____

❑ Are you satisfied with the scope of the indemnification?
Yes _____ No _____

❑ Does the organization have adequate assets to back up this indemnification?
Yes _____ No _____

❑ Does the organization have an officers' and directors' liability insurance policy? If not, why not? Yes _____ No _____

❑ Have you read the policy? Yes _____ No _____

❏ Are you aware that the largest single section of the policy is likely to be the portion that details *exclusions*—what the policy does *not* cover?
Yes _____ No _____

❏ Do you know and understand the exclusions in your policy?
Yes _____ No _____

❏ Are you comfortable with these exclusions? Yes _____ No _____

❏ Is the indemnification broader than the insurance coverage?
Yes _____ No _____

❏ Is the insurance coverage broader? Yes _____ No _____

❏ Does the law in your state provide some form of statutory immunity by which personal liability arising out of service for a nonprofit organization is avoided as a matter of law? Yes _____ No _____

❏ If conditions are attached to the immunity, do you (and/or the organization) satisfy these conditions? Yes _____ No _____

❏ In some states, the language that triggers the immunity must be in the organization's articles of incorporation/organization or bylaws. If this is required, does your organization's organizational documents contain this language?
Yes _____ No _____

(If the organization operates in more than one state, be certain to check on the immunity laws in each of those states.)

If a director or officer follows these guidelines and maximizes use of the *four I's*—indemnification, insurance, immunity, and incorporation—he or she can almost be guaranteed that personal liability for service for a nonprofit organization will be avoided. In any event, the individual will know that he or she did everything possible to avoid liability.

Nonprofit organizations need and deserve the best leadership they can find. It is important to serve. It is also important to serve prudently.

Epilogue

Nonprofit organizations are an expanding component of today's American society. They affect the lives of people nationwide. They are, as stressed in Chapter 1, a most distinguishing characteristic that differentiates the United States from all other countries. When grappling with problems, our nation is willing to rely on institutions other than governmental ones. They are a treasured national resource—or are they?

Many individuals truly treasure nonprofit organizations and demonstrate this feeling by giving of their money, expertise, and time, because they comprehend the value of pluralism and voluntarism. Most Americans generally have a positive attitude toward nonprofit entities—their church, synagogue, hospital, or alma mater. Yet, a growing minority is not particularly sympathetic toward nonprofits, and is, in some instances, hostile toward them. Persons in this latter category serve in legislatures; are employees of legislators; preside in courtrooms; or are federal, state, or local regulators. There are some in the U.S. Congress, for example, who see nonprofit organizations as the most unregulated of sectors in our society or who see "too many" of them—and they are working to remedy either or both perceived "deficiencies." (See Chapter 3, Myth 23.)

Nonprofit organizations are not on the brink of extinction; they undoubtedly have decades of service yet to come. Some troubling signs, however, suggest that the law climate for nonprofit organizations may soon be dramatically different.

UNDERSTANDING THE MODERN NONPROFIT

Many today do not understand (or profess to not understand) the contemporary nonprofit organization. From one quarter or another, this refrain persists: "I can no longer tell the difference between nonprofit and for-profit organizations." Tax-exempt hospitals, for example, hear this almost daily. As today's exempt colleges and universities know all too well, accumulation of wealth (traditionally known as endowments) is being trumpeted as evidence that tax exemption has been forfeited. Nonprofit organizations are often seen as competing with or "acting just like" commercial businesses.

Two aspects of all of this are constantly bandied about. In a way, they are the two sides of the same coin. It is said by some (too many actually, and often by those who should know better) that for an organization to be charitable, it should provide its goods or services without charge. This matter is amplified in Chapter 3 (see Myth 22). It is also often noted that an organization should not be tax-exempt if it charges fees. This view is also amplified in Chapter 3 (see Myth 21).

Thus, in the years to come, many nonprofit organizations will be struggling as the law changes and swirls about, with its focus on commerciality, competition, fee-charging, and the presence or absence of charitable giving. More forms of excise taxes, new payout requirements, and expansion of the private benefit doctrine are likely to prove vexing for the nonprofit community.

WHERE ARE NONPROFITS HEADED?

From a lawyer's vantage point, this question is easy to answer: Nonprofit organizations are headed for more regulation. More regulation does not (necessarily) mean elimination of nonprofits, but additional regulation is a threat. It raises suspicions in the minds of some public donors, tempts more than a few legislators into seeking even more regulatory control, and generally is a drag on the system (most notably, when it comes to charitable giving).

There are two things the members of the nonprofit community can do to improve their prospects for keeping some autonomy. Probably neither will be done, in part because the recommendations are somewhat inconsistent but largely because of human nature's adherence to the status quo, inertia, and fear of the unknown. One entails self-restraint; the other, more involvement in the political process.

Addressing the second point first, the nonprofit community has come a long way in recent years in participation in the legislative process at the federal level. It is more adept than ever in influencing the legislative process as practiced by the U.S. Congress. And this is not easy. If approaches are not handled with some sensitivity and skill, the nonprofit world's emissaries to the legislatures become perceived as merely another pack of lobbyists—often a counterproductive development—instead of a well-intentioned group pursuing the public weal. Also, as Chapters 14 and 15 point out, when nonprofit organizations venture into the realm of legislative and political campaign activities, they face numerous sanctions.

Still, much more action can be taken. Here are some suggestions:

- *More interaction with grass-roots resources.* Federal legislators (particularly those in the House of Representatives) pay attention to their constituencies. Representatives of nonprofit organizations must befriend their members of Congress and visit them often, in Washington and in the local districts. These legislators can become informed as to the organizations' programs and other activities, including fundraising plans and problems. (Legislators can identify with this: They are fundraisers too.) Nonprofits must learn to lobby when adverse legislation is not imminent; keeping up the relationships month to month, year in and year out, makes the real lobbying easier and more effective—and, in the long run, less necessary. Not all of this type of activity is involvement in the legislative process, so the sanctions are not always a problem. Besides, nonprofit organizations, including charitable ones, can usually lobby much more than they believe they can.

- *More activities that affect public opinion.* Ideally, there would be ongoing media coverage of nonprofit organizations' good works. Articles, press releases, studies, op-ed columns, and the like should routinely flow. Nonprofit organizations can engage in research activities and other projects that yield substantive results to community and business leaders and to legislators and their staffs. Expanded public relations would enhance the image of nonprofits, educate and remind the public of their heritage and role in contemporary society, and—in the process—probably pave the way for more successful fundraising. When the public is favorable toward a particular subject, the politicians tend to be as well, and the opponents find the opposing harder going.

- *More self-education.* Those who manage and advise nonprofit organizations must learn more about the basics of the law affecting them. (This book is written in that spirit.) Much difficulty could be avoided—whether from an IRS audit or a suit of personal liability against a director—if just the fundamentals were mastered. Conferences and seminars abound, but for some reason, those who need the word are not getting it. There are massive gaps in understanding of, for example, fundraising regulation (and techniques), the requirements for keeping tax-exempt status, the unrelated income rules, the intermediate sanctions penalties, and the annual reporting obligations.

- *Making better use of political action committees (PACs).* Like nonprofit organizations, members of Congress and other legislators need financial support—and they tend to be responsive to those who provide it to them. The world needs some PACs for the nonprofits' causes. Even those in the charitable community could experiment with the use of independent PACs.

Regarding self-restraint, one aspect of it is directly associated with the *pig theory*. This theory has it that a good idea can evolve into a massive mistake that adversely affects everyone, when the idea is pushed to its outer limits. The idea as implemented in the early stages is a good one; but, as others begin to use it, the idea becomes transformed into something different and certainly something more extensive. The practice expands until it attracts the attention of a legislature, which either taxes the income involved or outlaws the practice altogether. The lawmakers may pass very restrictive legislation that not only wipes out the entire undertaking (including the original good idea) but leaves the community more restricted and regulated than it was before the good idea was initially implemented. (A case in point is Congress's reaction to the very idea of charitable split-dollar insurance plans; see Chapter 16.) Another example of the pig theory can be seen in the evolving doctrine of commerciality. This doctrine cuts across tax exemption and unrelated income issues and applies to nearly all forms of nonprofit organizations.

Many nonprofit organizations have become obligated to sustain themselves and their beneficiaries by pursuing funding from new sources, now that some of the conventional ones are proving insufficient. (This is, by the way, no secret in Washington, D.C.; the General Accounting Office observed that "[a]s a result of growing federal deficits and reduced government spending for social services, tax-exempt organizations are being asked to assume a greater share in the funding of these services" and "[t]herefore, it is likely that in seeking sources of funds, tax-exempt organizations will continue to increase their UBI [unrelated business income] activity.") As they turn to the service-provider approach, they embark on fundraising ventures that, while innocent enough at the outset, expand economically and in visibility until the business community is antagonized and until some legislative body is activated.

Four examples of this are the enactment by Congress, in 1984, of the tax-exempt entity leasing rules; in 1986, of the tax rule causing the offering of commercial-type insurance to be either a basis for loss of tax exemption or an unrelated business; in 1996, of the intermediate sanctions penalties; and, in 2006, legislation that severely damaged supporting organizations and brought statutory regulation of donor-advised funds. Before the doctrine of commerciality matures, it is likely to challenge many existing notions of what is required to qualify as a tax-exempt organization, rewrite portions of the law of unrelated income taxation, and pit some nonprofit organizations against others.

The overall future for nonprofit organizations is bright, although along the way they are going to have to achieve a better public understanding of their role in society and, to some extent, learn to live with a redefinition of that role. There is much that nonprofit organizations can do to affect these developments. The proactive techniques suggested above can be blended with self-restraint. It is, admittedly, a tall order.

THE LONGER VIEW

Too many people regard tax-exempt organizations as quaint anachronisms of another era—forms of institutional life no longer suited for today and the future. The thought that exempt organizations, or most of them, are destined for extinction may be tested against the thinking of futurists.

For example, Alvin Toffler, writing in *The Third Wave*, envisioned great change in the nature of "increased diversity" in "ideas, political convictions, sexual proclivities, educational methods, eating habits, religious views, ethnic attitudes, musical tastes, fashions, and family forms." This development (stimulated by what he termed the "de-massification" of society), he believed, will lead to a splintering and/or reshaping of many of society's institutions—both a decentralizing and a fragmenting process. If nothing else, this result would mean more tax-exempt (or at least, nonprofit) organizations. As an illustration, Toffler saw this demassification occurring in U.S. political life when he described the "sudden, bewildering proliferation of high-powered splinter groups." Concerning the future of nonprofit organizations, Toffler clearly expected not only more of them but an expanded role for them.

Toffler predicted a greater diversity in organized religion and the emergence of new religions. He expected that a "host of new religions, new conceptions of science, new images of human nature, new forms of art will arise—in far richer diversity than was possible or necessary during the industrial age." He foresaw new educational organizations and new educational methods. Toffler predicted restructuring of curricula, revisions in the concept of grading, increased parental influence on the schools, and a lessening in the number of years of compulsory schooling; in general, he expected new forms of consultancies, massive changes in the modes of educational instruction (because of the advent of word processors, home computers, and telecommunications), and new opportunities in instruction and publishing. He predicted new advances and diversification of organizations in the fields of health and science. Nonprofit organizations should be in the forefront of what Toffler termed "[f]antastic scientific advances," yet ironically also very much involved in the resistance to new technology, being part of the organizational effort of "humanizing the technological thrust." He foresaw significant changes in health care delivery systems, with obvious implications for the nonprofit community.

Concerning the nation's political system, Toffler called for nothing less than the "design of new, more appropriate political structures." One of the pathways to this objective, he said, was "imaginative new arrangements for accommodating and legitimating diversity—new institutions that are sensitive to the rapidly shifting needs of changing and multiplying minorities." Nonprofit organizations will certainly be a part of this process, both as entities that help to design the new political process and as participatory elements of it.

In his wide-ranging analysis of life tomorrow, Toffler speculated on some of the needs arising in the future and on ways to satisfy them. Many of these ways would require the use of nonprofit organizations.

For example, Toffler discussed some of the problems that cannot be solved by national governments individually (such as inflation, activities of transnational corporations, arms trade, outer space governance, and interlocking currencies). He stated that "[w]e desperately need, therefore, to invent imaginative new institutions at the transnational level to which many decisions can be transferred" and called for "consortia and teams of nongovernmental organizations to attack various global problems."

Likewise, he wrote of the need to enable a variety of minorities to regulate more of their own affairs. To this end, he speculated, "We might, for example, help the people in a specific neighborhood, in a well-defined subculture, or in an ethnic group, to set up their own youth courts under the supervision of the state, disciplining their own young people rather than relying on the state to do so." He rationalized this suggestion in terms embodying some well-recognized tax law doctrines for such groups: "Such institutions would build community and identity, and contribute to law and order, while relieving the overburdened government institutions of unnecessary work."

In still another example of new nonprofit organization life forms, Toffler postulated the use of "semi-cults"—organizations that "lie somewhere between [the application of] structureless freedom and tightly structured regimentation." These groups were envisioned by him as a means to impose a certain degree of structure where and as long as it was required, yet persons would be able to return freely to productive life in society. He also suggested a variant of these entities to provide community services.

The conclusions of another futurist, John Naisbitt, parallel those of Toffler. Writing in *Megatrends*, Naisbitt also found, in the shift from an industrial society to an information society, the "evolution of a highly personal value system to compensate for the impersonal nature of technology," the transformation from national economics to a world economy, the emphasis on long-term concepts rather than short-term thinking, the change from centralization to decentralization, the shift from institutional help to self-help, the evolution from representative democracy to participatory democracy (within both government and large corporations), and the change from hierarchies to networking.

While Naisbitt, like Toffler, found no occasion to specifically address the future of nonprofit organizations as such, he foresaw growth in the human potential and self-help movements, massive changes in the delivery of education and healthcare, new political initiatives, the development of networking, and the emergence of new religions—all of which would inevitably utilize nonprofit organizations. Neither of these futurists wrote of any need to preserve tax exemption for nonprofit organizations—perhaps they simply assumed that it will continue. Toffler, for one, is not opposed to this type of use of the tax system, however; in his book, he calls for the application of tax incentives to help accomplish particular objectives.

This citation of futurists' suggestions and predictions is not intended to endorse any particular vein of futurist thinking or the necessary evolution of any particular form of tax-exempt organization, but only to suggest that unfolding societal needs are likely to heavily entail the active involvement of nonprofit (tax-exempt) organizations. Toffler's prognostications indicate an exciting and meaningful future, replete with a large dosage of the American tendency to create *associations*. Toffler's premise suggests that nonprofit organizations are an integral part of the American societal and political structure and that the concern for the immediate future is not whether nonprofit groups are a dying breed but whether they are to be seriously endangered by evolving tax and fundraising regulation policy.

It is projected that nonprofit (hopefully, tax-exempt) organizations will very much remain in the nation's future. The future, however, holds considerable changes in tax law, fundraising law, and other matters such as governance of nonprofit organizations, personal liability, and compensation forms. These changes will heavily impact the operations of the nation's nonprofit organizations as they cope with the new regulatory climate in the twenty-first century.

Glossary

Some of the terms listed here may seem deceptively simple. What could be plainer, for example, than *additional tax*? The law of nonprofit organizations, however, has some complex and specialized definitions and applications for apparently ordinary terms. In some instances, it is inadvisable to try to paraphrase or "popularize" them. My best advice to readers, generally, is to supplement the Glossary by going directly to the Internal Revenue Code sections cited here and reading the original definitions and discussions. A key factor in successfully starting and managing a nonprofit organization is to know what the IRS says about a particular topic and what it means when it says it.

Abatement. In general, a decrease or diminution; in the nonprofit organization tax law context, relief from a tax liability. For example, the IRS has the ability to abate an *intermediate sanctions* penalty and nearly all of the *excise taxes* imposed on *private foundations* (IRC § 4962).

Actuary. A specialist in projecting amounts of income, interest, or expense over future periods of time. Actuaries create the tables used in calculating *income interests* and *remainder interests*, which are important in implementing planned giving.

Additional tax. Under the tax rules that apply to private foundations, *initial* (excise) *taxes* are assessed first, on the foundations and their managers, as a method of enforcing the rules. If the offense is not corrected, *additional* (excise) *taxes* or "second-tier taxes" are added to encourage compliance with the rules. A similar two-tiered tax structure is part of the *intermediate sanctions* tax regime.

Adjusted gross income. In the case of an individual, the before-taxes amount that results when certain deductions are subtracted from his or her gross income (IRC § 62).

Advisory committee. A group of individuals who make their expertise and experience—and sometimes their celebrity—available to the *board of directors* of a *nonprofit organization*; a technique for attracting well-known persons to service for an organization without causing them to become involved in its actual governance.

Advocacy. The active espousal of a position, a point of view, or a course of action; it can include *lobbying, political activity*, demonstrations, boycotts, litigation, and various forms of program activity.

Affinity card. This is a credit card issued by, or in connection with, a commercial financial institution, where the users of the cards are confined to the membership or other constituency of a *tax-exempt organization*; a percentage of the resulting profit is paid to the exempt organization. If the card arrangement is structured properly, the exempt organization receives the payments (as income) as a tax-excludable *royalty*.

Agricultural organization. An organization described in IRC § 501(c)(5).

Amateur sports organization. An organization formed and operated exclusively to foster national or international amateur sports competition, to conduct national or international competitive sports events, or to support and develop amateur athletes for national or international competition in sports (IRC § 501(j)).

Annual information return. The return that is required to be filed by most *tax-exempt organizations* annually with the IRS (Form 990).

Annuity. A regular payment of a set amount of money for a person's life (or persons' lives), or for a period of years. An annuity may be payable as the result of creation of a *charitable gift annuity* or a *charitable remainder annuity trust*.

Apostolic association. A religious organization that has a common treasury or community treasury, even if it engages in business for the common benefit of its members. The members of the organization include in their gross income their entire pro rata shares, whether or not distributed, of the taxable income of the organization (IRC § 501(d)).

Application for recognition of exemption. The IRS form by which a *nonprofit organization* seeks recognition of tax-exempt status from the IRS (usually Form 1023 or 1024).

Appraisal. The determination of the fair market value of a property, as in the valuation of property that is the subject of a *charitable contribution*.

Appraiser. An individual who is in the business of making *appraisals*. An independent appraiser is mandated in connection with charitable gifts of property with a value in excess of $5,000.

Appreciated property. Property that has increased in value so that its fair market value has become greater than its cost basis (IRC §§ 170(b)(1)(C) and 170(e)).

Appreciation element. The component of value that represents the difference between the cost basis and the fair market value of an item of property.

Articles of incorporation. See *articles of organization*.

Articles of organization. The generic term for the document used to create a *nonprofit organization*; articles of incorporation in the case of a corporation; a constitution in the case of an unincorporated association; a *trust agreement* or *declaration of trust* in the case of a trust.

Association. An organization, usually nonprofit and tax-exempt, that has a membership, whether of individuals or organizations. Generally, a membership association is a tax-exempt organization described in IRC § 501(c)(6).

Attorney. A word commonly used as a synonym for "lawyer"; anyone who is acting on behalf of another and who has the authority to do so (as in power of attorney).

Audit. The process whereby the IRS examines the books and records of an organization, as well as witnesses, in search of compliance with the internal revenue laws (IRC §§ 7601–7611).

Award. A gift of cash or property in recognition of an achievement, usually taxable to the recipient unless immediately transferred to a *charitable organization* (IRC § 74).

Bargain sale. A transaction whereby a person transfers property to a *charitable organization* for less than its fair market value, thereby making the transaction part sale and part gift (IRC § 1011(b)).

Basis. The cost amount for the acquisition of an item of property, plus certain subsequent expenditures (IRC § 1012).

Benevolent. A term sometimes used as a synonym for *charitable*, although it is of broader scope than charitable. It is not formally used in the federal tax law rules, but sometimes is found in state and local laws.

Benevolent life insurance association. An organization described in IRC § 501(c)(12).

Bequest. A gift of personal property made by means of a will.

Black Lung benefit trust. An organization described in IRC § 501(c)(21).

Board of directors. Two or more individuals who serve as the governing body of an organization; see *board of trustees*.

Board of trade. An organization described in IRC § 501(c)(6).

Board of trustees. The same as a *board of directors*, except that the organization involved is usually a trust or a *charitable* entity.

Business league. An organization described in IRC § 501(c)(6).

Bylaws. The document of an organization that contains its rules of operation; in some jurisdictions, the term "code of regulations" is used.

Byrd Amendment. This body of law restricts the use of federal funds that are awarded to recipients of federal contracts, grants, loans, or cooperative agreements. The funds received may not be used to pay persons to influence or attempt to influence government agency employees or legislative decision makers in connection with the awarding of any contract, grant, loan, or cooperative agreement. Certain reporting requirements are imposed as well.

Capital asset. Property held by a person, whether or not connected with a trade or business; does not include inventory, depreciable property used in a business, certain literary or artistic compositions, and certain publications of the U.S. Government (IRC § 1221).

Capital campaign. A *fundraising* program designed to generate *contributions* for a *charitable* organization's capital, usually for a building, a major item of equipment, or an *endowment fund*.

Cause-related marketing. Fundraising techniques used to generate nongift revenues, involving *related* and/or *unrelated* activities; the term usually includes *charitable sales promotions* and other forms of *commercial co-ventures*.

Cemetery company. An organization described in IRC § 501(c)(13).

Chairperson of the board. An individual selected, usually by a *board of directors*, to be the leader of the board; this is not usually an *officer* position, although it can be when so provided in *articles of organization* or *bylaws*; in some instances, an individual denominated "chairman" or "chair" of the board.

Chamber of commerce. An organization described in IRC § 501(c)(6).

Charitable. The description of a purpose, activity, or organization that the applicable law, such as the federal tax law (principally, IRC § 501(c)(3)), regards as meeting at least one of the required *charitable* objectives (see Chapter 4).

Charitable contribution. A *contribution* made to a *charitable* organization; sometimes, a contribution made to a noncharitable organization for a *charitable* purpose.

Charitable contribution deduction. A *deduction* available, under certain federal, state, and local laws, for an amount of money or property transferred to a *charitable* organization (e.g., IRC § 170).

Charitable gift annuity. An arrangement whereby property is transferred to a *charitable* organization in exchange for an *annuity*. The donated value of the property in excess of the value of the annuity is a *charitable contribution*.

Charitable lead trust. A trust used to facilitate the contribution of a *lead interest* or *income interest* to a *charitable organization* (IRC § 514(c)(5)).

Charitable organization. An organization that is formed and operated for what the applicable law, such as the federal tax law (principally, IRC § 501(c)(3)), regards as a *charitable* purpose.

Charitable remainder trust. A form of *split-interest trust* that is used to split an item of property into an *income interest* and a *remainder interest*, usually to facilitate a deductible contribution of the remainder interest to a *charitable* organization.

Charitable sales promotion. An undertaking that essentially is the same as a *commercial co-venture*.

Charitable solicitation acts. State laws that regulate the process of soliciting *contributions* for *charitable* purposes.

Charity care standard. A standard of law that was once the basis of tax exemption for non-profit hospitals. It is premised largely on the view that tax-exempt status for hospitals should be based on a definition of the term *charitable*, which emphasizes relief of the poor. Under this standard (which is the law in some states), a hospital, to be tax-exempt, must provide a substantial portion of its health care services without cost or on a reduced-rate basis.

Civic league. An organization described in IRC § 501(c)(4); also known as a *social welfare organization.*

Civil society. A society organized as a democratic state, in that it has a pluralization of institutions; it has a governmental sector, a nonprofit sector, and a for-profit sector.

Code of ethics. A statement of principles established by a nonprofit membership organization and used to affect the professional behavior of its members. Ethical principles are not necessarily the same as law; typically they are loftier and idealistic. The ability of an individual or other person to remain a member of an organization may require compliance with its code of ethics.

Commensurate test. This test, which the IRS is planning to apply more frequently, assesses whether a *charitable organization* is maintaining program activities to a sufficient extent in relation to, or commensurate in scope with, its financial resources; failure to pass this text can cause an organization to lose its exemption.

Commercial. Conduct of an activity by a *nonprofit organization* in a manner similar to the way in which for-profit organizations conduct the same activity; the only federal law statutory illustration of this to date is the set of rules concerning *commercial-type insurance* (IRC § 501(m)).

Commercial co-venture. An arrangement between a for-profit organization and a *charitable* organization (sometimes more than one), whereby the for-profit entity agrees to make a *contribution* to the charitable entity, with the amount of the contribution determined by the volume of sales of products or services by the for-profit organization during a particular time period.

Commerciality. An emerging doctrine stating that an activity conducted in a *commercial* manner is deemed, for that reason alone, to be a nonexempt activity.

Commercial-type insurance. Generally, any insurance that is typically provided by commercial insurance companies. A *charitable organization* or a *social welfare organization* cannot be tax-exempt if a substantial part of its activities consists of the provision of commercial-type insurance (IRC § 501(m)).

Community benefit standard. The basis for the present-day rationale for the federal tax exemption of nonprofit hospitals; it is predicated on the fact that one of the definitions of the term *charitable* is the promotion of health. Thus, to be tax-exempt under federal law, a hospital must promote the health of a class of persons broad enough to represent an entire community and must be operated to serve a public interest.

Community chest. One of the types of organizations described in IRC § 501(c)(3).

Conflict-of-interest policy. This is a policy by which a *tax-exempt organization* defines, for its purposes, what a conflict of interest is and to whom the policy applies, and provides for periodic disclosure and, if necessary, resolution of conflicts.

Consideration. The element of value in a bargain; something exchanged to receive something in return, as when both parties to a *contract* receive consideration.

Constitution. See *articles of organization.*

Constructive receipt. A doctrine that applies to tax funds received by an individual or other person, at the time he, she, or it has the right to possession of or access to the money. The person may not yet have actual receipt of the funds, but the law treats the person as if that were the case; this is also known as the rule of "economic benefit."

Consultant.   One who provides services to an organization in a capacity other than as an *employee*, such as an accountant, fundraising counsel, or lawyer; an independent contractor.

Contract.   A set of promises between two or more persons that creates, revises, or eliminates a legal relationship; a set of promises underlain by *consideration*.

Contribution.   A transfer by one person to another of money or property without an expectation of any material return; a transfer of money or property without *consideration*.

Contribution base.   An amount equal to what is, essentially, an individual's *adjusted gross income*; used in computing the extent to which *charitable contributions* are deductible in a year (IRC § 170(b)(1)(F)).

Cooperative hospital service organization.   An organization that performs, on a centralized basis, one or more specified services solely for two or more hospitals and is operated on a cooperative basis (IRC § 501(e)).

Cooperative service organization of educational organizations.   An organization that is formed and operated solely to collectively invest in securities for the benefit of public and private schools, colleges, and universities (IRC § 501(f)).

Cooperative telephone company.   An organization described in IRC § 501(c)(12).

Credit union.   An organization described in IRC § 501(c)(14).

Crop financing organization.   An organization described in IRC § 501(c)(16).

Cruelty prevention organization.   One of the organizations described in IRC § 501(c)(3).

Damages.   A form of compensation or restitution paid to a person, usually as the consequence of a lawsuit, for an injury or other loss (suffered personally in the case of an individual or by an organization, or caused by harm to property or violation of rights) occasioned by commission of an unlawful act or some failure to act.

Declaration of trust.   A proclamation by a person of the existence of a trust; see *articles of organization, trust agreement*.

Declaratory judgment.   A declaration by the U.S. Tax Court, the U.S. Court of Federal Claims, or the U.S. District Court for the District of Columbia as to whether an organization is tax-exempt as described in IRC § 501(c)(3), a *charitable* organization (IRC § 170(c)(2)), a *private foundation* or *public charity* (IRC § 509), or a *private operating foundation* (IRC § 4942(j)(3) and IRC § 7428).

Deduction.   An item (usually an expenditure) that is subtracted from *adjusted gross income* to arrive at *taxable income*. An example is the *charitable contribution deduction*.

Defamation.   The effect of one person's publishing something that injures the reputation of another; a written defamation is a "libel" and an oral defamation is a "slander."

Deferred compensation plan.   A program whereby one or more employees of an organization are compensated for services rendered currently but the receipt of the compensation is deferred until a subsequent point in time (such as retirement).

Determination letter.   A letter from the IRS indicating *recognition of tax exemption* for a *nonprofit organization*.

Development program.   In many ways, a program that is the same as a *fundraising* program, although this type of program usually emphasizes *capital campaigns* or planned giving programs.

Devise.   A gift of real property by means of a will.

Direct lobbying.   An attempt to influence the development of *legislation* by contact with legislators, their staffs, or staffs of legislative committees, such as by meetings, correspondence, or testimony at hearings. (See *grass-roots lobbying*.)

Disqualified person.   A person who is a trustee, director, officer, or some other type of *insider* with respect to a *tax-exempt organization*, usually a *charitable* one.

Document-retention and -destruction policy. This policy, adopted by a *tax-exempt organization*, is designed to protect and preserve an organization's important documents, while also facilitating periodic destruction of unneeded documents.

Donor acquisition. A *fundraising* program where the emphasis is on the acquisition of new donors to a *charitable organization* (who, hopefully, will continue to give); also known as "prospecting."

Donor-advised fund. A fund (not a separate organization) maintained by a *public charity* for contributions from one or more donors as to which there is an understanding that the donor(s) may advise the charity regarding the distribution of amounts held in the fund; the fund often bears the name of the donor(s) (IRC §§ 4966, 4967).

Donor renewal. A *fundraising* program where the emphasis is on acquiring *contributions* from those who have previously given (the donor base) to a *charitable organization*.

Dues. Amounts of money paid to an organization for membership services; where these services are *consideration* and the organization is a *charitable* one, the dues are not deductible as *charitable contributions*.

Economic benefit. See *constructive receipt*.

Electioneering. The process of intervening or otherwise participating in a campaign for or against the election of a candidate for public office.

Employee. One who provides services to an organization (the "employer") where he or she is under the direct supervision and control of the organization; usually, the services are provided on the premises of the employer, using the resources of the employer, and under working hours and conditions set by the employer.

Employee's beneficiary association. An organization described in IRC § 501(c)(9).

Employer retirement claim organization. An organization described in IRC § 501(c)(22).

Endowment. An accumulation of *contributions* that are not expended for programs but are held for investment. The earnings (if any) are devoted to program activities, either generally or in a "restricted" manner.

Estate. A term with many meanings, including the property an individual owns at his or her death; federal tax law defines a "taxable estate" (IRC §§ 2051–2057).

Easement. A right, created by an agreement, to make lawful and beneficial use of land owned by another. For example, a *charitable organization* may be given a conservation easement (IRC § 170(h)).

Excess benefit transaction. A transaction where an economic benefit is provided by a *tax-exempt organization* to a *disqualified person*, where the benefit provided is greater than the value of the *consideration* received by the exempt organization for providing the benefit (IRC § 4958).

Excise tax. In the *tax-exempt organizations* context, the sanctions sometimes used to enforce tax law prohibitions—for example, the private foundation rules and the *expenditure test* in the charitable organizations lobbying field.

Exclusion. In the tax context, an item of income that is excluded from the concept of *gross income*, such as a scholarship (IRC § 117).

Exclusivity arrangement. This is a contractual arrangement between a *tax-exempt organization* and a for-profit corporation, by which the latter pays the former a sum of money for selling only the for-profit entity's products or services (that is, for not selling the products or services of a competitor). One of the current issues is whether this type of revenue is taxable as *unrelated business income*.

Executive committee. A subgroup of directors of an organization that has particular influence over the affairs of the organization.

Executive director. An employee of an organization who is assigned the principal responsibility for administering the organization; sometimes termed "president" or "executive vice president"; this may be an *officer* position.

Exempt-function revenue. Funds derived by a tax-exempt organization from the performance of an exempt function, such as revenue from the sale of publications or fees received for conferences or seminars.

Expenditure test. In the context of *lobbying* activities by *public charities*, a test that enables qualifying *charitable organizations* to elect to come under certain standards for more mechanically determining allowable lobbying (IRC § 501(h)).

Farmers' cooperative. An organization described in IRC § 521.

Federal Agents Registration Act. A body of law requiring lobbyists and other agents of foreign governments to register with and report to the Department of Justice.

Feeder organization. An organization, not tax-exempt, that distributes all of its net income of a tax-exempt organization (IRC § 502).

Felony. A criminal act of serious character—it is a graver act than a "misdemeanor." The punishment for the commission of a felony may be death or imprisonment for a period of time longer than one year; most of the state charitable solicitation laws contain penalties by which some violations of these laws are felonies.

Fiduciary. One who is bound to look after the affairs of another, using the same standards of care and prudence as he or she would use in attending to his or her own affairs, as in a trustee of a trust.

Foundation. See *private foundation*.

Fraternal society. An organization described in IRC § 501(c)(8) or § 501(c)(10).

Fundraiser. One who is employed (see *employee*) or retained (see *consultant*) to assist a tax-exempt organization (usually a *charitable* one) in the raising of funds, conventionally in the form of *contributions* and grants, and more recently in the form of *exempt function revenue* or *unrelated* revenue; also known as "professional fundraiser" or "professional fundraising counsel."

Fundraising. In the broadest sense, *fundraising* is the process of soliciting and receiving contributions, usually for a *charitable organization*; there are several categories of fundraising activities, most notably direct mail solicitation, in-person solicitation, private foundation grant solicitation, telemarketing, radio and television solicitation, Internet solicitation, special events (dinners, dances, auctions, and the like), and planned giving.

Gaming. Also known as gambling, this term embraces games of bingo, poker, other card games, raffles, pickle cards, casino nights, and a variety of coin-operated gambling devices.

General partnership. A partnership in which all of the partners are equally liable for satisfaction of the obligations of the partnership.

Grass-roots lobbying. An attempt to influence the legislative process by contacting the general public, or a segment of it, for the purpose of encouraging those individuals to contact the appropriate legislators; see *direct lobbying*.

Gross income. Except as otherwise provided in the IRC, all income from whatever source derived, including compensation for services (IRC § 61(a)); gross income does not include gifts (IRC § 102).

Homeowners' association. An organization described in IRC § 528.

Horticultural organization. One of the organizations described in IRC § 501(c)(5).

Identification number. A number assigned to organizations by the IRS; also termed an "employer identification number" (used even when the organization does not have any employees) (IRC § 6109).

Income interest.   The right to receive all or some portion of the income from property for a stated period of time, either alone or with others.

Independent sector.   The segment of U.S. society represented by nonprofit, principally *charitable*, organizations; also known as the "voluntary sector," "nonprofit sector," or "private sector."

Initial tax.   In the *intermediate sanctions* and *private foundations* contexts, the *excise taxes* that are initially assessable in enforcement of the rules; also known as "first-tier" taxes.

Insider.   This is a *person*, usually an individual, who is in a position to exercise a significant degree of control over the affairs of a *tax-exempt organization*. Generally, an insider is a trustee, director, or officer. The term can also include key employees, members of an insider's family, and entities that an insider controls.

Institutions.   In the *tax-exempt organizations* context, entities such as churches, universities, colleges, schools, and hospitals; these entities are not *private foundations* (IRC § 509(a)(1)).

Intermediate sanctions.   One or more tax penalties that can be levied by the IRS on a *disqualified person* when the person engages in an *excess benefit transaction* with an *applicable tax-exempt* organization (IRC § 4958).

Internal Revenue Code.   The statutory body of federal tax law developed by Congress and administered by the *Internal Revenue Service* (IRS). The current version of the law is the Internal Revenue Code (IRC) of 1986, as amended.

Internal Revenue Service.   The agency of the federal government with the principal responsibility for regulating the activities of *tax-exempt organizations*. The IRS is a component of the Department of the Treasury.

Joint venture.   An undertaking of two or more organizations and/or individuals for the accomplishment of a particular purpose; an arrangement closely akin to a *general partnership*.

Labor organization.   An organization described in IRC § 501(c)(5).

Lead interest.   The same right to income as an *income interest*; so named because, in the planned giving context, an income interest precedes (leads) the *remainder interest*.

Legislation.   General rules of human conduct that are consciously and deliberately stated by a law-making body; a declaration of general principles by a law-making body, to be applied (usually prospectively) to all persons or general classes of persons governed by the laws.

Limited partnership.   A partnership composed of at least one "general partner" and at least one "limited partner," the latter being one whose liability for acts of the partnership is limited to the amount of investment.

Literary organization.   One of the organizations described in IRC § 501(c)(3).

Lobbying.   An activity usually associated with an attempt to influence a legislative process; generically, it means being in the lobby, so it can also mean attempts to influence the outcome of executive branch or regulatory agencies' decisions, or actions of a legislative branch that are not *legislation*.

Low-cost article.   An article that is distributed by a *tax-exempt organization* (usually a *charitable* one) in connection with the solicitation of *charitable contributions*; the fundraising community terms these items "premiums." This type of distribution is not an *unrelated activity* where the article has a cost not in excess of $5 to the organization (IRC § 513(h)).

Medical care coverage organization.   An organization described in IRC § 501(c)(26).

Material restriction.   A restriction placed by a donor or grantor on what might otherwise be a *charitable contribution* or grant, such that the donor's or grantor's full right, title, and interest in the money or other property is not transferred. This restriction, for example, could prevent the transfer from being a deductible gift.

Mission statement. A statement, often adopted by an organization's *board of directors*, as to why a *tax-exempt organization* exists and what it plans to accomplish; this is essentially the same as a statement of purposes.

Modifications. Term used in the unrelated business tax context to describe the rules that exclude certain forms of income, such as *passive income*, from taxation (IRC § 512(b)).

Mutual ditch and irrigation company. One of the organizations described in IRC § 501(c)(12).

Mutual telephone company. One of the organizations described in IRC § 501(c)(12).

Net earnings. Gross earnings less operating expenses; in for-profit organizations, net earnings are often passed along to owners (e.g., dividends paid to stockholders).

Nonprofit organization. An entity that is organized so that its *net earnings* do not inure to the benefit of individuals or other *persons* in their private capacity.

Not-for-profit activities. Activities for which a business expense deduction is not available (IRC § 183); often confused with "nonprofit" activities.

Officer. An individual who, by reason of an organization's *articles of organization* or *bylaws*, or by law, is assigned certain duties in the operation of an organization.

Operational test. Rules applied (most frequently in the IRC § 501(c)(3) context) to determine whether an organization's operations will merit IRS recognition of its tax-exempt status.

Organizational test. Rules applied (most frequently in the IRC § 501(c)(3) context) to determine whether an organization's *articles of organization* will merit IRS recognition of its tax-exempt status.

Paid solicitor. See *solicitor*.

Partnership. See *general partnership* and *limited partnership*.

Passive income. Income that is not generated from active participation in a business; usually annuities, capital gain, dividends, interest, rents, and royalties.

Person. An entity, either an organization (corporation, unincorporated association, trust, partnership, or estate) or an individual.

Political activity. Generally, activity to advance some political end. Some political activity can cause loss of tax-exempt status for charitable and some other types of tax-exempt organizations, if these activities usually have to constitute activities for the benefit of or in opposition to political candidates for a public office.

Political organization. An organization described in IRC § 527.

Pooled income fund. A form of *split-interest trust*, by which *contributions* of *remainder interests* in money or property are made to *charitable organizations* (IRC § 642(c)(5)).

Private benefit. The doctrine, most prevalent in the IRC § 501(c)(3) context, that is much like the *private inurement* doctrine; the principal difference is that the private benefit doctrine does not require the involvement of an *insider*.

Private foundation. A *charitable organization* that is usually funded from one source (an individual, family, or business), that receives its ongoing funding from investment income (rather than contributions), and that makes grants for *charitable* purposes to other persons rather than conduct its own programs (IRC § 509(a)). See *private operating foundation* and *public charity*.

Private inurement. The doctrine, most prevalent in the IRC § 501(c)(3) context, that causes a *tax-exempt organization* to lose or be denied tax-exempt status because the organization is judged by the IRS to be operated for the private gain of a *person*.

Private operating foundation. A *private foundation* that operates one or more *charitable* programs (IRC § 4942(j)(3)).

Professional solicitor. See *solicitor*.

Public charity. A charitable organization that qualifies as an institution, is a *publicly supported charity*, or is a *supporting organization*, and thus is not a *private foundation* (IRC § 509(a)(1)).

Publicly supported charity. A *charitable organization* that is not a *private foundation* because it receives the requisite amount of financial support from the public (IRC §§ 170(b)(A)(vi) and 509(a)(1) or 509(a)(2)).

Qualified amateur sports organization. See *amateur sports organization.*

Qualified state tuition program. A program described in IRC § 529.

Real estate board. An organization described in IRC § 501(c)(6).

Recognition of tax exemption. The process engaged in by the IRS in determining that a *nonprofit organization* is a *tax-exempt organization.*

Regular income tax. Term used to describe the basic federal income tax, to distinguish it from the alternative minimum tax.

Related activity. A program activity that furthers the purposes of a *tax-exempt organization* (IRC § 512).

Remainder interest. The element of an item of property that causes outright title of the property to pass to a person (usually *a charitable* one) after the *income interest* in the property has expired.

Restricted gift. A *contribution*, usually to a *charitable organization*, that is accompanied by documentation mandating that it must be applied to a particular purpose of the organization, rather than used for its general operations.

Royalty. Payment made for the right to use property, usually as a fixed amount paid each time the item of property is sold or otherwise used.

Self-perpetuating board. A *board of directors* that is elected to office by their own votes rather than those of a membership.

Semi–tax-exempt organizations. These are organizations that must pay the federal income tax, not only on their *unrelated business taxable income* but also on their net investment income. These are *homeowners' associations, political organizations,* and *qualified state tuition programs.*

Shipowners' protection and indemnity association. An organization described in IRC § 526.

Social club. An organization described in IRC § 501(c)(7).

Social welfare organization. An organization described in IRC § 501(c)(4).

Solicitor. A *person* who is paid by a *charitable organization* to engage in the act of requesting *contributions* to the organization; also known as a "paid solicitor" or "professional solicitor."

Split-interest trust. A trust that is established for the purpose of creating an *income interest* and a *remainder interest* in one or more items of property (IRC § 4947).

Supplemental unemployment benefit trust. An organization described in IRC § 501(c)(17).

Supporting organization. A *charitable organization* that is not a *private foundation*, because it has a supportive relationship to one or more other organizations. The supported organization or organizations usually are *institutions* or *publicly supported charities* (IRC § 509(a)(3)).

Tax preference item. A money amount, usually a deduction or credit, that enables a taxpayer to reduce taxable income for *regular income tax* purposes.

Taxable income. For individuals who elect to itemize deductions, *adjusted gross income* less itemized deductions and the personal exemptions; for individuals who do not itemize their deductions, *adjusted gross income* less the standard deduction and the personal exemptions (IRC § 63).

Tax-exempt organization. A *nonprofit organization* that is exempt from one or more federal, state, or local taxes, most frequently the federal income tax (IRC § 501); also known as "tax-exempt entities."

Teachers' retirement fund association.   An organization described in IRC § 501(c)(11).

Testamentary trust.   A trust created by a will.

Title-holding company.   An organization described in IRC § 501(c)(2) or 501(c)(25).

Trade association.   A form of *business league* that is attempting to improve conditions in a particular trade, business, or profession.

Trade or business.   An activity carried on for the production of income from the sale of goods or the performance of services (IRC § 513(c)).

Trade show.   A function, usually of a *trade association*, consisting of the exhibiting of products and services of interest to the association's membership; usually undertaken in conjunction with the association's annual membership convention.

Trust agreement.   An agreement between two or more *persons* for the purpose of creating a trust; see *declaration of trust*.

Union.   One of the labor organizations described in IRC § 501(c)(5).

Unrelated activity.   An activity of a *tax-exempt organization* that is not undertaken in order to further the organization's tax-exempt purposes, other than most administrative, investment, and *fundraising* activities (IRC § 512).

Veterans' organization.   An organization described in IRC § 501(c)(19) or 501(c)(23).

Voluntary employee beneficiary association.   An organization described in IRC § 501(c)(9).

Whistleblower policy.   A policy, adopted by a *tax-exempt organization*, that facilitates employee complaints about an aspect of the organization's operations, by which the employees are enabled to report in confidence and without retaliation (such as loss of employment).

Workmen's compensation insurance organization.   An organization described in IRC § 501(c)(27).

Index